# CONTEMPORARY PERSPECTIVES ON RELIGIOUS EPISTEMOLOGY

# CONTEMPORARY PERSPECTIVES ON RELIGIOUS EPISTEMOLOGY

EDITED BY

## R. DOUGLAS GEIVETT
Biola University

## BRENDAN SWEETMAN
Rockhurst College

New York    Oxford

OXFORD UNIVERSITY PRESS

1992

*To Dianne*

—R. D. G.

---

*To Margaret*

—B. S.

Oxford University Press

Oxford   New York   Toronto
Delhi   Bombay   Calcutta   Madras   Karachi
Kuala Lumpur   Singapore   Hong Kong   Tokyo
Nairobi   Dar es Salaam   Cape Town
Melbourne   Auckland

and associated companies in
Berlin   Ibadan

Published by Oxford University Press, Inc.
198 Madison Avenue, New York, New York 10016-4314

Oxford is a registered trademark of Oxford University Press

Library of Congress Cataloging-in-Publication Data
Contemporary perspectives on religious epistemology
edited by R. Douglas Geivett, Brendan Sweetman.
p. cm.   Includes bibliographical references.
ISBN 0-19-507323-1
ISBN 0-19-507324-X (pbk.)
1. Knowledge, Theory of (Religion)
2. God—Proof.
3. Atheism.
I. Geivett, R. Douglas.
II. Sweetman, Brendan.
BL51.C6369   1992   210—dc20
91-43956

6 8 10 9 7 5

Printed in the United States of America

# Acknowledgments

We would like to express our appreciation to several people who assisted us at various stages in the preparation of this volume. We are very greatly indebted to our friend and teacher, Professor Dallas Willard of the University of Southern California, not only for countless rewarding philosophical discussions over the past several years, but also for his encouragement with this project and for his advice on the preparation of the manuscript. As a teacher of philosophy, Dallas Willard is, in our considerable experience, unchallenged.

We also owe our gratitude to Stephen T. Davis, John Hick, James Kellenberger, and Richard Purtill, all of whom provided enthusiastic support for the project. Thanks are also due to all at Oxford University Press who saw the book through to completion, but especially to Cynthia Read, Angela Blackburn, Peter Olin, and Melinda Wirkus. Ross Scimeca, of the Hoose Library of Philosophy at the University of Southern California, and Robin Vergoz, at Taylor University, greatly assisted us with bibliographical information. We also wish to thank the faculty personnel committee of Taylor University for a generous research grant toward the project.

We wish to record our appreciation for the contribution to religious epistemology made by all of the philosophers whose work appears in this collection. And we thank their various publishers for granting us permission to reprint here. (Spelling, punctuation, and occasionally italicization have been adjusted in this volume to conform to American usage.)

Finally, we owe our very deepest thanks and appreciation to our wives, Dianne Geivett and Margaret Sweetman. Without their encouragement, support, and companionship this work would not have seen the light of day. This volume is dedicated to them.

# Contents

# III   Reformed Epistemology

# IV   Natural Theology

# V   Prudential Accounts of Religious Belief

## VI   Rational Belief and Religious Experience

# CONTEMPORARY PERSPECTIVES ON RELIGIOUS EPISTEMOLOGY

# Introduction

The question of whether or not it is rational to believe in the existence of God is one of the most important of all human concerns. The answer to this question, whether positive or negative, will have profound importance for how we understand our world, and for how we live and act. It would not be an overstatement to say that it is our *duty* as rational human beings to confront the God question given the enormous implications the answer carries for human existence. Most people, of course, at one time or another make some attempt to consider seriously the issue of the rationality of belief in God. If one comes to hold that it is rational to believe in the existence of God, then one must attempt to discover the meaning and purpose of human life as planned by God. If one comes to hold that God does not exist, then one must attempt to come to terms with the consequences of this view, that there is no larger personal scheme of things in which human life makes sense. The universe, and even human life itself, would appear to be merely the products of chance. The implications of this "chance" occurrence of humanity for religion, morality, justice, law, and other important human pursuits must then be seriously addressed, however difficult or unpalatable they may turn out to be.

However, it has proved difficult to decide the issue of the rationality of belief in God, and philosophers have debated it from the beginning of time without producing any clear-cut or decisive solution which has come to be generally accepted. This does not mean, of course, that the issue is ultimately undecidable. It is, however, a complex and difficult issue which demands a great effort—intellectual, perhaps moral, or even spiritual—on the part of the individual inquirer; an effort, moreover, which demands an honest objective inquiry, not governed by prejudice, or by cultural or other biases. Whether or not a decisive solution is forthcoming in the human quest for God, it is necessary and worthwhile to examine serious arguments on all sides of the debate so that one can make an informed decision about this profound issue. All of the philosophers whose work appears in this book are engaged in inquiry about the existence of God. More particularly, this volume is concerned with the issue of the *justification of belief in God,* as we survey the important new developments in *religious epistemology* which have arisen in the philosophy of religion in recent decades.

Religious epistemology is concerned with what has always been one of the central issues in the philosophy of religion, the rational *justification* of religious belief.

Until recent years in the philosophy of religion, one particular approach in religious epistemology has dominated, namely, natural theology. This traditional approach to religious epistemology basically involved examining any *evidence* for the existence of God that could be found in the world of nature, and then attempting to draw some conclusion about whether or not God's existence could be *inferred* on the basis of the evidence found. Natural theology has always reached a favorable conclusion on this issue. One of the most famous of all natural theologians was St. Thomas Aquinas (1225–1274), who held that the existence of God could be proved in five ways, each based on an examination of certain features of the natural world. These "five ways," or demonstrations, of Aquinas set much of the agenda within the philosophy of religion for many centuries. Yet there were, of course, philosophers who disputed the view that the existence of God could be *deduced* from features of the natural world. Some argued that the existence of God could not even be regarded as probable considering the lack of evidence for God's existence in the natural world, and that, therefore, religious belief was not a "reasonable belief," in the sense of being philosophically defensible.

One of the most notable critics of the program of natural theology was the eighteenth-century Scottish philosopher, David Hume (1711–1776). However, Hume and his supporters agreed with Aquinas and his supporters that one should approach the question of the rationality of belief in God by considering whether or not there is sufficient evidence for God's existence. They simply disagreed with Aquinas, and with other natural theologians, that an examination of the "evidence" in the natural world afforded a *positive* answer to the God question. However, much of recent philosophy of religion has been very significant for its opposition to both natural theology and atheistic replies to natural theology arguments. Further, there have appeared in recent decades several new and exciting approaches to religious epistemology, all of them engaged in the attempt to find alternative ways of justifying the rationality of belief in God.

One of the main reasons for the emphasis on religious epistemology in recent philosophy of religion is the sustained attack made in this century upon the traditional epistemological theory known as foundationalism, a theory which once enjoyed wide favor. Briefly stated, foundationalism is the view that although some propositions are "basic," that is, they are not accepted on the basis of any other propositions or beliefs, many propositions are not basic. It further holds that those beliefs that are not basic can be rationally accepted only on the basis of evidence, and this evidence must ultimately be founded upon some set of the basic propositions. Those who subscribe to foundationalism have generally agreed that the proposition that *there is a God* is not basic, and that therefore this proposition can only be *rationally* accepted on the basis of evidence. Indeed, the project of natural theology is an attempt to provide this evidence, and it consequently must involve some version of foundationalism. This strategy is also sometimes called "evidentialism." But with the falling out of favor of foundationalist epistemology, under the influence of philosophers from all sides—including Wittgenstein in England, the analytic movement in America, and recent Continental thought—philosophers have begun to search for, and to explore, new ways of justifying religious belief. They seek ways which do not depend upon an epistemological theory which has been seriously called into question. Of course, many contemporary philosophers of religion are also keen to point out that *criticisms* of the rationality of religious belief which rely upon a foundationalist epistemology are also misplaced.

In recent decades within philosophy of religion another specialized development, in addition to that of religious epistemology, is especially noteworthy. This is the emergence of the subdiscipline of "philosophical theology." This field of inquiry is devoted to an exploration of the *concept* of God and of the data of revealed theology. Philosophical theology inquires about the coherence of theism and, assuming the coherence of theism, pursues the question of how to think about the divine nature and about God's relationship to the world. This development, along with those in religious epistemology, now dominates contemporary philosophy of religion. Both tendencies, we believe, can be attributed to the *general* stress laid on epistemology in philosophy during this century. Of the two areas of development just mentioned, religious epistemology is, in our view, the more fundamental. This is therefore a book in religious epistemology, not philosophical theology.

We have selected five broad epistemological approaches to the *justification* of religious belief. They are represented here by a sample of expositional papers on each view, along with a paper critical of that view. The *new* approaches we have identified and selected are:

|  | Expositional | Critical |
| --- | --- | --- |
| Wittgensteinan Fideism | D. Z. Phillips<br>Norman Malcolm<br>Paul L. Holmer | Kai Nielsen |
| Reformed Epistemology | Alvin Plantinga<br>Nicholas Wolterstorff<br>Robert Pargetter | Stewart C. Goetz |
| Prudential Accounts of Religious Belief | Thomas V. Morris<br>William G. Lycan and<br>  George N. Schlesinger | James Cargile |
| Rational Belief and Religious Experience | William P. Alston<br>John Hick<br>James Kellenberger | Wayne Proudfoot |

We have also included a section of contemporary work representing the traditional approach to the justification of religious belief, both for and against:

|  | Expositional | Critical |
| --- | --- | --- |
| Atheism | Antony Flew<br>William L. Rowe<br>Michael Martin | Scott A. Shalkowski |
| Natural Theology | William Lane Craig<br>Richard Swinburne<br>Dallas Willard<br>Robert M. Adams | Steven M. Cahn |

The *Wittgensteinian fideists* hold that natural theology is a totally misguided way of attempting to address the age-old question of the rationality of belief in God. Their view emphasizes that the epistemological approach finally settled on must be one which is appropriate for the subject matter under investigation. We cannot assume that one particular epistemological approach will yield knowledge of many different subject matters. Once we are over this hurdle in our thinking, these philosophers claim, we can then concentrate on the discovery and development of the proper epistemological approach to the question of the rationality of belief in God. For the Wittgensteinian fideists, this discovery will involve the insight that religious belief, like science and all other central human activities, is a language game which establishes its own internal criteria of meaning and rationality.

The *Reformed epistemologists* argue that the evidentialist approach of both natural theologians and many atheists relies upon a foundationalist epistemology, and that this approach is now called into question with the falling out of favor of foundationalism in this century. They argue that the classical foundationalist criteria for proper basicality—being self-evident, or incorrigible, or evident to the senses—are not necessary conditions of proper basicality, and that there is no reason why belief in God cannot be among the set of foundational beliefs. According to them, belief in God should be understood to be what they call a "properly basic" belief. By this they mean that, in order to be considered rational, belief in God need not be accepted on the basis of any other beliefs or propositions, that is, it need not be accepted on the basis of evidence. However, they claim that asserting the proper basicality of belief in God does not mean that such a belief is either groundless or irrational. Belief in God is warranted by virtue of its being basic to one's noetic structure.

Those who advocate *prudential accounts* of religious belief argue that one does not need overwhelming evidence for one's belief in God to be rational, and that much of the debate between natural theologians and their atheistic critics over whether there is sufficient evidence to warrant belief in God is beside the point. Their view is that, given that there is *some* evidence for the existence of God, it is rational on purely *prudential* grounds to assent to belief in God. This is because there is the possibility of infinite gain if it should turn out that God exists and that such gain is contingent upon believing in God. However, they emphasize that prudential considerations are only a prelude to the development of a full and mature religious faith.

An additional group of philosophers, working in the area of *religious experience,* are exploring the possibility that one might be able to experience God *directly* through one's experiences, thus bypassing the need for evidence from which one might then *infer* the existence of God. For them, religious experience does not constitute a range of evidence which might best be explained in terms of the activity of God. Rather, the reality of God is somehow immediately carried in the experience. And having an experience which seems to one to present the existence of God directly is what warrants belief in God for one who has the experience. It may even provide warrant for others who only know of such experiences secondhand.

What is common to all of these philosophical approaches is a dissatisfaction with natural theology and with the traditional "evidentialist" critique of theism by atheists. Their proponents thus share a common desire to develop alternative epistemological approaches to the God question. It is with these new developments, and with the latest work of those philosophers (both theists and atheists) who still maintain that the strategy of natural theology is the best way to approach the question of the existence of God, that this volume is concerned.

Our aim is to bring together the most significant and influential of these new efforts to justify the rationality of religious belief. Although there are quite a number of works devoted to one or another of the particular epistemological approaches which have arisen over the past few decades, none brings together the various contemporary perspectives on religious epistemology. Indeed, this omission seems to have led some to think that only one or two epistemological approaches prevail. In this scenario, natural theology has often been the biggest loser, with many under the impression that natural theology has no contemporary proponents. To be sure, the alternative approaches to religious epistemology mentioned above have individually generated much attention and even controversy. Bringing them all together for study and comparison in one volume, as we have done, can only help to further enlightened discussion in the philosophy of religion.

## II

We believe our six sections provide a balanced presentation of contemporary work in religious epistemology. We begin the volume with a section on atheism; the other five sections may be viewed as different epistemological "responses" to the charges made by atheistic philosophers. This arrangement of the material enables the reader to study different epistemological approaches to religious belief side by side: comparing the merits of each, and the problems each must face, evaluating the criticisms each approach makes of opposing views, and evaluating the individual attempt of each approach to justify belief in God. It also allows the reader to assess the strength of the case both for and against theism *in one volume* while taking into account a very wide range of contemporary material and spectrum of philosophical positions. Each section of the book ends with a quite substantial bibliography of work done in the last few decades broadly relating to the perspective represented in that section. Taken together, the bibliographies provide a fairly comprehensive survey of scholarly activity on religious epistemology in this generation.

### Atheism

Atheism continues to be an important particular response to the God question. It therefore deserves to be included in any survey of the major contemporary perspectives on religious epistemology. While most atheists do not propose a new epistemological approach to the God question, but abide by the evidentialist strategy of natural theologians, they nevertheless do hold that the correct response to the God question is a negative one. So it is interesting to consider recent work on this point of view and, indeed, to compare the atheistic arguments with the five theistic "responses" in the remainder of the anthology.

According to Antony Flew, whose paper begins the section on atheism, the debate about the existence of God should properly begin from "The Presumption of Atheism." The onus of proof, in other words, is on the theist. Flew believes that this presumption of atheism will provide a fresh perspective on the debate and help to clarify some central issues which are often overlooked. In his paper, he offers reasons why the presumption of atheism should be accepted and considers some objections that might be offered against the presumption.

William L. Rowe, in his contribution, considers the significance of the problem of evil for both the atheist and the theist. He argues that the problem of evil does provide sufficient justification for adopting a position of atheism. Rowe's paper is also of particular interest for distinguishing three varieties of atheism and for considering their place and significance in the debate about the rationality of belief in the existence of God.

Michael Martin aims in his selection to illustrate how various forms of traditional theological arguments, as discussed by David Hume, lead to the conclusion not that the theistic God exists, but that disbelief in the theistic God is more appropriate. Martin first considers the claim that the universe is a created object and argues that, even if this is true, it *probably* was not created by the theistic God. He concludes by discussing whether it is even reasonable to think that the universe is a created object.

Scott A. Shalkowski, in his paper critical of the atheistic position, directly attacks Flew's argument for the presumption of atheism. Shalkowski believes that Flew has got it wrong and that there is no general burden of proof that the theist must bear. He then considers how the argument in favor of atheism would fare in the hypothetical context of a society where it is the reigning intellectual and social predisposition to think that theism is the liberal view which frees one from the shackles of narrow, atheistic explanations of the cosmos, human beings, and the meaningfulness of life. Shalkowski claims that in such a context the arguments and evidence for "atheology" appear very tenuous indeed. According to him, it is much easier for atheists to punch holes in theistic arguments than it is for them to actually *argue for* the truth of atheism. When this is the strategy, Shalkowski holds, it is clear that atheism is at least as inadequately defended as atheists claim theism is.

## Wittgensteinian Fideism

Wittgensteinian fideism is a movement in the philosophy of religion which has developed over the last few decades as a direct consequence of the influence of the central insights of Ludwig Wittgenstein (1889–1951). The current major figure of this movement in philosophy of religion is the Welsh philosopher, D. Z. Phillips. The central thesis of the Wittgensteinian fideists is that religion, like science and all other central human activities, is a *form of life* which establishes its own internal criteria of meaning and rationality. In this view, the task of the philosopher is not to engage in the profoundly misguided endeavor of seeking "evidence" or "justification" for the rationality of belief in God; it is, rather, to describe and make explicit the various practices which make up the religious form of life and which give this form of life its particular meaning.

In "Faith, Skepticism, and Religious Understanding," D. Z. Phillips argues that we need to rethink the relationship between religion and philosophical reflection in order to understand that religion *is* a language game, and that the search for what he calls "external reasons"—for what would be, in his view, no more than a purely theoretical belief in God—is mistaken. Phillips examines the kind of philosophical inquiry the concept of divine reality calls for and goes on to develop his view by arguing that an affirmation of God is synonymous with seeing the possibility of eternal love.

Norman Malcolm also attacks that approach in philosophy of religion which calls for "evidence" and for "objective justification" of religious belief. He explores the notion of a language game and attempts to illustrate that in the end all language games are ultimately groundless. Indeed, according to Malcolm, most of the lives of educated, sophisticated adults are formed by such "groundless beliefs." Chemistry is just as "groundless" as religion, in Malcolm's view. The obsession with the justification of religious belief, as exemplified in the countless discussions of the proofs for the existence of God, is misguided. Given the groundlessness of all forms of life, Malcolm argues, the religious form of life is just as legitimate as any other form of life.

Paul Holmer reflects upon some of the broader themes discussed by both Phillips and Malcolm, and attempts to show that theism versus atheism is a pseudoissue and that theism, in its pretentious philosophical sense, is not fundamental to Judaism and Christianity. He also argues that the new sophisticated existential and ontological theologies, which propose atheistical or nontheistical conceptual schemes, are largely irrelevant. He tries to show that for religious belief no such conceptual scheme is needed at all, since the rich concepts already operative in religious life and practice are adequate for coming to understand the meaning and value of religious language.

Kai Nielsen, whose paper in this volume is part of a larger attempt to defend atheism, examines critically the major themes of Wittgensteinian fideism as they have been discussed by the three figures in the section and makes reference to the work of all three in his critique. His basic criticism is that Wittgensteinian fideism does not do full justice to the meaning of religious language. In particular, this approach fails in its attempt to reinterpret those bits of religious language which are, according to Nielsen, making factual claims about how things really are.

## Reformed Epistemology

In recent years, the philosophy of religion, especially in the United States, has seen the emergence of an influential new movement of "Reformed" epistemology, inspired chiefly by the work of Alvin Plantinga and Nicholas Wolterstorff. "Reformed" epistemology is so called because of the intellectual sympathies of its proponents with the Protestant tradition reaching back to John Calvin. The movement reflects a new epistemological approach to religious belief because its proponents argue that belief in God is "properly basic," that is, it is not accepted on the basis of *any* other beliefs or propositions, and yet it is justified. Therefore, the traditional epistemological approach, as exemplified in natural theology, is misguided in its attempt to provide arguments and evidence for God's existence. This view has much affinity with Wittgensteinian form-of-life views.

The classic early statement of Reformed epistemology is contained in Alvin Plantinga's paper "Is Belief in God Properly Basic?," reprinted in this volume. He argues that what he calls the "evidentialist objection" to theistic belief is beside the point because this objection is based upon a "classical" foundationalist epistemology. Since, according to Plantinga, classical foundationalists are unable to provide compelling reasons for why one should accept their criteria for what counts as a foundational or basic belief, and since the evidentialist *objection* to theism is rooted in classical foundationalism, this standard attempt to criticize theism is poorly rooted indeed. Plantinga argues, in contrast, that *belief in God* is itself properly basic; that is, one is justified in believing in God without basing that belief on any other beliefs or propositions. In the article reprinted here, Plantinga explains what he means by this claim and defends his view against various possible objections, arguing that none of the modern foundationalist's criteria for proper basicality— being self-evident, or incorrigible, or evident to the senses—are necessary conditions for proper basicality. He claims, moreover, that one who holds that belief in God *is* properly basic is not thereby committed to the idea that belief in God is groundless.

In his review essay, Nicholas Wolterstorff critiques the apologetic strategy of Clark Pinnock as presented in his book, *Reason Enough: A Case for the Christian Faith*. Pinnock's approach is to show the typical unbeliever, who might be wondering whether it is rational to accept the Christian faith, that it is indeed *rational* to do so, not because there are deductive arguments for the truth of religious belief, but because Christianity is *more probable than not* with respect to our perceptual knowledge. Wolterstorff challenges Pinnock's analysis of the typical situation of unbelief. Wolterstorff favors John Calvin's view that what is operative in many cases of unbelief is not so much insufficient awareness of the evidence, but *resistance* to the available evidence due to the effects of sin. His paper nicely complements Plantinga's by providing a further statement of the position of Reformed epistemology on the relationship between faith and reason.

Robert Pargetter attempts, first, to develop in some detail an account of properly basic belief, in order, second, to provide an evaluation of the contention that belief in God is properly basic. He appeals throughout to Plantinga's position and concludes that belief in God is only properly basic when at least two conditions are fulfilled: the believer must be reliable, and the believer's system of beliefs must cohere with "a holistic evaluation for rationality."

Stewart C. Goetz argues that "Belief in God is Not Properly Basic." This is because belief in God is an *inferred* belief, and this inference is crucial if belief in God is to be considered rational.

## Natural Theology

It is now widely assumed that natural theology has breathed its last and that there are no plausible arguments for the existence of God worthy of the consideration of enlightened twentieth-century thinkers. This attitude is due, in part, to the strident successes of science which have seemed to leave little for God to do. But the assumption, we think, is mistaken. For there are arguments of considerable philosophical subtlety which recent philosophers have offered in renewed attempts at natural theology. We include four of them here. They have in common an appropriate regard for the advances of science in the modern age.

William Lane Craig offers a version of the cosmological argument that seeks to exploit recent developments in astrophysics and cosmology. He maintains that it is more rational to think that the universe has a beginning than to think that it does not, and that anything that has a beginning must have a cause. Further, Craig argues that there is good reason to believe that the cause is a personal creator. Therefore, it makes more sense to believe that God exists than it does to think that God does not exist. Craig's article is a popularization of the argument presented in his book, *The* Kalam *Cosmological Argument.*

In "The Argument from Design," Richard Swinburne defends a form of the teleological argument. After reconstructing the argument and exhibiting its pattern (he notes that this pattern of argument is common in scientific inference), he discusses eight objections raised by David Hume in his *Dialogues Concerning Natural Religion* and *An Enquiry Concerning Human Understanding.* In his response to each of these objections, Swinburne clarifies the structure of this argument by analogy. He concludes that there are no formal weaknesses in the argument from design, and that it therefore has some force and a role to play in "the web of Christian apologetic."

Dallas Willard presents a three-stage argument for the existence of God which combines cosmological and teleological considerations. In the first stage he seeks to demonstrate that the universe is "ontologically haunted," in the sense that some non-natural Reality (which *might* be God) must exist apart from the natural or physical world as the cause of the natural or physical world. Stage two marks out the explanatory limits of evolutionary theory by showing that there is order in the world which logically *could not* have simply evolved. Stage three exhibits the need to interpret human life, as it is actually experienced, within the context of the "extranaturalism" and "cosmic intellectualism" defended in the first two stages. With each successive stage in the argument, Willard claims, the possibility of there being a God "in the full theistic sense" becomes increasingly substantial.

In "Flavors, Colors, and God," Robert M. Adams presents a version of the argument from consciousness, concentrating on that modification of mind known as perception. He argues that natural science cannot explain the correlation between phenomenal qualia and physical states manifested in perceptual experience, and that therefore a theological explanation is needed. There is, he suggests, "no atheistic escape from the problem of phenomenal qualia." His is an essay in the philosophy of mind as well as the philosophy of religion.

We have included an article by Steven M. Cahn which poses a challenge that is general enough to apply to all arguments of the natural theology type. He suggests that arguments are not, after all, very *relevant* to religion. He maintains that religious believers are fundamentally concerned to know the moral will of God and that no proof for the existence of God can provide this sort of knowledge. Cahn concludes that a demonstration is practically irrelevant for the religious life, and that the rationality of religious belief does not depend upon the fortunes of philosophic proofs for the existence of God.

## Prudential Accounts of Religious Belief

Blaise Pascal (1623–1662) earned permanent recognition in the philosophy of religion when he formulated his famous Wager argument. He was interested in the possibility that reason could not finally decide whether God exists since there appears to be evidence both for and against the existence of God. He reasoned that when the contrary propositions "God exists" and "God does not exist" are equiprobable relative to the evidence available to an individual, the prudent person will judge that God does exist because of the infinite gain (eternal life) to be achieved if he is right, and the relatively little to be lost if he is wrong. There is also the possibility of an infinite loss (eternal damnation) if he does not believe in God, and it turns out that God does exist.

The *prudential* line of reasoning continues to fascinate philosophers of religion. We have included two papers which defend "Pascal's Wager" against standard objections. Thomas V. Morris, in "Pascalian Wagering," attempts to clarify the epistemic context in which the Wager is intended to be an aid. He distinguishes between "epistemically unconcerned" and "epistemically concerned" versions of the Wager. He holds that the epistemically unconcerned version of the argument faces insuperable difficulties, and then argues that the epistemically concerned version can meet all common objections to the Wager. In an important section of his paper Morris discusses the possible ways for theism and atheism to be in *rough epistemic parity* for an individual, such that the Wager has special significance.

In contrast to Morris, William G. Lycan and George N. Schlesinger adopt what Morris calls the "epistemically unconcerned" interpretation of Pascal's Wager. In their article, "You Bet Your Life: Pascal's Wager Defended," they respond briskly to five "misguided objections" and then concentrate their attention on two "serious objections" to the Wager. The first serious objection asks whether an individual faced with martyrdom would be prudent to bet on God. Following a relatively brief reply to this worry, the authors develop a detailed response to the "Many Gods problem": "What if instead of the Christian God there is a Baal, a Moloch, a Wotan, or a Zeus, who prepares a particularly nasty fate for devout Christians?" Lycan and Schlesinger conclude that it is most rational to bet on "that superbeing which is the very most worthy of worship." They end with an exhortation to pray.

The reader who begins with the articles by Morris and Lycan and Schlesinger will be familiar with many objections to the Wager before coming to the critical paper by James Cargile. Cargile suggests that the argument as commonly formulated is simply invalid. He then notes other difficulties facing the Wager once it has been rearranged to deal with the initial difficulty he spells out.

## Rational Belief and Religious Experience

A number of theists have argued that an individual's religious experience can make it rational for that individual to believe in God. There are many different types of arguments that appeal to religious experience, however. Some of them resemble the sort of arguments used by natural theologians in that they involve an *inference from* a range of evidence drawn from experience *to* the existence of God. We have selected papers by philosophers who, in contrast to this, appeal to religious experience in a *noninferential* or *direct* manner in order to justify belief in God.

In his paper, "Religious Experience and Religious Belief," William P. Alston argues that religious experience *can* provide *direct* justification for religious belief. He does this by comparing the epistemology of religious experience with the epistemology of ordinary sense experience. Alston allows that this sort of justification of religious belief is defeasible, and he attempts to identify some of the possible defeaters of direct experiential justification of religious belief. Nevertheless, he concludes that Christian epistemic practice, like ordinary perceptual practice, is innocent until proven guilty. In the absence of defeaters, religious experience provides positive epistemic warrant for religious belief. The ways that Christian epistemic practice and ordinary perceptual practice are otherwise relevantly different do not affect their comparative epistemic status. That is, Christian epistemic practice enjoys basically the same epistemic status as ordinary perceptual practice. For this reason, anyone who subscribes to ordinary perceptual practice cannot consistently criticize Christian epistemic practice.

John Hick also seeks to show that religious belief is rational by comparing religious experience, as a ground for religious belief, with our experience of our natural environment. According to him, certain modifications of human consciousness are constituted by religious experience. Theistic belief is a form of "natural belief," in the Humean sense. That is, it is the sort of belief one inevitably adopts when one has certain types of experiences.

James Kellenberger describes three models of faith in God, one that is "biblical" and two that are "existential," and explores the relationship of each to the requirements of rationality. He suggests that religious experience is the ground for certainty on the biblical model of faith. In contrast, "absurd faith" believes against all reason, and "paradoxical faith" is the non-faith of those who wish they had faith but find that they do not. He seeks to clarify how one's faith in God might be deemed appropriate even when the religious believer is unable or unwilling to articulate his or her reasons for faith in God in terms of traditional standards of evidence.

Wayne Proudfoot reviews kinds of religious experience and examines the issue of reductionism. In his examination of the epistemic status of religious experience, he distinguishes between descriptive and explanatory reduction and traces the implications of each for the study of religious phenomena. He concludes that descriptive reduction is to be avoided, whereas explanatory reduction is not. He emphasizes the appropriateness of explaining religious phenomena in terms of concepts and beliefs held by those who have religious experiences. He argues that it is not possible to identify an experience as "religious" apart from concepts and beliefs which are not themselves conveyed by the religious experience. As he says, "explanatory commitments are assumed in the identification of an experience as religious," and "religious experience is constituted by concepts and beliefs." The question then becomes: Why does the subject employ concepts and beliefs which constitute the experience as religious? Proudfoot ends with the suggestion that the impulse to interpret an experience as religious is inculcated by cultural and historical patterns. He proposes that an accurate explanation of the religious experience of believers "requires a mapping of the concepts and beliefs that were available to them, the commitments they brought to the experience, and the contextual conditions that might have supported their identification of their experiences in religious terms."

# III

Obviously, no anthology can do justice to the vast range of work that is available on religious epistemology. Due to our method of organization for this volume, which we feel provides an accurate reflection of recent developments in religious epistemology, and due to pressures of space, the work of some philosophers one might have expected to find here may not have been included. This is unfortunate, but unavoidable. Our task has been to do justice to the main movements in religious epistemology which have arisen over the past thirty years or so by providing a broadly representative selection of work on each perspective. All of the papers in this collection have been previously published. As well as selecting work from major philosophers long associated with each view, we have attempted to include some of the more recent work in religious epistemology by philosophers who are newer to the field. We have also been guided in our selection process by a determination not to include items that have been widely anthologized.

One objective of this collection is to provide a useful textbook for courses in the philosophy of religion. We believe that students will find it both intellectually exciting and philosophically challenging to work through the main perspectives on religious epistemology, reading side by side expositional and critical work on each, and having the opportunity to compare the different approaches. The student using this volume may want to consider, for example, how the section on natural theology might be related to the other sections. Obviously, for natural theologians, arguments for the existence of God will constitute part of an overall response to Antony Flew's challenge. William Rowe's appeal to evil as evidence that God does not exist might be countered by the suggestion that there is independent evidence which strongly supports theism, whether or not there is evil in the world. The natural theologians' views contrast sharply with those of the Wittgensteinian fideists. What is the nature of their disagreement? What is significant about it? Might the Reformed epistemologist also be a natural theologian?

What is the possible relationship between natural theology and the material presented in the section on prudential considerations? Prudential accounts tend to argue that there is *some* good evidence for the existence of God. Must this evidence be of the same general kind favored by natural theologians? Can natural theology produce evidence that makes the existence of God so much more probable than not that prudential considerations become irrelevant? Is religious experience a possible component in the natural theologian's total case for the existence of God? If religious experience is incorporated into the natural theology approach, must it be in terms of an inference from religious experience to the existence of God, or might it involve the kind of direct awareness of God described by Alston and Hick? Does religious experience complement the prudential approach to the justification of religious belief? One might want to consider the differences and similarities between Wittgensteinian fideism and Reformed epistemology as possible responses to atheism's challenge. These are matters the student might profitably pursue.

It is fairly traditional to arrange textbooks on the philosophy of religion according to standard topics: the problem of evil, the credibility of miracles, the nature of religious language, the soundness of theistic arguments. Countless volumes have followed this pattern. But in an important sense this organization is inadequate. It can even be misleading. For it disguises the variety of epistemological approaches which now dominate the practice of philosophy of religion. It assumes a *pattern of investigation* which (as this volume clearly illustrates) is not uniformly accepted even among religious believers. Therefore, a volume like this will be very useful for laying the groundwork for further work in the philosophy of religion.

Special topics in religious philosophy—such as miracles, the problem of evil, religious language—can be explored with greater advantage after the most basic issues in religious *epistemology* have been carefully examined. One illustration of this can be found in the work of Alvin Plantinga, for whom, as we have noted, belief in God is properly basic. This outlook is motivated in part by a dim view of the possibility of constructing a viable natural theology. And the refusal to invest in the resources of natural theology seems to have led Plantinga to distinguish between a "theodicy" and a "defense" when dealing with the problem of evil.[1] His preference is for a "defense," which is not tied to the possibility of natural theology. In contrast, those who favor a "theodicy" in response to the problem of evil tend to be more optimistic about the prospects of natural theology. The point is that Plantinga's approach to religious epistemology would, if accepted, have significant implications for traditional problems associated with the philosophy of religion (such as the problem of evil). This is true of the other views as well.

It is worth pointing out to those who use this volume in the classroom that many of the papers can be used as study material for discussion of other important topics in the philosophy of religion. This feature makes this anthology useful for teachers wishing to teach other topics in their philosophy of religion courses, in addition to religious epistemology. Thus, for example, William Rowe's paper can be used as material to discuss the problem of evil, D. Z. Phillips's and Nicholas Wolterstorff's papers can be used to discuss the relationship between philosophy and theology, and William Lane Craig's and Robert M. Adams's papers can be used to discuss the significance for religious belief of some of the current developments in the philosophy of science and in the philosophy of mind, respectively. The section on religious experience can be used for a more general discussion of that topic. The section on Wittgensteinian fideism can be used for a general discussion of the nature of religious language. The anthology can also be supplemented, of course, with more general textbooks in the philosophy of religion. Some may also find this volume beneficial for more general courses in epistemology as an illustration of the *practical application* of epistemological developments in recent philosophy to one of the most important areas of human inquiry, the rationality of religious belief.

In addition to the advantages this book will have as a text, we would like to emphasize that it is the first to present in one volume selections from the major movements in religious epistemology which have been prominent in recent decades. We hope, therefore, that the anthology will serve not only as a convenient reference work for scholars, but also as a contribution to the field of philosophy of religion in its own right.

# Note

1. See Alvin Plantinga, *God, Freedom, and Evil* (Grand Rapids, MI: Eerdmans, 1977), pp. 26–28; idem, "The Reformed Objection to Natural Theology," *Christian Scholar's Review* 11 (1982): 187–98; Michael Peterson et al., *Reason and Religious Belief: An Introduction to the Philosophy of Religion* (New York: Oxford University Press, 1991), pp. 101–2; and Kelly James Clark, *Return to Reason: A Critique of Enlightenment Evidentialism and a Defense of Reason and Belief in God* (Grand Rapids, MI: Eerdmans, 1990), pp. 63–68.

# I

# ATHEISM

# 1

# The Presumption of Atheism

## *Antony Flew*

### A. Introductory

At the beginning of Book X of his last work *The Laws,* Plato turns his attention from violent and outrageous actions in general to the particular case of undisciplined and presumptuous behavior in matters of religion:

> We have already stated summarily what the punishment should be for temple-robbing, whether by open force or secretly. But the punishments for the various sorts of insolence in speech or action with regard to the gods, which a man can show in word or deed, have to be proclaimed after we have provided an exordium. Let this be it: "No one believing, as the laws prescribe, in the existence of the gods has ever yet performed an impious action willingly, or uttered a lawless word. Anyone acting in such a way is in one of three conditions: either, first, he does not believe the proposition aforesaid; or, second, he believes that though the gods exist they have no concern about men; or, third, he believes that they can easily be won over by the bribery of prayer and sacrifice" (§ 885B).[1]

So Plato in this notorious treatment of heresy might be said to be rebuking the presumption of atheism. The word 'presumption' would then be employed as a synonym for 'presumptuousness'. But, interesting though the questions here raised by Plato are, the word has in my title a different interpretation. The presumption of atheism which I want to discuss is not a form of presumptuousness; indeed it might be regarded as an expression of the very opposite, a modest teachability. My presumption of atheism is closely analogous to the presumption of innocence in the English Law; a comparison which we shall later find it illuminating to develop. What I want to examine in this paper is the contention that the debate about the existence of God should properly begin from a presumption of atheism, that the onus of proof must lie on the theist.

The word 'atheism', however, has in this contention to be construed unusually. Whereas nowadays the usual meaning of 'atheist' in English is "someone who asserts that there is no such being as God," I want the word to be understood here much less positively. I want the originally Greek prefix "a" to be read in the same

Reprinted from the *Canadian Journal of Philosophy* 2 (1972), by permission of the author and the editor. Notes edited.

way in 'atheist' as it customarily is read in such other Greco-English words as "amoral," "atypical," and "asymmetrical." In this interpretation an atheist becomes: not someone who positively asserts the nonexistence of God; but someone who is simply not a theist. Let us, for future ready reference, introduce the labels 'positive atheism' for the former doctrine and 'negative atheism' for the latter.

The introduction of this new sense of the word 'atheism' may appear to be a piece of perverse Humpty-Dumptyism,[2] going arbitrarily against established common usage. "Whyever," it could be asked, "don't you make it not the presumption of atheism but the presumption of agnosticism?" But this pardonably petulant reaction fails to appreciate just how completely noncommittal I intend my negative atheist to be. For in this context the agnostic—and it was, of course, in this context that Thomas Henry Huxley first introduced the term[3]—is by the same criterion of established common usage someone who, having entertained the existence of God as at least a theoretical possibility, now claims not to know either that there is or that there is not such a being. To be in this ordinary sense an agnostic you have already to have conceded that there is, and that you have, a legitimate concept of God; such that, whether or not this concept does in fact have application, it theoretically could. But the atheist in my peculiar interpretation, unlike the atheist in the usual sense, has not as yet and as such conceded even this.

This point is important, though the question whether the word 'agnosticism' can bear the meaning which I want now to give to the word 'atheism' is not. What the protagonist of the presumption of atheism, in my sense, wants to show is: that the debate about the existence of God ought to be conducted in a particular way, and that the issue should be seen in a certain perspective. His thesis about the onus of proof involves that it is up to the theist: first, to introduce and to defend his proposed concept of God; and, second, to provide sufficient reason for believing that this concept of his does in fact have an application. It is the first of these two stages which needs perhaps to be emphasized even more strongly than the second. Where the question of existence concerns, for instance, a Loch Ness Monster or an Abominable Snowman this stage may perhaps reasonably be deemed to be more or less complete before the argument begins. But in the controversy about the existence of God this is certainly not so: not only for the quite familiar reason that the word 'God' is used—or misused—in more than one way; but also, and much more interestingly, because it cannot be taken for granted that even the would-be mainstream theist is operating with a legitimate concept which theoretically could have an application to an actual being.

This last suggestion is not really as newfangled and factitious as it is sometimes thought to be. But its pedigree has been made a little hard to trace. For the fact is that, traditionally, issues which should be seen as concerning the legitimacy or otherwise of a proposed or supposed concept have by philosophical theologians been discussed: either as surely disposable difficulties in reconciling one particular feature of the Divine nature with another; or else as aspects of an equally surely soluble general problem of saying something about the infinite Creator in language intelligible to his finite creatures. These traditional and still almost universally accepted forms of presentation are fundamentally prejudicial. For they assume: that there is a Divine being, with an actual nature the features of which we can investigate; and that there is an infinite Creator, whose existence—whatever difficulties we finite creatures may have in asserting anything else about Him—we may take for granted.

The general reason why this presumption of atheism matters is that its acceptance must put the whole question of the existence of God into an entirely fresh perspective. Most immediately relevant here is that in this fresh perspective problems which really are conceptual are seen as conceptual problems; and problems which have tended to be regarded as advanced and, so to speak, optional extras now discover themselves as both elementary and indispensable. The theist who wants to build a systematic and thorough apologetic finds that he is required to begin absolutely from the beginning; and this absolute beginning is to ensure that the word 'God' is provided with a meaning such that it is theoretically possible for an actual being to be so described.

Although I shall later be arguing that the presumption of atheism is neutral as between all parties to the main dispute, inasmuch as to accept it as determining a procedural framework is not to make any substantive assumptions, I must give fair warning now that I do nevertheless believe that in its fresh perspective the whole enterprise of theism appears even more difficult and precarious than it did before. In part this is a corollary of what I have just been suggesting; that certain difficulties and objections, which may previously have seemed peripheral or even factitious, are made to stand out as fundamental and unavoidable. But it is also in part, as we shall be seeing soon, a consequence of the emphasis which it places on the imperative need to produce some sort of sufficient reason to justify theist belief.

## B. The Presumption of Atheism and the Presumption of Innocence

1. One thing which helps to conceal this need is a confusion about the possible varieties of proof, and this confusion is one which can be resolved with the help of the first of a series of comparisons between my proposed presumption of atheism and the legal presumption of innocence. It is frequently said nowadays, even by professing Roman Catholics, that everyone knows that it is impossible to prove the existence of God. The first objection to this putative truism is, as my reference to Roman Catholics should have suggested, that it is not true. For it is an essential dogma of Roman Catholicism, defined as such by the First Vatican Council, that "the one and true God our creator and lord can be known for certain through the creation by the natural light of human reason."[4] So even if this dogma is, as I myself believe, false, it is certainly not known to be false by those many Roman Catholics who remain, despite all the disturbances consequent upon the Second Vatican Council, committed to the complete traditional faith.

To this a sophisticated objector might reply that the definition of the First Vatican Council speaks of knowing for certain rather than of proving or demonstrating; adding perhaps, if he was very sophisticated indeed, that the word "demonstrari" in an earlier draft was eventually replaced by the expression "certo cognosci." But though this is, I am told,[5] correct, it is certainly not enough to vindicate the conventional wisdom. For the word 'proof' is not ordinarily restricted in its application to demonstratively valid arguments; arguments, that is, in which the conclusion cannot be denied without thereby contradicting the premises. So it is too flattering to suggest that most of those who make this facile claim, that everyone knows that it is impossible to prove the existence of God, are intending only the strictly limited assertion that one special sort of proof is impossible.

The truth, and the danger, is that wherever there is any awareness of such a limited and specialized interpretation, there will be a quick and illegitimate move to the much wider general conclusion that it is impossible and, furthermore, unnecessary to provide any sufficient reason for believing. It is, therefore, worth underlining that when the presumption of atheism is explained as insisting that the onus of proof must be on the theist, the word 'proof' is being used in the ordinary wide sense in which it can embrace any and every variety of sufficient reason. It is, of course, in this and only this sense that the word is interpreted when the presumption of innocence is explained as laying the onus of proof on the prosecution.

2. A second element of positive analogy between these two presumptions is that both are defeasible; and that they are, consequently, not to be identified with assumptions. The presumption of innocence indicates where the court should start and how it must proceed. Yet the prosecution is still able, more often than not, to bring forward what is in the end accepted as sufficient reason to warrant the verdict "Guilty"; which appropriate sufficient reason is properly characterized as a proof of guilt. The defeasible presumption of innocence is thus in this majority of cases in fact defeated; whereas, were the indefeasible innocence of all accused persons an assumption of any legal system, there could not be within that system any provision for any verdict other than "Not Guilty." To the extent that it is, for instance, an assumption of the English Common Law that every citizen is cognizant of all that the law requires of him, that law cannot admit the fact that this assumption is, as in fact it is, false.

The presumption of atheism is similarly defeasible. It lays it down that thorough and systematic inquiry must start from a position of negative atheism, and that the burden of proof lies on the theist proposition. Yet this is not at all the same thing as demanding that the debate should proceed on a positive atheist assumption, which must preclude a theist conclusion. Counsel for theism no more betrays his client by accepting the framework determined by this presumption than counsel for the prosecution betrays the state by conceding the legal presumption of innocence. The latter is perhaps in his heart unshakeably convinced of the guilt of the defendant. Yet he must, and with complete consistency and perfect sincerity may, insist that the proceedings of the court should respect the presumption of innocence. The former is even more likely to be persuaded of the soundness of his brief. Yet he too can with a good conscience allow that a thorough and complete apologetic must start from, meet, and go on to defeat, the presumption of atheism.

Put as I have just been putting it, the crucial distinction between a defeasible presumption and a categorical assumption will, no doubt, seem quite obvious. But I know from experience that many do find it difficult to grasp, at least in its application to the present highly controversial case.[6] Theists fear that if once they allow this procedural presumption they will have sold the pass to the atheist enemy. Most especially when the proponent of this procedure happens to be a known opponent of theism, the theist is inclined to mistake it that the procedure itself prejudicially assumes an atheist conclusion. But this, as the comparison with the legal presumption of innocence surely makes clear, is wrong. Such presumptions are procedural and not substantive; they assume no conclusion, either positive or negative.

3. However, and here we come to a third element in the positive analogy, to say that such presumptions are in themselves procedural and not substantive is not to say that the higher-order questions of whether to follow this presumption or that are trifling and merely formal rather than material and substantial. These higher-order questions are not questions which can be dismissed cynically as "issues of principle as opposed to issues of substance." It can matter a lot which presumption is adopted. Notoriously, there is a world of difference between legal systems which follow the presumption of innocence, and those which do not. And, as I began to indicate at the end of Part A, to adopt the presumption of atheism does put the whole argument into a distinctive perspective.

4. Next, as a fourth element in the positive analogy, it is a paradoxical consequence of the fact that these presumptions are procedural and not substantive that particular defeats do not constitute any sort of reason, much less a sufficient reason, for a general surrender. The fact that George Joseph Smith was in his trial proved guilty of many murders defeats the original presumption of his innocence. But this particular defeat has no tendency at all to show that even in this particular case the court should not have proceeded on this presumption. Still less does it tend to establish that the legal system as a whole was at fault in incorporating this presumption as a general principle. It is the same with the presumption of atheism. Suppose that someone is able to prove the existence of God. This achievement must, similarly, defeat our presumption. But it does not thereby show that the original contention about the onus of proof was mistaken.

One may, therefore, as a mnemonic, think of the word 'defeasible' ( = defeatable) as implying precisely this capacity to survive defeat. A substantive generalization—such as, for instance, the assertion that all persons accused of murder are in fact innocent—is falsified decisively by the production of even one authentic counter-example. That is part of what is meant by the Baconian slogan: "Magis est vis instantiae negativae."[7] But a defeasible presumption is not shown to have been the wrong one to have made by being in a particular case in fact defeated. What does show the presumption of atheism to be the right one to make is what we have now to investigate.

## C. The Case for the Presumption of Atheism

1. An obvious first move is to appeal to the old legal axiom: "Ei incumbit probatio qui dicit, non qui negat." Literally and unsympathetically translated this becomes: "The onus of proof lies on the man who affirms, not on the man who denies." To this the objection is almost equally obvious. Given just a very little verbal ingenuity, contrary notions can be rendered alternatively in equally positive forms: either "That this house affirms the existence of God," or "That this house takes its stand for positive atheism." So interpreted, therefore, our axiom provides no determinate guidance.[8]

Suppose, however, that we take the hint already offered in the previous paragraph. A less literal but more sympathetic translation would be: "The onus of proof lies on the proposition, not on the opposition." The point of the change is to bring out that this maxim was offered in a legal context, and that our courts are institutions of debate. An axiom providing no determinate guidance outside that framework may nevertheless be fundamental for the effective conduct of orderly and decisive debate. Here the outcome is supposed to be decided on the merits of what is said within the debate itself, and of that alone. So no opposition can set about demolishing the proposition case until and unless that proposition has first provided them with a case for demolition.

Of course our maxim, even when thus sympathetically interpreted, still offers no direction on which contending parties ought to be made to undertake which roles. Granting that courts are to operate as debating institutions, and granting that this maxim is fundamental to debate, we have to appeal to some further premise principle before we become licensed to infer that the prosecution must propose and the defense oppose. This further principle is, once again, the familiar presumption of innocence. Were we, while retaining the conception of a court as an institution for reaching decisions by way of formalized debate, to embrace the opposite presumption, the presumption of guilt, we should need to adopt the opposite arrangements. In these the defense would first propose that the accused is after all innocent, and the prosecution would then respond by struggling to disintegrate the case proposed.

2. The first move examined cannot, therefore, be by itself sufficient. To have considered it does nevertheless help to show that to accept such a presumption is to adopt a policy. And policies have to be assessed by reference to the aims of those for whom they are suggested. If for you it is more important that no guilty person should ever be acquitted than that no innocent person should ever be convicted, then for you a presumption of guilt must be the rational policy. For you, with your preference structure, a presumption of innocence becomes simply irrational. To adopt this policy would be to adopt means calculated to frustrate your own chosen ends; which is, surely, paradigmatically irrational. Take, as an actual illustration, the controlling elite of a ruling Leninist party, which must, as such, refuse to recognize any individual rights if these conflict with the claims of the party, and which in fact treats all those suspected of actual or potential opposition much as if they were already known "counterrevolutionaries," "enemies of socialism," "friends of the United States," "advocates of free elections," and all other like things bad. I can, and do, fault this policy and its agents on many counts. Yet I cannot say that for them, once granted their scale of values, it is irrational.

What then are the aims by reference to which an atheist presumption might be justified? One key word in the answer, if not the key word, must be 'knowledge'. The context for which such a policy is proposed is that of inquiry about the existence of God; and the object of the exercise is, presumably, to discover whether it is possible to establish that the word 'God' does in fact have application. Now to establish must here be either to show that you know or to come to know. But knowledge is crucially different from mere true belief. All knowledge involves true belief; not all true belief constitutes knowledge. To have a true belief is simply and solely to believe that something is so, and to be in fact right. But someone may believe that this or that is so, and his belief may in fact be true, without its thereby and necessarily constituting knowledge. If a true belief is to achieve this more elevated status, then the believer has to be properly warranted so to believe. He must, that is, be in a position to know.

Obviously, there is enormous scope for disagreement in particular cases: both about what is required in order to be in a position to know; and about whether these requirements have actually been satisfied. But the crucial distinction between believing truly and knowing is recognized as universally as the prior and equally vital distinction between believing and believing what is in fact true. If, for instance, there is a question whether a colleague performed some discreditable action, then all of us, though we have perhaps to admit that we cannot help believing that he did, are rightly scrupulous not to assert that this is known unless we have grounds sufficient to warrant the bolder claim. It is, therefore, not only incongruous but also scandalous in matters of life and death, and even of eternal life and death, to maintain that you know either on no grounds at all, or on grounds of a kind which on other and comparatively minor issues you yourself would insist to be inadequate.

It is by reference to this inescapable demand for grounds that the presumption of atheism is justified. If it is to be established that there is a God, then we have to have good grounds for believing that this is indeed so. Until and unless some such grounds are produced we have literally no reason at all for believing; and in that situation the only reasonable posture must be that of either the negative atheist or the agnostic. So the onus of proof has to rest on the proposition. It must be up to them: first, to give whatever sense they choose to the word 'God', meeting any objection that, so defined, it would relate only to an incoherent pseudo-concept; and, second, to bring forward sufficient reasons to warrant their claim that, in their present sense of the word 'God', there is a God. The same applies, with appropriate alterations, if what is to be made out is, not that atheism is known to be true, but only—more modestly—that it can be seen to be at least more or less probable.

## D. Objections to the Presumption of Atheism

1. Once the nature of this presumption is understood, the supporting case is short and simple. One reason why it may appear unacceptable is a confusion of contexts. In a theist or post-theist society it comes more easily to ask why a man is not a theist than why he is. Provided that the question is to be construed biographically this is, no doubt, methodologically inoffensive. But our concern here is not at all with biographical questions of why people came to hold whatever opinions they do hold. Rather, it is with the need for opinions to be suitably grounded if they are to be rated as items of knowledge, or even of probable belief. The issue is: not what does or does not need to be explained biographically; but where the burden of theological proof should rest.

2. A more sophisticated objection of fundamentally the same sort would urge that our whole discussion has been too artificial and too general, and that any man's inquiries have to begin from wherever he happens to be. "We cannot begin," C. S.

Peirce wrote, "with complete doubt. We must begin with all the prejudices which we actually have. . . . These prejudices are not to be dispelled by a maxim. . . ."[9] With particular present reference Professor John Hick has urged:

> The right question is whether it is rational for the religious man himself, given that his religious experience is coherent, persistent, and compelling, to affirm the reality of God. What is in question is not the rationality of an inference from certain psychological events to God as their cause; for the religious man no more infers the existence of God than we infer the existence of the visible world around us. What is in question is the rationality of the one who has the religious experiences. If we regard him as a rational person we must acknowledge that he is rational in believing what, given his experiences, he cannot help believing.[10]

To the general point drawn from Peirce the answer comes from further reading of Peirce himself. He was, in the paper from which I quoted, arguing against the Cartesian programme of simultaneous, systematic, and (almost) universal doubt. Peirce did not want to suggest that it is impossible or wrong to subject any of our beliefs to critical scrutiny. In the same paragraph he continues: "A person may, it is true, find reason to doubt what he began by believing; but in that case he doubts because he has a positive reason for it, and not on account of the Cartesian maxim." One positive reason for being especially leery towards religious opinions is that these vary so very much from society to society; being, it seems, mainly determined, in Descartes' phrase, "by custom and example."[11]

To Hick it has at once to be conceded: that it is one thing to say that a belief is unfounded or well-founded; and quite another to say that it is irrational or rational for some particular person, in his particular time and circumstances, and with his particular experience and lack of experience, to hold or to reject that belief. Granted that his usually reliable Intelligence were sure that the enemy tank brigade was in the town, it was entirely reasonable for the General also to believe this. But the enemy tanks had in fact pulled back. Yet it was still unexceptionably sensible for the General on his part to refuse to expose his flank to those tanks which were in fact not there. This genuine and important distinction cannot, however, save the day for Hick.

In the first place, to show that someone may reasonably hold a particular belief, and even that he may properly claim that he knows it to be true, is at best still not to show that that belief is indeed well grounded, much less that it constitutes an item of his knowledge.

Nor, second, is to accept the presumption of atheism as a methodological framework, as such: either to deprive anyone of his right "to affirm the reality of God"; or to require that to be respectable every conviction should first have been reached through the following of an ideally correct procedure. To insist on the correctness of this presumption as an initial presumption is to make a claim which is itself procedural rather than substantive; and the context for which this particular procedure is being recommended is that of justification rather than of discovery.

Once these fundamentals are appreciated, those for whom Hick is acting as spokesman should at first feel quite content. For on his account they consider that they have the very best of grounds for their beliefs. They regard their "coherent, consistent, and compelling" religious experience as analogous to perception; and the man who can see something with his own eyes and feel it in his own hands is in a perfect position to know that it exists. His position is indeed so perfect that, as Hick says, it is wrong to speak here of evidence and inference. If he saw his wife in the act of intercourse with a lover, then he no longer needs to infer her infidelity from bits and pieces of evidence. He has now what is better than inference; although for the rest of us, who missed this display, his testimony still constitutes an important part of the evidence in the case. The idiomatic expression "the evidence of my own eyes" derives its paradoxical piquancy from the fact that to see for oneself is better than to have evidence.

All this is true. Certainly, too, anyone who thinks that he can, as it were, see God must reject the suggestion that in so doing he infers "from certain psychological events to God as their cause." For to accept this account would be to call down upon his head all the insoluble difficulties which fall to the lot of all those who maintain that what we see, and all we ever really and directly see, is visual sense-data. And, furthermore, it is useful to be reminded that when we insist that knowledge as opposed to mere belief has to be adequately warranted, this grounding may be a matter either of having sufficient evidence or of being in a position to know directly and without evidence. So far, therefore, it might seem that Hick's objection was completely at cross-purposes; and that anyway his protégés have no need to appeal to the distinction between actual knowledge and what one may rationally and properly claim to know.

Wait a minute. The passage of Hick which has been under discussion was part of an attempt to show that criticism of the Argument from Religious Experience is irrelevant to such claims to, as it were, see God. But on the contrary: what such criticism usually challenges is just the vital assumption that having religious experience really is a kind of perceiving, and hence a sort of being in a position to know about its putative object. So this challenge provides just exactly that positive reason, which Peirce demanded, for doubting what, according to Hick, "one who has the religious experiences . . . cannot help believing." If, therefore, he persists in so believing without even attempting to overcome this criticism, then it becomes impossible to vindicate his claims to be harboring rational beliefs; much less items of authentic knowledge.

3. A third objection, of a different kind, starts from the assumption, mentioned in section B(1) earlier, that any program to prove the existence of God is fundamentally misconceived; that this enterprise is on all fours with projects to square the circle or to construct a perpetual motion machine. The suggestion then is that the territory which reason cannot inhabit may nevertheless be freely colonized by faith: "The world was all before them, where to choose."[12]

Ultimately, perhaps, it is impossible to establish the existence of God, or even to show that it is more or less probable. But, if so, this is not the correct moral: the rational man does not thereby become in this area free to believe, or not to believe, just as his fancy takes him. Faith, surely, should not be a leap in the dark but a leap toward the light. Arbitrarily to plump for some particular conviction, and then stubbornly to cleave to it, would be—to borrow the term which St. Thomas employed in discussing natural reason, faith, and revelation[13]—frivolous. If your venture of faith is not to be arbitrary, irrational, and frivolous, you must have presentable reasons: first, for making any such commitment in this area, an area in which, by hypothesis, the available grounds are insufficient to warrant any firm conclusion; and, second, for opting for one particular possibility rather than any of the other available alternatives. To most such offerings of reasons the presumption of atheism remains relevant. For though, again by the hypothesis, these cannot aspire to prove their conclusions, they will usually embrace some estimation of their probability. If the onus of proof lies on the man who hopes definitively to establish the existence of God, it must also, by the same token, rest on the person who plans to make out only that this conclusion is more or less probable.

I put in the qualifications "most" and "usually" in order to allow for apologetic in the tradition of Pascal's Wager.[14] Pascal makes no attempt in this most famous argument to show that his Roman Catholicism is true or probably true. The reasons which he suggests for making the recommended bet on his particular faith are reasons in the sense of motives rather than reasons in our previous sense of grounds. Conceding, if only for the sake of the present argument, that we can have no knowledge here, Pascal tries to justify as prudent a policy of systematic self-persuasion, rather than to provide grounds for thinking that the beliefs recommended are actually true.

Another instructive feature of Pascal's argument is his unwarranted assumption that there are only two betting options, neither of which, on the assumption of total ignorance, can be awarded any measure of positive probability. Granted all this, it then appears compulsively reasonable to wager one's life on the alternative which promises and threatens so inordinately much. But the number of theoretically possible world-systems is infinite, and the subset of those making similar promises and threats is also infinite. The immediate relevance of this to us is that it will not do, without further reason given, to set up as the two mutually exclusive and together exhaustive alternatives (one sort of) theism and (the corresponding sort of) positive atheism; and then to suggest that, since neither position can be definitely established, everyone is entitled simply to take their pick. The objection that this way of constructing the book leaves out a third, agnostic, opinion is familiar; and it is one which Pascal himself tried to meet by arguing that to refuse to decide is in effect to decide against religion. The objection based on the point that the number of theoretically possible Hell-threatening and Heaven-promising world-systems is infinite, is quite different and, against the Wager as he himself sets it up, decisive. The point is that, on the given assumption of total ignorance, combined with our present recognition of the infinite range of alternative theoretical possibilities; to bet on any one of the, so to speak, positive options, none of which can, by the hypothesis, be awarded any measure of positive probability, must be in the last degree arbitrary and capricious.

## E.  The Five Ways as an Attempt to Defeat
## the Presumption of Atheism

I have tried, in the first four sections, to explain what I mean by "the presumption of atheism," to bring out by comparison with the presumption of innocence in law what such a presumption does and does not involve, to deploy a case for adopting my presumption of atheism, and to indicate the lines on which two sorts of objection may be met. Now, finally, I want to point out that St. Thomas Aquinas presented the Five Ways in his *Summa Theologica* as an attempt to defeat just such a presumption. My hope in this is both to draw attention to something which seems generally to be overlooked, and, by so doing, to summon a massive authority in support of a thesis which many apparently find scandalous.

These most famous arguments were offered there originally, without any inhibition or equivocation, as proofs, period: "I reply that we must say that God can be proved in five ways"; and the previous second Article, raising the question "Whether the existence of God can be demonstrated?," gives the categorical affirmative answer that "the existence of God . . . can be demonstrated."[15] Attention usually and understandably concentrates on the main body of the third Article, which is the part where Aquinas gives his five supposed proofs. But, as so often, it is rewarding to read the entire Article, and especially the second of the two Objections to which these are presented as a reply:

> Furthermore, what can be accounted for by fewer principles is not the product of more. But it seems that everything which can be observed in the world can be accounted for by other principles, on the assumption of the nonexistence of God. Thus natural effects are explained by natural causes, while contrived effects are referred to human reason and will. So there is no need to postulate the existence of God.[16]

The Five Ways are thus, at least in one aspect, an attempt to defeat this presumption of (an Aristotelian) atheist naturalism, by showing that the things "which can be observed in the world" cannot "be accounted for . . . on the assumption of the nonexistence of God," and hence that there is "need to postulate the existence of God."[17] One must never forget that Aquinas composed his own Objections, and hence that it was he who introduced into his formulation here the idea of (this Aristotelian) scientific naturalism. No such idea is integral to the presumption of atheism as that has been construed in the present paper. When the addition is made the presumption can perhaps be labeled "Stratonician." (Strato was the next but one in succession to Aristotle as head of the Lyceum, and was regarded by Bayle and Hume as the archetypal ancient spokesman for an atheist scientific naturalism.)

By suggesting, a century before Ockham, an appeal to an Ockhamist principle of postulational economy, Aquinas also indicates a reason for adopting such a presumption. The fact that the Saint cannot be suspect of wanting to reach atheist conclusions can now be made to serve as a spectacular illustration of a point labored in Part B above, that to adopt such a presumption is not to make an assumption. And the fact, which has been put forward as an objection to this reading of Aquinas, that "Thomas himself was never in the position of a Stratonician, nor did he live in a milieu in which Stratonicians were plentiful,"[18] is simply irrelevant. For the thesis that the onus of proof lies upon the theist is entirely independent of these biographical and sociological facts.

What is perhaps slightly awkward for present purposes is the formulation of the first Objection: "It seems that God does not exist. For if of two contrary things one were to exist without limit the other would be totally eliminated. But what is meant by this word 'God' is something good without limit. So if God were to have existed no evil would have been encountered. But evil is encountered in the world. Therefore, God does not exist."

It would, from my point of view, have been better had this first Objection referred to possible difficulties and incoherencies in the meaning proposed for the word 'God'. Unfortunately, it does not, although Aquinas is elsewhere acutely aware of such problems. The changes required, however, are, though important, not extensive. Certainly, the Objection as actually given is presented as one of the God hypothesis falsified by familiar fact. Yet a particular variety of the same general point could be represented as the detection of an incoherence, not in the proposed concept of God as such, but between that concept and another element in the theoretical structure in which it is normally involved.

The incoherence—or perhaps on this occasion I should say only the ostensible incoherence—is between the idea of creation, as necessarily involving complete, continual, and absolute dependence of creature upon Creator, and the idea that creatures may nevertheless be sufficiently autonomous for their faults not to be also and indeed primarily His fault. The former idea, the idea of creation, is so essential that it provides the traditional criterion for distinguishing theism from deism. The latter is no less central to the three great theist systems of Judaism, Christianity, and Islam, since all three equally insist that creatures of the immaculate Creator are corrupted by sin. So where Aquinas put as his first Objection a statement of the traditional Problem of Evil, conceived as a problem of squaring the God hypothesis with certain undisputed facts, a redactor fully seized of the presumption of atheism as expounded in the present paper would refer instead to the ostensible incoherence, within the system itself, between the concept of creation by a flawless Creator and the notion of His creatures flawed by their sins.

# Notes

1. This and all later translations from the Greek and Latin are by me.
2. See Chapter VI of Lewis Carroll's *Through the Looking Glass:*

   "But 'glory' doesn't mean 'a nice knock-down argument,'" Alice objected.
   "When I use a word," Humpty Dumpty said in rather a scornful tone, "it means just what I choose it to mean—neither more nor less."
   "The question is," said Alice, "whether you can make words mean so many different things."
   "The question is," said Humpty Dumpty, "which is to be master—that's all."

3. See the essay "Agnosticism," and also that on "Agnosticism and Christianity," in Volume 5 of his *Collected Essays* (London: Macmillan, 1894). I may perhaps also refer to my own article on "Agnosticism" for the 1972 revision of the *Encyclopaedia Britannica.*
4. H. Denzinger, ed., *Enchiridion Symbolorum* (29th rev. Freiburg im Breisgau: Herder, 1953), section 1806.
5. By Professor P. T. Geach of Leeds.
6. This was brought home to me most forcibly by studying some of the reviews of my *God and Philosophy* (London: Hutchinson; New York: Harcourt Brace, 1966). It can be both interesting and instructive to notice the same confusion occurring in an equally controversial socio-political case. A. F. Young and E. T. Ashton, in their *British Social Work in the Nine-*

*teenth Century* (London: Routledge and Kegan Paul, 1956), quote Lord Attlee as reproaching the "general assumption that all applicants are frauds unless they prove themselves otherwise" (p. 111). It should by now be clear that to put the onus of proof of entitlement upon the applicant for welfare payments is emphatically not to assume that all or most of those who apply are in fact cheats.

This last example is the more salutary since the mistake is made by a former leader of the Labour Party who was above suspicion of any dishonourable intention to twist or to misrepresent. Would it were ever thus!

7. "The force of the negative instance is greater." For, whereas a single positive, supporting instance can do only a very little to confirm a universal generalization, one negative, contrary example would be sufficient decisively to falsify that generalization.

8. See the paper "Presumptions" by my former colleague Patrick Day in the *Proceedings of the XIVth International Congress of Philosophy* (Vienna, 1968), Vol. 5, p. 140. I am pleased that it was I who first suggested to him an exploration of this unfrequented philosophical territory.

9. C. S. Peirce, "Some Consequences of Four Incapacities," pp. 156–57 of Volume 5 of the *Collected Papers* (Cambridge, MA: Harvard University Press, 1934).

10. In his review of *God and Philosophy* in *Theology Today* (1967): 86–87. He makes his point not against the general presumption but against one particular application. (See John Hick's paper, "The Rationality of Religious Belief," in Part IV of this volume, pp. 304–19.)

11. Rene Descartes, *Discourse on the Method,* Part II. It occurs almost immediately after his observation: "I took into account also the very different character which a person brought up from infancy in France or Germany exhibits, from that which . . . he would have possessed had he lived among the Chinese or with savages."

12. John Milton, *Paradise Lost,* Bk. XII, line 646.

13. St. Thomas Aquinas, *Summa contra Gentiles,* Bk. I, Ch. VI. The whole passage, in which Aquinas gives his reasons for believing that the Christian candidate does, and that of Mohammed does not, constitute an authentic revelation of God, should be compared with some defense of the now widely popular assumption that the contents of a religious faith must be without evidential warrant.

Professor A. C. MacIntyre, for instance, while he was still himself a Christian, argued with great vigor for the Barthian thesis that "belief cannot argue with unbelief: it can only preach to it." Thus, in his paper on "The Logical Status of Religious Belief" in *Metaphysical Beliefs* (London: Student Christian Movement Press, 1957), MacIntyre urged: ". . . suppose religion could be provided with a method of proof . . . since the Christian faith sees true religion only in a free decision made in faith and love, the religion would by this vindication be destroyed. For all possibility of free choice would have been done away. Any objective justification of belief would have the same effect . . . faith too would have been eliminated" (p. 209).

Now first, insofar as this account is correct, any commitment to a system of religious belief has to be made altogether without evidencing reasons. MacIntyre himself concludes with a quotation from John Donne to illustrate the "confessional voice" of faith, commenting: "The man who speaks like this is beyond argument" (p. 211). But this, we must insist, would be nothing to be proud of. It is certainly no compliment, even if it were a faithful representation, to portray the true believer as necessarily irrational and a bigot. Furthermore, second, it is not the case that where sufficient evidence is available there can be no room for choice. Men can, and constantly do, choose to deceive themselves about the most well-evidenced, inconvenient truths. Also, no recognition of any facts, however clear, is by itself sufficient to guarantee one's allegiance and to preclude its opposite. MacIntyre needs to extend his reading of the Christian poets to the greatest of them all. For the hero of Milton's *Paradise Lost* had the most enviably full and direct knowledge of God. Yet Lucifer, if any creature could, chose freely to rebel.

14. See Blaise Pascal, *Pensées,* section 233 in the Brunschvicg arrangement. For a discussion of Pascal's argument see Chapter 6, section 7 of my *An Introduction to Western Philosophy* (London: Thames & Hudson; New York: Bobbs-Merrill, 1971). (See Part V of this volume for a detailed discussion of prudential accounts of religious belief.)

15. It is worth stressing this point, since nowadays it is frequently denied. Thus L. C. Velecky, in an article in *Philosophy* (1968), asserts: "He did not prove here the existence of God, nor indeed, did he prove it anywhere else, for a very good reason. According to Thomas, God's existence is unknowable and, hence, cannot be proved" (p. 226). The quotations from Aquinas given in my text ought to be decisive. Yet there seems to be quite a school of devout interpretation which waives aside what the Saint straightforwardly said as almost irrelevent to the question of what he really meant.

16. St. Thomas Aquinas, *Summa Theologica,* I, Q2 A3.

17. In this perspective it becomes easier to see why Aquinas makes so much use of Aristotelian scientific ideas in his arguments. That they are in fact much more dependent on these now largely obsolete ideas is usefully emphasized in Anthony Kenny's *The Five Ways* (London: Routledge & Kegan Paul; New York: Schocken Books, 1969). But Kenny does not bring out that they were deployed against a presumption of atheist naturalism.

18. Velecky, pp. 225–26.

# 2

# The Problem of Evil and Some Varieties
# of Atheism

## *William L. Rowe*

This paper is concerned with three interrelated questions. The first is: Is there an argument for atheism based on the existence of evil that may rationally justify someone in being an atheist? To this first question I give an affirmative answer and try to support that answer by setting forth a strong argument for atheism based on the existence of evil.[1] The second question is: How can the theist best defend his position against the argument for atheism based on the existence of evil? In response to this question I try to describe what may be an adequate rational defense for theism against any argument for atheism based on the existence of evil. The final question is: What position should the informed atheist take concerning the rationality of theistic belief? Three different answers an atheist may give to this question serve to distinguish three varieties of atheism: unfriendly atheism, indifferent atheism, and friendly atheism. In the final part of the paper I discuss and defend the position of friendly atheism.

Before we consider the argument from evil, we need to distinguish a narrow and a broad sense of the terms "theist," "atheist," and "agnostic." By a "theist" in the narrow sense I mean someone who believes in the existence of an omnipotent, omniscient, eternal, supremely good being who created the world. By a "theist" in the broad sense I mean someone who believes in the existence of some sort of divine being or divine reality. To be a theist in the narrow sense is also to be a theist in the broad sense, but one may be a theist in the broad sense—as was Paul Tillich—without believing that there is a supremely good, omnipotent, omniscient, eternal being who created the world. Similar distinctions must be made between a narrow and a broad sense of the terms "atheist" and "agnostic." To be an atheist in the broad sense is to deny the existence of any sort of divine being or divine reality. Tillich was not an atheist in the broad sense. But he was an atheist in the narrow sense, for he denied that there exists a divine being that is all-knowing, all-powerful, and perfectly good. In this paper I will be using the terms "theism," "theist," "atheism,"

Reprinted from the *American Philosophical Quarterly* 16 (1979), by permission of the editor. Notes edited.

"atheist," "agnosticism," and "agnostic" in the narrow sense, not in the broad sense.

# I

In developing the argument for atheism based on the existence of evil, it will be useful to focus on some particular evil that our world contains in considerable abundance. Intense human and animal suffering, for example, occurs daily and in great plenitude in our world. Such intense suffering is a clear case of evil. Of course, if the intense suffering leads to some greater good, a good we could not have obtained without undergoing the suffering in question, we might conclude that the suffering is justified, but it remains an evil nevertheless. For we must not confuse the intense suffering in and of itself with the good things to which it sometimes leads or of which it may be a necessary part. Intense human or animal suffering is in itself bad, an evil, even though it may sometimes be justified by virtue of being a part of, or leading to, some good which is unobtainable without it. What is evil in itself may sometimes be good as a means because it leads to something that is good in itself. In such a case, while remaining an evil in itself, the intense human or animal suffering is, nevertheless, an evil which someone might be morally justified in permitting.

Taking human and animal suffering as a clear instance of evil which occurs with great frequency in our world, the argument for atheism based on evil can be stated as follows:

1.  There exist instances of intense suffering which an omnipotent, omniscient being could have prevented without thereby losing some greater good or permitting some evil equally bad or worse.[2]
2.  An omniscient, wholly good being would prevent the occurrence of any intense suffering it could, unless it could not do so without thereby losing some greater good or permitting some evil equally bad or worse.

3.  There does not exist an omnipotent, omniscient, wholly good being.

What are we to say about this argument for atheism, an argument based on the profusion of one sort of evil in our world? The argument is valid; therefore, if we have rational grounds for accepting its premises, to that extent we have rational grounds for accepting atheism. Do we, however, have rational grounds for accepting the premises of this argument?

Let's begin with the second premise. Let $s_1$ be an instance of intense human or animal suffering which an omniscient, wholly good being could prevent. We will also suppose that things are such that $s_1$ will occur unless prevented by the omniscient, wholly good ($OG$) being. We might be interested in determining what would be a *sufficient* condition of $OG$ failing to prevent $s_1$. But, for our purpose here, we need only try to state a *necessary* condition for $OG$ failing to prevent $s_1$. That condition, so it seems to me, is this:

*Either*  (i)  there is some greater good, $G$, such that $G$ is obtainable by $OG$ only if $OG$ permits $s_1$,[3] *or*  (ii)  there is some greater good, $G$, such that $G$ is obtainable by $OG$ only if $OG$ permits either $s_1$ or some evil equally bad or worse,

*or*  (iii)  $s_1$ is such that it is preventable by $OG$ only if $OG$ permits some evil equally bad or worse.

It is important to recognize that (iii) is not included in (i). For losing a good greater than $s_1$ is not the same as permitting an evil greater than $s_1$. And this because the *absence* of a good state of affairs need not itself be an evil state of affairs. It is also important to recognize that $s_1$ might be such that it is preventable by $OG$ *without* losing $G$ (so condition (i) is not satisfied) but also such that if $OG$ did prevent it, $G$ would be lost *unless* $OG$ permitted some evil equal to or worse than $s_1$. If this were so, it does not seem correct to require that $OG$ prevent $s_1$. Thus, condition (ii) takes into account an important possibility not encompassed in condition (i).

Is it true that if an omniscient, wholly good being permits the occurrence of some intense suffering it could have prevented, then either (i) or (ii) or (iii) obtains? It seems to me that it is true. But if it is true then so is premise (2) of the argument for atheism. For that premise merely states in more compact form what we have suggested must be true if an omniscient, wholly good being fails to prevent some intense suffering it could prevent. Premise (2) says that an omniscient, wholly good being would prevent the occurrence of any intense suffering it could, unless it could not do so without thereby losing some greater good or permitting some evil equally bad or worse. This premise (or something not too distant from it) is, I think, held in common by many atheists and nontheists. Of course, there may be disagreement about whether something is good, and whether, if it is good, one would be morally justified in permitting some intense suffering to occur in order to obtain it. Someone might hold, for example, that no good is great enough to justify permitting an innocent child to suffer terribly.[4] Again, someone might hold that the mere fact that a given good outweighs some suffering and would be lost if the suffering were prevented, is not a morally sufficient reason for permitting the suffering. But to hold either of these views is not to deny (2). For (2) claims only that *if* an omniscient, wholly good being permits intense suffering *then* either there is some greater good that would have been lost, or some equally bad or worse evil that would have occurred, had the intense suffering been prevented. (2) does not purport to describe what might be a *sufficient* condition for an omniscient, wholly good being to permit intense suffering, only what is a *necessary* condition. So stated, (2) seems to express a belief that accords with our basic moral principles, principles shared by both theists and nontheists. If we are to fault the argument for atheism, therefore, it seems we must find some fault with its first premise.

Suppose in some distant forest lightning strikes a dead tree, resulting in a forest fire. In the fire a fawn is trapped, horribly burned, and lies in terrible agony for several days before death relieves its suffering. So far as we can see, the fawn's intense suffering is pointless. For there does not appear to be any greater good such that the prevention of the fawn's suffering would require either the loss of that good or the occurrence of an evil equally bad or worse. Nor does there seem to be any equally bad or worse evil so connected to the fawn's suffering that it would have had to occur had the fawn's suffering been prevented. Could an omnipotent, omniscient being have prevented the fawn's apparently pointless suffering? The answer is obvi-

ous, as even the theist will insist. An omnipotent, omniscient being could have easily prevented the fawn from being horribly burned, or, given the burning, could
have spared the fawn the intense suffering by quickly ending its life, rather than
allowing the fawn to lie in terrible agony for several days. Since the fawn's intense
suffering was preventable and, so far as we can see, pointless, doesn't it appear that
premise (1) of the argument is true, that there do exist instances of intense suffering
which an omnipotent, omniscient being could have prevented without thereby losing some greater good or permitting some evil equally bad or worse.

It must be acknowledged that the case of the fawn's apparently pointless suffering does not *prove* that (1) is true. For even though we cannot see how the fawn's
suffering is required to obtain some greater good (or to prevent some equally bad
or worse evil), it hardly follows that it is not so required. After all, we are often surprised by how things we thought to be unconnected turn out to be intimately connected. Perhaps, for all we know, there is some familiar good outweighing the
fawn's suffering to which that suffering is connected in a way we do not see. Furthermore, there may well be unfamiliar goods, goods we haven't dreamed of, to
which the fawn's suffering is inextricably connected. Indeed, it would seem to
require something like omniscience on our part before we could lay claim to *knowing* that there is no greater good connected to the fawn's suffering in such a manner
that an omnipotent, omniscient being could not have achieved that good without
permitting that suffering or some evil equally bad or worse. So the case of the fawn's
suffering surely does not enable us to *establish* the truth of (1).

The truth is that we are not in a position to prove that (1) is true. We cannot
know with certainty that instances of suffering of the sort described in (1) do occur
in our world. But it is one thing to *know* or *prove* that (1) is true and quite another
thing to have *rational grounds* for believing (1) to be true. We are often in the position where in the light of our experience and knowledge it is rational to believe that
a certain statement is true, even though we are not in a position to prove or to know
with certainty that the statement is true. In the light of our past experience and
knowledge it is, for example, very reasonable to believe that neither Goldwater nor
McGovern will ever be elected President, but we are scarcely in the position of
knowing with certainty that neither will ever be elected President. So, too, with (1),
although we cannot know with certainty that it is true, it perhaps can be rationally
supported, shown to be a rational belief.

Consider again the case of the fawn's suffering. Is it reasonable to believe that
there is some greater good so intimately connected to that suffering that even an
omnipotent, omniscient being could not have obtained that good without permitting that suffering or some evil at least as bad? It certainly does not appear reasonable to believe this. Nor does it seem reasonable to believe that there is some evil at
least as bad as the fawn's suffering such that an omnipotent being simply could not
have prevented it without permitting the fawn's suffering. But even if it should
somehow be reasonable to believe either of these things of the fawn's suffering, we
must then ask whether it is reasonable to believe either of these things of *all* the
instances of seemingly pointless human and animal suffering that occur daily in our
world. And surely the answer to this more general question must be no. It seems
quite unlikely that *all* the instances of intense suffering occurring daily in our world

are intimately related to the occurrence of greater goods or the prevention of evils at least as bad; and even more unlikely, should they somehow all be so related, that an omnipotent, omniscient being could not have achieved at least some of those goods (or prevented some of those evils) without permitting the instances of intense suffering that are supposedly related to them. In the light of our experience and knowledge of the variety and scale of human and animal suffering in our world, the idea that none of this suffering could have been prevented by an omnipotent being without thereby losing a greater good or permitting an evil at least as bad seems an extraordinarily absurd idea, quite beyond our belief. It seems, then, that although we cannot *prove* that (1) is true, it is, nevertheless, altogether *reasonable* to believe that (1) is true, that (1) is a *rational* belief.[5]

Returning now to our argument for atheism, we've seen that the second premise expresses a basic belief common to many theists and nontheists. We've also seen that our experience and knowledge of the variety and profusion of suffering in our world provides *rational support* for the first premise. Seeing that the conclusion "There does not exist an omnipotent, omniscient, wholly good being" follows from these two premises, it does seem that we have *rational support* for atheism, that it is reasonable for us to believe that the theistic God does not exist.

## II

Can theism be rationally defended against the argument for atheism we have just examined? If it can, how might the theist best respond to that argument? Since the argument from (1) and (2) to (3) is valid, and since the theist, no less than the nontheist, is more than likely committed to (2), it's clear that the theist can reject this atheistic argument only by rejecting its first premise, the premise that states that there are instances of intense suffering which an omnipotent, omniscient being could have prevented without thereby losing some greater good or permitting some evil equally bad or worse. How, then, can the theist best respond to this premise and the considerations advanced in its support?

There are basically three responses a theist can make. First, he might argue not that (1) is false or probably false, but only that the reasoning given in support of it is in some way *defective*. He may do this either by arguing that the reasons given in support of (1) are *in themselves* insufficient to justify accepting (1), or by arguing that there are other things we know which, when taken in conjunction with these reasons, do not justify us in accepting (1). I suppose some theists would be content with this rather modest response to the basic argument for atheism. But given the validity of the basic argument and the theist's likely acceptance of (2), he is thereby committed to the view that (1) is false, not just that we have no good reasons for accepting (1) as true. The second two responses are aimed at showing that it is reasonable to believe that (1) is false. Since the theist is committed to this view I shall focus the discussion on these two attempts, attempts which we can distinguish as "the direct attack" and "the indirect attack."

By a direct attack, I mean an attempt to reject (1) by pointing out goods, for example, to which suffering may well be connected, goods which an omnipotent, omniscient being could not achieve without permitting suffering. It is doubtful, however, that the direct attack can succeed. The theist may point out that some suffering leads to moral and spiritual development impossible without suffering. But it's reasonably clear that suffering often occurs in a degree far beyond what is required for character development. The theist may say that some suffering results from free choices of human beings and might be preventable only by preventing some measure of human freedom. But, again, it's clear that much intense suffering occurs not as a result of human free choices. The general difficulty with this direct attack on premise (1) is twofold. First, it cannot succeed, for the theist does not know what greater goods might be served, or evils prevented, by each instance of intense human or animal suffering. Second, the theist's own religious tradition usually maintains that in this life it is not given to us to know God's purpose in allowing particular instances of suffering. Hence, the direct attack against premise (1) cannot succeed and violates basic beliefs associated with theism.

The best procedure for the theist to follow in rejecting premise (1) is the indirect procedure. This procedure I shall call "the G. E. Moore shift," so-called in honor of the twentieth century philosopher, G. E. Moore, who used it to great effect in dealing with the arguments of the skeptics. Skeptical philosophers such as David Hume have advanced ingenious arguments to prove that no one can know of the existence of any material object. The premises of their arguments employ plausible principles, principles which many philosophers have tried to reject directly, but only with questionable success. Moore's procedure was altogether different. Instead of arguing directly against the premises of the skeptic's arguments, he simply noted that the premises implied, for example, that he (Moore) did not know of the existence of a pencil. Moore then proceeded indirectly against the skeptic's premises by arguing:

> If the skeptic's principles are correct I cannot know of the existence of this pencil.
> ──────────────────────────────────────────────────────
> ∴. The skeptic's principles (at least one) must be incorrect.

Moore then noted that his argument is just as valid as the skeptic's, that both of their arguments contain the premise "If the skeptic's principles are correct Moore cannot know of the existence of this pencil," and concluded that the only way to choose between the two arguments (Moore's and the skeptic's) is by deciding which of the first premises it is more rational to believe—Moore's premise "I do know that this pencil exists" or the skeptic's premise asserting that his skeptical principles are correct. Moore concluded that his own first premise was the more rational of the two.[6]

Before we see how the theist may apply the G. E. Moore shift to the basic argument for atheism, we should note the general strategy of the shift. We're given an argument: *p, q,* therefore, *r.* Instead of arguing directly against *p,* another argument is constructed—not-*r, q,* therefore, not-*p*—which begins with the denial of the conclusion of the first argument, keeps its second premise, and ends with the denial of the first premise as its conclusion. Compare, for example, these two:

| I. $p$ | II. not-$r$ |
|--------|-------------|
| $q$    | $q$         |
| ——     | ——          |
| $r$    | not-$p$     |

It is a truth of logic that if I is valid II must be valid as well. Since the arguments are the same so far as the second premise is concerned, any choice between them must concern their respective first premises. To argue against the first premise ($p$) by constructing the counter argument II is to employ the G. E. Moore shift.

Applying the G. E. Moore shift against the first premise of the basic argument for atheism, the theist can argue as follows:

Not-3. There exists an omnipotent, omniscient, wholly good being.
2. An omniscient, wholly good being would prevent the occurrence of any intense suffering it could, unless it could not do so without thereby losing some greater good or permitting some evil equally bad or worse.

Therefore,

not-1. It is not the case that there exist instances of intense suffering which an omnipotent, omniscient being could have prevented without thereby losing some greater good or permitting some evil equally bad or worse.

We now have two arguments: the basic argument for atheism from (1) and (2) to (3), and the theist's best response, the argument from (not-3) and (2) to (not-1). What the theist then says about (1) is that he has rational grounds for believing in the existence of the theistic God (not-3), accepts (2) as true, and sees that (not-1) follows from (not-3) and (2). He concludes, therefore, that he has rational grounds for rejecting (1). Having rational grounds for rejecting (1), the theist concludes that the basic argument for atheism is mistaken.

## III

We've had a look at a forceful argument for atheism and what seems to be the theist's best response to that argument. If one is persuaded by the argument for atheism, as I find myself to be, how might one best view the position of the theist. Of course, he will view the theist as having a false belief, just as the theist will view the atheist as having a false belief. But what position should the atheist take concerning the *rationality* of the theist's belief? There are three major positions an atheist might take, positions which we may think of as some varieties of atheism. First, the atheist may believe that no one is rationally justified in believing that the theistic God exists. Let us call this position "unfriendly atheism." Second, the atheist may hold no belief concerning whether any theist is or isn't rationally justified in believing that the theistic God exists. Let us call this view "indifferent atheism." Finally, the atheist may believe that some theists are rationally justified in believing that the theistic God exists. This view we shall call "friendly atheism." In this final part of the paper I propose to discuss and defend the position of friendly atheism.

If no one can be rationally justified in believing a false proposition, then friendly atheism is a paradoxical, if not incoherent, position. But surely the truth of a belief is not a necessary condition of someone's being rationally justified in having that belief. So in holding that someone is rationally justified in believing that the theistic God exists, the friendly atheist is not committed to thinking that the theist has a true belief. What he is committed to is that the theist has rational grounds for his belief, a belief the atheist rejects and is convinced he is rationally justified in rejecting. But is this possible? Can someone, like our friendly atheist, hold a belief, be convinced that he is rationally justified in holding that belief, and yet believe that someone else is equally justified in believing the opposite? Surely this is possible. Suppose your friends see you off on a flight to Hawaii. Hours after take-off they learn that your plane has gone down at sea. After a twenty-four hour search, no survivors have been found. Under these circumstances they are rationally justified in believing that you have perished. But it is hardly rational for you to believe this, as you bob up and down in your life vest, wondering why the search planes have failed to spot you. Indeed, to amuse yourself while awaiting your fate, you might very well reflect on the fact that your friends are rationally justified in believing that you are now dead, a proposition you disbelieve and are rationally justified in disbelieving. So, too, perhaps an atheist may be rationally justified in his atheistic belief and yet hold that some theists are rationally justified in believing just the opposite of what he believes.

What sort of grounds might a theist have for believing that God exists? Well, he might endeavor to justify his belief by appealing to one or more of the traditional arguments: Ontological, Cosmological, Teleological, Moral, etc. Second, he might appeal to certain aspects of religious experience, perhaps even his own religious experience. Third, he might try to justify theism as a plausible theory in terms of which we can account for a variety of phenomena. Although an atheist must hold that the theistic God does not exist, can he not also believe, and be justified in so believing, that some of these "justifications of theism" do actually rationally justify some theists in their belief that there exists a supremely good, omnipotent, omniscient being? It seems to me that he can.

If we think of the long history of theistic belief and the special situations in which people are sometimes placed, it is perhaps as absurd to think that no one was ever rationally justified in believing that the theistic God exists as it is to think that no one was ever justified in believing that a human being would never walk on the moon. But in suggesting that friendly atheism is preferable to unfriendly atheism, I don't mean to rest the case on what some human beings might reasonably have believed in the eleventh or thirteenth century. The more interesting question is whether some people in modern society, people who are aware of the usual grounds for belief and disbelief and are acquainted to some degree with modern science, are yet rationally justified in accepting theism. Friendly atheism is a significant position only if it answers this question in the affirmative.

It is not difficult for an atheist to be friendly when he has reason to believe that the theist could not reasonably be expected to be acquainted with the grounds for disbelief that he (the atheist) possesses. For then the atheist may take the view that some theists are rationally justified in holding to theism, but would not be so were they to be acquainted with the grounds for disbelief—those grounds being sufficient to tip the scale in favor of atheism when balanced against the reasons the theist has in support of his belief.

Friendly atheism becomes paradoxical, however, when the atheist contemplates believing that the theist has all the grounds for atheism that he, the atheist, has, and yet is rationally justified in maintaining his theistic belief. But even so excessively friendly a view as this perhaps can be held by the atheist if he also has some reason to think that the grounds for theism are not as telling as the theist is justified in taking them to be.[7]

In this paper I've presented what I take to be a strong argument for atheism, pointed out what I think is the theist's best response to that argument, distinguished three positions an atheist might take concerning the rationality of theistic belief, and made some remarks in defense of the position called "friendly atheism." I'm aware that the central points of the paper are not likely to be warmly received by many philosophers. Philosophers who are atheists tend to be tough minded—holding that there are no good reasons for supposing that theism is true. And theists tend either to reject the view that the existence of evil provides rational grounds for atheism or to hold that religious belief has nothing to do with reason and evidence at all. But such is the way of philosophy.[8]

# Notes

1. Some philosophers have contended that the existence of evil is *logically inconsistent* with the existence of the theistic God. No one, I think, has succeeded in establishing such an extravagant claim. Indeed, granted incompatibilism, there is a fairly compelling argument for the view that the existence of evil is logically consistent with the existence of the theistic God. (For a lucid statement of this argument see Alvin Plantinga, *God, Freedom, and Evil* [New York: Harper & Row, 1974], pp. 29–59.) There remains, however, what we may call the *evidential* form—as opposed to the *logical* form—of the problem of evil: the view that the variety and profusion of evil in our world, although perhaps not logically inconsistent with the existence of the theistic God, provides, nevertheless, *rational support* for atheism. In this paper I shall be concerned solely with the evidential form of the problem, the form of the problem which, I think, presents a rather severe difficulty for theism.

2. If there is some good, $G$, greater than any evil, (1) will be false for the trivial reason that, no matter what evil, $E$, we pick, the conjunctive good state of affairs consisting of $G$ and $E$ will outweigh $E$ and be such that an omnipotent being could not obtain it without permitting $E$. (See Alvin Plantinga, *God and Other Minds* [Ithaca, NY: Cornell University Press, 1967], p. 167.) To avoid this objection we may insert "unreplaceable" into our premises (1) and (2) between "some" and "greater." If $E$ isn't required for $G$, and $G$ is better than $G$ plus $E$, then the good conjunctive state of affairs composed of $G$ and $E$ would be *replaceable* by the greater good of $G$ alone. For the sake of simplicity, however, I will ignore this complication both in the formulation and discussion of premises (1) and (2).

3. Three clarifying points need to be made in connection with (i). First, by "good" I don't mean to exclude the fulfillment of certain moral principles. Perhaps preventing $s_1$ would preclude certain actions prescribed by the principles of justice. I shall allow that the satisfaction of certain principles of justice may be a good that outweighs the evil of $s_1$. Second, even though (i) may suggest it, I don't mean to limit the good in question to something that would

*follow in time* the occurrence of $s_1$. And, finally, we should perhaps not fault $OG$ if the good $G$, that would be lost were $s_1$ prevented, is not actually greater than $s_1$, but merely such that allowing $s_1$ and $G$, as opposed to preventing $s_1$ and thereby losing $G$, would not alter the balance between good and evil. For reasons of simplicity, I have left this point out in stating (i), with the result that (i) is perhaps a bit stronger than it should be.

4. See Ivan's speech in Book V, Chapter 4 of *The Brothers Karamazov.*

5. One might object that the conclusion of this paragraph is stronger than the reasons given warrant. For it is one thing to argue that it is unreasonable to think that (1) is false and another thing to conclude that we are therefore justified in accepting (1) as true. There are propositions such that believing them is much more reasonable than disbelieving them, and yet are such that *withholding judgment* about them is more reasonable than believing them. To take an example of Chisholm's: it is more reasonable to believe that the Pope will be in Rome (on some arbitrarily picked future date) than to believe that he won't; but it is perhaps more reasonable to suspend judgment on the question of the Pope's whereabouts on that particular date, than to believe that he will be in Rome. Thus, it might be objected that, while we've shown that believing (1) is more reasonable than disbelieving (1), we haven't shown that believing (1) is more reasonable than withholding belief. My answer to this objection is that there are things we know which render (1) probable to the degree that it is more reasonable to believe (1) than to suspend judgment on (1). What are these things we know? First, I think, is the fact that there is an enormous variety and profusion of intense human and animal suffering in our world. Second is the fact that much of this suffering seems quite unrelated to any greater goods (or the absence of equal or greater evils) that might justify it. And, finally, there is the fact that such suffering as is related to greater goods (or the absence of equal or greater evils) does not, in many cases, seem so intimately related as to require its permission by an omnipotent being bent on securing those goods (the absence of those evils). These facts, I am claiming, make it more reasonable to accept (1) than to withhold judgment on (1).

6. See, for example, the two chapters on Hume in G. E. Moore, *Some Main Problems of Philosophy* (London: Allen & Unwin, 1953).

7. Suppose that I add a long sum of numbers three times and get result $x$. I inform you of this so that you have pretty much the same evidence I have for the claim that the sum of the numbers is $x$. You then use your calculator twice over and arrive at result $y$. You, then, are justified in believing that the sum of the numbers is *not x*. However, knowing that your calculator has been damaged and is therefore unreliable, and that you have no reason to think that it is damaged, *I* may reasonably believe not only that the sum of the numbers is $x$, but also that you are justified in believing that the sum is not $x$. Here is a case, then, where you have all of my evidence for $p$, and yet I can reasonably believe that you are justified in believing not-$p$—for I have reason to believe that your grounds for not-$p$ are not as telling as you are justified in taking them to be.

8. I am indebted to my colleagues at Purdue University, particularly to Ted Ulrich and Lilly Russow, and to philosophers at the University of Nebraska, Indiana State University, and the University of Wisconsin at Milwaukee for helpful criticisms of earlier versions of this paper.

# 3

# Atheistic Teleological Arguments

## Michael Martin

. . . The traditional teleological argument and its various modern formulations are not sound arguments for the existence of God.[1] . . . What has not been fully appreciated is that the sort of criticisms of the traditional teleological argument developed by Hume can be used *against* the existence of an all-knowing, all-powerful, and all-good God. That is to say, Hume's arguments, if properly understood . . . can be used to support disbelief in the existence of a theistic God. In this [paper] I develop and defend arguments of this sort. I call them atheistic teleological arguments.

### Salmon's Argument

Philo in Hume's *Dialogues Concerning Natural Religion* maintained that there is no strong argument from analogy from our experience to the conclusion that the universe was created out of nothing by an infinite disembodied being. A stronger argument from analogy, he says, is from our experience to the conclusion that the universe was created from preexisting material by a plurality of finite embodied gods. If we take Philo's argument seriously, it suggests that the *nonexistence* of a theistic God is supported by analogical arguments from experience.

A recent argument by Wesley Salmon can be understood as building upon this insight. Salmon uses probabilistic considerations derived from a reformulation of Philo's argument to show that the existence of God is improbable.[2] Salmon estimates these probabilities: (1) that an entity created by an intelligent agency exhibits order, (2) that an entity that is not created by an intelligent agency does not exhibit order, (3) that an entity is created by an intelligent agency, (4) that an entity is not so created, (5) that an entity exhibits order, and (6) that an entity does not. Given these estimates and Bayes's theorem, he argues that it is much more probable that an entity such as the universe whose origin is unknown was not created by intelligent agency than that it was.

The argument, stated more formally and in greater detail, is this: Let D designate the class of objects created by an intelligent agency. Let O refer to the class of objects that exhibit order. Then

$P(D,O)$ = the probability that an object created by an intelligent agency exhibits order.

$P(\sim D,O)$ = the probability that an object not created by an intelligent agency exhibits order.

$P(D)$ = the probability of an object created by an intelligent agency.

$P(O)$ = the probability of an object exhibiting order.

$(P \sim D)$ = the probability of an object not created by an intelligent agency.

$P(O,D)$ = the probability that an object exhibiting order is created by an intelligent agency.

$P(O,\sim D)$ = the probability that an object exhibiting order is not created by an intelligent agency.

According to Bayes's theorem:

$$P(O,D) = [P(D,O) \times P(D)]/P(O)$$
$$P(O,\sim D) = [P(\sim D,O) \times P(\sim D)]/P(O)$$

Salmon attempts to assess the various probabilities involved in this theorem. He maintains that given the incredibly large number of entities in our universe that are not the result of intelligence—galaxies, planets, atoms, molecules—$P(D)$ is very low whereas $P(\sim D)$ is very high. Further, he maintains that although $P(D,O)$ is high, it may not be near unity. This is because intelligent design may in fact produce chaos such as one finds in war. He maintains that $P(\sim D,O)$ is not negligible since biological generation and mechanical causation often produce order. Salmon argues that given this assessment, "we are in a position to say, quite confidently," that $P(O,D)$ is very low for any unspecified entity.[3]

But Salmon maintains that this does not settle the matter in the case of the creation of the universe, since we are dealing with a single unique event. Where a unique event is at issue one should refer the case to the broadest homogeneous reference class—that is, to the broadest class that cannot be relevantly subdivided. When this is applied to the design argument, Salmon says, one must take into account the type of order that the universe exhibits and the sort of intelligent creator that theists believe the teleological argument proves. Following Philo's argument, he maintains that if one takes these considerations into account, far from improving the probability of the theists' conclusion, the situation is worsened.

For example, the creator of the universe is regarded as pure spirit, a disembodied intelligence. But in no instance in our experience has a disembodied intelligence produced order. Thus where $D_i$ is the class of disembodied intelligences, $P(D_i) = 0$. Further, as far as our experience is concerned, order of a large magnitude is never produced by a single designer. Thus if $D_s$ is the class of single designers and $O_m$ is the class of extremely large objects, $P(D_s,O_m) = 0$. Since the universe is an entity with a large magnitude it is improbable that it was created by a single designer. Thus, when one takes into account the particular attributes involved in the unique case of the creation of the universe, the probability that the universe was created by an intelligent being becomes vanishingly small.

## Cartwright's Critique

Nancy Cartwright maintains that Salmon has begged the question in supposing that galaxies, planets, atoms, molecules, and so on are not the result of design.[4] Consequently, he cannot assume that P(D) is very low whereas P($\sim$D) is very high. She argues that in fact it is very hard to assess these probabilities inductively since there are few cases on whose origin the theist and the atheist agree. Therefore, to determine the frequency at which ordered objects arise from a random process, she suggests a controlled experiment. For example, she suggests that we might put the parts of a watch in a box and shake the box. The probability of getting the watch together in this way is, according to Cartwright, "as near zero as can be."[5] As Cartwright points out, atheists may argue that given billions of years there is a great likelihood that the watch would come together in this random way. But there is no way of knowing this with any confidence, she says, and it is best to use experimental results. On the basis of these results, and contrary to Salmon's claim, P(D,O), is much higher than P($\sim$D,O).

## Salmon's Retort

In a reply[6] to Cartwright, Salmon maintains that the proposed experiment is irrelevant. He never supposed, he argues, that watches and other human artifacts could result from unintelligent causes: "I rested my case on things like atoms and molecules, stars and galaxies."[7] Salmon says that on the best cosmological knowledge, "everything from atoms to galaxies" was formed without intelligent design. Although cosmology is not an experimental science, Salmon adds, "it is built upon physical disciplines, such as thermodynamics and quantum mechanics, which are extensively supported by experimental evidence."[8]

## Assessment of the Debate

Has Salmon answered Cartwright's charge that he has begged the question? What does it mean to beg the question? As this expression is usually understood, to beg the question is to assume what one is supposed to prove. Salmon was out to show that it is probable that the universe was not designed by an intelligent being, and he assumed in his premises that atoms, molecules, and galaxies were not the result of intelligent design. This is not what he was out to prove unless one supposes that the universe is nothing more than atoms, molecules, and galaxies. But it is not clear that Salmon assumes this. At the very least, Cartwright's criticism is mislabeled. Cartwright can be understood, however, as simply saying that some of Salmon's premises are now unjustified and could only be justified by experimental evidence that is all but impossible to acquire. But Salmon provides indirect experimental evidence from scientific cosmology to support the premises that Cartwright questioned. Unless Cartwright finds problems with this evidence it would seem not only that no question has obviously been begged but that the disputed premises have a good degree of empirical support. Given these premises, it is improbable that the universe was created by an intelligent being.

Furthermore, even if Salmon has begged the question in assuming that atoms, molecules, and galaxies are not the result of an intelligent agency, or if at least he has not provided enough support for this assumption, his arguments that turn on the special properties of the universe and the alleged creator of this universe would not be affected. Recall that he maintained:

$$P(D_i) = 0$$
$$P(D_s, O_m) = 0$$

It is difficult to see that any question has been begged or why these propositions are not justified by our experience. Experience surely teaches that there are no disembodied beings. As Salmon puts it: "In no instance within our experience . . . has a disembodied intellect produced any kind of artifact, whether or not it might have exhibited any order. Indeed, since disembodied intelligence has never operated in any fashion, to the best of our knowledge, we must conclude from experience that for such an intelligence," $P(D_i) = 0$, and $P(D_iO)$ is simply undefined.[9] Furthermore, experience teaches that the agency of a single being does not produce extremely large objects with order; that is, $P(D_s, O_m) = 0$. Substituting in Bayes's theorem we obtain the following results: $P(O, D_i)$ is undefined and $P(O_m, D_s) = 0$. In terms of our experience, then, the probability that a unique disembodied being created the universe is "as near to zero as can be." $P(O_m, D_s) = 0$ yields this result when substituted in Bayes's theorem, and $P(D_i) = 0$ yields this directly without need of substitution.

I conclude, therefore, that unless a better refutation is offered, Salmon's argument gives good grounds for supposing that God did not create the universe.

## Expansion of the Argument

If Salmon's arguments concerning the unique properties of God are restated and expanded, they provide a powerful inductive case for positive atheism in the narrow sense.[10] The theistic God is an all-powerful, all-knowing, all-good, disembodied person who created the universe out of nothing. If it can be shown that, in the light of the evidence, such a being is improbable, then disbelief that the theistic God exists is justified. Consequently, positive atheism in the narrow sense is justified.

The general form an expanded argument takes is this:

1. In terms of our experience, created entities of kind K that have been examined are always (or almost always, or usually) created by a being (or beings) with property P.
2. The universe is a created entity.
2a. If the universe is a created entity, it is of kind K.

[Probably]

3. The universe was created by a being with property P.
4. If the theistic God exists, then the universe was not created by a being with property P.

5. Therefore, the theistic God does not exist.

The first part of the argument takes the form of an acceptable inductive argument. The inference from premises (1), (2), and (2a) to the conclusion (3)—sometimes called a predictive inference—moves from a property shared by all or most of the examined members of a class to some unexamined member that has this property. Premises (1), (2), and (2a) do not entail (3), they only make (3) probable. On the other hand, (3) and (4) do entail (5). Nevertheless, since (3) is only probable and it is one of the premises used in the derivation of (5), (5) is not established with certainty. Premise (1) is established by empirical observation. That is, in all cases that we have observed, created entities of a certain kind are created by a being or beings with certain properties. Premise (2) is assumed by theists. Premise (2a) is justified unless we have independent evidence to suppose that the universe should not be classified as an entity of type K. Premise (4) is an analytic truth; given our usual understanding of "God," it is true by definition. Let us now consider some instantiations of this argument.

## *The Argument from Embodiedness*

. . . Theists believe that God is a disembodied person and that He created the universe.[11] Some people have questioned whether the concept of a disembodied person is meaningful and, if it is, whether it is coherent. In the present argument I assume that the concept is both meaningful and coherent. It maintains that it is unlikely that a being who is disembodied created the universe, and since this is unlikely, it is unlikely that God exists.

The argument proceeds as follows:

1. In terms of our experience, all created entities of the kinds that we have so far examined are created by one or more beings with bodies. [Empirical evidence]
2. The universe is a created entity. [Supposition]
2a. If the universe is a created entity, then it is of the same kind as the created entities we have so far examined. [Empirical evidence]

[Probably]
3. The universe was created by one or more beings with bodies. [From (1), (2), and (2a) by predictive inference]
4. If the theistic God exists, then the universe was not created by a being with a body. [Analytic truth]

5. Therefore, the theistic God does not exist. [From (3) and (4) by *modus tollens*]

Since premises (2) and (4) seem unproblematic and the deductive inference from (3) and (4) to (5) seems uncontroversial, let us concentrate on premises (1) and (2a) and the inference from (1), (2), and (2a) to (3).

Consider premise (1). What possible objections could there be to this premise? One objection that could be raised is that premise (1) begs the question against theism by assuming what needs to be proved: that if the universe was created, it was not created by a being without a body. It may be said that this is already assumed in premise (1), for it is assumed that all created entities are created by one or more beings with bodies. However, this objection is mistaken. Premise (1) does not assume that all created entities are created by one or more beings with bodies. It simply says that, as far as we can tell from our experience, all created entities of the kinds we have so far examined are created by one or more beings with bodies.

There might be cases for which there is no evidence as to whether some entity is created by some being or beings. Perhaps in the case of living organisms we do not have this kind of evidence. Perhaps this is also true in the case of stars and atoms. Then again, taking into account Salmon's retort to Cartwright, perhaps we do. For the purpose of the argument this need not be decided. What *is* clear is that in all uncontroversial cases of created objects, these were created by one or more beings with bodies. Or to put it in a slightly different way, we know of no cases where an entity is created by one or more beings without bodies.

Our experience does not rule out the possibility of an entity created by a disembodied being. Indeed, some of the entities we see every day may be of that sort. But we have no experience to support the belief that there are such entities. We have seen created entities that are large, old, complex, and so on that are created by one or more beings with bodies. We have not seen any created entities that are large, beautiful, difficult to understand, and so on that are created by a disembodied entity or entities. The universe is large, old, complex, and so on. We cannot observe whether it is created by one or more beings with or without bodies. But from the evidence we do have, we can infer that if it was created, it was probably created by one or more beings with bodies. Thus there is no reason to suppose that the question has been begged. We do not *assume* that the universe was created by one or more beings with bodies. We *infer* this from the available evidence.

It may also be objected that premise (2a) is dubious, and therefore the argument fails. The universe, it is said, is unique; it is one of a kind. Consequently, it is a mistake to put it in the same class as other created objects. For example, the universe is infinitely larger, older, and more complex than any created object we have ever experienced. Because of these differences, we have no right to assimilate the universe to the kind of created object that we normally experience.

What reason is there to suppose that the vast size, age, or complexity of the universe is relevant? There does not seem to be any evidence supporting this view. For example, as we examine larger and larger entities that we know are created, we do *not* find that more and more of them are created by beings that are disembodied. In fact, as far as our evidence is concerned, the size of the created object is irrelevant. All created objects from the smallest (a pinhead) to the largest (a battleship or a city) are created by beings with bodies. Similar points can be made about age and complexity. As far as our experience is concerned, neither the age nor the complexity of a created object is relevant to whether it is created by a being that is disembodied. Indeed, as far as our experience is concerned, no property of a created thing is relevant to whether it is created by a disembodied entity. No matter what kinds of things known to be created we have examined, none of them is known to be created by a disembodied entity. We must conclude that this objection does not show that (2a) is a dubious premise.

Finally, it may be argued that the inductive inference from (1), (2), and (2a) to (3) is weak in that the sample on which it is based is relatively small. For most of the objects we experience in our lives, we do not know if they are created or not. For all we know, atoms, molecules, stars, living organisms, and grains of sand may be created objects. Relative to this class, the class of objects that we know to be created is small. Yet it is this latter class that our inference is based on. If, for example, we had knowledge of whether atoms, molecules, stars, living organisms, and grains of sand were created, our sample might well give us good grounds for concluding that the universe is a created object. But we do not.

As Salmon has argued, scientific theory and evidence strongly support the view that entities such as stars and molecules are not created. But let us suppose that such evidence and theory do not exist. We must base our rational beliefs on the available evidence, which indicates that in all noncontroversial cases of objects known to be created, these objects were created by beings with a body. Our sample would be changed if new evidence came to light, and our present belief would not be rational in relation to this enlarged sample. Yet this is irrelevant to our present situation. Our sample as it stands is large and varied. It consists of literally billions of known created entities that have not been created by a disembodied being or beings and contain no known created entity that has been created by a disembodied being or beings. Furthermore, it contains evidence of all the various kinds of known created entities. It is surely irrelevant that the sample would be larger or more varied if, for example, we knew that atoms, molecules, stars, living organisms, and grains of sand were created and if these were included in it. The larger sample might give us more confidence in any inference made on its basis, but it would not show that an inference made on the basis of a smaller and less varied sample was unreliable.

Since the argument from embodiedness has the form of a strong inductive argument, the premises are well supported, and objections to it can be met, we conclude that it is a strong argument for the nonexistence of the theistic God.

## The Argument from Multiple Creators

Theism is a monistic view in that God and not a plurality of supernatural beings is said to have created the universe. Yet our experience indicates that all large and complex entities are created by a group of beings working together. Although we have no direct experience of the universe's being created by a group of beings, from our experience one should infer inductively that if the universe is a created entity, it was created by a group of beings. But if so, then the existence of a theistic God is unlikely. The argument can be stated more formally as follows:

1. In terms of our experience, all large and complex created entities of the kinds that we have so far examined are created by a group of beings working together. [Empirical evidence]
2. The universe is a created entity. [Supposition]

2a. If the universe is a created entity, then it is a large and complex created entity of the same kind as some of the created large and complex entities we have so far examined. [Empirical evidence]

[Probably]

3. The universe was created by a group of beings working together. [From (1), (2), and (2a) by predictive inference]
4. If the theistic God exists, then the universe was not created by a group of beings working together. [Analytic truth]
5. Therefore, the theistic God does not exist. [From (3) and (4) by *modus tollens*]

Presumably the same sort of objections that just were discussed in relation to the argument from embodiedness could be raised against this argument, and they can be disposed of in exactly the same way. For example, it may be argued that the universe is unique; it is infinitely larger and more complex than any known created object. Consequently, it cannot be classified with the known created entities that are large and complex. But why should the universe's infinitely greater size and complexity make any difference? Indeed, as far as experience is concerned, the larger and more complex a created entity becomes the greater the likelihood that it was created by a group of beings working together. The largest and most complex created entities—cities, battleships, hydroelectric plants, interstate highway systems—are in all cases created by many individuals working together. In general, the larger and more complex the entity, the more beings are involved in its creation. Thus the vastness and complexity of the universe would show not the inappropriateness of the argument from multiple creators but that its conclusion is even better supported than one might have supposed. This conclusion about the number of entities involved in the creation of large and complex entities is supported also by a large and varied sample. We have found that large and complex created objects are created by multiple entities in numerous cases and in a wide variety of circumstances—for example, the pyramids and Hoover Dam. It seems to be true no matter what the object is made of, no matter what the moral views of the participants, no matter what the technology of the creators.

We must conclude, then, that there is strong inductive reason to suppose that if the universe was created, it was created by multiple beings and, consequently, that the theistic God does not exist.

## The Argument from Apparent Fallibility

In our observation of created objects we sometimes notice what appear to be mistakes and errors. It usually turns out that these are the result of the fallibility of the creator or creators. The universe also appears to have mistakes and errors. If it is a created object, chances are that any and all of its creators are fallible. But if the creator of the universe is fallible, then God does not exist, since God is infallible and the creator of the universe. The argument, stated more formally, is as follows:

1. In terms of our experience, most seeming errors or mistakes in the kinds of created entities we have so far examined are the result of the fallibility of one or more creators of the entities. [Empirical evidence]

2. The universe is a created entity. [Supposition]
2a. If the universe is a created entity, then it is an entity of a kind we have so far examined, with seeming errors or mistakes. [Empirical evidence]

[Probably]

3. The seeming errors or mistakes in the universe are the result of the actions of a fallible being or beings. [From (1), (2), and (2a) by predictive inference]
4. If the theistic God exists, then the seeming errors or mistakes in the universe are the results of the actions of a being who is infallible. [Analytic truth]
5. Therefore, the theistic God does not exist. [From (3) and (4) by *modus tollens*]

Consider premise (1). This is well confirmed by our experience. For example, we are told that a recently constructed building has poor ventilation; we notice that getting the spare tire out of the trunk in our new car is awkward because of the way the trunk is constructed; we read about a new city in Brazil that has been constructed with inadequate sanitation facilities for the estimated population.

Sometimes, of course, we are mistaken in our judgments about what is an error. The evidence of poor ventilation may stem from our failure to understand how the new system works. The city in Brazil may have adequate sanitation facilities despite reports. Our mistaken suppositions about errors are usually corrected as we become acquainted with the created objects. Indeed, it would be most unusual if the misapprehension persisted after a few years of acquaintance. Moreover, whatever the problems with the created entity, we usually discover that they result from the fallibility of the creator or creators. For example, the failure of the architects of the building to anticipate certain factors resulted in poor circulation of air; the automotive engineers did not forsee that building the trunk in a certain way would make it awkward to remove the spare tire; the city planners made errors in their calculations.

Sometimes, of course, we find that the problem was anticipated, yet there was a compelling reason for creating the object in that way. For example, the automotive engineers built the trunk in a certain way, knowing it would be awkward to remove a tire, because it was much cheaper to do so. If this is not so, we can usually tell. For example, we reason that if the trunk was built in this way to save money, we can expect that other design aspects of the automobile will reflect similar attempts at economy. But we may not find other attempts at economy. Moreover, there may be other reasons to suppose that economy was not an issue. For example, we may also estimate that getting a tire out of the trunk could have been made much easier without any more expense by raising one part of the trunk and lowering another. We could be wrong in our reasoning, but experience teaches that we usually are not. What appear to be mistakes because of the fallibility of the creators of objects are usually just that.

If the universe is a created entity, it contains what appear to be errors or mistakes of its creator or creators. For example, there appear to be great inefficiencies in the process of evolution: some of the organs of animals have no apparent function; some organisms seem to have no function in the ecological whole. There are apparent errors also in the genetic endowment of certain organisms: for example, because of genetic deficiencies, children are born blind and crippled. Our experience indicates that in most of the cases we have examined when a created entity seems to have some mistakes, the mistakes are due to the fallibility of the creator or creators. So it is probable that this is true of the apparent errors or mistakes found in the universe; the creator or creators of the universe are fallible. However, since God is supposed to be infallible and the creator of the universe, God does not exist.

The same sort of objections can be raised against this argument as against the argument from embodiedness and the argument from multiple creators, and they can be handled in exactly the same way. However, a new objection can be raised against this argument. It can be maintained that, to the eye of the believer, the universe does not seem as if it contains errors or mistakes. It may be said that what the nonbeliever sees as the uselessness of certain organs and organisms, a theist sees as God's mysterious but perfect handiwork.

This objection has no force, however. First, the way the universe appears to the believer is irrelevant. The question is how it appears to those who have not made up their minds and are basing their beliefs on the evidence. Second, very often the universe appears to theists to contain mistakes and errors of creation. They attempt to explain these appearances away by assumptions such as that God cannot logically create a better universe. The force of the present argument is that all these ways of explaining away the appearance of error fly in the face of the evidence. If we remain true to the evidence, we must suppose, if the universe was created at all, that what seems like an error is just that and is based on what most apparent errors are based on: the fallibility of the creator or creators.

We must therefore conclude that there is good reason to suppose that the theistic God does not exist.

## The Argument from Finiteness

Our experience with entities known to be created is that they are created by beings with finite power. No matter what the object—be it small or large, old or new, simple or complex—if we know that it was created, we have found that it was created by a being or beings with finite power. If the universe is a created object, then probably it was created by a being or beings with finite power. However, since the theistic God has unlimited power and is supposed to be the creator of the universe, the theistic God does not exist. More formally, the argument can be stated in this way:

1. In terms of our experience, all created entities of the kinds that we have so far examined were created by a being or beings with finite power. [Empirical evidence]
2. The universe is a created entity. [Supposition]
2a. If the universe is a created entity, then it is of the same kind as some of the created entities we have so far examined. [Empirical evidence]

[Probably]
3. The universe was created by a being or beings with finite power. [From (1), (2), and (2a) by predictive inference]

4. If the theistic God exists, then the universe was not created by a being with finite power. [Analytic truth]

5. Therefore, the theistic God does not exist. [From (3) and (4) by *modus tollens*]

The same sort of objections can be raised against this argument as against the preceding ones, and they can be handled in exactly the same way. Again, however, a new objection can be raised. It can be maintained that the vast size and complexity of the universe suggest that the creator or creators of the universe would have to have infinite power. If we extrapolate to the universe from the amount of power it takes to produce the things we know are created, we can reasonably infer that the universe, if it was created, was created by a being or beings with unlimited power.

This argument is not warranted by our experience, however. Of course, one could imagine a world in which experience supports to some extent the extrapolation assumed in the argument. But even in that case it is unclear that an inference to an infinitely powerful being would be warranted. Consider a world in which the larger and more complex the entities known to have been created, the larger and more powerful the beings who created the objects. For example, in this world there might be a series of progressively larger giants. If an object of x size and complexity were found, we would discover that it was created by 20-foot-tall giants; if an object of $x^2$ size and complexity were found, we would discover that it was created by 200-foot-tall giants. And so on. In this world we might infer that if galaxies were created, they were created by giants of truly enormous size and power. In this world we also might infer that if the universe was created at all, then it was created by giants of even greater size and power than those that created the galaxies. However, it is unclear that we would be justified in inferring that the universe was created by giants of infinite size and power.

In any case, the world is not our world. In our world all known created objects are created by finite beings. The size of the beings seems to be roughly the same; the power of the beings is increased only through technological means. If modern creators have more power than the ancients, it is only because of advanced technology. The ancients were able to compensate for inferior technology by the use of mass labor. Given this experience we may infer that if the world was created, it was created by finite beings, perhaps with their power greatly enhanced through superadvanced technology. Any inference that goes beyond this is simply flying in the face of the evidence.

We again must conclude that if the universe was created, it was probably created by a being or beings with finite power. Consequently, the theistic God does not exist.

## The Argument from Preexisting Material

In all cases of created objects that have been investigated, the created object was created on the basis of preexisting material. This is true of all the various kinds of created objects we know, small and large, old and new, complex and simple, useful and useless. We can infer, then that the universe, if it was created, was probably created on the basis of preexisting material. However, although creation *ex nihilo* is perhaps not an essential tenet of theism, it has been claimed to be a distinctive feature of Christianity.[12] If it is, we can infer that the Christian God does not exist. The argument, stated more formally, is this:

1. In terms of our experience, all created entities of the kinds that we have so far examined are created from preexisting material. [Empirical evidence]
2. The universe is a created entity. [Supposition]
2a. If the universe is a created entity, it is of the same kind as some of the created entities we have so far examined. [Empirical evidence]

[Probably]
3. The universe was created from preexisting material. [From (1), (2), and (2a) by predictive inference]
4. If the Christian God exists, then the universe was not created from preexisting material. [Analytic truth]

5. Therefore, the Christian God does not exist. [From (3) and (4) by *modus tollens*]

The same sort of objections can be raised against this argument as against the preceding ones, and they can be handled in exactly the same way. So again we must conclude that there are good inductive reasons to suppose that the Christian God does not exist.

### The Universe as a Created Object

In all the arguments considered above I have supposed for the sake of argument that the universe is a created object. I have shown that if it is, then it probably was not created by the theistic God. But is there any reason to believe that the universe is a created entity? There is Salmon's argument against this. It may be possible, moreover, to develop an argument similar to his that does not make any assumptions about the size of the relative classes of created and noncreated objects. . . . [Wallace Matson has] maintained that both proponents and critics of the argument assume that "the properties according to which we judge whether or not some object is an artifact, are accurate adjustments of parts and curious adapting of means to ends."[13] However, Matson argues that this assumption is false. In actual practice an artifact is distinguished from a natural object by the evidence of machinery and the material from which the object was made.

Matson's insight can be developed in the following way. Let T be the tests that anthropologists and other scientists use to determine whether some item is a created object. We know that almost always when an object meets test T it turns out to be a created object. For example, we know almost always that when an object has certain peculiar marks on it, these have been left by a flaking tool and, consequently, that the object was created. We also know that usually when an object does not meet test T it is not a created object. As Matson points out, the tests actually used by anthropologists and other scientists are not aimed at determining whether the object serves some purpose—that is, whether it shows a fine adjustment of parts and a curious adaptation of means to ends. To illustrate his point, Matson suggests the thought experiment of separating into two piles a heap of created and non-created objects that one has not seen before:

> Let us put in the heap a number of "gismos"—objects especially constructed for the test by common methods of manufacture, i.e., metallic, plastic, painted, machined, welded, but such that the subject of the test has never seen such things before, and they do not in fact display any "accurate adjustment of parts" or "curious adaptating of means to ends." Put into the heap also a number of natural objects which the subject has never seen. Will he have any more difficulty [in separating the objects into two piles]? He will not. The gismos go into one pile, the platypuses and tektites into the other, quite automatically.
>
> Of course one might conceivably make mistakes in this sorting procedure. And it is perhaps hazardous to predict that human visitors to another planet would be entirely and immediately successful in determining, from an inventory of random objects found on its surface, whether it was or had been the abode of intelligent beings. But space explorers would not be at a loss as to how to proceed in the investigation. They would look for evidences of machining, materials that do not exist in nature, regular markings, and the like. Presence of some of these would be taken as evidence, though perhaps not conclusive, of artifice.[14]

Let us call the argument for the nonexistence of God developed on the basis of Matson's insight the argument from the tests of artifice and state it more formally as follows:

1. In almost all the cases examined so far, if an object does not meet test T, it is not created. [Empirical observation]
2. The universe does not meet test T. [Empirical observation]

[Probably]

3. The universe is not created. [From (1) and (2) by predictive inference]
4. If the theistic God exists, then the universe is created. [Analytic truth]

5. Therefore, the theistic God does not exist. [From (3) and (4) by *modus tollens*]

This argument may be criticized in much the same way as the other ones considered here, and these criticisms can be just as easily answered. First, it may be maintained that it begs the question of whether the universe is created. But no question has been begged. I have not assumed that the universe is not created; I inferred this from the evidence. Second, it may be argued that premise (1) is not established. But it has been established in the same way that Salmon's assumption was established that planets, atoms, and galaxies are not created objects. According to the best scientific theory and evidence we have, if some object is not made of certain material, does not have certain markings, and so on, it is usually not a created object. Such evidence and theory could be mistaken, but it is the best we have to go on.

Third, it may be objected that the universe is unique and should not be judged by the same tests we use to judge other objects. Although it may be true that the universe is unique, there is no reason to suppose, in the light of our present evidence, that this is relevant in judging whether it is created or not. We have no reason to suppose it cannot be judged by the same criteria we use to judge whether planets, rocks, and gismos are created. Fourth, it may be urged that as our technology advances, we may be able to create objects that resemble more and more the natural objects we find in the universe. If so, then test T will no longer be a reliable method of distinguishing some created objects from noncreated objects. Whether our technology will ever advance to a stage where it would be possible to distinguish by any conceivable test, for example, a created platypus from a noncreated one seems unlikely. Of course, it is certainly likely that our technology will advance to a stage where it would be impossible to tell a created object from a noncreated one by test T. But there is every reason to suppose that our tests for an artifice will improve with our technology and that a new test will be devised that will be able to distinguish the created from the uncreated. In any case, the argument from the tests of artifice is based on our *present* evidence and may have to be given up as new evidence is gathered. This possibility does not affect the present force of the argument.

We can conclude that there is good reason to suppose that the universe is not created and, consequently, that the theistic God does not exist.

## Conclusion

I have shown that if we take seriously the evidence at our disposal, we can infer that the theistic God does not exist. If we assume that the universe is a created object, the creator is probably not the theistic God. However, if we use the criteria for creation that are used by scientists, it is probable that the universe is not created and consequently that the theistic God does not exist.

## Notes

1. This point is defended by Michael Martin in his *Atheism: A Philosophical Justification* (Philadelphia: Temple University Press, 1990), Chapter 5.

2. Wesley C. Salmon, "Religion and Science: A New Look at Hume's *Dialogues,*" *Philosophical Studies* 33 (1978):143–76.

3. Salmon, "Religion and Science," p. 151.

4. Nancy Cartwright, "Comments on Wesley Salmon's 'Science and Religion . . . ,'" *Philosophical Studies* 33 (1978):177–83.

5. Cartwright, "Comments," p. 182.

6. Wesley Salmon, "Experimental Atheism," *Philosophical Studies* 35 (1979):101–4.

7. Salmon, "Experimental Atheism," p. 102.

8. Salmon, "Experimental Atheism," p. 103.

9. Salmon, "Religion and Science," p. 153.

10. Students of David Hume will recognize that I do little more than expand some of the arguments in *Dialogues Concerning Natural Religion.* (Eds.: Martin defines "positive atheism in the narrow sense" as "the position of disbelieving that God exists,"on the strength of a posteriori arguments that God does not exist. This is contrasted with what he calls "negative atheism," which is "the position of not believing that a theistic God exists," on the grounds that religious utterances are cognitively meaningless, that traditional theistic arguments do not succeed, and that no other approach to religious epistemology (i.e., Wittgensteinian fide-

ism, or Reformed epistemology) can provide warrant for belief in God. See Martin, *Atheism,* p. 26.)

11. In recent literature one theist has gone so far as to argue that God does indeed have a body. God's body is the world. See, for example, Grace Jantzen, *God's World, God's Body* (Philadelphia: Westminster Press, 1984). Apparently, this unorthodox theology is in response to arguments attempting to show that the notion of a disembodied being is incoherent. Whether Jantzen's theology succeeds we need not decide here. The problem with this position, from the perspective of the present argument, is that either the world is created or it is not. If it is created, then it is improbable that God exists, even if we grant that He has a body, since in our experience there have been no cases of beings creating their own bodies. If it is not created, then an essential aspect of theism has been given up. For a discussion of Jantzen's views, see Charles Taliaferro, "The Incorporeality of God," *Modern Theology* 3:2 (1987):179–88; Grace Jantzen, "Reply to Taliaferro," *Modern Theology* 3:2 (1987):189–92.

12. See Ronald W. Hepburn, "Religious Doctrine of Creation," in *Encyclopedia of Philosophy,* ed. Paul Edwards (New York: Macmillan, 1967), vol. 2, p. 252.

13. Wallace I. Matson, *The Existence of God* (Ithaca, NY: Cornell University Press, 1965), p. 129.

14. Matson, *Existence of God,* pp. 129–30.

# 4

# Atheological Apologetics

## *Scott A. Shalkowski*

The philosophy of religion game has generally been played according to the following rules: a theist puts forth an inference from evidence to the conclusion that God
exists; then, a skeptic tries to find fault with the inference or undermine the truth
of the evidential claims. The explanation of this pattern may differ from case to
case. Anselm and Aquinas sought not to bolster their faith or that of others, but to
exhibit connections between the deliverances of faith and the dictates of reason,
that faith might become knowledge. In the twentieth century, I suspect, the reason
has been somewhat different.[1] Theistic belief is not intellectually respectable in the
way it was in the days of Anselm and Aquinas. In many cases the game is still played
by the same rules, since theists think they have something to prove and nontheists
do not seem to disagree. Most think that the burden of proof is on the theist,
whereas there is no such corresponding burden on the atheist.

My task here has two main parts. First, I will argue from completely general
grounds that there is no special burden of proof that the theist must bear—that the
traditional arrangement is arbitrary. Such burdens are context-sensitive matters
and there is no a priori presumption in favor of atheism. Second, I will chart out
the difficulties for deductive atheological apologetics. While it seems common, and
sometimes fashionable, to say that one can neither prove nor disprove God's existence, and while there has been extensive literature exhibiting the failings of traditional theistic apologetics, there has been very little done by way of exhibiting the
failings of atheism. I will argue that if one takes up the task of providing sound arguments for atheism, formidable difficulties arise. Further, if theism is suspect due to
the failings of its apologetics, atheism is suspect due to the failings of its apologetics.

## I

Who has the burden of proof in the debate over the existence of God? Antony Flew
explicitly claims that theists bear the burden of proof because there is a "presumption of atheism."[2] What is it for there to be a presumption against theism? If one

Reprinted from the *American Philosophical Quarterly* 26 (1989), by permission of the editor. Notes
edited.

means only that one cannot assume the existence of God when trying to prove the existence of God, then surely it is correct to think that in certain contexts, there is a presumption against theism. In other contexts, though, there will also be a presumption against atheism, when it is being supported by an argument. Flew wants to maintain, however, that the presumption against theism is not context-relative in the way I have suggested. Rather, it is a non–context-relative presumption that warrants what I will call the "default strategy" for defending atheism, i.e., the presumption has the force of providing the framework of an automatic defense of atheism simply on the condition that there are no good theistic apologetics. If theists cannot win the day, the result is not a standoff; rather, atheism wins by default. Why might one think that there is a non–context-relative presumption against theism? . . . Flew gives an argument for the presumption of atheism by saying that some general features regarding knowledge claims require that a defensible presumption against theism be in force. . . . For Flew, "atheism" does not refer to the position I will discuss, the denial of God's existence. Rather, it is simply a position regarding God's existence that fails to be theism.[3] Flew says that

> What the protagonist of the presumption of atheism, in my sense, wants to show is: that the debate about the existence of God ought to be conducted in a particular way, and that the issue should be seen in a certain perspective. His thesis about the onus of proof involves that it is up to the theist: first, to introduce and to defend his proposed concept of God; and, second, to provide sufficient reason for believing that this concept of his does in fact have an application.[4]

Flew construes the problem in terms of a debate. In every debate there must be a side that starts things off. The affirmative side makes some claims and gives some reasons for those claims that the negative side tries to undermine by showing there is no need to change the status quo. The worry here is why theism should be the side that starts the debate. In addition, setting the problem in the context of a debate deviates from the way we ordinarily think about knowledge and justification. If theistic apologists fail to win a debate, does it follow that either they or the ordinary believer are unjustified in their belief in theism? If so, it is not clear how. Suppose Sextus Empiricus were debating a realist about physical objects. Given what I take is common philosophical lore, that defeating the skeptic is well nigh impossible, it follows that we are unjustified in our common-sense beliefs. So, for atheists who are not also ready to accept general skepticism, this way of posing the problem about theism is contrary to the way *they* generally think about justification and violates what Flew maintains about the similarity of the requirements for justification in both religious and nonreligious contexts.

The first portion of this account of how the debate about God's existence should be conducted is acceptable only if it does not entail that theists possess a fully adequate and completely comprehensible description of God. All that is necessary for this, or any other debate, to get going is an accounting of some properties God is thought to have, e.g., supernatural creative power, great intelligence, benevolence, and wide-ranging knowledge. Some of these may entail a fuller conception of God, but will still leave many things out.

Flew has said to what the presumption of atheism amounts. What is crucial, though, is whether there is any reason to think that this is an appropriate presumption. In addition, maybe alongside the presumption of atheism there is also a presumption of theism such that the atheist must formulate an adequate conception of what is denied and provide sufficient reasons for denying that this conception has application. Flew argues that this is not so along the following lines.

> It is . . . not only incongruous but also scandalous in matters of life and death, and even of eternal life and death, to maintain that you know either on no grounds at all, or on grounds of a kind which on other and comparatively minor issues you yourself would insist to be inadequate.[5]

> It is by reference to this inescapable demand for grounds that the presumption of atheism is justified. If it is to be established that there is a God, then we have to have good grounds for believing that this is indeed so. Until and unless some such grounds are produced we have literally no reason at all for believing . . . our concern here . . . is with the need for opinions to be suitably grounded if they are to be rated as items of knowledge, or even probable belief.[6]

The main problem with Flew's justification for the presumption of atheism is that everything he says in its defense is completely general. There is nothing peculiar about the debate over God's existence which forces this presumption. It is supposed to follow from a general demand for grounds. This generality may be expressed as

(E)  If it is to be established that _____, then we must have good grounds for believing that this is indeed so.

The blank may be filled with any proposition. It may be filled with the proposition that God does not exist as easily as it can be filled with the proposition that God exists. Flew admits this, but thinks that somehow his claim regarding the requirement for grounds forces the theist to embark on the procedure of establishing theism and not forcing the atheist to establish atheism. This is because for him "atheism" includes agnosticism. As yet, we still have found no reason to think that there is this differential responsibility between one who affirms and one who denies theism. It is perfectly consistent with all Flew has said that no position can be established in the context of a debate without providing good grounds for it. The unanswered questions at this point are why one ought to construe the debate so that theism always has the affirmative side and why one should identify rational or nonscandalous belief with what can be successfully argued in a debate. So far, there has been no answer to these questions. Put another way, this is to rig the case, not argue for it. Of course, if the task is to show in a debate that "God" properly applies to some object, the onus is on the theist. But, if the context is inquiring about who, if anyone, knows the correct propositions about the application of "God," then both sides have work to do. Flew's point about knowledge is if anyone knows anything, it is in virtue of having good grounds for believing it. This applies to theism and atheism equally.

Flew does not really say what he means by grounds here. If he means grounds as propositions from which one's belief in God is inferred, as he seems to, then this requirement is too strong. Many of our perceptual beliefs are items of knowledge without such grounds and would be unwarranted from the general epistemological position that there is an initial, methodological presumption against any belief and this presumption requires the holder of that belief to provide reasons before it is a justified belief. To admit that there are some nonscandalous beliefs which do not have this type of grounds, Flew must weaken his account of grounds. One might say that perceptual beliefs are grounded, not because they are inferred from other beliefs, but because they are rooted in some nonpropositional evidence, thereby allowing that there are cases in which this evidence is not entertained *as* evidence. Its evidential value may not be transparent to the knower. This saves our perceptual beliefs, but will be of little use in the context of a debate since only something entertained as propositional evidence is of use in a debate, and this is how Flew is setting up the problem. The warranted believer may not know what it is that grounds some beliefs or may not be able to *show* how they are grounded, in some manner acceptable in a debate. It follows that propositional evidentialism is not a general requirement on justified, nonscandalous beliefs. To claim that propositional evidence is required for justified, nonscandalous theistic belief we need something that will distinguish theistic belief from other beliefs where propositional evidence is not required. Observations about what is required in a debate do not provide what is needed.

One might concede these points and forsake a completely general defense of the presumption of atheism. One might try to heap the burden of proof on the theist . . . by adopting some principle like: positive existence claims require proof or evidence.[7] Is there a coherent distinction to be drawn between positive and negative existence claims? I am not sure there is. Suppose one fully delineated all the things in one's ontology and added that these are all the individuals there are. Is such a claim a positive claim, since it says only what there is and does not directly say anything about nonexistence, or is it a negative claim by virtue of the fact that it says the given list is exhaustive? By saying that the list is complete, one can certainly infer that many things do not exist. If negative existence claims are characterized by syntactic markers, like occurrences of negated forms of "exists," it is a positive claim. If negative claims are characterized by semantic markers, e.g., entailing that certain things do not exist, it is a negative claim. This worry needs to be cleared away before we can know whether this defense of the presumption of atheism can succeed.

For now, let us suppose that this worry can be satisfied. Why might one adopt a principle of this sort? A point in its favor is that we do not tend to assert positive existence claims without reasons. We do not habitually assert that things of various kinds exist unless there is some evidence from the senses or testimony for their existence because there are innumerably many mutually incompatible claims that could be made. Though this is not an absolute guide for epistemic conduct, we often try to avoid false belief and if we form beliefs about contingent existence without evidence of some kind, we run the very great risk of forming many false beliefs.

This seems right, but of little consequence here. All of this can be said regarding negative existence claims. So, this principle cannot be justified on the basis of some general epistemic guidelines to avoid false beliefs. One might try to support this principle by claiming that relatively few of all the possible existents actually exist. Hence, one is more likely to get things right if one affirms existence only on the basis of grounds and fails to affirm on the basis of no grounds. There are two problems with this response. First, it is not obviously true and would require some hefty metaphysical argument, yet to be given, to prove it. Second, without such an argument this is just a replay of the intrinsic probabilities gambit. It will not work under this guise any more than it did before.

Further, there is no reason to think that the burden of proof borne by the advocate of a positive existence claim is absolute. Rather, it seems to be context-sensitive. Suppose someone claimed, in the context of our current scientific community, that there are no electrons (and this is not claimed for instrumentalist reasons). Clearly, in the current context, someone who denies the existence of electrons must show how we can explain various phenomena without such an appeal to electrons. This will hold for any denial of an apparently well-established claim of science or ordinary experience. The one who denies the existence of trees has the burden of proof, not the one who affirms their existence. Of course, if no one ever had any of the relevant experiences, then the situation would be reversed. This shows us only that even though there was a time when those affirming the existence of electrons bore the burden of proof, this was merely a context-sensitive burden. Flew has done nothing to show that in the absence of evidence, the presumption in force is not a presumption of agnosticism.[8]

Michael Scriven provides a related, but different, argument for the presumption of atheism. He reflects on what theists and atheists believe and notes that there is much in common between them.

> . . . every sane theist also believes in the claims of ordinary experience, while the reverse [that atheists believe the claims of religion] is not the case. Hence, the burden of proof is on the theist to show that the *further step* he wishes to take will not take him beyond the realm of truth.[9]

This is to justify the general atheological strategy of taking atheism to be secure and in no need of further, independent justification if the theistic arguments, both deductive and inductive, are unsound. Atheism can be defended if we construe the theistic arguments to include all arguments which support theism to any significant degree. If the theistic arguments fail, we have a default defense of atheism.

Scriven's remarks about the beliefs shared by theists and atheists will not bear the weight of justifying this claim. The phenomenon of widely shared beliefs can be put in the following way to show, in parallel fashion, that it is really the atheist which bears the burden of proof. Every sane atheist also believes the denials of ordinary experience, while the reverse—that theists believe the denials of atheism—is not the case. Hence, the burden of proof is on the atheist to show that the *further step* he wishes to take will not take him beyond the realm of truth.[10] Scriven's argument seems to be that if not everyone, or a majority of people, believe something, then one who believes it needs some argument to justify that belief. Mere departure from consensus generates the need for argument. But this cuts both ways and will generate a burden of proof for the theist in some contexts and a burden for the atheist in others. This is not a sufficient basis for the default strategy. What Scriven needs to argue is that we should focus on positive existence claims rather than denials, and I have argued that there is no reason why we should until we know more about the evidential context.[11]

Scriven tries one more tack. Why do mature adults not believe in Santa Claus?[12] Not because anyone has produced any very good argument to show that he does not exist, but because there is no good reason to think that he does. And we do not merely suspend our belief in the absence of good arguments against the Santa Claus hypothesis, rather we disbelieve. Likewise, the appropriate course of action in the case of God is to disbelieve, if it turns out that the theistic arguments fail.

This example does not serve Scriven's purposes very well. The reason adults disbelieve in Santa Claus is not simply that there is no good reason to think that he exists, but because we have good reason to think he does *not*. At some point in our lives we found that those who let us in on the myth were conscious of the fact that they were telling us a falsehood. Our parents knew that they were telling us a lie and later we found this out. We disbelieve rather than suspend belief because at some point we learned of the willful deception, participate in the process of decorating trees and putting presents under them and (possibly) propagating the deception ourselves. But, this is not the situation with belief in God for most atheists. Atheists do come to hold the belief that theism is false and that there is some deception present in religious teaching and practice, but in the vast majority of cases this is not because someone like a parent confesses deceiving them at an early age, nor do atheists typically begin to participate in the production of the phenomena that is allegedly explained by the activity of God. So, some of the crucial elements that cause us to disbelieve in Santa Claus are absent in the case of belief in God and nothing has been said to justify a default defense of atheism.

In addition, this ignores the fact that there *is* evidence for the existence of God—"religious" experience, testimony, alleged miracles, and the like. Scriven may well think that this is insufficient to warrant belief in God. I will say more about how such evidence must be dealt with by the atheological apologist below. For now, let it suffice to say that if there were no evidence at all for belief in God, this would legitimize merely agnosticism unless there is evidence *against* the existence of God. Atheism would be at least partially legitimized, then, because one could use such evidence to fuel some argument against the existence of God and that would be a defense of atheism, not by some presumption in its favor, but by some plausible case to be made in its favor. . . .

It might be argued that while theism is not intrinsically suspicious, it is a second-rate position given the current evidential situation. Given what we know about the physical world and its workings, there is no need to posit God; God is an ontological or explanatory dangler. Lurking behind this general line of thought is that what is open to all are the deliverances of science. These things are open to all in that experiments can be repeated and certain events are publicly observable, even if not publicly observed. These things are not private like allegedly religious experience or the persuasiveness of certain theistic arguments like the Argument from Design.[13] However, to make this claim about burdens to be borne in our situation, one must have already embarked on the project of atheological apologetics. There must be some case such that on its basis, it looks as though God does not exist. Otherwise, there is no reason to think that on the present evidence things are not good for the theist. So, the only way to avoid atheological apologetics is if either (i) there is an a priori, non–context-sensitive presumption in favor of atheism and all the known and plausibly constructible theistic arguments fail, or (ii) it is possible to justifiedly believe whether God exists independently of evidence for God's existence. I have argued that the first part of (i) has not been well supported by its advocates, and Flew and company are loathe to accept (ii).

## II

Let us suppose we begin the philosophy of religion game in a different manner. The only change needed is not one of evidence, but of the predominant attitude toward theism. Suppose we begin teaching philosophy of religion to a class and the reigning intellectual and social predisposition is to think that theism is the liberal view which frees one from the shackles of narrow, atheistic explanations of the cosmos, human history, and the meaningfulness of life. We ask whether there is any reason to think otherwise. There have historically been people of high degrees of intelligence, sophistication, and integrity who have disbelieved the existence of God, and for a long period our social and intellectual tradition was atheistic, but after a religious enlightenment this has changed, though there are still conservative strongholds of unbelief and skeptical revivals. What is the case to be made for atheism? I think that a general accounting of atheological apologetics will show that the same moves actually made against defenses of theism can also be made against atheological apologetics and would seem equally plausible in the context described above. Since the shift in context I have envisioned requires no shift in the weight of evidence, we will see that atheism is no better off than theism, contrary to the reigning intellectual climate.

Until fairly recently in the history of theistic arguments, the predominant strategy has been to provide sound arguments for the existence of God rather than producing probabilistic apologetics. Let us see how atheology fairs under similar strictures. What is the grist for the atheological mill? There are at least three sorts. First, there is the evidence, if true, that all the theistic arguments fail. Second, there are reasons to think that theistic claims are internally incoherent. Third, there are reasons to think that while certain versions of theism are coherent, they conflict with the facts and, hence, are false. I will discuss these claims in turn, noting the difficulties that the atheist encounters which are in many ways parallel to the difficulties traditionally raised for theistic apologetics. I will argue that the same difficulties that motivated the move to inductive theistic apologetics, will also show that if there is to be any successful atheological apologetics, they must be inductive.

The major reason cited for thinking that theism is intellectually disreputable is that the theistic arguments are unsatisfactory. They are either invalid or plagued with at least one false premise. Plantinga's modal version of the ontological argument is taken by some as an instance of this.[14] Fine and Mackie concede its validity, but reject a crucial premise as unjustified.[15] Suppose this criticism is correct. What are we to make of it in the present context? If the objection can be sustained in the face of independent arguments in favor of the offending premise, the most we get is that one argument against atheism is unsuccessful.

The Cosmological and Design arguments meet similar fates. Here, though, it is more common to show that the argument is invalid by arguing that the data appealed to in the premises could be present on, or explained by, some nontheistic alternative. If such attacks are justified, they show that it is not inconsistent to suppose that the world is as it is without a creator or sustainer. While no successful, deductive proof will fail to entail this result, it is hardly enough.[16] A justified atheist requires more than is established so far, i.e., that it is not *necessary* to appeal to God in explaining the existence of the world, or its design. There are alternative explanations. But, this is no better than a stalemate, since theism is a possible explanation as well. Exposing weaknesses in an opponent's argument merely establishes that possibly an alternative position is true.

What is needed is some sound argument to the conclusion that no God exists. What will count as disproving the existence of God? Surely, one would have a successful disproof of the existence of God, if one could show that there is some internal metaphysical impossibility in the matter. To arrive at this conclusion, the argument must be formulated in terms of a specifically determined set of divine attributes. If it is impossible for any being to possess all of the attributes in the set, then surely there is no being that exemplifies all of these attributes. This points to a systematic difficulty in providing this type of argument for atheism. There are many forms of theism and atheism, each corresponding to a well-defined set of properties attributable to a deity. Proving atheism by this course will require proving each set of divine attributes to be unexemplifiable. A full-blooded atheism will require many proofs. To avoid this situation, an atheist must generate an argument to the effect that there is a unique set, or small number of sets, of attributes that must be exemplified by any being that is any decent sort of God. Similarly, looking only at power properties for illustration, one might argue that a divine being must have power greater than P. If it can be shown that it is impossible to have power greater than P, one could show in one fell swoop that there are no divine beings. Theological divergence over the nature of God gives us pause regarding the feasibility of providing such a proof.

A second problem which besets this general defense of atheism is that it is questionable whether the problematic sets of attributes are required by Western theism. Suppose omnipotence is found to be unexemplifiable. This would show that any set containing the attribute is unexemplifiable. But, while this proves a large number of atheisms, it does not show clearly that Christianity, Judaism, or Islam are false. The major phenomena to be saved is the testimony of the relevant revelations associated with each religious tradition. It is contentious whether omnipotence rather than almightiness is required by Christianity, say.[17] If it is not, then we could hardly be satisfied with proofs of atheism which are consistent with the truth of Christianity.[18] So, atheological arguments of this sort require empirical investigation into the claims of the religions, in addition to philosophical arguments.[19]

Noting these systematic problems looming in the foreground for atheological apologetics, one might opt for a weaker defense of atheism—showing that the existence of God is inconsistent with the contingent facts of the world. After all, the reason for showing an inconsistency in this context is to show that no god *does* exist. Atheism follows from the conclusion that no god *can* exist as well as from the conclusion that no god can in a world like ours. It is possible to construe the problem of evil as a well-known example of this sort of argument. While Mackie formulates the argument to show an internal inconsistency for theism, the inconsistency essentially derives from a contingent proposition that theists take to be true. If theists gave up some propositions about the existence of evil as an important part of their credo, the argument could be reformulated in the way I have in mind. If this argument is successful, it shows that it is not possible for a being with certain attributes to exist in our world. But, what about the God of Christianity? The just-mentioned worry arises in this context as well. The Christian God is to be creator, ruler, judge, worthy of worship, savior, sanctifier, morally superior to humans, etc. So far as I can see, none of these roles requires any of the offending attributes employed in arguments from evil.[20] And this is the best situation for atheologians who use this type of argument, since philosophers of religion have cast serious doubt on whether there even is any inconsistency involving the appropriate propositions regarding evil and God's alleged properties. Any argument of this sort will require the aforementioned religious investigation *and* the successful proof of the supposed incompatibility. The versions offered so far have not met these conditions. It appears that an atheist has a systematically difficult time in showing that it is not possible for God to exist or that it is not possible for God to exist in a world that is much like ours.

One might try other ways to prove that the nature of our world is such that it excludes anything that remotely resembles a deity. Such arguments must show more than that atheism can form a part of a consistent package which includes the observable data about our world; they must show that such a package is the *correct* one. If this is shown, then atheism has been shown. There are at least two ways in which this could be proven. Atheism would be proven if it could be shown that the physical world is all that exists; there is nothing but atoms and the void.[21] A second approach is to allow the existence of nonphysical things, even agents, but argue that none of them is God. This approach concedes the falsity of materialism, but not the truth of theism. I will discuss these in turn.

How can one show that the material world is all that exists? One could argue that all events are explained by the activities of material objects. Physical properties leave all things explained. How can this be proven? To make the atheist's task easier, let us first assume that we actually know the laws of nature completely. If we know the laws, then we know what physical objects do, when left to their own devices. This transforms the question to whether all events have been in accord with the laws of nature. To prove that they are, one can run tests. Set up known initial conditions and see if the results are in accord with the predictions of our correct theory. If the outcomes of these experiments are not in accord with the predictions, then there is more at work in the world than physical objects. If the predictions are all matched with the appropriate results, then this defense of atheism is still viable.

Of course, it is not quite this easy. Typically, when the experimental results are not in accord with predictions, a good scientist does not give up and conclude that materialism is false. Most often one concludes that either (i) we have not got the laws right yet, (ii) the initial conditions were not as we supposed, or (iii) the experimental device did not function properly. In the situation envisioned, (i) is no longer open to the atheist. Though the other two options are open, suppose that failed predictions continue to occur. While one can continue to maintain that we just are not as good at figuring out the relevant initial conditions or designing experimental devices as we would like, at a certain stage it looks as though the atheist will be engaged in a certain sort of nonempirical leap of faith. Claims are made in the face of disconfirming data that look much like the moves theists make in the face of disconfirming data like unanswered prayers, failed business transactions, or the loss of a loved one. In both cases the theory defended is saved by appeals to ignorance. For the atheist, it is ignorance of initial conditions or why our devices are not functioning properly; for the theist it is ignorance of why God is silent or allows certain heinous conditions to persist. Now if it is illegitimate for the theist to appeal to ignorance—and many atheists think it is—it is equally illegitimate for the atheist.[22] Faith is faith, whether the doctrine to which one is faithful is materialism or theism. The appeals seem to be quite on a par.

Having noted these worries, let us move on and suppose that when the empirical experimentation is done, the hypothesis that all events are materially explained is still viable. But, surely, this is not the end of the matter. The thesis that matter is all there is extends to all events, and determining whether all of them are explainable after the fashion of the experimental events is not straightforward. Even armed with a correct physical theory, the extrapolation goes well beyond the experimental data and in the face of some data—miracle reports. To avoid question begging, one must *show* that all of these reports are false. Merely showing that materialism is consistent with the phenomena that are supposed to be miraculous will not do. The question is not whether a purely physical world could have phenomena such as instantaneous "healings" of cancer, or the feeding of five thousand from a few loaves and fishes. The question is whether our world is one in which these events are *actually* explained in this way. Showing this will require a direct argument against the existence of nonphysical entities which are active in the physical world. Otherwise, claiming that mistakes about the initial conditions caused us to make incorrect predictions and the deviant events to appear miraculous simply begs the question. One can show that the events are not genuinely miraculous only when one can show that no nonphysical agency is at work in our world. Knowing the correct physical theory does not help the defender of atheism in the face of miracle reports, since it is not sufficient to claim that one *need* not appeal to nonphysical agency to explain events of these types. This would be to say just that some argument(s) that proceed from premises about apparently miraculous events to a conclusion about the falsity of materialism is (are) fallacious. The point to be established regards the nature of the *actual* causes of these token events, which is much more difficult.

The problem of extrapolating from laboratory data to the nature of all events at all points of space-time has historical parallels. Proponents of the Argument from Design are criticized because wide-ranging conclusions are drawn on the basis of a very small (spatially and temporally) segment of the universe. If this is a telling criticism against certain versions of the Argument from Design, then it is telling against the present type of argument. If there are acceptable moves that allow one to extrapolate and rule out miracles in other segments of the universe, these moves may prove acceptable in extrapolating from observed design to general conclusions about the entire world. However, there is one dissimilarity. We are concerned with how one might provide a sound argument for the denial of God's existence. Premises that warrant such extrapolations will be inductive premises and their insertion will change the argument into an inductive argument. In contrast, the insertion of similar premises will not change the nature of the Argument from Design, since it is intended as an inductive argument. So, it looks as though this attempt to save a deductive atheological argument changes the game and prevents the atheist from succeeding along this route.

Questions of theoretical simplicity, Occam's razor, and the like, are not to the point at hand. Whatever the merits of simplicity as a constraint on the acceptance of explanatory hypotheses, it is irrelevant to the possibility of producing a sound argument for the conclusion that atheism is true. Premises involving the preferability of a simpler hypothesis yield the conclusion that one hypothesis is preferable to another, not that atheism is true. Simplicity does not generate sound arguments.

Even here, I have been too easy on the atheist. First, there is no reason why genuine miracles must be extraordinary in the sense that they do not regularly happen, or that when they do, they are detectable by us as miracles.[23] Second, we do not know all physical laws. There are plenty of events which do not fit with current theories. Whether all can be accounted for within better theories is the hope of the materialist, and this may be a well-founded hope about laboratory phenomena, even by a theist's lights. But, as long as it is only a hope it thwarts attempts at sound arguments for materialism. Finally, the atheologian is actually in a state much worse. Suppose naturalism is sufficient to explain all physical events—no miracles occur. It still does not follow that God does not exist, that the world has no creator, or sustainer. "Non-miracleism" entails only that no nonnatural event has occurred in our space-time, not the nonexistence of nonphysical entities. A proof of no miracles, if such there be, is not sufficient to prove materialism. So, it looks as though any attempt to prove atheism by proving materialism, is fraught with enormous difficulties.

In light of these difficulties, one might give up trying to prove materialism and acquiesce in the epistemic possibility of nonphysical beings. Could one show that none of them is God because, say, they are like humans in their tendencies, capacities, and actions except that they are nonphysical? This will not be a matter of purely philosophical analysis. One is forced to quasi-empirical considerations. Normally, when we are concerned with the falsity of some proposition, we inspect the relevant portions of the world. Of course, this has its problems since we cannot observe and analyze everything and it is the nature of some things to be mysterious, for example, the Loch Ness monster and the Abominable Snowman, if they exist. If most religions are correct in their claims that God is not open to spectators, one who is anti- or non-religious may not find all there is to find. Those who *diligently* seek God are rewarded. Direct inspection on these matters is difficult for the diligent, and more so for certain sorts of skeptics. Let us waive the difficulties here and see the requirements of this defense.

To the extent direct inspection is possible, it will involve some combination of the observation of the behavior and testimony of the nonphysical beings and others who have directly observed the behavior and testimony of these beings. Deciding what to make of this evidence will be parallel to what the theist does when evaluating putative religious experiences and revelation. Arguments which show that religious experience and revelation ought to be discounted as less than sufficient, or even good, evidence for theism will also entail that this is deficient for the atheist's purposes. If this evidence is admitted for the atheist, it must be admitted (with the same caveats) for the theist. A defense of this weaker atheism requires concessions to the traditional believer who believes, at least in part, on the basis of the testimony of the Bible, acquaintances, and personal experience. It turns out that precisely the same type of evidence gathering theists often use is what the atheist needs to justify premises about the nature of nonphysical beings. The sort of information obtainable from direct inspection would be what these beings do. When we observe behavior, what can we infer about the nature of the beings? Suppose we try to tell by observation whether some agent is omnipotent. From the fact that someone does not do something one cannot infer that they cannot. If they appear to try and do not, then we can infer that they cannot only on the condition that we know that they actually tried. To know this is to rely upon the testimony of the agent or others. But, testimony can be inadequate either because it may not be given or because we may be deceived, thus not giving us insight into whether a genuine attempt was made.[24] This procedure is fallible and many inferences that believers make on the basis of the witness of the Bible or their own experiences may go beyond the data, but so will the inferences drawn by one trying to show that no God exists on the basis of quasi-empirical considerations.

Similar difficulties arise for the investigation of the other divine attributes. To know whether one has committed a moral transgression (due either to moral imperfection or ignorance of either moral or non-moral truths that affect which action is the proper one in the circumstances), one must have more than observations of apparently immoral behavior. One needs to know the motivation for the action and/or whether there *is* a morally sufficient reason for engaging in this sort of apparently immoral behavior. This is particularly hard to determine in light of the fact that in Christianity God is to have said, "My ways are higher than your ways," and this may involve not only that God always chooses the high road whereas sometimes we do not. It may also involve the fact that God's moral insight is greater than ours in such a way that the moral facts, which we see all too dimly, render the apparently immoral behavior virtuous; there is a morally sufficient reason for the action that we do not, and maybe this side of glorification cannot, see or understand.

If the direct inspection fails to yield satisfactory grist for the atheist's mill, we might inquire about the direct experience of others. This may give us some new evidence about the nature of these nonphysical beings and is analogous not only to the use of testimony by theists for the justification of beliefs regarding the existence and nature of God, but it is also analogous to the procedure we use in the study of the physical world. We often rely on expert testimony on the nature of leptons and bosons rather than do the investigation ourselves. Oral and written testimony is open to one camp just in case it is open to the other. When we consider this weaker atheism, we find that when failures force one to its defense, one must tacitly admit that traditional sources of evidence for the theist should be countenanced as embodying legitimate means of obtaining evidence on these matters.

A final point about this very weak type of apologetics. The admission of quasi-empirical procedures of evidence gathering seems to make it hard to formulate an argument which has a hope of being sound. The evidence will be about things done and undone, said and unsaid. In order to show that this evidence entails that there is no God, one will first need to show that the evidence entails that the agent under investigation does not have some necessary attribute(s) of divinity. It is this part of the argument that runs the very great risk of being invalid, since so many auxiliary hypotheses will need to be invoked to link the observations with the conclusion that the agent lacks some crucial attribute, and these hypotheses will be tendentious and very hard to justify *via* a sound argument.[25]

## III

The consequences of what I have argued here are straightforward. First, there is no good reason for the presumption of atheism that is prevalent in many Western intellectual circles. I, at least, have been unable to construct or find a good argument which places differential burdens of proof on theists and atheists. There is no justification for the current atheistic rage, if such there be, in the absence of atheological apologetics, and the absence of such apologetics is quite striking.[26]

Second, if we put the same burden of proof on the atheist as was traditionally heaped upon the theist, the atheist runs into systematic difficulties. It is much easier to punch holes in theistic arguments and show that some brand of atheism is possibly correct, than to actually argue for its truth. This is generally taken as all that is necessary. If we move beyond this, we find that the needs of and problems of the atheist are parallel to those of the theist. This situation should be recognized and the current presumption in favor of atheism removed, since in other areas we readily recognize that the bearing of a burden is a context-dependent and dialectically sensitive matter. To impose the same argumentative restrictions upon the atheist is to show that the position is at least as inadequately defended as theism. It might be useful to reverse intentionally the burden of proof to help make it clear that whatever the reasons for its widespread acceptance, atheism is no less a matter of faith than theism, and from these considerations we can say this with good reason.

I will close with two comments on how this bears on more recent discussions in the philosophy of religion. First, there is no reason given here to think that one needs to engage in apologetics in order to hold either theism or atheism in a rationally acceptable manner. Under certain (presumably different) circumstances one could rationally hold either of these positions as a basic belief, one not inferred on the basis of reasons. We all hold plenty of beliefs of this sort, so it seems that one needs to put forth some positive argument that (ir)religious beliefs cannot be rationally held in this fashion. I do not rule out that such an argument can be given; it is just not given here nor entailed by anything said here.[27] Second, the move away from deductive apologetics to probabilistic apologetics will not affect the points made here. If we allow one side to retreat to this weaker defense, the other may as well. If the use of inductive procedures is acceptable for the atheist, it is acceptable for the theist. I have not argued here that this is so, but I suspect that the needs and difficulties will be very similar on both sides of the probabilistic dispute. This will better equip us to guard against jumping to hasty conclusions about the virtues of our own favored positions. Whether the atheologian can produce apologetics that is superior to that of the theist will be a matter that we can decide only after more attempts at atheological apologetics have been made.[28]

# Notes

1. For an account of the different ways theistic arguments have been used, see Nicholas Wolterstorff, "The Migration of the Theistic Arguments: From Natural Theology to Evidentialist Apologetics," *Rationality, Religious Belief, and Moral Commitment: New Essays in the Philosophy of Religion,* eds. Robert Audi and William J. Wainwright (Ithaca, NY: Cornell University Press, 1986), pp. 38–81.

2. Anthony Flew, "The Presumption of Atheism," *Canadian Journal of Philosophy* 2 (1972): 29–46. (Reprinted in Part I of this volume, pp. 19–31. All subsequent page references to Flew's article in Shalkowski refer to the pages of this volume.)

3. Such an atheism may involve the outright denial of theism (what he calls positive atheism), agnosticism, or failing to have the belief in God due, possibly, to the fact that the atheist simply has not even considered whether there is a God.

4. Flew, p. 20.

5. Flew, p. 25.

6. Flew, p. 25.

7. This was suggested to me in conversation, though not advocated, by John Biro.

8. Nicholas Rescher distinguishes two sorts of burden, one of which is constant, another which can be shifted between parties in a dispute. These two burdens are (1) probative burdens of an initiating assertion (I-burdens) and (2) evidential burdens of further reply in the face of contrary considerations (E-burdens). I-burdens are constant while E-burdens shift between debating parties. (See Rescher, *Dialectics* [Albany, NY: SUNY Press, 1977], p. 27.) However, this distinction will be of little use for Flew's purpose because I-burdens are constant only after one party initiates an assertion in a debate. After that, the initiating party must provide some grounds for the assertion. After some *prima facie* grounds have been given, the debate can get underway and the E-burden can shift between the responding party and the initiating party as counter-evidence and arguments are given. There is no reason given in Rescher's construal of the nature of the dialectical procedure that one party must begin the debate. Both can remain silent and each can begin the debate.

9. Michael Scriven, *Primary Philosophy* (New York: McGraw-Hill, 1966), p. 101.

10. The denials I have in mind here are claims like [that] there are no centaurs, mermaids, etc.

11. Scriven claims that there is a difference in how negative and positive existential claims can be supported. He writes: "Negative existential hypotheses in natural language can be supported by the failure of proofs of their contradictories, but positive existential hypotheses are not made plausible by the failure of disproofs [sic] of their denials" (in a footnote on p. 5). He gives no argument for this which would overturn the criticisms I have levelled against such a view. It should be clear that nothing I have argued here involves claiming that positive existence claims are *supported* by the failure of proofs of their denials. I maintain only that there is no difference between negative and positive existence claims on this count.

12. Scriven, *Primary Philosophy*, pp. 102–3.

13. I am doubtful that this account of the difference between science and religion is viable.

Theists can claim that religious experiences are no more private than any others. Those who have never had them just have not gone through the right procedures in the same way those who have never had experiences of sharks have not gone through the right procedures. (See the papers on religious experience in Part VI of this volume. For the development of theistic arguments by certain contemporary philosophers, see Part IV of this volume. Richard Swinburne defends the Argument from Design on pp. 201–11.)

14. See Alvin Plantinga, *The Nature of Necessity* (Oxford, Engl.: Clarendon Press, 1974), Ch. 10.

15. See Kit Fine, "Review of *The Nature of Necessity*," *The Philosophical Review* 85 (1976): 562–66; J. L. Mackie, *The Miracle of Theism* (Oxford, Engl.: Clarendon Press, 1982), pp. 55–63. Fine criticizes the argument by claiming that the premises entail a falsehood, while Mackie simply claims that we have no good reason for accepting a crucial premise (that a maximally great being possibly exists). Neither line of criticism, even if correct, precludes some other version of the ontological argument from being successful. One sort of criticism that precludes a successful version is showing that it is not possible for there to be a maximally great being. This would show wanting all ontological arguments for such a being. However, this goes beyond merely criticizing a theistic argument, since showing this premise of the argument to be false requires a prior argument that theism is impossible, and will fall prey to the claims I make below about such defenses of atheism.

16. This is no more than what a theist does when trying to show how some argument against the existence of God, like the problem of evil, fails. One shows how God can fit into a picture which contains evil. But, showing such consistency does not show that God is actually in the picture. Atheists rightly do not take theodicies or defenses as sufficient reason to think that theism is true, and likewise we should not take potshots at theistic arguments to show that atheism is true. If theodicies are accounts of what God's reasons are for permitting evil, this is not quite correct. If one provides God's actual reasons for permitting evil, one has provided something which entails that God exists, and such a theodicy is sufficient to prove the existence of God. Neither theists nor critics tend to think that successful theodicies accomplish this much. Perhaps, then, it is better to construe the difference between theodicies and defenses against the problem of evil (for example, Plantinga's free-will defense) in one of the following ways. First, theodicies provide some positive reason God might have for allowing evil, while defenses do not need to make any claim about God's actual reasons and merely show that the existence of evil is consistent with the existence of God. The proponent of a defense could claim to have no idea whatever about what reasons a being worthy of worship does have for allowing evil. Second, we might construe the difference according to some difference in the conditional theses advocated. A theodicy might involve a conditional such as "If God exists, then God's reason for permitting evil *is* R." On the other hand, a defense might involve a conditional that makes reference to a possible reason God might have as "If God exists, then God's reason *would* (*could*) be R. In either case, theodicies would not be sufficient for thinking theism true.

17. I construe almightiness as an attribute involving great, unsurpassed, power but also allowing that there are things metaphysically possible for that being to do, that it cannot do.

18. A case in point: Kai Neilsen provides arguments to show that the Western concept of God is incoherent, stemming from the alleged incoherence of a necessary being; a God which transcends the world, yet is the object of religious experience; and disembodied agency. (See Nielsen, "In Defense of Atheism," *Philosophy and Atheism* [Buffalo, NY: Prometheus Press, 1985], pp. 77–106.) Even if these arguments are valid, atheism is not established for the reasons cited here. A theist could take these arguments to show three things: (i) God is a contingent being, (ii) God's transcendence involves God's not being a part of or constituted by the physical world and does not prohibit human experience of God, and (iii) when theists claim disembodied existence for God, the motivation is to claim no essential *physical* embodiment

for God. If agency really requires a body, then God has some non-physical body. Instead, a theist could challenge the validity of the arguments and show that there is no incoherence in these notions at all. This just shows that much less is ruled out by such arguments than is commonly supposed.

19. This empirical investigation may well not yield the desired results and philosophers like Richard Swinburne have taken pains to show that the philosophical arguments are unsuccessful anyway. (See Swinburne, *The Coherence of Theism* [Oxford, Engl.: Clarendon Press, 1977]).

20. Some might think that worthiness of worship requires various perfections. If so, then the atheist's task is easier than I have suggested. I want to point out only that this is not obvious. One who takes the constraints of the Bible, say, as the only requirements an orthodox conception of God must meet could make a strong case that the Bible does not require these perfections of God. There are those who think that Christian theology should not be tied to such restrictive Biblicism; see, for example, Thomas V. Morris's symposium paper on "Perfect Being Theology," presented at the Central Division meetings of the American Philosophical Association in May of 1987. (Eds.: see also Thomas V. Morris, *Our Idea of God: An Introduction to Philosophical Theology* [Downers Grove, IL: InterVarsity Press, 1991], especially Chapter 2.) I will not try to adjudicate this debate here. What is important is that we recognize that the moves I have suggested are open to the theist. In addition, perhaps there is no coherent concept of perfection in the same way there is no coherent concept of the best of all possible worlds. This is plausible when thinking about power. It may be that no matter how powerful a being is, it is possible for there to be one more powerful with no sense to be made of infinite power. If so, then even the theist will be in a position of saying that a divine being must have power at least at level $P$, while allowing that there are powers surpassing $P$.

21. Atheism is often associated with some broad version of materialism. See Scriven, *Primary Philosophy*, p. 88, n. 2.

22. In fact the situation may be worse for the scientific defender of atheism. The connections between the initial conditions are to be tighter when considering physical experiments than in religious "experiments" like praying and seeing whether the prayer is answered. From the outset, it is granted that God may not answer prayers in the way desired by the one making the prayer for any number of reasons, like lack of genuine faith and trust in God, evil motives of the person, evil consequences unforeseen by the one offering the prayer, etc.

23. For a very useful discussion of these matters, see Robert Hambourger, "Need Miracles Be Extraordinary?" *Philosophy and Phenomenological Research* 47 (1987): 435–49.

24. If we are intentionally deceived by the agent, then we have some evidence that the person is not God.

25. Witness the failings of logical behaviorism. For a nice summary of this type of difficulty for behaviorism, see Christopher Peacocke, *Holistic Explanation* (Oxford, Engl.: Clarendon Press, 1979).

26. In recent years there has been the beginnings of an atheological apologetic industry. An example of this is George Smith, *Atheism: The Case Against God* (Buffalo, NY: Prometheus Press, 1979). I have not discussed this work in detail here since it focuses on issues other than deductive arguments for atheism. (Eds.: The recent work by Michael Martin, *Atheism: A Philosophical Justification,* is another example. See the bibliography on pp. 74–77 for this and other sources on atheism. A selection by Michael Martin is included in this volume, pp. 43–57.)

27. (Eds.: see Part III, on "Reformed Epistemology," in this volume for a discussion of this strategy.)

28. Research for this paper was supported by a fellowship in the Center for Philosophy of Religion at the University of Notre Dame during the 1986–1987 academic year. Members of the Center provided many valuable comments on a previous draft of this paper.

# Bibliography

Abraham, William J. "Natural Atheology," in his *An Introduction to the Philosophy of Religion*. Englewood Cliffs, NJ: Prentice-Hall, 1985.

Angeles, Peter, ed. *Critiques of God* (The Skeptics Bookshelf). Buffalo, NY: Prometheus Books, 1979.

Anscombe, G.E.M. "A Reply to Mr. C. S. Lewis' Argument that 'Naturalism' is Self-refuting," in her *Collected Philosophical Papers*. Vol. 2: *Metaphysics and the Philosophy of Mind*. Minneapolis: University of Minnesota Press, 1981.

Baier, Annette. "Secular Faith," in *Revisions: Changing Perspectives in Moral Philosophy*, eds. Stanley Hauerwas and Alasdair MacIntyre. Notre Dame, IN: University of Notre Dame Press, 1983.

Berman, David. *A History of Atheism in Britain from Hobbes to Russell*. London: Routledge & Kegan Paul, 1988.

Brinton, Alan. "Agnosticism and Atheism." *Sophia* 28 (1989): 2–6.

Buckley, Michael J., S. J. *At the Origins of Modern Atheism*. New Haven, CT: Yale University Press, 1987.

Clifford, William K. "The Ethics of Belief," reprinted in *Philosophy of Religion: An Anthology*, ed. Louis P. Pojman. Belmont, CA: Wadsworth, 1987.

Dore, Clement. "Agnosticism and the Atheistic Argument from Suffering," in his *Moral Scepticism*. New York: St. Martin's Press, 1991.

Edwards, Paul. "Atheism," in *Encyclopedia of Philosophy*, ed. Paul Edwards. New York: Macmillan, 1967.

———. "A Critique of the Cosmological Argument." *The Rationalist Annual* (1959): 63–77.

———. "Some Notes on Anthropomorphic Theology," in *Religious Experience and Truth*, ed. Sydney Hook. New York: New York University Press, 1961.

Evans, Donald. "A Reply to Flew's 'The Presumption of Atheism.'" *Canadian Journal of Philosophy* 2 (1972): 47–50.

Findlay, J. N. "Can God's Existence Be Disproved?" *Mind* 57 (1948): 176–83.

Fitzpatrick, F. J. "The Onus of Proof in Arguments about the Problem of Evil." *Religious Studies* 17 (1981): 19–38.

Flew, Antony. *God, Freedom and Immortality*. Buffalo, NY: Prometheus Books, 1984.

———. *God and Philosophy*. London: Hutchinson, 1966.

———. *The Presumption of Atheism*. New York: Harper & Row, 1976.

———. "Reply to Evans." *Canadian Journal of Philosophy* 2 (1972): 51–53.

Flew, Antony, and Alasdair MacIntyre, eds. *New Essays in Philosophical Theology*. New York: Macmillan, 1955.

Friedman, Joel I. "The Natural God: A God Even an Atheist Can Believe In." *Zygon* 21 (1986): 53–60.

Gale, Richard M. *On the Nature and Existence of God.* Cambridge, Engl.: Cambridge University Press, 1991.

Gaskin, J.C.A. *The Quest for Eternity: An Outline of the Philosophy of Religion.* Harmondsworth, Middlesex (Engl.): Penguin, 1984.

————, ed. *Varieties of Unbelief: From Epicurus to Sartre.* New York: Macmillan, 1989.

Geivett, R. Douglas. *Evil and the Evidence for God: The Challenge of John Hick's Theodicy.* Philadelphia: Temple University Press, in press.

Goulder, Michael, and John Hick. *Why Believe in God?* London: SCM Press, 1983.

Hanson, Norwood Russell. "What I Don't Believe," in *What I Do Not Believe and Other Essays,* eds. Stephen Toulmin and Harry Woolf. Dordrecht, Neth.: D. Reidel, 1971.

Hepburn, Ronald W. "Agnosticism," in *Encyclopedia of Philosophy,* ed. Paul Edwards. New York: Macmillan, 1967.

Herrick, Jim. *Against the Faith.* London: Glover & Blair, 1985.

Johnson, B. C. *The Atheist Debater's Handbook.* Buffalo, NY: Prometheus Books, 1983.

Kolenda, Konstantin. *Religion Without God.* Buffalo, NY: Prometheus Books, 1976.

Kvanvig, Jonathan L. "The Evidentialist Objection." *American Philosophical Quarterly* 20 (1983): 47–55.

Lamont, Corliss. *The Philosophy of Humanism.* New York: Frederick Ungar, 1985.

Lewis, C. S. *The Abolition of Man: How Education Develops Man's Sense of Morality.* New York: Macmillan, 1947.

————. "De Futilitate," in his *Christian Reflections.* Grand Rapids, MI: Eerdmans, 1967.

Lewis, Delmas. "The Problem with the Problem of Evil." *Sophia* 22 (1983): 26–35.

Luijpen, William A., and Henry J. Koren. *Religion and Atheism.* Pittsburgh, PA: Duquesne University Press, 1971.

McGrath, P. J. "Atheism or Agnosticism?" *Analysis* 47 (1987): 54–57.

MacIntyre, Alasdair. *Difficulties in Christian Belief.* London: SCM Press, 1956.

————. "The Logical Status of Religious Belief," in *Metaphysical Beliefs,* eds. Stephen Toulmin et al. London: SCM Press, 1957.

MacIntyre, Alasdair, and Paul Ricoeur. *The Religious Significance of Atheism.* New York: Columbia University Press, 1969.

Mackie, J. L. *The Miracle of Theism: Arguments for and against the Existence of God.* Oxford, Engl.: Clarendon Press, 1982.

Martin, C. B. *Religious Belief.* Ithaca, NY: Cornell University Press, 1959.

Martin, Michael. *Atheism: A Philosophical Justification.* Philadelphia: Temple University Press, 1990.

————. "A Disproof of the God of the Common Man." *Question* 7 (1974): 115–24.

————. "Does the Evidence Confirm Theism More Than Naturalism?" *International Journal for Philosophy of Religion* 16 (1984): 257–62.

————. "Pascal's Wager as an Argument for Not Believing in God." *Religious Studies* 19 (1983): 57–64.

Masterson, Patrick. *Atheism and Alienation: A Study of the Philosophical Sources of Contemporary Atheism.* Dublin, Ireland: Gill & Macmillan, 1973.

Matson, Wallace I. *The Existence of God.* Ithaca, NY: Cornell University Press, 1965.

Molnar, Thomas. *Theists and Atheists: A Typology of Non-Belief.* The Hague: Mouton, 1980.

Moreland, J. P., and Kai Nielsen. *Does God Exist? The Great Debate.* Nashville, TN: Thomas Nelson, 1990.

Morris, Thomas V. "Agnosticism." *Analysis* 45 (1985): 219–24.

Nagel, Ernest. "Philosophical Concepts of Atheism," in *Critiques of God,* ed. Peter Angeles. Buffalo, NY: Prometheus Books, 1976.

Nielsen, Kai. "Agnosticism," in *Dictionary of the History of Ideas,* ed. P. P. Wiener. New
    York: Charles Scribner, 1973–74.
———. "Atheism." *Encyclopedia Britannica.* 1983.
———. *Contemporary Critiques of Religion.* New York: Herder & Herder, 1971.
———. *Ethics Without God,* rev. ed. Buffalo, NY: Prometheus Books, 1990.
———. *God and the Grounding of Morality.* Ottawa: University of Ottawa Press, 1991.
———. *God, Scepticism and Modernity.* Ottawa: University of Ottawa Press, 1989.
———. *An Introduction to the Philosophy of Religion.* New York: St. Martin's Press, 1983.
———. *Philosophy and Atheism: In Defense of Atheism.* Buffalo, NY: Prometheus Books,
    1985.
———. *Scepticism.* London: Macmillan; New York: St. Martin's Press, 1973.
———. *Why Be Moral?* Buffalo, NY: Prometheus Books, 1989.
O'Hear, Anthony. *Experience, Explanation, and Faith.* London: Routledge & Kegan Paul,
    1984.
Parsons, Keith. *God and the Burden of Proof.* Buffalo, NY: Prometheus Books, 1989.
———. *Science, Confirmation and the Theistic Hypothesis.* New York: Peter Lang, 1990.
Penelhum, Terence. *Problems of Religious Knowledge.* London: Macmillan, 1971.
Plantinga, Alvin. "Epistemic Probability and Evil." *Archivo di Filosofia* 56 (1988): 557–84.
———. "The Sceptic's Strategy," in *Faith and the Philosophers,* ed. John Hick. London:
    Macmillan, 1966.
Quinn, Philip L. "Epistemic Parity and Religious Argument," in *Philosophical Perspectives:
    5. Philosophy of Religion, 1991,* ed. James E. Tomberlin. Atascadero, CA: Ridgeview
    Publishing Co., 1991.
Rachels, James. "God and Human Attitudes." *Religious Studies* 7 (1971): 325–38.
Robinson, Richard. *An Atheist's Values.* Oxford, Engl.: Clarendon Press, 1964.
Rowe, William. "The Empirical Argument from Evil," in *Rationality, Religious Belief, and
    Moral Commitment,* eds. Robert Audi and William J. Wainwright. Ithaca, NY: Cor-
    nell University Press, 1986.
———. "Evil and the Theistic Hypothesis: A Response to Wykstra." *International Journal
    for Philosophy of Religion* 16 (1984): 95–100.
———. "Evil and Theodicy." *Philosophical Topics* 16 (1988): 119–32.
———. *Philosophy of Religion: An Introduction.* Belmont, CA: Wadsworth, 1978.
———. "Ruminations About Evil," in *Philosophical Perspectives: 5. Philosophy of Religion,
    1991,* ed. James E. Tomberlin. Atascadero, CA: Ridgeview Publishing, 1991.
Rümke, H. C. *The Psychology of Unbelief: Character and Temperament in Relation to Unbe-
    lief.* London: Rockliffe, 1952.
Russell, Bertrand. *Why I Am Not a Christian, and Other Essays on Religion and Related
    Subjects* (ed. Paul Edwards). New York: Simon & Schuster, 1957.
Schulmann, Frank. "Atheism's Challenge." *Religious Humanism* 20 (1986): 137–41.
Scriven, Michael. *Primary Philosophy.* New York: McGraw-Hill, 1966.
Shotwell, David A. "Is the Universe Improbable?" *Skeptical Inquirer* 11 (1987): 376–82.
Smart, J.J.C. "The Existence of God." *Church Quarterly Review* 156 (1955): 178–94.
Smith, George H. *Atheism: The Case Against God* (The Skeptics Bookshelf). Buffalo, NY:
    Prometheus Books, 1979.
Stein, Gordon, ed. *An Anthology of Atheism and Rationalism* (The Skeptics Bookshelf). Buf-
    falo, NY: Prometheus Books, 1980.
Sutherland, Stewart R. *Atheism and the Rejection of God.* Oxford, Engl.: Basil Blackwell,
    1977.
Swinburne, Richard. *The Coherence of Theism.* Oxford, Engl.: Clarendon Press, 1977.
———. *The Existence of God.* Oxford, Engl.: Clarendon Press, 1979.

————. *Faith and Reason.* Oxford, Engl.: Clarendon Press, 1981.

————. "Mackie, Induction and God." *Religious Studies* 19 (1983): 385–91.

————. Review of *The Miracle of Theism,* by J. L. Mackie. *Journal of Philosophy* 82 (1985): 46–53.

Trethowan, Dom Illtyd. "In Defense of Theism: A Reply to Professor Kai Nielsen." *Religious Studies* 2 (1966): 37–48.

Wells, G. A. *Religious Postures: Essays on Modern Christian Apologists and Religious Problems.* La Salle, IL: Open Court, 1988.

Wykstra, Stephen J. "Difficulties in Rowe's Case for Atheism." Paper presented at the Pacific Division Meeting of the American Philosophical Association, March 1984.

————. "The Humean Obstacle to Evidential Arguments from Suffering: On Avoiding the Evils of 'Appearance'." *International Journal for Philosophy of Religion* 16 (1984): 73–93.

# II

# WITTGENSTEINIAN FIDEISM

# 5

# Faith, Skepticism, and Religious Understanding

## D. Z. Phillips

The relation between religion and philosophical reflection needs to be reconsidered. For the most part, in recent philosophy of religion, philosophers, believers, and nonbelievers alike have been concerned with discovering *the grounds* of religious belief. Philosophy, they claim, is concerned with reasons; it considers what is to count as good evidence for a belief. In the case of religious beliefs, the philosopher ought to inquire into the reasons anyone could have for believing in the existence of God, for believing that life is a gift from God, or for believing that an action is the will of God. Where can such reasons be found? One class of reasons comes readily to mind. Religious believers, when asked why they believe in God, may reply in a variety of ways. They may say, "I have had an experience of the living God," "I believe in the Lord Jesus Christ," "God saved me while I was a sinner," or "I just can't help believing." Philosophers have not given such reasons very much attention. The so-called trouble is not so much with the content of the replies as with the fact that the replies are made by believers. The answers come from *within* religion, they presuppose the framework of Faith, and therefore cannot be treated as *evidence* for religious belief. Many philosophers who argue in this way seem to be searching for evidence or reasons for religious beliefs *external* to belief itself. It is assumed that such evidence and reasons would, if found, constitute the grounds of religious belief.

The philosophical assumption behind the ignoring of religious testimony as begging the question, and the search for external reasons for believing in God, is that one could settle the question of whether there is a God or not without referring to the form of life of which belief in God is a fundamental part. What would it be like for a philosopher to settle the question of the existence of God? Could a philosopher say that he believed that God exists and yet never pray to Him, rebel against Him, lament the fact that he could no longer pray, aspire to deepen his devotion, seek His will, try to hide from Him, or fear and tremble before Him? In short, could a man believe that God exists without his life being touched *at all* by the belief? Norman Malcolm asks with good reason, "Would a belief that he exists, if it were completely non-affective, really be a belief that he exists? Would it be anything at all? What is 'the form of life' into which it would enter? What difference would it make whether anyone did or did not have this belief?"[1]

Yet many philosophers who search for the grounds of religious belief claim, to their own satisfaction at least, to understand what a purely theoretical belief in the existence of God would be. But the accounts these philosophers give of what religious believers seem to be saying are often at variance with what many believers say, at least, when *they* are not philosophizing. Every student of the philosophy of religion will have been struck by the amount of talking at cross-purposes within the subject. A philosopher may say that there is no God, but a believer may reply, "You are creating and then attacking a fiction. The god whose existence you deny is not the God I believe in." Another philosopher may say that religion is meaningless, but another believer may reply, "You say that when applied to God, words such as 'exists', 'love', 'will', etc., do not mean what they signify in certain nonreligious contexts. I agree. You conclude from this that religion is meaningless, whereas the truth is that you are failing to grasp the meaning religion has." Why is there this lack of contact between many philosophers and religious believers? One reason is that many philosophers who do not believe that God exists assume that they know what it means to say that there is a God. Norman Kemp Smith made a penetrating analysis of this fact when commenting on the widespread belief among American philosophers in his day of the uselessness of philosophy of religion.

> . . . those who are of this way of thinking, however they may have thrown over the religious beliefs of the communities in which they have been nurtured, still continue to be influenced by the phraseology of religious devotion—a phraseology which, in its endeavour to be concrete and universally intelligible, is at little pains to guard against the misunderstandings to which it may so easily give rise. As they insist upon, and even exaggerate, the merely literal meaning of this phraseology, the God in whom they have ceased to believe is a Being whom they picture in an utterly anthropomorphic fashion. . . .[2]

The distinction between religious believers and atheistical philosophers is not, of course, as clear-cut as I have suggested. It is all too evident in contemporary philosophy of religion that many philosophers who *do* believe in God philosophize about religion in the way which Kemp Smith found to be true of philosophical nonbelievers. Here, one can say either that their philosophy reflects their belief, in which case they believe in superstition but not in God, or, taking the more charitable view, that they are failing to give a good philosophical account of what they really believe.

Insufficient attention has been paid to the question of what kind of philosophical enquiry the concept of divine reality calls for. Many philosophers assume that everyone knows *what* it means to say that there is a God, and that the only outstanding question is *whether* there is a God. Similarly, it might be thought, everyone knows what it means to say that there are unicorns, although people may disagree over whether in fact there are any unicorns. If there were an analogy between the existence of God and the existence of unicorns, then coming to see that there is a

God would be like coming to see that an additional being exists. "I know what people are doing when they worship," a philosopher might say. "They praise, they confess, they thank, and they ask for things. The only difference between myself and religious believers is that I do not believe that there is a being who receives their worship." The assumption, here, is that the meaning of worship is contingently related to the question whether there is a God or not. The assumption might be justified by saying that there need be no consequences of existential beliefs. Just as one can say, "There is a planet Mars, but I couldn't care less," so one can say, "There is a God, but I couldn't care less." But what is one *saying* here when one says that there is a God? Despite the fact that one need take no interest in the existence of a planet, an account could be given of the kind of difference the existence of the planet makes, and of how one could find out whether the planet exists or not. But all this is foreign to the question whether there is a God. That is not something anyone could *find out*. It has been far too readily assumed that the dispute between the believer and the unbeliever is over a *matter of fact*. Philosophical reflection on the reality of God then becomes the philosophical reflection appropriate to an assertion of a matter of fact. I have tried to show that this is a misrepresentation of the religious concept, and that philosophy can claim justifiably to show what is meaningful in religion only if it is prepared to examine religious concepts in the contexts from which they derive their meaning.

A failure to take account of the above context has led some philosophers to ask religious language to satisfy criteria of meaningfulness alien to it. They say that religion must be rational if it is to be intelligible. Certainly, the distinction between the rational and the irrational must be central in any account one gives of meaning. But this is not to say that there is a paradigm of rationality to which all modes of discourse conform. A necessary prolegomenon to the philosophy of religion, then, is to show the diversity of criteria of rationality; to show that the distinction between the real and the unreal does not come to the same thing in every context. If this were observed, one would no longer wish to construe God's reality as being that of an existent among existents, an object among objects.

Coming to see that there is a God is not like coming to see that an additional being exists. If it were, there would be an extension of one's knowledge of facts, but no extension of one's understanding. Coming to see that there is a God involves seeing a new meaning in one's life, and being given a new understanding. The Hebrew-Christian conception of God is not a conception of a being among beings. Kierkegaard emphasized the point when he said bluntly, "God does not exist. He is eternal."[3]

The distinction between eternity and existence has been ignored by many philosophers of religion, and as a result they have singled out particular religious beliefs for discussion, divorcing them from the context of belief in God. Alasdair MacIntyre has pointed out the importance of recognizing the need, not simply to discuss specific religious utterances, but to ask why such utterances are called religious in the first place.

> Those linguistic analysts who have turned their attention to theology have begun to examine in detail particular religious utterances and theological concepts. This

examination of the logic of religious language has gone with a great variety of religious attitudes on the part of the philosophers concerned. Some have been sceptics,
others believers. But what their enterprise has had in common is an examination
of *particular* religious forms of speech and utterance, whether such examination
has been presented as part of an argument for or as part of an argument against
belief. What such examinations may omit is a general consideration of what it
means to call a particular assertion or utterance part of a religious belief as distinct
from a moral code or a scientific theory.[4]

In his more recent work in the philosophy of religion, MacIntyre has said that the
above distinction buys a position at the price of emptiness,[5] but I think his earlier
view is the correct one. It stresses the artificiality of separating the love, mercy, or
forgiveness of God from His nature. One cannot understand what praising, confessing, thanking, or asking mean in worship apart from belief in an eternal God.
The eternity of the Being addressed determines the meaning of all these activities.
One implication of this fact is that philosophers who do not see anything in belief
in God can no longer think of their rejection as the denial of something *with which
they are familiar.* Discovering that belief in God is meaningful is not like establishing that something is the case within a universe of discourse with which we are
already familiar. On the contrary, it is to discover that there *is* a universe of discourse we had been unaware of. The flattering picture that the academic philosopher may have of himself as possessing the key to reality has to be abandoned. The
philosopher, like anyone else, may fail to understand what it means to believe in an
eternal God.

In saying that one must take account of the concept of the eternal if one wishes
to understand various religious activities, I realize that I am laying myself open to
all kinds of misunderstandings. Some religious believers, when they have wanted
to turn aside the philosopher's questions, have said, "Finite understanding cannot
understand the eternal," or something similar. This is not what I am saying. There
is a proper place to say such things, that God is the inexpressible, for example, but
that place is within religious belief. These are religious utterances whose meaning
is seen in the role they play in the lives of believers. Sometimes, however, the utterances are used as a form of protectionism against intellectual inquiry. They began
as religious utterances, but end up as pseudo-epistemological theories. When this
happens, the philosopher's censure is deserved. In saying that human understanding cannot fathom the eternal, the believer is claiming that there is some higher
order of things that transcends all human discourse, that religion expresses "the
nature of things." In saying this, the believer falsifies the facts. Such a position
involves upholding what John Anderson calls "a hierarchical doctrine of reality."
Anderson has a powerful argument against this brand of religious apologetics. He
says that to speak in this way

> . . . is to speak on behalf of the principle of authority—and so again (whatever the
> actual power may be that is thus metaphysically bolstered up) to support a low way
> of living. It is low, in particular, because it is anti-intellectual, because it is neces-
> sarily dogmatic. Some account can be given of the relation of a particular 'rule' or
> way of behaving to a certain way of life, but it can have no demonstrable relation

to 'the nature of things'. To say that something is required by the nature of things is just to say that it is required—to say, without reason, that it 'is to be done'; and, as soon as any specification is attempted, the whole structure breaks down. If, for example, we are told to do something because God commands us to do so, we can immediately ask why we should do what God commands—and any intelligible answer brings us back to *human* relationships, to the struggle between opposing movements.[6]

I should like to make it quite clear that I agree with Anderson in the above criticism. In speaking of religion as turning away from the temporal towards the eternal, I am not putting forward any kind of epistemological thesis. On the contrary, I am referring to the way in which the concept of the eternal does play a role in very many human relationships. I am anxious to show that religion is not some kind of technical discourse or esoteric pursuit cut off from the ordinary problems and perplexities, hopes, and joys which most of us experience at some time or other. If it were, it would not have the importance it does have for so many people. By considering one example in detail—namely, eternal love or the love of God—I shall try to show what significance it has in human experience, the kind of circumstances which occasion it, and the kind of human predicament it answers. By so doing I hope to illustrate how seeing that there is a God in this context is synonymous with seeing the possibility of eternal love.[7]

Let me begin by speaking of a distinction with which we are all familiar: the distinction between *mine* and *yours*. The distinction is relevant to the concept of justice. If I take what is yours, or if you take what is mine, justice is thereby transgressed against. Our relationships with other people are pervaded by a wide range of rights and obligations, many of which serve to emphasize the distinction between *mine* and *yours*. But all human relationships are not like this. In erotic love and in friendship, the distinction between *mine* and *yours* is broken down. The lovers or the friends may say, "All I have is his, and what is his is mine." Kierkegaard says that the distinction between *mine* and *yours* has been transformed by a relationship in which the key term is *ours*. Nevertheless, he goes on to show that the *mine/yours* distinction is not completely transformed by such relationships, since the *ours* now functions as a new *mine* for the partners in the relationships. The distinguishing factor in the *mine/yours* distinction is now the relation of erotic love or friendship as opposed to the self-love which prevailed previously. *Mine* and *yours* now refer to those who are within and to those who are outside the specific relationship.

Now, Christianity wishes to speak of a kind of love which is such that no man is excluded from it. It calls this love "love of one's neighbor." What is more, it claims that this love is internally related to the love of God; that is, that without knowing what this love is, one cannot know what the love of God is either. An attempt to elucidate what is meant by love of the neighbor will therefore be an attempt to elucidate what is meant by the love of God.

If one considers self-love in its simplest form—namely, as the desire to possess the maximum of what one considers to be good for oneself—it is easy enough to imagine conditions in which such love could be thwarted. War, famine, or some other natural disaster might upset the normal conditions in which rights and obligations operate. Even given such conditions, the self-lover's ambitions may be thwarted by the greater ingenuity of his competitors. Sooner or later he may be forced to realize that the minimum rather than the maximum is going to be his lot. Self-love might be called temporal love in so far as it depends on states of affairs contingently related to itself. If a man's life revolves around self-love, it is obvious that he is forever dependent on the way things go, since it is the way things go that determines whether his self-love is satisfied or not.

It might be thought that erotic love and friendship avoid the predicament of self-love outlined above. The lovers or the friends may say to one another, "Come what may, we still have each other." Yet, such reliance shows that this love too is temporal; it depends on certain states of affairs being realized. To begin with, the point of such love depends on the existence of *the other*. Often, when the lovers or the friends love each other very much, the death of the beloved can rob life of its meaning; for what is love without the beloved? Again, erotic love and friendship depend on the unchangeability of the beloved. But the beloved may change. Friendship can cool, and love can fade. If the relationship is such that it depended on reciprocation, then a change in the beloved or in the friend may rob it of its point. So although erotic love and friendship are far removed from self-love, they too are forms of temporal love in so far as they are dependent on how things go.

Temporal love, then, is marked by certain characteristics: it depends on how things go, it may change, and it may end in failure. Eternal love, it is said, is not dependent on how things go, it cannot change, and it cannot suffer defeat. One must not think that this contrast presents the believer with an either/or. He is not asked to choose between loving God on the one hand and loving the loved one on the other. What he is asked to do is not to love the loved one in such a way that the love of God becomes impossible. The death of the beloved must not rob life of its meaning, since for the believer the meaning of life is found in God. The believer claims that there is a love that will not let one go whatever happens. This is the love of God, the independence of which from what happens is closely bound up with the point of calling it eternal.

The object of Christian love is the neighbor. But who is the neighbor? The neighbor is every man. The obligation to love the neighbor does not depend on the particularity of the relationship, as in the case of the love which exists between parents and children, lovers or friends. The neighbor is not loved because of his being a parent, lover, or friend, but simply because of his being. In relation to the agent, the love takes the form of self-renunciation. In this self-renunciation, man discovers the Spirit of God. Consider how love of the neighbor exhibits the three characteristics I mentioned earlier: independence of the way things go, unchangeability, and immunity from defeat. Kierkegaard brings out the contrast between love of one's neighbor on the one hand, and erotic love and friendship on the other, in these terms.

> The beloved can treat you in such a way that he is lost to you, and you can lose a friend, but whatever a neighbour does to you, you can never lose him. To be sure, you can also continue to love your beloved and your friend no matter how they treat you, but you cannot truthfully continue to call them beloved and friend when they, sorry to say, have really changed. No change, however, can take your neigh-

bour from you, for it is not your neighbour who holds you fast—it is your love which holds your neighbour fast.[8]

For someone with eyes only for the prudential, and common-sense considerations, the love which Kierkegaard is talking about seems to lead inevitably to self-deception, and to a kind of foolishness. On the contrary, Kierkegaard argues, eternal love is precisely the only kind of love which can never deceive one. After a certain stage of unrequited love, no one could be blamed for saying, "The lover has deceived me." It becomes intelligible and justifiable to say this because the love in question does not have much point without some degree of reciprocation. At first sight it looks as if the same conclusions apply to love of one's neighbor. But eternal love believes all things, and yet is never deceived! Ordinarily speaking, we say that only a fool believes all things; only a man who ignores the odds could be so stupid. Yet, Christianity says that eternal love cannot be deceived, for if a believer is wrong about a man but continues to love him, in what sense is he deceived? True, one can enumerate all the ways in which obvious deceptions have taken place: loans unreturned, promises broken, trusts betrayed, etc., but the believer continues to love the neighbor despite all this. Those who see little in the love of the neighbor will say, especially if the believer is reduced to a state which many would call ruin, that the believer has lost all. On the contrary, Kierkegaard tells us, the believer, in the act of self-renunciation, possesses all; he possesses love. To possess this love is to possess God. Indeed, the only way in which the believer can be deceived is by ceasing to love. Ordinarily, when we say, "I shall show no more love toward him," we envisage the loss as suffered by the person who is the object of one's love. But if the believer says, "I shall love the neighbor no longer," he is the victim of deception, since the loss of loving is his loss too. Kierkegaard brings this point out very clearly:

> When someone says, 'I have given up my love for this man,' he thinks that it is this person who loses, this person who was the object of his love. The speaker thinks that he himself possesses his love in the same sense as when one who has supported another financially says, 'I have quit giving assistance to him.' In this case the giver keeps for himself the money which the other previously received, he who is the loser, for the giver is certainly far from losing by this financial shift. But it is not like this with love; perhaps the one who was the object of love does lose, but he who 'has given up his love for this man' is the loser. Maybe he does not detect this himself; perhaps he does not detect that the language mocks him, for he says explicitly, 'I have given up my love.' But if he has given up his love, he has then ceased to be loving. True enough, he adds 'my love for this man', but this does not help when love is involved, although in money matters one can manage things this way without loss to oneself. The adjective *loving* does not apply to me when I have given up my love 'for this man'—alas, even though I perhaps imagined that he was the one who lost. It is the same with despairing over another person; it is oneself who is in despair.[9]

In this way, Kierkegaard illustrates the truth that for the believer, love itself is the real object of the relationship between himself and another person. This love is the Spirit of God, and to possess it is to walk with God. Once this is realized, one can see how love and understanding are equated in Christianity. To know God is to love Him. There is no theoretical understanding of the reality of God.

If anyone thinks he is a Christian and yet is indifferent towards his being a Christian, then he really is not one at all. What would we think of a man who affirmed that he was in love and also that it was a matter of indifference to him?[10]

"But, so far," the nonbeliever might complain, "you have simply concealed the advantage entailed in religion, namely, God's love for the sinner. Is not this the reason for love of the neighbor? Unless one loves the neighbor, God will not love one." There is truth in this *unless,* but not as conceived in the above objection. The love of the neighbor is not the means whereby a further end is realized—namely, one's own forgiveness. On the contrary, there is an internal relation between forgiving another and being forgiven oneself. I cannot hope to emulate Kierkegaard's analysis of this religious truth, so I must ask the reader to forgive a final quotation of two passages where his analysis is particularly forceful:

When we say, 'Love saves from death,' there is straightway a reduplication in thought: the lover saves another human being from death, and in entirely the same or yet in a different sense he saves himself from death. This he does at the same time; it is one and the same; he does not save the other at one moment and at another save himself, but in the moment he saves the other he saves himself from death. Only love never thinks about the latter, about saving oneself, about acquiring confidence itself; the lover in love thinks only about giving confidence and saving another from death. But the lover is not thereby forgotten. No, he who in love forgets himself, forgets his sufferings in order to think of another's, forgets all his wretchedness in order to think of another's, forgets what he himself loses in order lovingly to consider another's loss, forgets his advantage in order lovingly to look after another's advantage: truly, such a person is not forgotten. There is one who thinks of him, God in heaven; or love thinks of him. God is love, and when a human being because of love forgets himself, how then should God forget him! No, while the lover forgets himself and thinks of the other person, God thinks of the lover. The self-lover is busy; he shouts and complains and insists on his rights in order to make sure he is not forgotten—and yet he is forgotten. But the lover, who forgets himself, is remembered by love. There is one who thinks of him, and in this way it comes about that the lover gets what he gives.[11]

And again:

'Forgive, and you will also be forgiven.' Meanwhile, one might nevertheless manage to understand these words in such a way that he imagined it possible to receive forgiveness without his forgiving. Truly this is a misunderstanding. Christianity's view is: forgiveness *is* forgiveness: your forgiveness is your forgiveness; your forgiveness of another is your own forgiveness: the forgiveness which you give you receive, not contrariwise that you give the forgiveness which you receive. It is as if Christianity would say: pray to God humbly and believing in your forgiveness, for he really is compassionate in such a way as no human being is; but if you will test how it is with respect to the forgiveness, then observe yourself. If honestly before God you wholeheartedly forgive your enemy (but remember that if you do, God sees it), then you dare hope also for your forgiveness, for it is one and the same. God forgives you neither more nor less nor otherwise than *as* you forgive your trespassers. It is only an illusion to imagine that one himself has forgiveness, although one is slack in forgiving others.[12]

My purpose in discussing the Christian concept of love was to show how coming to see the possibility of such love amounts to the same thing as coming to see the possibility of belief in God. As I said earlier, to know God is to love Him, and the understanding which such knowledge brings is the understanding of love. Belief, understanding, and love can all be equated with each other in this context. There are, however, certain objections which can be made against this conclusion. Before ending, I want to consider one of the strongest of these made recently by Alasdair MacIntyre:

> And if the believer wishes to he can always claim that we can only disagree with him because we do not understand him. But the implications of this defence of belief are more fatal to it than any attack could be.[13]

One of the fatal implications of identifying understanding and believing, according to MacIntyre, is that one can no longer give an intelligible account of a rejection of religious belief. MacIntyre says that the Protestant who claims that grace is necessary before one can possess religious understanding is soon convicted of paradox.

> For the Protestant will elsewhere deny what is entailed by his position, namely that nobody ever rejects Christianity (since anyone who thinks he has rejected it must have lacked saving grace and so did not understand Christianity and so in fact rejected something else).[14]

Does MacIntyre's point hold for any identification of understanding and believing? I suggest not. To begin with, there is a perfectly natural use of the word *rejection* which is connected with the inability of the person who rejects to make any sense of what is rejected. I can see no objection to saying that the man who says that religion means nothing to him rejects the claims of religion on his life. Apparently, when Oscar Wilde was accused of blasphemy during his trial, he replied "Sir, blasphemy is a word I never use." Wilde is rejecting a certain way of talking. Similarly, the man who says, "Religion is mumbo-jumbo as far as I am concerned," is making a wholesale rejection of a way of talking or a way of life. That way of talking and that way of life mean nothing to him, but this does not mean that he cannot reject them.

On the other hand, I agree with MacIntyre that there are difficulties involved in the view I wish to maintain if the rejection of religion in question is not the rejection of the meaningless, but rebellion against God. Camus says of the rebel:

> The rebel defies more than he denies. Originally, at least, he does not deny God, he simply talks to Him as an equal. But it is not a polite dialogue. It is a polemic animated by the desire to conquer.[15]

But if the rebel knows God and yet defies Him, how can one say that to know God is to love Him? Clearly, some kind of modification of my thesis is called for. I agree. But what is not called for is a denial of the identification of belief and understanding in religion. The fact of rebellion makes one think otherwise because of a false and unnecessary assimilation of "I believe in God" to "I believe in John."

Belief in God has a wider range of application than belief in another person. This point has been made very clearly by Norman Malcolm:

> Belief in a person primarily connotes trust or faith: but this is not so of belief in God. A man could properly be said to believe in God whose chief attitude towards God was *fear*. ('A sword is sent upon you, and who may turn it back?') But if you were enormously afraid of another human being you could not be said to believe in him. At least you would not believe in him *in so far* as you were afraid of him: whereas the fear of God is one form of belief in Him.
>
> I am suggesting that *belief-in* has a wider meaning when God is the object of it than when a human being is. Belief in God encompasses not only trust but also awe, dread, dismay, resentment, and perhaps even hatred. Belief in God will involve some affective state or attitude, having God as its object, and those attitudes could vary from reverential love to rebellious rejection.[16]

I should still want to argue, however, that the love of God is the primary form of belief in God if only because the intelligibility of all the other attitudes Malcolm mentions is logically dependent on it. The rebel must see the kind of relationship God asks of the believer before he can reject and defy it. He sees the story from the inside, but it is not a story that captivates him. The love of God is active in his life, but in him it evokes hatred. To say that he does not believe in God is absurd, for whom does he hate if not God?

Similar difficulties to those mentioned by MacIntyre might be thought to arise in giving an account of seeking for God. If one must believe before one can know God, how can one know that it is God one is seeking for? The answer to this difficulty has been given by Pascal: "Comfort yourself, you would not seek me if you had not found me." One must not think of belief in God as an all-or-nothing affair. Whether the love of God means anything in a man's life can be assessed, not simply by his attainments, but also by his aspirations. So even if a man does not actually love God, his understanding of what it means to love God can be shown by his aspirations toward such love.

On the other hand, it would be a mistake to conclude that in the absence of religious attainments only religious aspirations could be the sign that religion held some meaning for a person. We have seen already in the case of the rebel that belief in God need not entail a worshipful attitude on the part of the believer. Neither need the believer aspire to attain love of God. On the contrary, he may want to flee from it. Instead of feeling sad because he spurns God's love, he may hate the fact that he cannot rid his life of God. If someone were to say to him, "You do not believe in God," he might reply, "How can you say that when God will not leave me alone?"

What, then, are our conclusions? The assertion that to know God is to love Him is false if it is taken to imply that everyone who believes in God loves Him. What it stresses, quite correctly, is that there is no theoretical knowledge of God. As Malcolm said, "belief in God involves some affective state or attitude." I think that love of God is fundamental in religion, since all other attitudes can be explained by reference to it. I believe that Kierkegaard says somewhere that in relation to God there are only lovers—happy or unhappy—but lovers. The unhappy or unruly lover has an understanding of what it means to believe in God as well as the happy lover. The man who construes religious belief as a theoretical affair distorts it. Kierkegaard emphasizes that there is no understanding of religion without passion. And when the philosopher understands that, *his* understanding of religion is incompatible with skepticism.

## Notes

1. Norman Malcolm, "Is it a Religious Belief that 'God Exists'?" in *Faith and the Philosophers,* ed. John Hick (London: Macmillan, 1964), p. 107.

2. Norman Kemp Smith, "Is Divine Existence Credible?" in *Religion and Understanding,* ed. D. Z. Phillips (Oxford, Engl.: Basil Blackwell, 1967), pp. 105–6.

3. Søren Kierkegaard, *Concluding Unscientific Postscript,* ed. N. K. Smith (Indianapolis: Bobbs Merrill, 1963), p. 296.

4. Alasdair MacIntyre, "The Logical Status of Religious Belief," in *Metaphysical Beliefs,* ed. Alasdair MacIntyre (London: Macmillan, 1957), p. 172.

5. See Alasdair MacIntyre, "Is Understanding Religion Compatible with Believing?" in *Faith and the Philosophers,* ed. John Hick.

6. John Anderson, "Art and Morality," *Australasian Journal of Psychology and Philosophy* 19 (December, 1941): 256–57.

7. Anyone acquainted with Kierkegaard's *The Works of Love* (New York: Harper & Row, 1962) will recognize in what follows how dependent I am on the second part of that work.

8. Kierkegaard, *Works of Love,* p. 76.

9. Kierkegaard, *Works of Love,* pp. 239–40.

10. Kierkegaard, *Works of Love,* p. 42.

11. Kierkegaard, *Works of Love,* p. 262.

12. Kierkegaard, *Works of Love,* pp. 351–52.

13. MacIntyre, "Is Understanding Religion Compatible with Believing?," p. 133.

14. MacIntyre, "Is Understanding Religion Compatible with Believing?," p. 116.

15. Albert Camus, *The Rebel: An Essay on Man in Revolt* (Peregrine Book ed.), trans. Anthony Bower (New York: Random House, 1958), p. 31.

16. Malcolm, "Is it a Religious Belief that 'God Exists'?," pp. 106–7.

# 6

# The Groundlessness of Belief

## Norman Malcolm

### I

In his final notebooks Wittgenstein wrote that it is difficult "to realize the ground-lessness of our believing."[1] He was thinking of how much mere acceptance, on the basis of no evidence, shapes our lives. This is obvious in the case of small children. They are told the names of things. They accept what they are told. They do not ask for grounds. A child does not demand a proof that the person who feeds him is called "Mama." Or are we to suppose that the child reasons to himself as follows: "The others present seem to know this person who is feeding me, and since they call her 'Mama' that probably is her name"? It is obvious on reflection that a child cannot consider evidence or even doubt anything until he has already learned much. As Wittgenstein puts it: "The child learns by believing the adult. Doubt comes *after* belief" (*OC*, 160).

What is more difficult to perceive is that the lives of educated, sophisticated adults are also formed by groundless beliefs. I do not mean eccentric beliefs that are out on the fringes of their lives, but fundamental beliefs. Take the belief that familiar material things (watches, shoes, chairs) do not cease to exist without some physical explanation. They don't "vanish in thin air." It is interesting that we do use that very expression: "I *know* I put the keys right here on this table. They must have vanished in thin air!" But this exclamation is hyperbole: we are not speaking in literal seriousness. I do not know of any adult who would consider, in all gravity, that the keys might have inexplicably ceased to exist.

Yet it is possible to imagine a society in which it was accepted that sometimes material things do go out of existence without having been crushed, melted, eroded, broken into pieces, burned up, eaten, or destroyed in some other way. The difference between those people and ourselves would not consist in their *saying* something that we don't say ("It vanished in thin air"), since we say it too. I conceive of those people as acting and thinking differently from ourselves in such ways as the following: if one of them could not find his wallet, he would give up the search sooner than you or I would; also he would be less inclined to suppose that it was stolen. In general what we would regard as convincing circumstantial evidence of theft those people would find less convincing. They would take fewer precautions than we would to protect their possessions against loss or theft. They would have less inclination to save money, since it too can just disappear. They would not tend to form strong attachments to material things. They would stand in a looser relation to the world than we do. The disappearance of a desired object, which would provoke us to a frantic search, they would be more inclined to accept with a shrug. Of course their scientific theories would be different; but also their attitude toward experiment, and inference from experimental results, would be more tentative. If the repetition of a familiar chemical experiment did not yield the expected result, this *could* be because one of the chemical substances had vanished.

The outlook I have sketched might be thought to be radically incoherent. I do not see that this is so. Although those people consider it to be possible that a wallet might have inexplicably ceased to exist, it is also true that they regard that as unlikely. For things that are lost usually do turn up later; or if not, their fate can often be accounted for. Those people use pretty much the same criteria of identity that we do; their reasoning would resemble ours quite a lot. Their thinking would not be incoherent. But it would be different, since they would leave room for possibilities that we exclude.

If we compare their view that material things do sometimes go out of existence inexplicably with our own rejection of that view, it does not appear to me that one position is supported by *better evidence* than is the other. Each position is compatible with ordinary experience. On the one hand it is true that familiar objects (watches, wallets, lawn chairs) occasionally disappear without any adequate explanation. On the other hand it happens, perhaps more frequently, that a satisfying explanation of the disappearance is discovered.

Our attitude in this matter is striking. We would not be willing to consider it even as *improbable* that a missing lawn chair had "just ceased to exist." We would not entertain such a suggestion. If anyone proposed it we would be sure he was joking. It is no exaggeration to say that this attitude is part of the foundations of our thinking. I do not want to say that this attitude is *un*reasonable; but rather that it is something that we do not *try* to support with grounds. It could be said to belong to "the framework" of our thinking about material things.

Wittgenstein asks: "Does anyone ever test whether this table remains in existence when no one is paying attention to it?" (*OC,* 163). The answer is: Of course not. Is this because we would not call it "a table" if that were to happen? But we do call it "a table" and none of us makes the test. Doesn't this show that we do not regard that occurrence as a possibility? People who did so regard it would seem ludicrous to us. One could imagine that they made ingenious experiments to decide the question; but this research would make us smile. Is this because experiments were conducted by our ancestors that settled the matter once and for all? I don't believe it. The principle that material things do not cease to exist without physical cause is an unreflective part of the framework within which physical investigations are made and physical explanations arrived at.

Wittgenstein suggests that the same is true of what might be called "the principle of the continuity of nature":

> Think of chemical investigations. Lavoisier makes experiments with substances in his laboratory and now concludes that this and that takes place when there is burning. He does not say that it might happen otherwise another time. He has got hold of a world-picture—not of course one that he invented: he learned it as a child. I say world-picture and not hypothesis, because it is the matter-of-course (*selbstverständliche*) foundation for his research and as such also goes unmentioned (*OC,* 167).

> But now, what part is played by the presupposition that a substance A always reacts to a substance B in the same way, given the same circumstances? Or is that part of the definition of a substance? (*OC,* 168).

Framework principles, such as the continuity of nature or the assumption that material things do not cease to exist without physical cause, belong to what Wittgenstein calls a "system." He makes the following observation, which seems to me to be true: "All testing, all confirmation and disconfirmation of a hypothesis takes place already within a system. And this system is not a more or less arbitrary and doubtful point of departure for all our arguments; no, it belongs to the nature of what we call an argument. The system is not so much the point of departure, as the element in which arguments have their life" (*OC,* 105).

A "system" provides the boundaries within which we ask questions, carry out investigations, and make judgments. Hypotheses are put forth, and challenged, *within* a system. Verification, justification, the search for evidence, occur *within* a system. The framework propositions of the system are not put to the test, not backed up by evidence. This is what Wittgenstein means when he says: "Of course there is justification; but justification comes to an end" (*OC,* 192); and when he asks: "Doesn't testing come to an end?" (*OC,* 164); and when he remarks that "whenever we test anything we are already presupposing something that is not tested" (*OC,* 163).

That this is so is not to be attributed to human weakness. It is a conceptual requirement that our inquiries and proofs stay within boundaries. Think, for example, of the activity of calculating a number. Some steps in a calculation we will check for correctness, but others we won't: for example, that $4 + 4 = 8$. More accurately, some beginners might check it, but grown-ups won't. Similarly, some grown-ups would want to determine by calculation whether $25 \times 25 = 625$, whereas others would regard that as laughable. Thus the boundaries of the system within which *you* calculate may not be exactly the same as my boundaries. But we do calculate; and, as Wittgenstein remarks, "In certain circumstances . . . we regard a calculation as sufficiently checked. What gives us a right to do so? . . . Somewhere we must be finished with justification, and then there remains the proposition that *this* is how we calculate" (*OC,* 212). If someone did not accept any boundaries for calculating, this would mean that he had not learned *that* language-game: "If someone supposed that *all* our calculations were uncertain and that we could rely on none of them (justifying himself by saying that mistakes are always possible) perhaps we would say he was crazy. But can we say he is in error? Does he not just react differently? We rely on calculations, he doesn't; we are sure, he isn't" (*OC,* 217). We are taught, or we absorb, the systems within which we raise doubts, make inquiries, draw conclusions. We grow into a framework. We don't question it. We accept it trustingly. But this acceptance is not a consequence of reflection. We do not *decide* to accept framework propositions. We do not decide that we live on the earth, any more than we decide to learn our native tongue. We do come to adhere to a framework proposition, in the sense that it shapes the way we think. The framework propositions that we accept, grow into, are not idiosyncrasies but common ways of speaking and thinking that are pressed on us by our human community. For our acceptances to have been withheld would have meant that we had not learned how to count, to measure, to use names, to play games, or even *to talk.* Wittgenstein remarks that "a language-game is only possible if one trusts something." Not *can,* but *does* trust something (*OC,* 509). I think he means by this trust or acceptance what he calls belief "in the sense of religious belief" (*OC,* 459). What does he mean by belief "in the sense of religious belief"? He explicitly distinguishes it from *conjecture* (*Vermutung:* ibid). I think this means that there is nothing tentative about it; it is not adopted as an hypothesis that might later be withdrawn in the light of new evidence. This also makes explicit an important feature of Wittgenstein's understanding of belief, in the sense of "religious belief," namely, that it does not rise or fall on the basis of evidence or grounds: it is "groundless."

## II

In our Western academic philosophy, religious belief is commonly regarded as unreasonable and is viewed with condescension or even contempt. It is said that religion is a refuge for those who, because of weakness of intellect or character, are unable to confront the stern realities of the world. The objective, mature, *strong* attitude is to hold beliefs solely on the basis of *evidence.*

It appears to me that philosophical thinking is greatly influenced by this veneration of evidence. We have an aversion to statements, reports, declarations, beliefs, that are not based on grounds. There are many illustrations of this philosophical bent.

For example, in regard to a person's report that he has an image of the Eiffel Tower we have an inclination to think that the image must *resemble* the Eiffel Tower. How else could the person declare so confidently what his image is *of*? How could he know?

Another example: a memory-report or memory-belief must be based, we think, on some mental *datum* that is equipped with various features to match the corresponding features of the memory-belief. This datum will include an image that provides the *content* of the belief, and a peculiar feeling that makes one refer the image to a *past* happening, and another feeling that makes one believe that the image is an *accurate* portrayal of the past happening, and still another feeling that informs one that it was *oneself* who witnessed the past happening. The presence of these various features makes memory-beliefs thoroughly reasonable.

Another illustration: if interrupted in speaking one can usually give a confident account, later on, of what one had been *about* to say. How is this possible? Must not one remember *a feeling of tendency to say just those words?* This is one's basis for knowing what one had been about to say. It justifies one's subsequent account.

Still another example: after dining at a friend's house you announce your intention to go home. How do you know your intention? One theory proposes that you are presently aware of a particular mental state or bodily feeling which, as you recall from your past experience, has been highly correlated with the behavior of going home; so you infer that *that* is what you are going to do now. A second theory holds that you must be aware of some definite mental state or event which reveals itself, not by experience but *intrinsically,* as the intention to go home. Your awareness of that mental item *informs* you of what action you will take.

Yet another illustration: this is the instructive case of the man who, since birth, has been immune to sensations of bodily pain. On his thirtieth birthday he is kicked on the shins, and for the first time he responds by crying out, hopping around on one foot, holding his leg, and exclaiming "The pain is terrible!" We have an overwhelming inclination to wonder, "How could he tell, *this first time,* that what he felt was *pain?*" Of course the implication is that *after* the first time there would be *no* problem. Why not? Because his first experience of pain would provide him with a sample that would be preserved in memory; thereafter he would be equipped to determine whether any sensation he feels is or isn't pain; he would just compare it with the memory-sample to see whether the two match! Thus he will have a *justification* for believing that what he feels is pain. But the *first time* he will not have this justification. This is why the case is so puzzling. Could it be that this first time he *infers* that he is in pain from his own behavior?

A final illustration: consider the fact that after a comparatively few examples and bits of instruction a person can go on to carry out a task, apply a word correctly in the future, continue a numerical series from an initial segment, distinguish grammatical from ungrammatical constructions, solve arithmetical problems, and so on. These correct performances will be dealing with new and different examples, situations, combinations. The performance output will be far more varied than the instruction input. How is this possible? What carries the person from the meager instruction to his rich performance? The explanation has to be that an effect of his training was that he abstracted the Idea, perceived the Common Nature, "internalized" the Rule, grasped the Structure. What else could bridge the gap between the poverty of instruction and the wealth of performance? Thus we postulate an intervening mental act or state which removes the inequality and restores the balance.

My illustrations belong to what could be called the *pathology* of philosophy. Wittgenstein speaks of a "general disease of thinking" which attempts to explain occurrences of discernment, recognition, or understanding, by postulating mental states or processes from which those occurrences flow "as from a reservoir" (*BB*, p. 143). These mental intermediaries are assumed to contribute to the causation of the various cognitive performances. More significantly for my present purpose, they are supposed to *justify* them; they provide our *grounds* for saying or doing this rather than that; they *explain how we know.* The Image, or Cognitive State, or Feeling, or Idea, or Sample, or Rule, or Structure, *tells* us. It is like a road map or a signpost. It guides our course.

What is "pathological" about these explanatory constructions and pseudo-scientific inferences? Two things at least. First, the movement of thought that demands these intermediaries is circular and empty, unless it provides criteria for determining their presence and nature *other than* the occurrence of the phenomena they are postulated to explain—and of course no such criteria are forthcoming. Second, there is the great criticism by Wittgenstein of this movement of philosophical thought: namely, his point that no matter what kind of state, process, paradigm, sample, structure, or rule is conceived of as giving us the necessary guidance, *it* could be taken, or understood, as indicating a *different* direction from the one in which we actually did go. The assumed intermediary Idea, Structure, or Rule does not and cannot reveal that because of it we went in the only direction it was reasonable to go. Thus the internalized intermediary we are tempted to invoke to bridge the gap between training and performance, as being that which shows us what we must do or say if we are to be rational, cannot do the job it was invented to do. It cannot fill the epistemological gap. It cannot provide the bridge of justification. It cannot put to rest the How-do-we-know? question. Why not? Because it cannot tell us how *it itself* is to be taken, understood, applied. Wittgenstein puts the point briefly and powerfully: "Don't always think that you read off your words from facts; that you portray these in words according to rules. For even so you would have to apply the rule in the particular case without guidance" (*PI*, 292). Without guidance! Like Wittgenstein's signpost arrow that cannot tell us whether to go in the direction of the arrow tip or in the opposite direction, so too the Images, Ideas, Cognitive Structures, or Rules that we philosophers imagine as devices for guidance cannot interpret themselves to us. The signpost does not tell the traveler how to read it. A second signpost might tell him how to read the first one; we can imagine such a case. But this can't go on. If the traveler is to continue his journey he will have to do something on his own, without guidance.

The parable of the traveler speaks for *all* of the language-games we learn and practice, even those in which there is the most disciplined instruction and the most rigorous standards of conformity. Suppose that a pupil has been given thorough training in some procedure, whether it is drawing patterns, building fences, or proving theorems. But then he has to carry on by himself in new situations. How does he know what to do? Wittgenstein presents the following dialogue: " 'However you instruct him in the continuation of a pattern—how can he *know* how he is to continue by himself?'—Well, how do *I* know?—If that means 'Have I grounds?', the answer is: the grounds will soon give out. And then I shall act, without grounds" (*PI*, 211). Grounds come to an end. Answers to How-do-we-know? questions come to an end. Evidence comes to an end. We must speak, act, live, without evidence. This is so not just on the fringes of life and language, but at the center of our most regularized activities. We do learn rules and learn to follow them. But our training was in the past! We had to leave it behind and proceed on our own.

It is an immensely important fact of nature that as people carry on an activity in which they have received a common training, they do largely *agree* with one another, accepting the same examples and analogies, taking the same steps. We agree in what to say, in how to apply language. We agree in our responses to particular cases.

As Wittgenstein says, "That is not agreement in opinions but in form of life" (*PI*, 241). We cannot explain this agreement by saying that we are just doing what the rules tell us—for our agreement in applying rules, formulae and signposts is what gives them their *meaning*.

One of the primary pathologies of philosophy is the feeling that we must *justify* our language-games. We want to establish them as well grounded. But we should consider here Wittgenstein's remark that a language-game "is not based on grounds. It is there—like our life" (*OC*, 559).

*Within* a language-game there is justification and lack of justification, evidence and proof, mistakes and groundless opinions, good and bad reasoning, correct measurements and incorrect ones. One cannot properly apply these terms to a language-game itself. It may, however, be said to be "groundless," not in the sense of a groundless opinion, but in the sense that we accept it, we live it. We can say, "This is what we do. This is how we are."

In this sense religion is groundless; and so is chemistry. Within each of these two systems of thought and action there is controversy and argument. Within each there are advances and recessions of insight into the secrets of nature or the spiritual condition of humankind and the demands of the Creator, Savior, Judge, Source. Within the framework of each system there is criticism, explanation, justification. But we should not expect that there might be some sort of rational justification of the framework itself.

A chemist will sometimes employ induction. Does he have evidence for a Law of Induction? Wittgenstein observes that it would strike him as nonsense to say, "I know that the Law of Induction is true." ("Imagine such a statement made in a law court.") It would be more correct to say, "I believe in the Law of Induction" (*OC*, 500). This way of putting it is better because it shows that the attitude toward induction is belief in the sense of "religious" belief—that is to say, an acceptance which is not conjecture or surmise and for which there is no reason—it is a groundless acceptance.

It is intellectually troubling for us to conceive that a whole system of thought might be groundless, might have no rational justification. We realize easily enough, however, that grounds soon give out—that we cannot go on giving reasons for our reasons. There arises from this realization the conception of a reason that is *self-justifying*—something whose credentials as a reason cannot be questioned.

This metaphysical conception makes its presence felt at many points—for example, as an explanation of how a person can tell what his mental image is *of*. We feel that the following remarks, imagined by Wittgenstein, are exactly right: " 'The image must be more similar to its object than any picture. For however similar I make the picture to what it is supposed to represent, it can always be the picture of something else. But it is essential to the image that it is the image of *this* and of nothing else' " (*PI*, 389). A pen and ink drawing represents the Eiffel Tower; but it could represent a mine shaft or a new type of automobile jack. Nothing prevents this drawing from being taken as a representation of something other than the Eiffel

Tower. But my mental image of the Eiffel Tower is *necessarily* an image of the Eiffel Tower. Therefore it must be a "remarkable" kind of picture. As Wittgenstein observes: "Thus one might come to regard the image as a super-picture" (ibid.). Yet we have no intelligible conception of how a super-picture would differ from an ordinary picture. It would seem that it has to be a *super-likeness*—but what does this mean?

There is a familiar linguistic practice in which one person *tells* another what his image is of (or what he intends to do, or what he was about to say) and no question is raised of how the first one *knows* that what he says is true. This question is imposed from outside, artificially, by the philosophical craving for justification. We can see here the significance of these remarks: "It isn't a question of explaining a language-game by means of our experiences, but of noting a language-game" (*PI*, 665). "Look on the language-game as the *primary* thing" (*PI*, 656). Within a system of thinking and acting there occurs, *up to a point*, investigation and criticism of the reasons and justifications that are employed in that system. This inquiry into whether a reason is good or adequate cannot, as said, go on endlessly. We stop it. We bring it to an end. We come upon something that *satisfies* us. It is *as if* we made a decision or issued an edict: "*This* is an adequate reason!" (or explanation, or justification). Thereby we fix a boundary of our language-game.

There is nothing wrong with this. How else could we have disciplines, systems, games? But our fear of groundlessness makes us conceive that we are under some logical compulsion to terminate at *those particular* stopping points. We imagine that we have confronted the self-evident reason, the self-justifying explanation, the picture or symbol whose meaning cannot be questioned. This obscures from us the *human* aspect of our concepts—the fact that what we call "a reason," "evidence," "explanation," "justification," is what appeals to and satisfies *us*.

## III

The desire to provide a rational foundation for a form of life is especially prominent in the philosophy of religion, where there is an intense preoccupation with purported proofs of the existence of God. In American universities there must be hundreds of courses in which these proofs are the main topic. We can be sure that nearly always the critical verdict is that the proofs are invalid and consequently that, up to the present time at least, religious belief has received no rational justification.

Well, of course not! The obsessive concern with the proofs reveals the assumption that in order for religious belief to be intellectually respectable it *ought* to have a rational justification. *That* is the misunderstanding. It is like the idea that we are not justified in relying on memory until memory has been proved reliable.

Roger Trigg makes the following remark: "To say that someone acts in a certain way because of his belief in God does seem to be more than a redescription of his action. . . . It is to give a reason for it. The belief is distinct from the commitment which may follow it, and is the justification for it."[2] It is evident from other remarks that by "belief in God" Trigg means "belief in the existence of God" or "belief that God exists." Presumably, by the *acts* and *commitments* of a religious person Trigg refers to such things as prayer, worship, confession, thanksgiving, partaking of sacraments, and participation in the life of a religious group.

For myself I have great difficulty with the notion of belief in *the existence* of God, whereas the idea of belief *in* God is to me intelligible. If a man did not ever pray for help or forgiveness, or have any inclination toward it; nor ever felt that it is "a good and joyful thing" to thank God for the blessings of this life; nor was ever concerned about his failure to comply with divine commandments—then, it seems clear to me, he could not be said to believe in God. Belief in God is not an all or none thing; it can be more or less; it can wax and wane. But belief in God in any degree does require, as I understand the words, some religious action, some commitment, or if not, at least a bad conscience.

According to Trigg, if I take him correctly, a man who was entirely devoid of any inclination to religious action or conscience might believe in *the existence* of God. What would be the marks of this? Would it be that the man knows some theology, can recite the Creeds, is well-read in Scripture? Or is his belief in the existence of God something different from this? If so, what? What would be the difference between a man who knows some articles of faith, heresies, Scriptural writings, and in addition believes in the existence of God, and one who knows these things but does not believe in the existence of God? I assume that both of them are indifferent to the acts and commitments of religious life.

I do not comprehend this notion of belief in *the existence* of God which is thought to be distinct from belief *in* God. It seems to me to be an artificial construction of philosophy, another illustration of the craving for justification.

Religion is a form of life; it is language embedded in action—what Wittgenstein calls a "language-game." Science is another. Neither stands in need of justification, the one no more than the other.

Present-day academic philosophers are far more prone to challenge the credentials of religion than of science. This is probably due to a number of things. One may be the illusion that science can justify its own framework. Another is the fact that science is a vastly greater force in our culture. Still another reason may be the fact that by and large religion is to university people an alien form of life. They do not participate in it and do not understand what it is all about. This nonunderstanding is of an interesting nature. It derives, at least in part, from the inclination of academics to suppose that their employment as scholars demands of them the most severe objectivity and dispassionateness. For an academic philosopher to become a religious believer would be a stain on his professional competence! Here I will quote from Nietzsche, who was commenting on the relation of the German scholar of his day to religious belief; yet his remarks continue to have a nice appropriateness for the American and British scholars of our own day:

> Pious or even merely church-going people seldom realize *how much* good will, one might even say willfulness, it requires nowadays for a German scholar to take the problem of religion seriously; his whole trade . . . disposes him to a superior, almost good-natured merriment in regard to religion, sometimes mixed with a mild contempt directed at the 'uncleanliness' of spirit which he presupposes wherever one still belongs to the church. It is only with the aid of history (thus *not* from his per-

sonal experience) that the scholar succeeds in summoning up a reverent seriousness and a certain shy respect towards religion; but if he intensifies his feelings towards it even to the point of feeling grateful to it, he has still in his own person not got so much as a single step closer to that which still exists as church or piety; perhaps the reverse. The practical indifference to religious things in which he was born and raised is as a rule sublimated in him into a caution and cleanliness which avoids contact with religious people and things; . . . Every age has its own divine kind of naïvety for the invention of which other ages may envy it—and how much naïvety, venerable, childlike and boundlessly stupid naïvety there is in the scholar's belief in his superiority, in the good conscience of his tolerance, in the simple unsuspecting certainty with which his instinct treats the religious man as an inferior and lower type which he himself has grown beyond and *above*.[3]

# IV

Someone could point out that within particular religions there are beliefs that are based on evidence or to which evidence is relevant. This is indeed so. Some doctrinal beliefs about Jesus and the Holy Spirit, for example, are based on New Testament texts. Here is an area where evidence and interpretation are appropriate. There are disputes between Christian sects (for example, the controversy over the authority of the Bishop of Rome)—disputes to which textual evidences are relevant.

In the present essay I have been talking not about this or that doctrinal belief but, more generally, about *religious belief*. It would be convenient if I could substitute the words "belief in God" for the words "religious belief"; but I hesitate to do so because the Buddhists, for example, do not describe themselves as believing in God, and yet Buddhism is undoubtedly a religion. Religious belief as such, not particular creeds or doctrines, is my topic.

I think there can be evidence for the particular doctrines of a faith only within the attitude of religious belief. Many people who read about incidents in the life of Jesus, as recounted in the Gospels, or about events in the lives of the Hebrew prophets, as recounted in the Old Testament, do not believe that the reported incidents actually occurred. But it is possible to believe that they occurred without regarding them as *religiously significant*. That a man should die and then come to life again is not necessarily of religious significance. That the apparent motion of the sun should be interrupted, as related in Joshua, does not have to be understood religiously. A well-known physicist once remarked to me, only *half*-humorously, that a study of the causation of miracles could be a branch of applied physics! Biblical miracles *can* be regarded as events of merely scientific interest. They can be viewed from either a scientific or a religious *Weltanschauung*. It is only from the viewpoint of religious belief that they have religious import.

It is such a viewpoint or *Weltbild* (to use Wittgenstein's term), whether religious or scientific, that I am holding to be "groundless." I am not saying, of course, that these different ways of picturing the world do not have *causes*. Education, culture, family upbringing, can foster a way of seeing the world. A personal disaster can destroy, or produce, religious belief. Religious people often think of their own belief as a result of God's intervention in their lives.

My interest, however, is not in causes. What I am holding is that a religious viewpoint is not based on grounds or evidence, whether this is the Five Ways of Aquinas, the starry heavens, or whatever. Of course, some people do *see* the wonders of nature as *manifestations* of God's loving presence. Someone might even be able to regard the Five Ways in that light. Anselm did thank God for His gift of the Ontological Proof. But seeing something as a manifestation of God's love or creative power is a very different thing from taking it either as evidence for an empirical hypothesis or as a kind of logical proof of the correctness of religious belief.

Some readers may want to know whether my position is that people do not *in fact* seek grounds for their religious belief, or whether, as a conceptual matter, there *could not* be grounds. I hold that both things are true, even though this may shock a well-trained analytic philosopher. When you are describing a language-game, a system of thought and action, you are describing concepts, and yet also describing what certain people do—how they think, react, live. Wittgenstein reminds us that in doing mathematical calculations we do not worry about the figures changing shape after being written down; and also that scientists usually are not in doubt as to whether they are in their laboratories. That such doubts are rare is an empirical fact; yet if it were not for this kind of fact we *could not* have some of our concepts. Consider these remarks by Wittgenstein:

> Mathematicians do not in general quarrel over the result of a calculation. (This is an important fact.)—If it were otherwise, if for instance, one mathematician was convinced that a figure had altered unperceived, or that memory had deceived either him or the other person, and so on—then our concept of "mathematical certainty" would not exist (*PI*, p. 225).

> If I am trying to mate someone in chess, I cannot be having doubts as to whether the pieces are perhaps changing positions of themselves and at the same time my memory is tricking me so that I don't notice it (*OC*, 346).

I know that some philosophers would like to have a *demonstration* that religious belief is groundless. I do not know what "demonstration" could mean here. But I will say this: it is obvious that the wonders and horrors of nature—the history of nations, great events in personal experience, music, art, the Ontological Proof, and so on—can be responded to either religiously or nonreligiously. Suppose there is a person who is untouched by any inclination toward religious belief, and another who wants to present him convincing grounds for religious belief. Can he do it? I don't see how. The first person can regard the presented "evidence" as psychologically, historically, mythologically, or logically interesting—perhaps fascinating. But even if he has an "open mind," the proffered phenomena or reasoning cannot have religious import for him unless he has at least an inclination toward a religious *Weltbild*. This is the necessary medium, the atmosphere, within which these "evidences" can have religious significance. Wittgenstein's remarks about "the language-game," namely that

It is not based on grounds.
It is not reasonable (or unreasonable)
It is there—like our life (*OC,* 559)

are meant to apply to all language-games, but seem to be true in an especially obvious way of religious belief.

Belief in a God who creates, judges, and loves humanity is *one form* of religious belief. Belief in a mystical principle of causality according to which good produces good and evil produces evil is *another form* of religious belief. Those perspectives on reality are not hypotheses for or against which evidence can be marshalled. You may invite someone to see the world as a heartless mechanism or, on the contrary, as throbbing with love. Once a person has the beginnings of such a vision you may strengthen it for him by means of luminous examples. But unless he already shares that vision in some degree, he will not take your examples in the way you want him to take them. It may be that your conviction, passion, love, will move him in the direction of religious belief. But this would be speaking of causes, not grounds.

## Notes

1. Ludwig Wittgenstein, *On Certainty,* ed. G.E.M. Anscombe and G. H. von Wright; trans. D. Paul and G.E.M. Anscombe (Oxford, Engl.: Basil Blackwell, 1969), paragraph 166. Henceforth I include references to this work in the text, employing the abbreviation "*OC*" followed by paragraph number. References to Wittgenstein's *The Blue and Brown Books* (Oxford, Engl.: Basil Blackwell, 1958) are indicated in the text by "*BB*" followed by page number. References to his *Philosophical Investigations,* ed. G.E.M. Anscombe and R. Rhees; trans. G.E.M. Anscombe (Oxford, Engl.: Basil Blackwell, 1967) are indicated by "*PI*" followed by paragraph number. In *OC* and *PI* I have mainly used the translations of Paul and Elizabeth Anscombe, but with some departures.

2. Roger Trigg, *Reason and Commitment* (Cambridge, Engl.: Cambridge University Press, 1973), p. 75.

3. Friedrich Nietzsche, *Beyond Good and Evil,* trans. R. J. Hollingdale (Harmondsworth, Middlesex [Engl.]: Penguin, 1972), para. 58.

# 7

# Theology, Atheism, and Theism

## *Paul L. Holmer*

### I

The cluster of views which we call "theism" is almost invariably associated with Christianity and Judaism (less often with most other religions). Many educated people are convinced that "theism" is the diagnosis and statement of the concepts already basic and elemental in one's thinking and behavior if one is conventionally religious. To get at such concepts is the task of technically trained students, but the task is of importance not just to them but to everyone.

Being religious is what one might call a first-level kind of activity. Perhaps it is something like being a scientist, or maybe an educator, or even a historian. In all of these latter endeavors, one indulges a range of intellectual activities. One learns to speak in the scientific manner about what one hopes are the facts of the matter. So, too, with the historical account, there is a game to be learned and a way and manner to promulgate it and size up the states of affairs from within it. In respect to all of these games, there is another kind of activity possible. One can think out a philosophy of science and a kind of philosophy of history, too. These are attempts to lay bare the methodologies, the presuppositions, the concepts, the axioms, the tacit beliefs, and perhaps other antecedent factors that are deemed to be present.

The philosophy of science ostensibly gets at something that is "in" science but that is not the same as the subject matter of scientific inquiry. And the philosophies of art, education, history, and even mathematics, along with other equally special- ized studies, purport to work out components that are said to be present, yet not quite explicit and clear. It is as if there were a conceptual background, accessible only to philosophical tools, against which these activities take place. In religious circles, theism is credited with being that conceptual ground. Part of the lament widely heard today is justified; for when it is said that theism is no longer relevant to science, art, history, etc., this is to remark upon the fact that most of these endeav- ors certainly do not depend upon a common metaphysical scheme and certainly not upon theism. The notion that there was a common and universal conceptual scheme, equally relevant to all intellectual and humane endeavors, is a large part of the enthusiasm for a metaphysics. Today we are not quite so sure of that singular scheme. Instead, there seem to be philosophical schemes in the plural, one for each kind of domain, and they have, in turn, rather little in common. Early statements of theism, like St. Thomas's, made all of learning appear to depend in subtle ways upon something metaphysical, which if not theistic was yet compatible with Christianity and other positive religious teachings and became equally ingredient in all kinds of learned domains.

For better or for worse, theism is still talked about as a kind of conceptual scheme. The claims made for it are widespread, long-established, and plausible—but plausible only if one does not examine them in great detail. Besides, theism is said to be fundamental to Christianity, Judaism, and Islam, as well as to many other convictional outlooks of the world. Though religions otherwise differ, it has been widely declared that they share this theistic scheme of concepts. Theism looks like a religion-neutral philosophical context within which one can discern common fundamentals.

Nonetheless, this theistic system, too, has come in for very serious criticism. All of us know about alternative schemes, some of which are clearly atheistic. Lucretius, Hobbes, Hume, Voltaire, materialists, determinists of certain kinds, positivists, and others have proposed substitute schemes. Atheisms are of diverse sorts, but one is an atheist (relative to theism) however one denies that theistic scheme. For a long while now, the problem of science versus religion has been leading some people to say that the conceptual scheme of science is atheistic, or if not that, at least nontheistic; and the incompatibility between science and religion has had more to do with the reputed philosophical bearings of each than with the respective claims of the religious and scientific teachings. Also, the very fact that this conflict between science and religion takes so many forms (psychological versus theological accounts of man, biological versus biblical descriptions of living things and their origins) brings out the point already made—namely, that there is no prevailing common metaphysical scheme holding between them. Nontheistic concepts are, because of science, more popular and more widely espoused today than heretofore. But this brings us to the heart of the matter.

In the pages that follow, I wish to argue that the theism/atheism issue is a pseudo-issue and that the issues covered by that rubric must be otherwise handled even to make sense, let alone to be resolved. Furthermore, I will try to show that theism, in its pretentious philosophical sense, is not fundamental to Judaism and Christianity; and that the denials of theism—even conceptual atheisms—are not necessarily denials of Christianity and Judaism. It will be suggested, in addition, that this negative case is not a warrant for saying that modern religion must be without God. In short, if the argument proposed is valid, then it should be clear that even some of the new sophisticated existential and ontological theologies, which propose atheistical or nontheistical conceptual schemes, are largely irrelevant. Their mistakes are logical, not factual. The point, crucial to all of the rest, is simply that no such conceptual scheme is needed at all. There are concepts enough, rich ones too, already operative in religious life and practice, and to make these clear would be more than a life's work for a theologian. Furthermore, it should be obvious in what follows that there is a way to talk about God's existence and his love and care of the world without thereby insisting upon the system ordinarily called theism.

Theism, which is claimed to be the conceptual ground of some religions, actually does justice to none. Besides being too general and having a smothering effect upon the peculiarities of Christian, Jewish, and other positive beliefs, the very logical moves constituting it are dubious.

## II

Philosophical theism, despite its long and hallowed history, is not the essence of Christian and Jewish religion; neither is the denial of that theism invariably and necessarily the denial of God Almighty. The point is, rather, that theism is not the standard and ineluctable conceptual part, there to be discovered every time one undoes faith by intellectual analysis. To deny that it is standard is not to say much of anything.

Through the centuries, it has become a very complicated matter either to defend or to attack, for example, Christianity. For the theistic contention is that the concepts making up theism are the essence of Christianity. Until one isolates theism and positively countermands it, one cannot even be a respectable critic of the Christian religion. On both sides, the attack and the defense, the task becomes terribly abstract. There is something absurd about this. Crucifying Jesus, living faithlessly, and loving the world with all one's heart, soul, mind, and strength tend then to become trivialities compared to denying theism. It is almost as if the academics have made crucial what was not so initially. Nonetheless, the theist will have us believe that to deny God's existence and the things said about him somehow are profoundly involved in doing all of the above things, just as he will have us believe that in following Jesus, behaving faithfully, and obeying the first commandment are contained the theistic concepts.

Put in another way, a defense of the faith is complicated. For obedience and following, loyalty and suffering, even for Jesus' sake, are all thought to be by-products of, or in some way consequents to, the more fundamental matter of believing in theism. Therefore, theism is what counts and what must be defended at all costs, whereas the specific sins and works of unrighteousness, of which Jesus and Paul speak so often as if they are to be avoided above all else, become too small even to mention. Christians (and one might include certain Jews and certain followers of Mohammed, among others) have accordingly been pledged to defend the existence of a kind of nonnatural realm, including God, vast purposes, indestructible values, and a lot else besides, which realm is only penetrable by the help of special philosophical and theological concepts. This tissue of sophisticated talk is said, besides, to describe reality and to be the very ground of everything in the life of faith. All of this has to do with "being," and lately with the "ground" of being.

Some years ago, a distinguished British philosopher, Gilbert Ryle, began to analyze the concept of "mind."[1] The word *mind* obviously is woven into the tapestry of our language, popular and technical. But the aim of Ryle's book was not to dislodge the word from our usage, but to examine the attempts of philosophers to take that word and show its spiritual referent, mind itself. For this is what concepts most often do, when properly used—namely, refer to something or other. However, Professor Ryle shows his readers that the nonmaterial, mental stuff called mind is a "gratuitous personification of an habitual way in which a human being acts." This "mind" is what he refers to sarcastically as "the ghost in the machine."

One need not grant Ryle every point in his book in order to recognize the merits of what is a major thrust. He is hard after a kind of metaphysics that keeps sneaking in and making us overlook the subtleties and multitudinous ways of thinking, feeling, and talking that our daily life entails. A metaphysical concern for "mind" and for big "category" words (like *consciousness, emotions,* and *thoughts*) causes the neglect of the little details of our natural everyday discourse and awareness. Certainly his book does not deprive us of the right to say: "Her mind was destroyed" or "He has a good mind." For this referential, everyday, and common usage can be a highly significant one, if the language is careful and the surroundings right. It need not obligate one to a spiritual conception of mental life or to a dualistic metaphysics.

Today we are quite accustomed to an empirical kind of psychology that describes behavior, including our thinking, without involving special metaphysical concepts like "mind," "soul," "faculties," and the rest.[2] So, too, other sciences are no longer dependent upon "entelechies," "substance," "being," and "potencies," once the peculiar province of transcendental insight and description. But theology—certainly that which pretends to be constructive, perhaps systematic, and exciting—is aimed at the task of giving one additional knowledge of an immaterial and divine realm. So much is this the case that most of philosophical and second-hand theology today is twisting about, this way and that, to refurbish those persistent philosophical concepts with a meaning that is viable and tough for our twentieth century.

In America, many earnest theologians are trying to give the concept of "God" meaning by suggesting that A. N. Whitehead's philosophical categories and concepts—metaphysical with a vengeance—will refurbish the theistic apparatus. Others, in Europe and America, are using the speculative biology of Teilhard de Chardin; and still others, the new sophisticated logics which look like a respectable way to reinstate Plato's ideal entities. Europeans, too, have discovered in Heidegger and Jaspers, "being," "existence," and other ontological concepts. It is no longer a secret that theologians were once greatly indebted to idealistic metaphysics; for whatever else one might say about the kinds of idealists, they did propose a scheme of concepts that marked what looked like the necessary, universal, and persistent features of our world. It was an easy step from such a scheme to the theological conviction that here were the bases and stuff for one's knowledge of God. Without this idealistic conceptual scheme, most theologians today have no way to be "theistic" or even to claim the intellectualistic position which they think theology must avow if it is to be knowledge at all.

There is something to the charge that most of this theistic metaphysics—whether time-honored idealism, scholasticism, other kinds of supernaturalism, or modern "process," logistical, or ontological schemes—is really a lot of nonsense. Certainly, we do not know how to argue the rightness or wrongness of such views;

for they are arbitrary and loosely related to the everyday world. Worse than that, though, is the fact that most of theistic metaphysics is as meaningless to contemporaries as the talk about invisible spirits and "anima" indwelling in trees and waters is to the students of botany and geology. Thus far, surely, there is a glorious intellectual irrelevance about theism, for it simply does not illuminate the world we live in or give substance to religious thinking. Instead, it looks—whether in old or new forms, whether Heideggerian, Whiteheadian, Platonic, or Rahnerian—like a gratuitous invention.

Besides that, theism is not a definitive analysis and depiction of what is involved in most Jewish and Christian thinking. Students of biblical literature in our time have produced a serious rift in the ranks by insisting that the conceptual scheme investing the Scripture with worth is that of *Heilsgeschichte,* or "holy history." So-called biblical theology, therefore, has produced in our century quite a different set of concepts from that of traditional theism, and these new notions are still said to get at the essence of biblical religion. My point is not to praise this effort; for it, too, is another schematism satisfying a metaphysical urge rather than actually illuminating much of anything. But whenever the theistic theologian insists that theistic concepts are the disclosure of what is involved in the Bible, it is well to remind him or her of the presence of the theologian of *Heilsgeschichte.* Both schemes have, in fact, a touch of the arbitrary about them; and this realization ought to impel us, instead of looking for a scheme of concepts, to look at ourselves and examine rather closely this intense desire for another more intellectual set of concepts. We all seem to be discontent with the concepts that the language of faith already provides. Yet, in the latter only is our hope for being emboldened to a life of faith and some thoughts with real integrity.

# III

There is no denying that theism is extremely subtle. The irony is that an attack upon theism seems also to be an attack upon the work of some of the most skillful and intellectually talented proponents of religious faith. Theistic theology even looks like a kind of religion-neutral spiritual knowledge, fundamental to all of the rest of religion, and ecumenical with a vengeance.

Being a theist as opposed to being an atheist purports to be an intellectual matter, something independent of being a Christian, a Jew, or what have you. On the other hand, being a Christian or a Jew or what have you binds one inextricably, it is said, to being a kind of theist. Theism is a "genus" word, and the positive religions and their theologies are like species within that genus. Recently, new ways of connecting these things have been invented. Being a Christian, for example, is said to be a matter that is often unclear and unanalyzed. One frequently does not know what it "means" to be a Christian, it is purported, until one gets at the concepts that are involved. This matter of connecting up concepts with "meaning" is another strange and subtle relation, quite tempting to intellectually oriented people. However, it is by no means obvious, even though it is widely held, that all meanings are made clear by intellectual analyses; nor is it clear, either, that all concepts are, for that matter, intellectualistic and only the names for abstract bits of *ens rationis.*

There is, however, this new use for theism—namely, to serve as the ultimate court of meaning, and also as the skein of reality to which *God, Spirit,* and other big religious words must refer. The charge is widely made that theism in our day has become meaningless because those big words and other long Latinate abstract nouns—*regeneration, temptation, resignation, consecration, sanctification*—tangled up in the theistic net, no longer mean anything. Therefore, some theologians have urged that we be atheistic, while others (like Tillich and Heidegger) have urged that we get rid of the dichotomous way of thinking—God "in" being or God *not* "in" being—and identify God altogether differently, perhaps as being itself or as the ground of being. In all these cases, "meaning" is still the goal; and the thesis is that a better set of concepts is needed to state the meanings or even to get the meanings launched.

It is a little difficult to oppose this. Any kind of opposition looks anti-intellectual and like a vote for plebeian piety. But the point of our analysis is not to make a case for grossness nor to veto logic and analytic skill. Neither is any kind of disparagement of abstract reflection intended. On the contrary, it can be asserted that the most detailed and seemingly disinterested analysis is very frequently also the most useful. Great detail and great skill are essential to becoming clear. Furthermore, religions, not least Christianity, do live in part by concepts, and these, in turn, become muddied by dubious associations and are frequently misconstrued by virtue of their resemblances to concepts found in the sciences, in aesthetics, and surely in morals. So the opposition here is not to the application of intellectual skills to religious affairs but rather to the odd intellectualist and quasi-metaphysical position that is difficult to ferret out and difficult, too, to state.

This intellectualist view is no longer argued and is seldom, therefore, made explicit. Of course, it probably is not (and never was) an arguable matter and thereby shows, besides, that it is somewhat arbitrary. Nonetheless, the conviction is powerful and causes us to look for all kinds of wrong things, to expect more than intelligence can ever proffer, and, generally, to misplace a wide range of problems and issues. Theism plays a large role in an intellectualist economy. Even people who have no regard for religious faith take it to be a matter of course that anyone who does take it seriously must therefore be a theist. On the other hand, the person who is not religious and who is an intellectual will most frequently say that he or she is an atheist, neglecting to mention, perhaps, that one is actually and instead a blasphemer, or indifferent, or lazy, or insensitive, or plainly disinclined, or any number of other things that a person can be by way of being nonreligious.

The point here is that theism is not an imposition. Rather, it fits a kind of academic prejudice and conviction quite handily. For one can be a theist without being otherwise religious, and one can be an atheist without being an irrationalist; but one seemingly cannot be neither a theist nor an atheist without a breach with the minimal conditions of rationality. For the academic prejudice here baldly stated is that if one is neither a theist nor an atheist, he does not care at all about how religious talk is grounded. It is as if theism/atheism is a serious affair and involves making up your mind on the ultimates. The dichotomy tends to exhaust the possibilities.

Perhaps this can be qualified a bit. It has been decreed for a long while that the dichotomy exhausted the rational options. But then came those who said theism and atheism are not quite exhaustive—for in both "God exists" and "God does not exist," the working assumption was that the first meant "God is in being" and the second "God is not in being." A note of the great idealist spiritual tradition has been sounded recently in Jaspers, Heidegger, Tillich, and numerous of their followers—namely, that God is not "in" being, but rather that he *is* being. Therefore neither *exists* nor *does not exist* applies to him at all. It is no wonder, then, that this kind of philosophizing seems to some people to be the hope for theology's being saved as a kind of knowledge, and to be a new and stout answer to the world's doubters. But the academic prejudice is still at work; for this kind of theology still has to ground everyday religious language and practice in something that only philosophical concepts can possibly reach. This "new" move is not radical at all—it merely restates the academic prejudice in another form.

This prejudice is very easy to succumb to. Most of the time, we think "with" ideas and "about" the world and a host of things. Only under special circumstances do we think about ideas. Ordinarily, all concepts, ideas, percepts, sensations, and the rest are "of" things, people, and places, and include what is called "reference" as part of their use and meaning. But a longstanding prejudice in Western intellectual circles has made us think that ideas or concepts are purely mental and only in the mind, and that their reference to anything outside of the mind requires another kind of intellectual job. Philosophical "isms" or schemes, conceptual to be sure, are necessary to show that ideas refer to something. And philosophical concepts always look like a promising way to get at the spiritual stuff where the ordinary language fails.

In religious contexts, this academic prejudice works in the following way. It can be admitted that first-level and ordinary religious beliefs and behavior produce and evince a wide array of concepts—"grace," "God," "love," "forgiveness," "faith," and numerous others. But it is believed that these concepts are, within the kind of context, uncertain, and in an exceedingly subtle way. For there is supposedly a real point to the question: Is there or is there not a God? Ordinary language supposedly treats matters "as if" there were a God, but doubts will creep in. Theism becomes both the way of treating the meaning of the term *God,* and thus of grounding it in its proper referent, and also the way of treating the question whether anything exists to which such a concept can refer.

The prejudice of which I have spoken is a prejudice of the learned and is therefore fiendishly difficult to eradicate. In part, this prejudicial proclivity was the target of Wittgenstein's *Philosophical Investigations,* as well as the subject of many of Kierkegaard's diatribes against the supposed dependence of Christianity upon philosophical and psychological concepts. This prejudice works to effect a separation between ideas, as if they were psychical, intellectual, and spiritual, and their referents, as if they must be of a different genre and quality. Clearly, most of the problems that philosophers try to resolve for religious men (as well as when they try to "ground" politics, science, morals, etc.) are created by conceiving of matters in this bifurcating way. Of course, the duality has to be overcome. In religious circles, theism, with its assertions that there is a God with such and such characteristics, seems to tell us that, after all, there just might be something to which biblical authors were referring and that there may be something on which to ground popular religion. The ordinary language of faith is thought to need a foundation and another learned formulation.

My point all along has been that this kind of learning is really a pseudo-learning. The concepts within such discourse as theism (or its modern substitutes) are invariably artificial anyway and have no real work to do except that provided by those who think them up. This is why there are so many alternative systems built around these ostensibly important matters and also why there is no limit to the number that can be proposed. It is only "conceivability" and nothing else that finally puts restraints upon the enterprises. Furthermore, the concepts in the theistic schemes are not genuine concepts. For example, the concept of God as "first cause" is not an analysis of God as described in the first few chapters of Genesis; so there is little obvious connection, if any, between the two concepts. But more, the concept of "first cause" has little working significance; for insofar as it trades on the general concept of "cause," it turns out that there is no general working concept. All concepts of "cause" occur only within specific domains, and they seem to be quite different therein. The generalized concept was a philosophical creation and is another instance of an almost useless and overgeneralized concept. To add "first" to it, whether "primary" or "first in time," is to compound the verbiage but not much else. But those words also have to be concepts; they survive because their working context is the very philosophical prose in which they are created.

This is the intellectual stuff with which the theism/atheism issues are ensnared. It is about time that Christian theologians, let alone the philosophers, stop inventing concepts that work only in contrived contexts, and begin to study those we already have. We already have a working language of faith. We do not need "theism." Neither do we need substitutes for theism. For our point is that neither affirming nor denying theism is an important matter. Philosophically it is a kind of gratuitous business; religiously it is simply trivial. And I suspect the same can be said about other schemes, early and late, that try to replace the theistic apparatus. Theism once purported to be the understanding of, for example, Christianity. Clearly, today, theism is itself something to understand. It has become not an aid to understanding but that which must be explained, proved, justified, and clarified before it can itself be understood. Therefore, the critics are right when they say that theism is not viable any longer. But I am here pushing matters even further by insisting that we are wrong in assuming that an intellectual scheme like theism (or its substitutes) is needed at all.

Logically, the notion that we must have a conceptual philosophical scheme in order to understand is a howler. For if we do not understand, we sometimes need explanations, training, information, skills, and patient teachers. The assertion that philosophical theism is the "understanding" of Christianity can only be a downright mistake. For finally there is no ultimate court of understanding. Furthermore, even biblical language *was* the understanding of some people, and one must recover the conditions for understanding that language not by creating another one, but by understanding with it.

## IV

Instead of the theism/atheism issue, we must once more return to the common ways of speaking about God, grace, Jesus, and Spirit, and to the common ways of behaving that Scripture enjoins. There are, clearly enough, a host of difficulties in doing either. But one thing we must avoid above all else, and that is the perpetual and restless philosophical seeking for knowledge about God. This drives us to neglect doing even what we can and ought to do and to attempt what in principle cannot satisfy us. Most people of any academic pretentions, also exposed to Christianity, soon forsake altogether trying to obey Jesus or Paul, let alone other admonitions of their church and literature, and begin instead to try to "understand" the teachings. Then they are off. Stirred by an insatiable curiosity, and kept envious by vague notions of perfect knowledge and infallible facts, each reflective person progressively reduces his claims to know and then his ability to act. All of this becomes an intellectual virtue. Agnosticism about some things becomes agnosticism about all things—God, reality, and everything the church teaches. The long pursuit for a limited but invulnerable knowledge of God has then begun. Philosophic doubt has begun, and only a theism—a scheme of rather precise but generalized concepts, logically a little more pure—promises surcease.

Fortunately, there are primitive credenda that keep us sensible. Both David Hume and J. G. Hamann noted how these reasserted themselves the moment one takes up again the affairs of daily life or speaks the everyday language. Surely, being a Christian has much more to do with "how" one takes up the affairs of everyday life than it does with glimpsing into transnatural realms, more to do with loving neighbors than with a reality to which they are unwitting testimonies, and more to do with common sense than with a finespun system making it dubious. However, the doubter wants more than "how," more than the admonition to love, more than commands and parables, stories and recommendations. It is as if he must know something more, something lying behind the miscellany, something existing, true, real, and more meaningful. So while he suspends his decisions and delicately makes a religious virtue of his search for God, he endeavors to get behind and beneath Scripture, church, commandments, and ordinary believing. The doors are closed, but he finds the keys in the philosophical concepts. Here is the promise of objectivity, existence, and reference. And theism tells us that God is omniscient, omnipotent, omnipresent, omnicompetent, and invisible. It is almost as if, these things being true, now one can trust God, love him, and maybe obey him; but, of course, there is the small matter: Is the conceptual scheme, in turn, really true?

Nowadays there appears to be no one quite qualified to say. For the conceptual ways of getting behind the appearances and the sayings are rather tenuous. Theism is no longer obvious, and, because of difficulties, the contemporary theistic notions are becoming highly specialized. Of course, Christians do learn to use concepts of love, hope, grace, prayer, God, holiness, forgiveness, and many many more in rather workaday ways. Liturgy, prayers, hymns, sermons, the Bible, and other forms of religious language also serve to put such concepts to work upon a wide range of phenomena. The web of language catches up and construes a wide variety of everyday things for us, and with more or less success does a variety of jobs for us. Perhaps this is one reason why being a religious person requires also that one practice that faith; for the practice is also the matter of saying prayers and reading Scripture—in other words, using that faithful language as one's own, thereby keeping the words of faith as the ruling motifs for daily life. Here the Christians indeed do use religious concepts. Here we do not find the words of theistic metaphysics at all. In fact, the only way to get in on theistic metaphysical words is by doing up special theories about God's existence and his nature, which is a very special and a very artificial and contrived thing to do.

In church and home, we do not need an abstract set of concepts at all. Our situation is perhaps comparable to that of the automobile mechanic who repairs cars—generators, ignitions, bearings, engines, and transmissions. Indeed he uses concepts, and quite responsibly. It is a mistake to insist that he is bereft of anything important for the repair of cars if he does not know the atomic weights, molecular structures, and the coefficients of expansion for various materials with which he is working. The point is that in most circumstances the repairman does not need such concepts at all. Just as we learn to use the concepts of "hearing" and "seeing" without correspondingly needing to know the concepts of "sense impression," so the metalworker gets along without the concept of "valence." Because we say that every metal has a coefficient of expansion, a valence, and an atomic weight, we tend to think that the concepts for metals in cars include the chemical concepts of metals. But this is not the case. One need not know anything about atomic weight in order to talk well about automobiles and their pathology. The concepts for small things are not *in* concepts for large things the way atoms are *in* supposedly everything else. This is why the matter of doing philosophy and theology by analysis can also be deceptive, for it often feeds upon the notion that concepts are ingredient the way molecules are in a glass of water, or vitamins are in food—or God is in Christ. But in all the examples, it is clear that using concepts like those for foods, for cars, and for everyday things does not presuppose knowledge of the concepts for vitamins, atomic weights, and other specialist-described ingredients. Likewise, the concepts of theistic metaphysics are not components in most of the concepts of God wrought for us by Scripture, prayers, and liturgy—perhaps, too, by most sermons.

The argument that the meaning of saying "I believe in God the Father, maker of heaven and earth" can only be ascertained by recourse to a theistic metaphysics is a case in point. The notion of a timeless deity who exists anterior to everything else that exists is, obviously enough, an attempt to do justice to both the Creed of the Apostles and to the Genesis narrative. But the argument is invalid, because saying the Creed does not suppose that the concepts of God must always include everything that is said about him in the specialist context, any more than speaking of engines supposes knowledge of atomic weights. The mechanic has enough concepts to identify and to repair cars and their parts—other concepts serve other roles and are often used by other people. The able mechanic also "understands" the workings of the automobile in his ordinary concepts. It would be a mistake to say that he needs the concepts of chemistry and physics to get the "true" understanding.

Again, the Creed secures the worshipper's attention, straightens his dispositions, and shakes him loose from worldly and transitory loyalties. If the concept of God works to this effect in that context, that is quite enough. Here there are all kinds of meaning; and it is only a play upon the word *meaning* that makes it seem that the concept of God in the highly abstract and specialized context is more meaningful.

On the contrary. The specialized concepts often mean less rather than more.

For such concepts in these abstruse and artificial contexts often have very little work to do. Typically it is only the special metaphysical context that keeps such concepts alive. The irony is that the longstanding academic prejudice about which we are speaking has conditioned the intelligentsia to believe that every use of religious language is ipso facto an employment of theistic concepts. The case is no longer argued; it is simply assumed. Thus, many people are made anxious by the decay of metaphysical allegiances, arguing that if these evaporate, then one cannot hope to convert people to the true faith, or then religious language will clearly be meaningless. This is as mistaken as to assume that the concept of iron for the miner depends upon getting the concept of iron also clear in the contexts of chemistry and physics. Even if "iron" should prove to be no longer a viable chemical concept, still "iron" has an established role for miners, ironmongers, manufacturers, and probably even for the chemist when he works around his house. So, too, the concepts of Christian and Jewish faith are not derived from specialist contexts, nor from philosophical or psychological concepts referring to spiritual entities.

The theistic conceptual scheme is not then "in" ordinary religious language at all. But this is not to say that one must therefore think "secularly," as a certain contemporary fashion has it, or that one must revert to a kind of premetaphysical and maybe mythical kind of thinking. The language of prayers, liturgy, and Scripture is by itself neither mythical nor metaphysical, secular nor divine. When put to work in a very responsible and exacting way, the words of prayer, liturgy, and Scripture come to have meaning just as they are. They do not need to be interpreted in order to mean something when they become efficacious for a whole variety of tasks. It is only when they are put to hard and continuing tasks, as they are when we think with them and through them, that we get any kind of conceptual worth at all. Concepts are, after all, chiefly the concentrations of practice and behavior, intent and thought, that give shape and constancy and therefore meaning to our discourse and to our lives.

It is tempting, too, to assume that a theistic scheme is like a code or a table for a game, which we can look up, and by which we fix thereafter the concepts of our religion. Theism is no such code. The truth here is a little hard, for we can only surmise the codes for the meaning of everyday religious concepts out of the conduct of such concepts in religious behavior and literature; and in the last analysis, not even the Bible is so conclusive a reference work that it tells us about every possible misreading. This is said in order to remind us that the meanings of religious words are laden with freight picked up in the religious life. But this does not say that the religious life is theory-free. Just as terms for automobiles in the repairman's vocabulary become laden by the learning that he and countless others have slowly acquired, so too are the special terms of a scientist describing iron and other elements fraught with chemical theory. The words are saturated by their associations within chemical theory, but not by philosophical or other kinds of theories. Therefore, there is a dependence of terms upon theory, and to change the theory often means to change the meaning of the terms; for theories are also one kind of context in which words work, and in which they get and lose their meanings.

Accordingly, we wish to note here that theological terms are not dependent upon philosophical theories, nor even upon the scheme called theism. This does not say that they are "only words," or "atomistic," or "nominalistic," or "relativistic," or without conceptual meaning. The situation is that religious concepts (and specifically Christian concepts, the only ones I have a standing familiarity with) depend upon the somewhat piecemeal outlook and piecemeal theories that bind them together. Creeds, the Bible, prayers, and liturgies call up views of the way people, the world, God, and everyday things are, and they enjoin behavior. There is quite enough theory in these pieces of literature to satisfy one with that kind of hunger. On the other hand, to invoke a philosophical scheme like theism in order to constitute that embedded theory, and to serve as the foundation or the conceptual meaning for all the rest, seems to be as confused an endeavor as to suggest to the automobile mechanic that he get in on chemical valences before he touches the car—or worse, that we ask both the mechanic and the inorganic chemist to get in on a philosophical scheme of reality before they repair a car or do their chemistry.

Atheism and theism are positions generated by mistaking the way Christian and other religious concepts come to mean something. Both of these positions once seemed to have a kind of merit precious to intellectuals. They placed the religious concepts in a kind of scheme where they became systematized and capable of being addressed en masse. A kind of labeling and ordering became possible; and one exulted in being able to reject or to accept a large number at once. But this apparent virtue of homogenizing concepts is sillier in religious matters than it is in science. For the religious life involves, on the conceptual side, a veritable welter of concepts, just as on the behavioral side we have to say that it consists of all kinds of things, from prayers to praise, from faith to hope, from patience to obedience, and from loving God to loving one's neighbor. Its concepts are variegated and heterogeneous, but are no poorer for that.

## Notes

1. Gilbert Ryle, *The Concept of Mind* (New York: Barnes & Noble, 1949). See especially pp. 15 ff.

2. One has to be very careful here, however. Many of the sciences today, including psychology, all too quickly get rid of one kind of metaphysics and then quickly espouse another like "behaviorism" or kinds of materialism. Some matters are more subtle. Notions of "general law," "explanation," "causality," and others often introduce the metaphysical issues in disguised form. But these matters must be addressed separately.

# 8

# Does Religious Skepticism
# Rest on a Mistake?

## *Kai Nielsen*

### I

There are those who will say that the skeptic's . . . questions indicate that he has got religion all wrong and that we can, if we have a feel for what religion is all about, only be radically skeptical of such skepticism.

Paul Holmer and D. Z. Phillips, working out of a tradition deeply influenced by both Wittgenstein and Kierkegaard, try to make such a case.[1] . . . I want to examine this anti-skeptical argument that there is no such skeptical case to meet since it is a mistake to look for some rational foundation for religious belief or for some general standards of significance or rationality. Philosophy, such philosophers contend, cannot supply such standards as foundations for there are none; but Judaism and Christianity are none the worse off for all of that, for they neither need nor require such general criteria. No philosophical, logical, or scientific sanction is required or indeed possible for religion; no sustainable case can be made for looking externally to the practices of religion themselves for criteria of intelligibility, rationality, and truth in religion; outside of the discourse itself there is nothing in virtue of which we could come to see how, after all, there is a religiously viable concept of God or how fundamental religious beliefs could be seen to be true or, for that matter, false. There are, it is argued, within religion itself, good reasons for believing that there are religious truth-claims and that these truth-claims are indeed true. But they are not the type the skeptic expects and regards as relevant to the establishment of the intelligibility or truth of the claims of religion. The skeptic has a conception of what would satisfy claims of intelligibility and truth for a putative truth-claim, but doubts, for religious utterances of a nonanthropomorphic sort, that either of these conditions can be satisfied. But, Holmer and Phillips maintain, the skeptic's quest is a mistaken one, for there is and can be no question of confirming "religious hypotheses" or giving evidence for religious beliefs or displaying the facts which show them to be true or the possible facts which, if they indeed turned out to be the facts, would show them to be false. Not all beliefs need be so related to evidence and not all legitimate uses of language need be used to make confirmable or infirmable statements. Religious utterances, it is maintained, are not even of the type that should pass tests for intelligibility applicable to genuine empirical statements of fact. They do not play or even purport to play that role in religious life and to so construe them is to misunderstand their very logic.

In short, the claim is that it is not the case that the body of truths embedded in our religious forms of life are truths which require evidence or support by the facts. The "grammar of belief" should be differently understood. We need to understand that religious beliefs are not bits of speculative metaphysics or parts of isolated language-games (esoteric forms of discourse) separated from the stream of life. Religious beliefs indeed play an important role in the lives of many people; they are closely meshed with the whole of our life and are not isolated from the facts. But they are not and cannot be assessed by the facts; rather, as Phillips puts it, they assess the facts, "bring a characteristic emphasis to bear on the facts."[2] They are the framework, the onlook, within which the believer meets and understands "the fortune, misfortune, and the evil that he finds in his own life and in the life about him."[3] To think that they are assessable by reference to the facts is utterly to confuse how religious discourse works. They regulate our lives and they have a regulative function in certain domains over what it makes sense to say, over what constitutes an explanation, and over what is taken to be reasonable and unreasonable.

The thing to see, Phillips maintains, is how religious beliefs are a distinctive kind of belief. They are not conjectures, opinions, something we hold tentatively, and they are less closely linked with predictions than with conceptions of how we shall strive to live and how we view the value and significance of life. Religious beliefs are differently related to knowledge claims than are empirical beliefs. They are not beliefs which can be so generalized and systematized that we can ask for a verification of or an external check on "religion as such."[4]

There remains, however, on this account, a real difference between believers and skeptics . . . The essential difference, Phillips claims, is the "difference between someone who does look on his life in a certain way and regulates it accordingly and someone who has no time for such a response or who sees nothing in it."[5] It is a critical mistake on the skeptic's part to "think that nothing can be believed unless there is evidence or grounds for that belief."[6] "Belief" when we are talking about religion and when we are talking about empirical matters of fact has very different employments. . . . Phillips maintains that in coming to have a religious belief—say a firm faith in God's providence—what is most essentially involved is the viewing and regulating of one's life in a certain way and not the coming to have an opinion which is based on the weighing of evidence.[7] The difference between a believer and a skeptic is not that the believer knows something that the skeptic doesn't, but the difference is in commitment and orientation. The core confusion for skeptics and for many believers as well is to assume, indeed to hold as a very fundamental presupposition, "that the relation between religious beliefs and the non-religious facts is that between what is justified and its justification, or that between a conclusion and its grounds."[8] It is a pervasive mistake in thinking about religion to take it as just evident that if religious beliefs are to be sustained they must have such a foundation.

Holmer stresses, even more than Phillips, both that there is no underlying philosophical, scientific, or indeed just plainly factual support for religious beliefs and that no underlying conceptual scheme or foundation for belief is needed. There are plenty of concepts actually functioning in the religious life and they are sufficient.[9] It is a mistake to think either that philosophy can supply a convincing answer to the skeptic or that it can support the skeptic's negations and doubts. Philosophy can give us no new knowledge of God nor can it even reconfirm any old knowledge to bolster up the leaky vessel of faith. In this way neither philosophical theology nor philosophical atheology is possible. Philosophy cannot give us something crucial for our religious lives which Christianity or Judaism cannot; it can neither provide the ground for nor the critique of everyday religious language and practice. It is a pervasive confusion among philosophers and theologians to think that some philosophical scheme can "become both the way of treating the meaning of the term 'God' and thus of grounding it in its proper referent, and also the way of treating the question whether anything exists to which such a concept can refer."[10] The assumption is that there is a real point to the question: Is there or is there not a God? But this is an illusion. There is no "ultimate court of understanding" or transfield criteria of rationality or intelligibility in virtue of which this "question" could be answered. Religion is a form of life and within this form of life there are established criteria for truth, intelligibility, and rationality, but there are no transfield criteria of truth, rationality, and intelligibility, in virtue of which one could justifiably claim that religious beliefs are either true or false, reasonable or unreasonable, or even intelligible or unintelligible. The skeptic can have no place to stand. His very core assumptions concerning religion rest on mistakes.

## II

We must put aside, Holmer and Phillips would have us understand, such philosophical preconceptions and recognize that to understand religion we must see it in its own context. In such a context we see orthodox Christians and Jews confessing their sins to God and praying to God. But, in trying to attain such a participant's understanding, it is surely natural to ask: To whom or to what are they praying or confessing when they pray or confess? Here the believer is very likely to be "uptight," utterly at a loss to know what to say. Almost anyone who has grown up in a Jewish or Christian culture can readily play such religious language-games; that is, such a person knows how to pray and confess to God, yet even with this skill, this mastery of the language, and the religious employment of the key "pictures" used in this form of discourse, he can remain utterly skeptical about the coherence of such concepts and at sea about the alleged reality for which the key religious terms stand. Such a person may have a very good understanding of how to engage in religious practices and he will, if he has such an understanding, also have a good grasp of religious language-games (forms of discourse). But the crucial point to see is that he can very well have such an understanding while remaining utterly agnostic about whether these practices make sense or whether such talk is intelligible. It may be true, as Phillips avers, that within Jewish and Christian forms of life, love of God is the primary form of religious belief, but the nagging question still remains: What are we talking about here? Where our God is not the God of religious idolatry, *what* is it that we are trying to love or are supposed to love when we love God?

With even a rudimentary understanding of the underlying structure of this discourse, it should be evident to us that God is not something which could be located and that believing in God is very different from believing that the world is round. Our "belief in" here is indeed not the mere holding of an opinion. And it *may* even be true that for some sorts of X the only way of discovering what belief in X is like is by believing in X. But before we treat God as that sort of X, we should bear in mind that there have been countless people who have believed in God, who have thrown themselves wholeheartedly into these forms of life, and who have gradually, as they have explored the logic of their faith, come to find such beliefs not simply mysterious but incoherent. Perhaps they have made philosophical blunders in coming to think such concepts incoherent, but it is surely not correct to say of these people, as Phillips does, that they once understood and then later failed to understand. They plainly have a religious understanding and sometimes, at least, it is the case that this very religious understanding drives them into perplexity about and sometimes into a rejection of religion. Sometimes, as Phillips and Holmer show, loss of belief does not have such conceptual roots and indeed is far less intellectually defendable or (for some other cases) arguable. But there are also men with the need to believe or at least with the wish to believe who find they can no longer believe because they have become convinced that the key religious concepts of their faith are unintelligible or incoherent. And coming as it does out of religious and philosophical reflection from within this very form of life, it surely is question-begging to assert that this skepticism must simply be the result of conceptual blunders.

When we believe, we must believe something. That is what Wittgenstein would call a grammatical remark. But what is it that we believe in when we love, confess to, or pray to God? Is believing in God like believing in justice, i.e., is it *simply* to subscribe to a set of moral principles and to hope these principles will prevail? This, though it would relieve us of some philosophical difficulties, would hardly appear to be a characterization of Christian or Jewish religious forms of life. Surely to believe is to do that, but it is not *simply* to do that any more than to be an M.D. is simply to be able to give first aid.

Phillips believes that one comes very close to superstition or idolatry when one treats a religious form of life as a form of life which takes belief in God to be belief in an ultimate order of fact. "True religion," Phillips argues, does not essentially consist in trusting that a certain state of affairs is going to be the case or perhaps even in believing that a certain state of affairs is the case. Belief in God, as Phillips sees it, is *entirely independent* of the way things go. But then it becomes, to put it conservatively, doubly difficult to say what belief in God comes to. Phillips, and Holmer as well, stress how religious belief involves trust and regulating one's life in a certain way. But religious belief involves trust *in God* and that involves believing that (thinking that) there is a God. It makes no sense to say "I trust in God but I don't think there is a God." So we have another component in belief in God that cannot be understood in terms of trusting or anything like trusting. Moreover, the other factor does not have to do just with the regulating of one's life, for there are people who have ceased to believe or are unable to believe, who still continue to regulate their lives in very Jewish or Christian ways.

Phillips maintains, as has Norman Malcolm as well, that to give an account of belief in God one must take "the distinction between existence and eternity seriously." He tries to give an account of what it is to "come to see meaning in the eternal."[11] To understand how this links up with belief in God, it is necessary to recognize and take to heart the fact that in developed forms of the Hebrew-Christian tradition "the conception of God is not a conception of a being among beings."[12] Coming to see that there is a God is not like coming to see that some additional being exists. It is not, as Kierkegaard paradoxically put it, like coming to see that something exists, but it is a coming to an acknowledgment of eternity. But again, what we are talking about here remains intolerably obscure. What is it to acknowledge eternity? What is it to come to understand that God does not exist but is eternal?

Let us see if we can get a purchase on this. I, of course, agree with Holmer and Phillips that the philosopher may indeed fail to understand what it means to believe in an eternal God.[13] We cannot, they point out, be confident that we, even as participants, have an adequate religious understanding even of first-order discourse. But this has an unwelcome consequence for Holmer and Phillips, for it also means that we cannot be sure that our first-order religious discourse is intact as it is and that we are only confused about the proper *analysis* of the discourse in question. I understand what it is to believe or to know that there are physical objects (e.g., sticks and stones), though I am quite unclear about the proper analysis of 'physical object', but by contrast, I am actually unclear (a) about what I am to believe in order to believe in an eternal God and (b) about the correct *analysis* of 'eternal God'. I am in doubt about the proper analysis of 'physical object' but in no doubt whatsoever about whether there are sticks and stones; however, in the religious case I am in doubt both about the proper analysis of 'God' *and* about whether there actually is or even could be such a reality.

Presumably, in Christian-Jewish discourses 'eternal God' is a pleonasm, but pleonasm or not, how are we to understand such a phrase? In fact—to push the matter a little further—if we are honest with ourselves can we really rightly claim we understand it? In trying to understand and then give an account of what it is to believe in such a kind of reality, to believe in a kind of order of eternity which transforms and gives a new meaning to one's life, one should start, Phillips argues, with trying to understand what it means to speak of 'eternal love' and what role such a concept has in the stream of life. The aim of this exercise is to show how "there is a God in this context is synonymous with seeing the possibility of eternal love. . . ."[14]

A Jew or Christian is distinguished from a skeptic, according to Phillips, in believing that besides temporal love there is a "love that will not let one go whatever happens."[15] If one's aspirations and desires are thwarted, if one's friendships go dry, and if one's love dies, one's life, if one has such a belief, is not robbed of its meaning, for *whatever* happens to one, one's life has significance. . . . In loving in this way, one engages in self-renunciation, one loves one's neighbor no matter what he does and thus one cannot be deceived. . . .

It is true that one could not believe in God without loving or at least having some affective attitude toward God. Knowledge of God—if indeed there is such—cannot be a purely theoretical knowledge. Kierkegaard is perfectly correct in maintaining that "if anyone thinks he is a Christian and yet is indifferent towards being a Christian he is not one at all."[16] But to equate belief, understanding, and loving here is to confuse a necessary condition for religious belief with a sufficient one, and it is to convert atheists like myself who have such supposed exclusively Christian or religious attitudes toward love into believers by stipulative redefinition. I do indeed believe in eternal love, characterized as Phillips characterizes it—though I do not like to talk in this way—but I do not believe in God. A man who really cares about humanity will indeed have such agapeistic attitudes toward his fellow men: he will love them come what may. It is a commitment which for him is categorical. And if this is what is meant by 'eternal love', he believes in eternal love. But a man with such attitudes need not believe in God or even understand the word 'God'.

To reply in the manner of Phillips that such a man is really a believer for to love in this manner is to believe in God is not to characterize the Christian religion from within, as Phillips would have us do, but to select from within this form of life *some* of the criteria for what constitutes religious belief and by *persuasive* definition to *make* them *the* criteria of 'true religion'. But this is not to keep to the pure Wittgensteinian task of conceptual analysis that Phillips takes to be the sole legitimate philosophical task. Rather it is an oblique way of doing what he thinks ought *not* to be done in *philosophy,* i.e., to advocate and to engage in apologetics.[17] And such an advocacy is all the more insidious for not being straightforward, for it appears to be a conceptual analysis of a form of language, when in reality it is the identifying of religious belief with a particular subset of religious beliefs by the simple expedient of selecting and labeling as the sole legitimate claimant for genuine religious discourse, expressive of religious beliefs, the portion of that discourse which is not "a scandal to the intellect." That is to say he simply ignores those bits of religious discourse which at least prima facie appear to contain incoherent or at least very problematical claims. (He does exactly the same thing with the concept of immortality in his *Death and Immortality.*) Here we have what in effect, if not in intention, is a form of apologetic advocacy of a radically reconstructed Christianity masquerading as a neutral conceptual analysis of Christian discourse. Through an arbitrary *persuasive* definition of "true religion," our religious options get circumscribed. The difference between a believer and a nonbeliever on such an account becomes simply a difference in attitude and picture preference; what appear at least to be substantial, nonattitudinal clashes between Christianity and atheism are whisked away by linguistic legerdemain. . . .

We are left, Holmer's and Phillips's arguments to the contrary notwithstanding, in the following situation. Given the type of form of life and mode of discourse that Judaism and Christianity have become, 'God', though purportedly functioning as a referring expression, is not taken to denote anything locatable. But if "belief in God" is to be an intelligible notion, we must believe in something when we sincerely say we believe in God. But no criteria of identification have been given for identifying the referent, the alleged reality, that 'God' supposedly denotes. God is plainly not some locatable reality "out there." Phillips makes this evident enough. But then *what* are we talking about when we speak of God?

If God is construed as 'creator of the universe', 'pure spirit', 'pure act', or 'necessary being', we are still at a loss to identify what it is we are talking about. Thus, if a man asserts that there is indeed a necessary being, there is no way of deciding or even gaining an educated hunch whether his assertion is true or false or even probably true or false and this is, in effect, to confess that we do not understand what he is trying to claim. That is, we are trying to take it as an assertion, but we do not understand what it could conceivably assert. The trouble in the utterance "There is a necessary being" is with 'necessary being'. We are given to understand that a necessary being is an 'independent being', 'eternal being', i.e., "a being which could not begin to exist or cease to exist," "a being without sufficient conditions," "an unlimited being," and the like. But we still have no effective understanding here, for such terms are expressive of a network of notions, all of which suffer from the same conceptual difficulty: we do not know if any of them are in any way *exemplifiable.* We do not know and seem to have no way of finding out, for example, if there is an eternal being, though we do know that *if* there is an eternal being, it makes no sense to ask when it started to exist or if it could cease to exist. Assuming for a moment that 'necessary being' or 'necessary existence' is in *some way* intelligible, we need to ask in a timeless, tenseless way, whether there is or could be such a being. Part of what is involved here is this: we know that if God is a necessary being or existence, that if He does not exist now, His existence is eternally precluded; furthermore, it at least seems to be the case that if this necessary being does exist now, He always existed and must always continue to exist. But we still have no idea of what would or logically could constitute an answer to our putative question, i.e., whether there is or could be a necessary being. Since this is so, the concept (notion) in question is an *ersatz*-concept. Its sign-vehicle 'necessary being' purports to stand for something but actually does not. Similar arguments can be made for 'pure spirit', 'the creator of the universe', 'pure act', and the like.

Holmer and Phillips could respond that I have not really taken to heart or come to grips with their claims about the contextual (form-of-life-dependent) nature of criteria of truth, intelligibility, and rationality. In my account, they could say, something is going on that is typical of philosophers, namely a confused "craving for generality, a desire to give an all embracing unitary account of reality."[18] But, they could add, the search for such a unit is a delusion. The distinction between 'the real and the unreal' does not come to the same thing in every context. Moreover, we have no criteria for or an independent test of whether language corresponds to reality. It is not reality which gives language its sense. It is not reality which shows which words, if any, in our discourse are empty, idling words. Rather, what is real and what is unreal shows itself in the very workings of our language, in the actual and varied uses of language in live contexts. There is no general way of talking about how language corresponds to reality and there is no general way in which we can usefully talk about criteria of rationality either. Rather, the criteria of rationality and coherence are *internal* to each mode of discourse.

I have discussed this issue elsewhere and I must be brief here.[19] First, Phillips admits that there "will be no strict lines of demarcation between different modes of discourse at many points." But, given this overlap, what really is the argument for believing that the criteria for truth, rationality, intelligibility, and evidence are contained within the particular mode of discourse in question? The very mode of discourse is not on Phillips's own account self-contained. Why, then, should we think that each mode of discourse has within itself its distinctive and self-contained criteria for truth or rationality? The concept of consistency is a part of the concept of rationality, and consistency is not utterly form-of-life-dependent. Moreover, to be rational is—though this is not all that it is—to be objective. That is, where we are talking about rational action, it is to be willing, where it is possible, to examine the evidence or reasons for a belief and to hear argument before acting or judging. Now, what in a given situation will count "as evidence" or "as relevant reasons" is indeed partly a function of a particular form of life but not entirely so. If someone tells me that God created the heavens and the earth, there is in English an ordinary sense of 'created' which is not utterly form-of-life-dependent and without which we would not understand that religious claim, and given this common use of 'created', I know what counts as evidence for something's being created and thus I know what, if anything, would count as evidence for that alleged claim. Because of features in common to all uses of 'created', evidence for something's being created is not utterly idiosyncratic to each mode of discourse. Moreover, we should not forget that forms of life change, drop out of existence, come into existence, and overlap. We once believed in ghosts and engaged in explicit magical practices. They once were our forms of life. But our very pervasive concepts of truth, evidence, and knowledge and our expanding knowledge of the world led us to criticize and finally to abandon such forms of life. Phillips's argument commits him to the a priori claim that it is impossible to assess rationally whole forms of life. A blunder, he would have us believe, can only be a blunder within a particular system. But to say we could have no rational grounds for criticizing belief in ghosts or our own Western magical practices constitutes a reductio of his argument.

It is not unnatural to respond that, in arguing as I have, I neglected to consider an important page that both Phillips and Holmer take from Wittgenstein about the distinctive features of religious belief. I have spoken about the need for evidence or reasons for or against as something that must go with an assertion which could in turn be believed or disbelieved. But Phillips directly and indeed Holmer by implication have asserted that religious claims are not claims for which there can be evidence or grounds. The logic of the discourse is such that the very idea is deemed to be irrelevant.

While this may be true of some religious utterances, it has not been shown to be true of all of them. There appears to be no conceptual ban on asking (to take a key example) for the evidence for "God created the heavens and the earth." When someone wants to know how, if at all, it is known to be true or believed with justification to be true, he has not said something deviant or logically or conceptually odd as he would have if he had asked how we know "Stop yelling" is true.

Phillips, however, remarks that we cannot grasp the nature of religious beliefs "by forcing them into the alternatives: empirical positions or human attitudes."[20]

When I avow, "I believe in God the Father, maker of heaven and earth" or "God is in Christ" or "God is truth," I indeed typically would be expressing an attitude, and, with respect to the first utterance quoted, perhaps in some sense I am necessarily doing that. However, this is not all that I mean to be doing; and this holds for any of the above utterances. . . .

In believing in any of these religious claims one believes firmly: they are unshakeable for believers, they do not think of them as conjectures or hypotheses for which the evidence is not particularly good. Rather, to be a religious believer, one must subscribe to them with one's whole heart and whole mind and, moreover, they are the framework or picture in accordance with which believers view crucial areas of their lives. That is to say, their view of birth, death, joy, misery, despair, hope, fortune, and misfortune is deeply affected by this framework. Religious beliefs are firm in that they categorically regulate the believer's life in those domains on which they touch.

Religious beliefs either are or necessarily involve pictures or frameworks doing the work characterized above. But what is meant by 'framework' or 'picture' here? Plainly these terms are not being used literally, but beyond that bare acknowledgment it is difficult to know what is intended. Phillips claims that we know that when we assert religious beliefs we are not asserting empirical propositions or purely moral or purely normative claims (e.g., purely moral or normative in the way that "You ought to think more of the feelings of others" is moral or "Rigorous training makes good athletes" is normative). As Phillips puts it himself, religious beliefs are neither "empirical propositions . . . [nor] human attitudes, values conferred, as it were, by individuals on the world about them."[21] Rather the religious pictures "have a life of their own, a possibility of sustaining those who adhere to them."[22] Believers believe that these pictures are not pictures they can pick and choose and about whose adequacy they can make a judgment. Rather these pictures come to measure them. They simply find themselves adhering to them and subscribing to them in a quite categorical way. For them they have a value which is absolute. They are, after all, their picture of the divine for which they have and can have no substitute, since they have and can have no independent access to or notion of divinity.

This is a very odd use of 'picture' in which we are to adhere to a picture and yet can have no independent access to what is pictured. Moreover, if 'picture' *here* connotes anything similar to what 'image' connotes, there must be some notion of representation in virtue of which there must be something which the picture is a picture of. But we seem barred from any understanding of this 'something that is pictured' in religious contexts because there can be no independent access to what is pictured. And if (like an abstract painting) the picture is in no way a representation, it is difficult to understand how it can be a model and a guide.

In general, the notions of picture and framework remain so obscurely characterized by Phillips that we can make little of them or put little weight on such notions. Moreover, if these beliefs, which are also pictures or frameworks, are not, when we express them, empirical propositions or simply moral or normative ones, then, what we should say is that no alternative characterization has been given of what they mean or how they function. Their logical status is utterly problematical.

Consider:

1. To love God is to know the truth.
2. God is the truth.
3. God is in Christ.
4. I believe in God the Father, maker of heaven and earth.

None of these, according to Phillips, are empirical propositions and they are not analytic either. Well, then they are some other kind of proposition. Well and good. But what kind and how are we to understand them? They are said to be key religious truths, but no hint—once we exclude all evidential considerations—is given as to how we could have the slightest reason for believing them to be true or false. But if this is so, then it is difficult to understand what could be meant in saying they are truths (claims or statements) which could actually be true or false. Phillips comes perilously close to saying that truth here comes to truthfulness, that is, sincerity of avowal and commitment. But then religious claims are being modeled too nearly even for Phillips's taste on moral ones. Religion, so construed, is too close for comfort to morality touched with emotion and the distinctive putative truth-claims of religion have been lost. But if Phillips backs off here, how are we to understand (1) through (4)? Presumably they have some statement-making role (constative force). But if that is so, then they have truth-values and if they have truth-values, it should be possible at least in principle to find out what their truth-values are. Phillips and Holmer have made us keenly aware of the commissive force of religious utterances: how, in sincerely avowing "Christ is the truth and the way," I am committing myself to a norm in accordance with which I evaluate my own life and the quality of life around me. But religious utterances certainly appear at least to have a constative, statement-making force as well. But about this Phillips and Holmer are unhelpful. It seems to me that we should say of them what W. D. Hudson has said of Wittgenstein: ". . . what he seems at times to have come near to suggesting is that, because religious beliefs have commissive force, that somehow entitles us to by-pass the troublesome problem of their constative force."[23] Furthermore, as Mitchell has recognized, that we commit ourselves quite categorically to being regulated by certain claims—in this case religious doctrines—says something about "the pragmatics of belief" but does not imply that there cannot be evidence for or against a religious belief.[24] It only means (by definition) that for the *believer* his belief is in an important way unshakeable. If his belief is nevertheless shaken such that he no longer accepts the belief because he does not believe that it is true, he ceases (again by definition) to be a believer. But this does not mean that he cannot acknowledge that there is evidence for or against religious beliefs, it is only that he, *as a believer,* is committed to treating that evidence in a certain way, namely to regarding it as not sufficiently strong to warrant abandoning his faith. But he need not contend that in some way it is logically impossible that his religious beliefs could be false. But it is impossible for him to be a believer and actually believe that his religious beliefs are false. (Again we see that even truisms can be true.)

Once we abandon anthropomorphism, it is unclear what constative force or what truth-value (if any) religious utterances have. Phillips and Holmer leave us without a clue here; indeed they are of no help beyond suggesting that we cannot establish truth here in the way we can over a question of empirical fact. But we are left entirely in the dark about how else we might go about understanding what truth-value putative religions truth-claims have and this leaves their meaning or at least their constative force problematical.

These utterances which express beliefs which are said to be pictures may very well only have what has been characterized as having a 'pictorial meaning' or a 'pictorial sense'.[25] "There is a time machine in the basement of the Chrysler Building" is a good example. Here we have some understanding of the utterance, for we have some relevant images or pictures—we could even have a governing picture of a "time machine"—but the utterance still could not be used to make a true or false statement. People characteristically care about (1) through (4) in the way they do not about the above utterance, but, as to their "claims" they appear to be parallel. At the very least we have much to remain skeptical about and it does not at all seem to be the case that it has been established that [religious] skepticism rests on a mistake. . . .

# Notes

1. See Paul L. Holmer, "Wittgenstein and Theology," in *New Essays on Religious Language,* ed. Dallas M. High (New York: Oxford University Press, 1969); "Atheism and Theism," *Lutheran World,* 12 (1963) (reprinted in revised form in this anthology as "Theology, Atheism, and Theism," pp. 104–15) and "Metaphysics and Theology: The Foundations of Theology," *The Lutheran Quarterly* (1967). See D. Z. Phillips, *The Concept of Prayer* (London: Routledge & Kegan Paul, 1965); *Faith and Philosophical Enquiry* (London: Routledge & Kegan Paul, 1970) (reprinted as "Faith, Skepticism, and Religious Understanding" in this volume); *Death and Immortality* (London: Macmillan, 1970); the essays by Phillips in *Religion and Understanding,* ed. D. Z. Phillips (Oxford, Engl.: Basil Blackwell, 1967); "Religion and Epistemology: Some Contemporary Confusions," *Australasian Journal of Philosophy* 44 (1966): 316–30; and "Religious Belief and Philosophical Enquiry," *Theology* 71, 573 (March 1968).
2. Phillips, *Faith and Philosophical Enquiry,* p. 166.
3. Phillips, *Faith and Philosophical Enquiry,* p. 113.
4. Phillips, *Faith and Philosophical Enquiry,* p. 157.
5. Phillips, *Faith and Philosophical Enquiry,* p. 157.
6. Phillips, *Faith and Philosophical Enquiry,* p. 87.
7. Phillips, *Faith and Philosophical Enquiry,* p. 89.
8. Phillips, *Faith and Philosophical Enquiry,* p. 101.
9. Holmer, "Atheism and Theism," p. 15
10. Holmer, "Atheism and Theism," p. 20
11. Phillips, *Religion and Understanding,* p. 6.
12. Phillips, *Religion and Understanding,* p. 68.
13. Phillips, *Religion and Understanding,* p. 70.
14. Phillips, *Religion and Understanding,* p. 71.
15. Phillips, *Religion and Understanding,* p. 73.
16. Søren Kierkegaard, *The Works of Love* (New York: Harper & Row, 1962), p. 42.
17. Phillips, "Religious Belief and Philosophical Enquiry," pp. 120–21.

18. Phillips, "Religious Belief and Philosophical Enquiry," pp. 115.

19. Kai Nielsen, "Wittgensteinian Fideism," *Philosophy* 42 (July 1967): 191–209.

20. Phillips, *Faith and Philosophical Enquiry,* p. 111.

21. Phillips, *Faith and Philosophical Enquiry,* p. 117.

22. Phillips, *Faith and Philosophical Enquiry,* p. 117.

23. W. D. Hudson, "Some Remarks on Wittgenstein's Account of Religious Belief," in Royal Institute of Philosophy Lectures *Talk of God,* Vol. 2 (London: Macmillan, 1969), p. 44.

24. Basil Mitchell, "The Justification of Religious Belief," *Philosophical Quarterly* 2 (1961), reprinted in *New Essays on Religious Language,* ed. D. M. High.

25. Robert C. Coburn, "A Budget of Theological Puzzles," *Journal of Religion* 43 (April 1963): 89–90.

# Bibliography

Armour, Leslie, and Mostafa Faghoury. "Wittgenstein's Philosophy and Religious Insight." *Southern Journal of Philosophy* 22 (1984): 33–48.

Bell, Richard H. "Theology As Grammar: Is God an Object of Understanding?" *Religious Studies* 11 (1975): 307–17.

———, ed. *The Grammar of the Heart: New Essays in Moral Philosophy and Theology.* San Francisco, CA: Harper & Row, 1988.

Braithwaite, R. B. *An Empiricist's View of the Nature of Religious Belief* (9th Arthur Stanley Eddington Lecture). Cambridge, Engl.: Cambridge University Press, 1955.

Brown, Stuart C. *Do Religious Claims Make Sense?* London: SCM, 1969.

Brunton, Alan. "A Model for the Religious Philosophy of D. Z. Phillips." *Analysis* 31 (1970–71): 43–48.

Cameron, J. M. "Reply to R. F. Holland, 'Religious Discourse and Theological Discourse'." *Australasian Journal of Philosophy* 34 (1956): 203–7.

Cell, Edward. *Language, Existence and God.* New York: Abingdon, 1971.

Charlesworth, M. J. "Philosophy and the Analysis of Religious Language," in *Philosophy of Religion: The Historic Approaches.* London: Macmillan, 1972.

———. *The Problem of Religious Language.* Englewood Cliffs, NJ: Prentice-Hall, 1974.

Clegg, J. S. "Faith." *American Philosophical Quarterly* 16 (1979): 225–32.

Cooke, Vincent M. "Wittgenstein and Religion." *Thought* 61 (1986): 348–59.

Crosson, Frederick, ed. *The Autonomy of Religious Belief.* Notre Dame, IN: University of Notre Dame Press, 1981.

Cupitt, Don. *The Sea of Faith.* Cambridge, Engl.: Cambridge University Press, 1988.

———. *Taking Leave of God.* London: SCM, 1981.

Foster, Michael B. *Mystery and Philosophy.* London: SCM, 1957.

Gill, Jerry H. "Wittgenstein and Religious Language." *Theology Today* 21 (1964): 59–72.

Gudmunsen, C. *Wittgenstein and Buddhism.* London: Macmillan, 1977.

Gutting, Gary. "A Dialogue on Wittgensteinian Fideism," in *Philosophy of Religion: An Anthology,* ed. Louis P. Pojman. Belmont, CA: Wadsworth, 1987.

———. "The Wittgensteinian Approach," in his *Religious Belief and Religious Skepticism.* Notre Dame, IN: University of Notre Dame Press, 1982.

Haikola, Lars. *Religion as Language Game.* Lund, Sweden: Wallin & Dalholm Boktrycheri, 1977.

Henderson, Edward H. "Theistic Reductionism and the Practice of Worship." *International Journal for Philosophy of Religion* 10 (1979): 25–50.

Hester, Marcus. "Foundationalism and Peter's Confession." *Religious Studies* 26 (1990): 403–13.

High, Dallas M. "Belief, Falsification and Wittgenstein." *International Journal for Philosophy of Religion* 3 (1972): 240–50.

————, ed. *New Essays on Religious Language.* New York: Oxford University Press, 1969.

Holland, R. F. "Religious Discourse and Theological Discourse." *Australasian Journal of Philosophy* 34 (1956): 147–63.

Holmer, Paul L. *The Grammar of Faith.* New York: Harper & Row, 1978.

————. *Theology and the Scientific Study of Religion.* Minneapolis, MN: T. S. Denison, 1961.

Hudson, H. D. Review of *The Autonomy of Religious Belief,* edited by Frederick Crosson. *Religious Studies* 19: 99–101.

————. Review of *Faith and Reason,* by Richard Swinburne. *Religious Studies* 19: 93–96.

Hudson, W. D. *Ludwig Wittgenstein: The Bearing of His Philosophy upon Religious Belief.* Richmond, VA: John Knox, 1968.

————. *A Philosophical Approach to Religion.* London: Macmillan, 1974.

————. "Some Remarks on Wittgenstein's Account of Religious Belief," in *Talk of God,* eds. G.N.A. Vesey et al. London: Macmillan, 1969.

————. "On Two Points Against Wittgensteinian Fideism." *Philosophy* 43 (1968): 269–73.

————. *Wittgenstein and Religious Belief.* New York: St. Martin's Press, 1975.

Jones, J. R., and D. Z. Phillips. "Belief and Loss of Belief: A Discussion." *Sophia* 9 (1970): 1–7.

Kasachkoff, Tziporah. "Talk about God's Existence." *Philosophical Studies* (National University of Ireland) 19 (1970): 181–92.

Keeling, L. Bryant, and Mario F. Morelli. "Beyond Wittgensteinian Fideism: An Examination of John Hick's Analysis of Religious Faith." *International Journal for Philosophy of Religion* 8 (1977): 250–62.

Keightley, Alan. *Religion and the Great Fallacy.* Bognor Regis, Engl.: New Horizon, 1983.

————. *Wittgenstein, Grammar and God.* London: Epworth, 1976.

Kellenberger, James. "The Language-Game View of Religion and Religious Certainty." *Canadian Journal of Philosophy* 2 (1972): 255–75.

Kenny, Anthony. *The Legacy of Wittgenstein.* Oxford, Engl.: Basil Blackwell, 1984.

————. *Wittgenstein.* London: Allen Lane, 1973.

Kerr, Fergus. *Theology After Wittgenstein.* Oxford, Engl.: Basil Blackwell, 1986.

Lewis, Charles. "Phillips, Barth and the Concept of God." *International Journal for Philosophy of Religion* 8 (1977): 151–68.

Lyas, Colin. "The Groundlessness of Religious Belief," in *Reason and Religion,* ed. Stuart C. Brown. Ithaca, NY: Cornell University Press, 1977.

Mackie, J. L. "Religion without Belief," in *The Miracle of Theism: Arguments for and against the Existence of God.* Oxford, Engl.: Clarendon Press, 1982.

Malcolm, Norman. "Is It a Religious Belief That 'God Exists'?" in *Faith and the Philosophers,* ed. John Hick. London: Macmillan, 1966.

Martin, Michael. "Faith and Foundationalism," in his *Atheism: A Philosophical Justification.* Philadelphia: Temple University Press, 1990.

Masterson, Patrick. "God and Grammar." *Philosophical Studies* (National University of Ireland) 27 (1980): 7–24.

Nielsen, Kai. "The Challenge of Wittgenstein: An Examination of His Picture of Religious Belief." *Studies in Religion* 3 (1973): 29–46.

————. "The Coherence of Wittgensteinian Fideism." *Sophia* 11 (1972): 4–12.

————. *Contemporary Critiques of Religion.* New York: Herder & Herder, 1971.

————. *An Introduction to Philosophy of Religion.* New York: St. Martin's Press, 1982.

————. *Scepticism.* London: Macmillan; New York: St. Martin's Press, 1973.

————. "Wittgensteinian Fideism." *Philosophy* 42 (1967): 191–209.

————. "Wittgensteinian Fideism: A Reply to Hudson." *Philosophy* 44 (1969): 53–65.

Penelhum, Terence. *Religion and Rationality.* New York: Random House, 1971.
Phillips, D. Z. *Belief, Change and Forms of Life.* London: Macmillan, 1986.
———. *The Concept of Prayer.* London: Routledge & Kegan Paul, 1965.
———. *Death and Immortality.* New York: St. Martin's Press, 1970.
———. *Faith after Foundationalism.* London: Routledge & Kegan Paul, 1988.
———. *Faith and Philosophical Enquiry.* London: Routledge & Kegan Paul, 1970; New
    York: Schocken Books, 1971.
———. *Religion without Explanation.* Oxford, Engl.: Basil Blackwell, 1976.
———, ed. *Religion and Understanding.* Oxford, Engl.: Basil Blackwell; New York: Mac-
    millan, 1967.
Plantinga, Alvin. "Malcolm, Norman," in *Encyclopedia of Philosophy,* ed. Paul Edwards.
    New York: Macmillan, 1967.
Rhees, Rush. *Without Answers.* New York: Schocken Books, 1969.
———, and Brian McGuinness, eds. *Wittgenstein and His Times.* Oxford, Engl.: Basil Black-
    well, 1982.
Richmond, James. "Religion without Explanation: Theology and D. Z. Phillips." *Theology*
    83 (1980): 34–43.
Sherry, Patrick. "Is Religion a 'Form of Life'?" *American Philosophical Quarterly* 9 (1972):
    159–67.
———. *Religion, Truth and Language-Games.* New York: Barnes & Noble, 1977.
———. "Truth and the 'Religious Language-Game'." *Philosophy* 47 (1972): 18–37.
Swenson, J. "Treating God as Real." *Theology Today* 45 (January 1989): 446–50.
Swinburne, Richard. "Attitude Theories," in his *The Coherence of Theism.* Oxford, Engl.:
    Clarendon Press, 1977.
Trigg, Roger. *Reason and Commitment.* Cambridge and London, Engl.: Cambridge Univer-
    sity Press, 1973.
Ward, Keith. *Holding Fast to God: A Reply to Don Cupitt.* London: SPCK, 1982.
Whittaker, John H. *Matters of Faith and Matters of Principle.* San Antonio, TX: Trinity Uni-
    versity Press, 1981.
Winch, Peter. *The Idea of a Social Science.* London: Routledge & Kegan Paul, 1958.
———. "Understanding a Primitive Society." *American Philosophical Quarterly* 1 (1964):
    307–24.
Wittgenstein, Ludwig. *Lectures and Conversations on Aesthetics, Psychology and Religious
    Belief* (compiled from notes by Y. Smythies, R. Rhees, and J. Taylor), ed. Cyril Bar-
    rett. Berkeley: University of California Press, 1967.
———. *Notebooks 1914–19,* trans. G.E.M. Anscombe. New York: Harper & Row, 1969.
———. *Philosophical Investigations,* 3rd ed., eds. G.E.M. Anscombe and R. Rhees; trans.
    G.E.M. Anscombe. Oxford, Engl.: Basil Blackwell, 1967.
———. *Tractatus Logico-Philosophicus,* trans. D. F. Pears and B. F. McGuinness. New
    York: Routledge & Kegan Paul, 1972.

# III

# REFORMED EPISTEMOLOGY

# 9

# Is Belief in God Properly Basic?

## *Alvin Plantinga*

Many philosophers have urged the *evidentialist* objection to theistic belief; they have argued that belief in God is irrational or unreasonable or not rationally acceptable or intellectually irresponsible or noetically substandard, because, as they say, there is insufficient evidence for it.[1] Many other philosophers and theologians—in particular, those in the great tradition of natural theology—have claimed that belief in God is intellectually acceptable, but only because the fact is there is sufficient evidence for it. These two groups unite in holding that theistic belief is rationally acceptable only if there is sufficient evidence for it. More exactly, they hold that a person is rational or reasonable in accepting theistic belief only if she has sufficient evidence for it—only if, that is, she knows or rationally believes some *other* propositions which support the one in question, and believes the latter on the basis of the former. In "Is Belief in God Rational?," I argued that the evidentialist objection is rooted in *classical foundationalism,*[2] an enormously popular picture or total way of looking at faith, knowledge, justified belief, rationality, and allied topics. This picture has been widely accepted ever since the days of Plato and Aristotle; its near relatives, perhaps, remain the dominant ways of thinking about these topics. We may think of the classical foundationalist as beginning with the observation that some of one's beliefs may be *based upon* others; it may be that there are a pair of propositions A and B such that I believe A *on the basis of B*. Although this relation isn't easy to characterize in a revealing and nontrivial fashion, it is nonetheless familiar. I believe that the word "umbrageous" is spelled u-m-b-r-a-g-e-o-u-s; this belief is based on another belief of mine: the belief that that's how the dictionary says it's spelled. I believe that $72 \times 71 = 5112$. This belief is based upon several other beliefs I hold: that $1 \times 72 = 72$; $7 \times 2 = 14$; $7 \times 7 = 49$; $49 + 1 = 50$; and others. Some of my beliefs, however, I accept but don't accept on the basis of any other beliefs. Call these beliefs *basic*. I believe that $2 + 1 = 3$, for example, and don't believe it on the basis of other propositions. I also believe that I am seated at my desk, and that there is a mild pain in my right knee. These too are basic to me; I don't believe them on the basis of any other propositions. According to the classical foundationalist, some propositions are *properly* or *rightly* basic for a person and some are not. Those that are not, are rationally accepted only on the basis of

Reprinted from *Nous* XV (1981), by permission of the author and of the editor. Notes edited.

*evidence,* where the evidence must trace back, ultimately, to what is properly basic. The existence of God, furthermore, is not among the propositions that are properly basic; hence a person is rational in accepting theistic belief only if he has evidence for it.

Now many Reformed thinkers and theologians[3] have rejected *natural theology* (thought of as the attempt to provide proofs or arguments for the existence of God). They have held not merely that the proffered arguments are unsuccessful, but that the whole enterprise is in some way radically misguided. In "The Reformed Objection to Natural Theology," I argue that the reformed rejection of natural theology is best construed as an inchoate and unfocused rejection of classical foundationalism.[4] What these Reformed thinkers really mean to hold, I think, is that belief in God need not be based on argument or evidence from other propositions at all. They mean to hold that the believer is entirely within his intellectual rights in believing as he does even if he doesn't know of any good theistic argument (deductive or inductive), even if he doesn't believe that there is any such argument, and even if in fact no such argument exists. They hold that it is perfectly rational to accept belief in God without accepting it on the basis of any other beliefs or propositions at all. In a word, they hold that *belief in God is properly basic.* In this paper I shall try to develop and defend this position.

But first we must achieve a deeper understanding of the evidentialist objection. It is important to see that this contention is a *normative* contention. The evidentialist objector holds that one who accepts theistic belief is in some way irrational or noetically substandard. Here 'rational' and 'irrational' are to be taken as normative or evaluative terms; according to the objector, the theist fails to measure up to a standard he ought to conform to. There is a right way and a wrong way with respect to belief as with respect to actions; we have duties, responsibilities, obligations with respect to the former just as with respect to the latter. So Professor Blanshard:

> . . . everywhere and always belief has an ethical aspect. There is such a thing as a
> general ethics of the intellect. The main principle of that ethic I hold to be the same
> inside and outside religion. This principle is simple and sweeping: Equate your
> assent to the evidence.[5]

This "ethics of the intellect" can be construed variously; many fascinating issues—issues we must here forebear to enter—arise when we try to state more exactly the various options the evidentialist may mean to adopt. Initially it looks as if he holds that there is a duty or obligation of some sort not to accept without evidence such propositions as that God exists—a duty flouted by the theist who has no evidence. If he has no evidence, then it is his duty to cease believing. But there is an oft-remarked difficulty: one's beliefs, for the most part, are not directly under one's control. Most of those who believe in God could not divest themselves of that belief just by trying to do so, just as they could not in that way rid themselves of the belief that the world has existed for a very long time. So perhaps the relevant obligation is not that of divesting myself of theistic belief if I have no evidence (that is beyond my power), but to try to cultivate the sorts of intellectual habits that will tend (we hope) to issue in my accepting as basic only propositions that are properly basic.

Perhaps this obligation is to be thought of *teleologically:* it is a moral obligation arising out of a connection between certain intrinsic goods and evils and the way in which our beliefs are formed and held. (This seems to be W. K. Clifford's way of construing the matter.) Perhaps it is to be thought of *aretetically:* there are valuable noetic or intellectual states (whether intrinsically or extrinsically valuable); there are also corresponding intellectual virtues, habits of acting so as to promote and enhance those valuable states. Among one's obligations, then, is the duty to try to foster and cultivate these virtues in oneself or others. Or perhaps it is to be thought of *deontologically:* this obligation attaches to us just by virtue of our having the sort of noetic equipment human beings do in fact display; it does not arise out of a connection with valuable states of affairs. Such an obligation, furthermore, could be a special sort of moral obligation; on the other hand, perhaps it is a sui generis non-moral obligation.

Still further, perhaps the evidentialist need not speak of duty or obligation here at all. Consider someone who believes that Venus is smaller than Mercury, not because he has evidence of any sort, but because he finds it amusing to hold a belief no one else does—or consider someone who holds this belief on the basis of some outrageously bad argument. Perhaps there isn't any obligation he has failed to meet. Nevertheless his intellectual condition is deficient in some way; or perhaps alternatively there is a commonly achieved excellence he fails to display. And the evidentialist objection to theistic belief, then, might be understood as the claim, not that the theist without evidence has failed to meet an obligation, but that he suffers from a certain sort of intellectual deficiency (so that the proper attitude toward him would be sympathy rather than censure).

These are some of the ways, then, in which the evidentialist objection could be developed; and of course there are still other possibilities. For ease of exposition, let us take the claim deontologically; what I shall say will apply mutatis mutandis if we take it one of the other ways. The evidentialist objection, therefore, presupposes some view as to what sorts of propositions are correctly, or rightly, or justifiably taken as basic; it presupposes a view as to what is *properly* basic. And the minimally relevant claim for the evidentialist objector is that belief in God is *not* properly basic. Typically this objection has been rooted in some form of *classical foundationalism,* according to which a proposition $p$ is properly basic for a person $S$ if and only if $p$ is either self-evident or incorrigible for $S$ (modern foundationalism) or either self-evident or 'evident to the senses' for $S$ (ancient and medival foundationalism). In "Is Belief in God Rational?," I argued that both forms of foundationalism are self-referentially incoherent and must therefore be rejected.[6]

Insofar as the evidentialist objection is rooted in classical foundationalism, it is poorly rooted indeed: and so far as I know, no one has developed and articulated any other reason for supposing that belief in God is not properly basic. Of course it doesn't follow that it *is* properly basic; perhaps the class of properly basic propositions is broader than classical foundationalists think, but still not broad enough to admit belief in God. But why think so? What might be the objections to the Reformed view that belief in God is properly basic?

I've heard it argued that if I have no evidence for the existence of God, then if I accept that proposition, my belief will be groundless, or gratuitous, or arbitrary. I think this is an error; let me explain.

Suppose we consider perceptual beliefs, memory beliefs, and beliefs which ascribe mental states to other persons: such beliefs as

1. I see a tree,
2. I had breakfast this morning,

and

3. That person is angry.

Although beliefs of this sort are typically and properly taken as basic, it would be a mistake to describe them as *groundless*. Upon having experience of a certain sort, I believe that I am perceiving a tree. In the typical case I do not hold this belief on the basis of other beliefs; it is nonetheless not groundless. My having that characteristic sort of experience—to use Professor Chisholm's language, my being appeared treely to—plays a crucial role in the formation and justification of that belief. We might say this experience, together, perhaps, with other circumstances, is what *justifies* me in holding it; this is the *ground* of my justification, and, by extension, the ground of the belief itself.

If I see someone displaying typical pain behavior, I take it that he or she is in pain. Again, I don't take the displayed behavior as *evidence* for that belief; I don't infer that belief from others I hold; I don't accept it on the basis of other beliefs. Still, my perceiving the pain behavior plays a unique role in the formation and justification of that belief; as in the previous case, it forms the ground of my justification for the belief in question. The same holds for memory beliefs. I seem to remember having breakfast this morning; that is, I have an inclination to believe the proposition that I had breakfast, along with a certain past-tinged experience that is familiar to all but hard to describe. Perhaps we should say that I am appeared to pastly; but perhaps this insufficiently distinguishes the experience in question from that accompanying beliefs about the past not grounded in my own memory. The phenomonology of memory is a rich and unexplored realm; here I have no time to explore it. In this case as in the others, however, there is a justifying circumstance present, a condition that forms the ground of my justification for accepting the memory belief in question.

In each of these cases, a belief is taken as basic, and in each case properly taken as basic. In each case there is some circumstance or condition that confers justification; there is a circumstance that serves as the *ground* of justification. So in each case there will be some true proposition of the sort

4. In condition $C$, $S$ is justified in taking $p$ as basic.

Of course $C$ will vary with $p$. For a perceptual judgment such as

5. I see a rose-colored wall before me,

*C* will include my being appeared to in a certain fashion. No doubt *C* will include more. If I'm appeared to in the familiar fashion but know that I'm wearing rose-colored glasses, or that I am suffering from a disease that causes me to be thus appeared to, no matter what the color of the nearby objects, then I'm not justified in taking (5) as basic. Similarly for memory. Suppose I know that my memory is unreliable; it often plays me tricks. In particular, when I seem to remember having breakfast, then, more often than not, I *haven't* had breakfast. Under these conditions I am not justified in taking it as basic that I had breakfast, even though I seem to remember that I did.

So being appropriately appeared to, in the perceptual case, is not sufficient for justification; some further condition—a condition hard to state in detail—is clearly necessary. The central point, here, however, is that a belief is properly basic only in certain conditions; these conditions are, we might say, the ground of its justification and, by extension, the ground of the belief itself. In this sense, basic beliefs are not, or are not necessarily, *groundless* beliefs.

Now similar things may be said about belief in God. When the Reformers claim that this belief is properly basic, they do not mean to say, of course, that there are no justifying circumstances for it, or that it is in that sense groundless or gratuitous. Quite the contrary. Calvin holds that God "reveals and daily discloses himself to the whole workmanship of the universe," and the divine art "reveals itself in the innumerable and yet distinct and well-ordered variety of the heavenly host." God has so created us that we have a tendency or disposition to see his hand in the world about us. More precisely, there is in us a disposition to believe propositions of the sort *this flower was created by God* or *this vast and intricate universe was created by God* when we contemplate the flower or behold the starry heavens or think about the vast reaches of the universe.

Calvin recognizes, at least implicitly, that other sorts of conditions may trigger this disposition. Upon reading the Bible, one may be impressed with a deep sense that God is speaking to him. Upon having done what I know is cheap, or wrong, or wicked I may feel guilty in God's sight and form the belief *God disapproves of what I've done.* Upon confession and repentence, I may feel forgiven, forming the belief *God forgives me for what I've done.* A person in grave danger may turn to God, asking for his protection and help; and of course he or she then forms the belief that God is indeed able to hear and help if he sees fit. When life is sweet and satisfying, a spontaneous sense of gratitude may well up within the soul; someone in this condition may thank and praise the Lord for his goodness, and will of course form the accompanying belief that indeed the Lord is to be thanked and praised.

There are therefore many conditions and circumstances that call forth belief in God: guilt, gratitude, danger, a sense of God's presence, a sense that he speaks, perception of various parts of the universe. A complete job would explore the phenomenology of all these conditions and of more besides. This is a large and important topic; but here I can only point to the existence of these conditions.

Of course none of the beliefs I mentioned a moment ago is the simple belief that God exists. What we have instead are such beliefs as

    6. God is speaking to me,
    7. God has created all this,
    8. God disapproves of what I have done,
    9. God forgives me,

and

    10. God is to be thanked and praised.

These propositions are properly basic in the right circumstances. But it is quite consistent with this to suppose that the proposition *there is such a person as God* is neither properly basic nor taken as basic by those who believe in God. Perhaps what they take as basic are such propositions as (6)–(10), believing in the existence of God on the basis of propositions such as those. From this point of view, it isn't exactly right to say that it is belief in God that is properly basic; more exactly, what are properly basic are such propositions as (6)–(10), each of which self-evidently entails that God exists. It isn't the relatively high level and general proposition *God exists* that is properly basic, but instead propositions detailing some of his attributes or actions.

    Suppose we return to the analogy between belief in God and belief in the existence of perceptual objects, other persons, and the past. Here too it is relatively specific and concrete propositions rather than their more general and abstract colleagues that are properly basic. Perhaps such items as

    11. There are trees,
    12. There are other persons,

and

    13. The world has existed for more than five minutes,

are not in fact properly basic; it is instead such propositions as

    14. I see a tree,
    15. That person is pleased,

and

    16. I had breakfast more than an hour ago,

that deserve that accolade. Of course propositions of the latter sort immediately and self-evidently entail propositions of the former sort; and perhaps there is thus no harm in speaking of the former as properly basic, even though so to speak is to speak a bit loosely.

    The same must be said about belief in God. We may say, speaking loosely, that belief in God is properly basic; strictly speaking, however, it is probably not that proposition but such propositions as (6)–(10) that enjoy that status. But the main point, here, is that belief in God, or (6)–(10), are properly basic; to say so, however, is not to deny that there are justifying conditions for these beliefs, or conditions that confer justification on one who accepts them as basic. They are therefore not groundless or gratuitous.

A second objection I've often heard: if belief in God is properly basic, why can't *just any* belief be properly basic? Couldn't we say the same for any bizarre abberation we can think of? What about voodoo or astrology? What about the belief that the Great Pumpkin returns every Halloween? Could I properly take *that* as basic? And if I can't, why can I properly take belief in God as basic? Suppose I believe that if I flap my arms with sufficient vigor, I can take off and fly about the room; could I defend myself against the charge of irrationality by claiming this belief is basic? If we say that belief in God is properly basic, won't we be committed to holding that just anything, or nearly anything, can properly be taken as basic, thus throwing wide the gates to irrationalism and superstitution?

Certainly not. What might lead one to think the Reformed epistemologist is in this kind of trouble? The fact that he rejects the criteria for proper basicality purveyed by classical foundationalism? But why should *that* be thought to commit him to such tolerance of irrationality? Consider an analogy. In the palmy days of positivism, the positivists went about confidently wielding their verifiability criterion and declaring meaningless much that was obviously meaningful. Now suppose someone rejected a formulation of that criterion—the one to be found in the second edition of A. J. Ayer's *Language, Truth and Logic,* for example. Would that mean she was committed to holding that

17. Twas brillig; and the slithy toves did gyre and gymble in the wabe,

contrary to appearances, makes good sense? Of course not. But then the same goes for the Reformed epistemologist; the fact that he rejects the classical foundationalist's criterion of proper basicality does not mean that he is committed to supposing just anything is properly basic.

But what then is the problem? Is it that the Reformed epistemologist not only rejects those criteria for proper basicality, but seems in no hurry to produce what he takes to be a better substitute? If he has no such criterion, how can he fairly reject belief in the Great Pumpkin as properly basic?

This objection betrays an important misconception. How do we rightly arrive at or develop criteria for meaningfulness, or justified belief, or proper basicality? Where do they come from? Must one have such a criterion before one can sensibly make any judgments—positive or negative—about proper basicality? Surely not. Suppose I don't know of a satisfactory substitute for the criteria proposed by classical foundationalism; I am nevertheless entirely within my rights in holding that certain propositions are not properly basic in certain conditions. Some propositions seem self-evident when in fact they are not; that is the lesson of some of the Russell paradoxes. Nevertheless it would be irrational to take as basic the denial of a proposition that seems self-evident to you. Similarly, suppose it seems to you that you see a tree; you would then be irrational in taking as basic the proposition that you don't see a tree, or that there aren't any trees. In the same way, even if I don't know of some illuminating criterion of meaning, I can quite properly declare (17) meaningless.

And this raises an important question—one Roderick Chisholm has taught us to ask. What is the status of criteria for knowledge, or proper basicality, or justified belief? Typically, these are universal statements. The modern foundationalist's criterion for proper basicality, for example, is doubly universal:

18.  For any proposition *A* and person *S, A* is properly basic for *S* if and only if *A* is incorrigible for *S* or self-evident to *S*.

But how could one know a thing like that? What are its credentials? Clearly enough, (18) isn't self-evident or just obviously true. But if it isn't, how does one arrive at it? What sorts of arguments would be appropriate? Of course a foundationalist might find (18) so appealing, he simply takes it to be true, neither offering argument for it nor accepting it on the basis of other things he believes. If he does so, however, his noetic structure will be self-referentially incoherent. (18) itself is neither self-evident nor incorrigible; hence in accepting (18) as basic, the modern foundationalist violates the condition of proper basicality he himself lays down in accepting it. On the other hand, perhaps the foundationalist will try to produce some argument for it from premises that are self-evident or incorrigible: it is exceedingly hard to see, however, what such an argument might be like. And until he has produced such arguments, what shall the rest of us do—we who do not find (18) at all obvious or compelling? How could he use (18) to show us that belief in God, for example, is not properly basic? Why should we believe (18), or pay it any attention?

The fact is, I think, that neither (18) nor any other revealing necessary and sufficient condition for proper basicality follows from clearly self-evident premises by clearly acceptable arguments. And hence the proper way to arrive at such a criterion is, broadly speaking, *inductive.* We must assemble examples of beliefs and conditions such that the former are obviously properly basic in the latter, and examples of beliefs and conditions such that the former are obviously *not* properly basic in the latter. We must then frame hypotheses as to the necessary and sufficient conditions of proper basicality and test these hypothesis by reference to those examples. Under the right conditions, for example, it is clearly rational to believe that you see a human person before you: a being who has thoughts and feelings, who knows and believes things, who makes decisions and acts. It is clear, furthermore, that you are under no obligation to reason to this belief from others you hold; under those conditions that belief is properly basic for you. But then (18) must be mistaken; the belief in question, under those circumstances, is properly basic, though neither self-evident nor incorrigible for you. Similarly, you may seem to remember that you had breakfast this morning, and perhaps you know of no reason to suppose your memory is playing you tricks. If so, you are entirely justified in taking that belief as basic. Of course it isn't properly basic on the criteria offered by classical foundationalists; but that fact counts not against you but against those criteria.

Accordingly, criteria for proper basicality must be reached from below rather than above; they should not be presented as ex cathedra, but argued to and tested by a relevant set of examples. But there is no reason to assume, in advance, that everyone will agree on the examples. The Christian will of course suppose that belief in God is entirely proper and rational; if he doesn't accept this belief on the basis of other propositions, he will conclude that it is basic for him, and quite properly so. Followers of Bertrand Russell and Madelyn Murray O'Hare may disagree, but how is that relevant? Must my criteria, or those of the Christian community, conform to their examples? Surely not. The Christian community is responsible to *its* set of examples, not to theirs.

Accordingly, the Reformed epistemologist can properly hold that belief in the Great Pumpkin is not properly basic, even though he holds that belief in God is properly basic and even if he has no full-fledged criterion of proper basicality. Of course he is committed to supposing that there is a relevant *difference* between belief in God and belief in the Great Pumpkin, if he holds that the former but not the latter is properly basic. But this should prove no great embarrassment; there are plenty of candidates. These candidates are to be found in the neighborhood of the conditions I mentioned in the last section that justify and ground belief in God. Thus, for example, the Reformed epistemologist may concur with Calvin in holding that God has implanted in us a natural tendency to see his hand in the world around us; the same cannot be said for the Great Pumpkin, there being no Great Pumpkin and no natural tendency to accept beliefs about the Great Pumpkin.

By way of conclusion then: being self-evident, or incorrigible, or evident to the senses is not a necessary condition of proper basicality. Furthermore, one who holds that belief in God *is* properly basic is not thereby committed to the idea that belief in God is groundless or gratuitous or without justifying circumstances. And even if he lacks a general criterion of proper basicality, he is not obliged to suppose that just any or nearly any belief—belief in the Great Pumpkin, for example—is properly basic. Like everyone should, he begins with examples; and he may take belief in the Great Pumpkin as a paradigm of irrational basic belief.

# Notes

1. See, for example, Brand Blanshard, *Reason and Belief* (London: Allen & Unwin, 1974), pp. 400ff.; W. K. Clifford, "The Ethics of Belief," in his *Lectures and Essays* (London: Macmillan, 1879), p. 345ff.; A.G.N. Flew, *The Presumption of Atheism* (London: Pemberton Publishing Co., 1976), p. 22 (see the paper by Flew in Part I of this volume, pp. 19–32); Bertrand Russell, "Why I Am Not a Christian," in his *Why I Am Not a Christian* (New York: Simon & Schuster, 1957), p. 3ff.; and Michael Scriven, *Primary Philosophy* (New York: McGraw-Hill, 1966), p. 87ff.

2. Alvin Plantinga, "Is Belief in God Rational?" in *Rationality and Religious Belief*, ed. C. F. Delaney (Notre Dame, IN: University of Notre Dame Press, 1979), pp. 7–27.

3. A Reformed thinker or theologian is one whose intellectual sympathies lie with the Protestant tradition going back to John Calvin (not someone who was formerly a theologian and has since seen the light).

4. Alvin Plantinga, "The Reformed Objection to Natural Theology," *Proceedings of the American Catholic Philosophical Association* 15 (1980), 49–63.

5. Blanshard, *Reason and Belief*, p. 401.

6. Platinga, "Is Belief in God Rational?"

# 10

## Is Reason Enough?

### Nicholas Wolterstorff

One of the characteristic differences between the Reformed and the Anglo-American Evangelical traditions of Christendom is their difference in attitude toward the project of giving arguments for the Christian faith. Reformed people characteristically have a deep intuitive revulsion against this project. They are convinced that it is useless, or worse, pernicious and idolatrous, to give preeminence to Reason rather than to Christ. Yet they have not been reluctant to meet head-on the arguments of the objectors to the faith. Neither have they been reluctant to give theoretical articulation to the Christian faith. Nor have they been reluctant to engage in the academic disciplines in the light of the Christian faith. In short, though Reformed people are profoundly convinced of the importance of theoretical activity in the life of the Christian community and in the life of humanity generally, of the giving of arguments for the faith they want no part.

Evangelicals are typically just the opposite. Often they have been suspicious of the worth of academic theology. Only episodically have they been persuaded of the worth—or even the *sense*—of engaging in the academic disciplines in the light of the Christian faith. What leaps to their attention when they read the history of culture is the dangerous and seductive character of theorizing. They perceive that over and over the theoretician has served the false god of Reason. And yet the project of giving evidences for the Christian faith exercises an irresistible lure for them.

Reformed persons have no taste at all for undergirding the Christian faith with evidences. Yet they are deeply committed to expressing their faith by way of theorizing. Evangelicals have little taste for expressing the faith by way of theorizing. Yet they are profoundly committed to assembling evidences to undergird the faith. What strange and surprising oppositions!

### I

What brings these reflections to mind is my recent reading of a new book by an articulate theologian from the Evangelical tradition, Clark H. Pinnock. The book is entitled *Reason Enough: A Case for the Christian Faith.*[1] I should say at once,

Reprinted from *The Reformed Journal* 31 (April 1981), by permission of the editor. Notes edited.

however, that Pinnock is not at all a typical member of the Evangelical tradition—at least if I have represented that tradition correctly above. He is not suspicious of theorizing; he sees its importance as one of the ways in which the Christian community gives expression to its faith. He is characteristic, though, in his insistence that giving evidence for the faith is both legitimate and important.

I want here to engage him in discussion on what he says. And I do mean *engage him in discussion.* I do not propose to trot out all the old positions and arguments and do battle. The times for that are over, if ever they were present. I want to put my questions to Pinnock in the expectation that there is something here for each to learn from the other.

For whom is Pinnock's book meant? To whom does he wish to present his evidences for the truth of the Christian faith? To the person considering whether or not to accept the Christian faith. The person Pinnock has in mind is not the person ignorant of Christianity, nor the person who already has faith and is confident therein; rather, his concern is the person who pretty much knows the content of the faith and is wondering whether to accept it or not (or to continue accepting it):

> My purpose in writing this book is to communicate with people who are interested in investigating the truth claims made on behalf of the Christian message. Is Christianity, in fact, true? . . . I am writing, then, for those who do not believe and for those who experience difficulties in their believing.[2]

However, not every person considering whether to accept the faith is Pinnock's intended audience here. The person he has in mind is the one who, before she accepts the faith, wants to be sure that it would be rational for her to do so. The person Pinnock is addressing is the person who is willing to consider accepting the faith but not at the cost of sacrificing her intellect. And what Pinnock proposes to do is meet her demand. Pinnock proposes to show her that it would be rational to accept the faith. For Pinnock regards this demand as appropriate. "I do not believe," he says, "that we need to commit ourselves without reasonable grounds."[3] Pinnock urges that his apologetic efforts be placed "in the proper context, which is to test belief in God from the point of view of its rationality."[4]

Thus Pinnock sees himself as a fair-minded lawyer before what he hopes will be an equally fair-minded jury:

> I see my task as that of Christian persuasion. I am in the role of a fair-minded lawyer seeking to convince you the jury of the truth of the Christian message through the presentation of the evidences at my disposal. . . . I am . . . aiming at . . . a testing of faith in the light of knowledge which will enable you to take that step of commitment without sacrificing your intellect.[5]

"I am committed," says Pinnock,

> to appealing to reason to try to persuade those yet unconvinced to make a decision for Jesus Christ. Faith according to the Bible does not involve a rash decision made without reflection or a blind submission in the face of an authoritarian claim.[6]

But do not expect too much of the evidential arguments that he will offer, says Pinnock. He is not, in the fashion of Thomistic natural theology, going to offer *dem-*

*onstrations*—deductive arguments from premises which are self-evident to the attentive mind or evident to the senses. Rather, he is going to argue that Christianity is the best available explanation of various phenomena. And this gives us something weaker than demonstrations.

> I am not aiming at rational proof. . . . We will be dealing here with reasonable probabilities. No world view offers more than that, and Christianity offers nothing less. There will come a day I believe when God will reveal his glory in an unmistakable way and there will no longer be any room for doubt and hesitation. But that day is not yet, and in the meantime we work with reasonable probabilities which, while they do not create or compel belief, do establish the credible atmosphere in which faith can be born and can grow.[7]

What does Pinnock hope for as the outcome of his efforts at persuasion? A more or less tentative acceptance of Christianity as the best explanation of various phenomena? Not at all. What he asks of his jury is that, once he has met their demand to show them that it would be rational to accept the Christian faith, they *commit* themselves to Jesus Christ. God's "way is to provide us with good and sufficient evidence of reasonable, persuasive force, and then to invite us to enter into the trustful certitude of faith."[8] Such faith "is the act of wholehearted trust in the goodness and promises of the God who confronts us with his reality and gives us ample reason to believe that he is there."[9] And so, says Pinnock, "open yourself up to God, confess your failure to live a just and holy life, and determine to follow the Lord Jesus. Act upon the evidence that stands before you and accept the saving offer that is being extended."[10] Pinnock never explicates the relation between believing with some tentativity that Christianity is the best explanation of various phenomena and adopting the trustful certitude of faith. But clearly he does not blur the difference between the two.

Pinnock's project then is to show to the person who wonders whether Christianity is rational that it is indeed that. And he proposes to accomplish this by giving evidence for the truth of Christianity.

What does he propose to allow as evidence? A proposition that is evident with respect to one body of propositions may not be such with respect to another. Or to put it the other way round: one set of propositions may be good evidence for a certain proposition while another set is not. So when someone proposes to give evidence for Christianity, we must ask what he proposes to take as evidence. Where does he start? Well, since the project is to persuade the unbeliever, we have to start with something that the unbeliever accepts, and is justified in accepting. What Pinnock proposes to start with is our perceptual knowledge. This will provide us the evidence. And from this we are to make what anyone recognizes as reasonable inferences to Christianity:

> I do not want to make any special demands in the area of knowledge. I have no hidden assumptions, no special philosophy. My contention is that the truth claims of the Christian gospel can be checked out in the ordinary ways we verify the things we know.[11]

The full picture then is this: Pinnock is addressing himself to that person wondering whether to accept the Christian faith who has stipulated that before he accepts it he be shown that it is rational to do so. Pinnock then undertakes to meet this demand. He does so by, as he sees it, trying to show that Christianity is more probable than not with respect to our perceptual knowledge. In particular, he tries to show that Christianity is the best explanation of various phenomena. And then, having met the demand to show that it is rational to accept the faith, he urges the person to commit himself to Christ.

## II

I do not here wish to scrutinize Pinnock's actual arguments. I wish rather to reflect on the project he has set to himself. Before I do so, however, let me say that among my acquaintances is one for whom the decisive step in his conversion to Christianity some years back was his consideration of the evidence for the truth of Christianity. So let the Reformed person not leap into the fray here insisting that arguments presented to unbelievers for the truth of Christianity are always useless, or even pernicious. They are not. One can appropriately ask what exactly they do, under what circumstances they do it, etc., but what is not in question is that sometimes they work beneficially.

The person Pinnock has in mind is the person who is considering whether or not to accept Christianity and who has resolved to do so only if he or she is assured that it is rational to do so. Now evidently Pinnock believes that the characteristic difficulty for such a person—that which hinders him from accepting the faith—is that the evidence for the truth of Christianity is not available to him or has not been presented vividly enough to him. He hasn't perceived the evidential hookup between his perceptual knowledge and Christian teaching. For what Pinnock addresses to this person is a discourse in which he presents to him evidence for the truth of Christianity.

The first question I want to pose is whether Pinnock's analysis of the typical situation is correct. Characteristic of the Reformed tradition is quite a different analysis. What the Reformed person would suspect as operative in this and other cases of unbelief is not so much insufficient awareness of the evidence, as it is *resistance* to the available evidence. Calvin's thought, for example—which he bases in part on Romans 1—is that God has planted in every human being a disposition to believe in the existence of a divine Creator, and that this disposition is triggered, or activated, by our awareness of the richly complex design of the cosmos and of ourselves. It was not Calvin's thought that we *inferred* the existence of a divine Creator from perceptual knowledge of the existence of design. It was rather his thought that the awareness of the design immediately causes the belief—just as having certain sensations immediately convinces us that we are in the presence of another human person. It is possible, though, said Calvin, to resist the workings of this disposition. And one of the characteristic effects of sin is that we do resist it. The sinner prefers *not* to acknowledge the existence of a divine Creator. Thus Calvin's picture of the unbeliever is of one who characteristically resists acknowledging what he really knows, not of course because he has any evidence for its falsehood, rather because he does not *like* to believe it.

Of course it's perfectly compatible with what Calvin says to acknowledge that a given person may feel very little or none of this resistance anymore. It may now be only a dim memory with him; he may feel little or no impulse anymore to believe that God exists.

Now of course one treats differently the person one views as resisting God than the person one views as having insufficient evidence of God. And one of the reasons the Reformed tradition has been so skeptical of the benefit of giving evidence is that it sees resistance as the key factor. For what, after all, does one do to overcome resistance to this truth? Well, for one thing, one attacks whatever defenses have been built up; thus it is that the Reformed tradition has characteristically gone on the attack against objections to Christianity. For the rest, one tries to bring to light the roots of the resistance, in the hope that God through his Spirit will work in the heart of the unbeliever so as to move him or her from resistance to love.

Let me give an analogy. Marx and Freud have taught us that often what shapes our beliefs is more or less hidden desires to protect our economic position or overcome our sense of insecurity. We construct ideologies, or rationalizations. Given its sources, the way to relieve someone of an ideology or rationalization is not to lay in front of him or her evidence for its falsehood. Usually that won't work. One must get at those hidden dynamics and bring them to light. Critique or therapy, rather than presenting evidence, is what is required.

Who is right here? Well, is it not in fact characteristic of converts to the Christian faith to confess that they had been resisting? And is this not the biblical picture of our human situation as well? But perhaps we must distinguish here, as Calvin himself did. Perhaps the person who refuses to be a theist knows better, and is resisting. But perhaps sometimes the person who is a theist but not a Christian has never had the reasons for accepting the gospel of Jesus Christ forcefully laid before him. Perhaps he has never been presented with the authenticity of the apostolic teaching, and its testimony to the resurrection of Jesus Christ. It is true that there are those who, when presented with this, resist. But probably there are also those who, having imbibed the anti-religious spirit of the modern Western world, have never seriously faced up to the grounds for accepting the Christian faith. To such a person, then, one presents as forcefully as one can the evidence for the truth of Christianity.

My guess, then, is that sometimes Pinnock's strategy is relevant. I judge, though, that it is relevant to fewer people than he seems to suppose. And in any case, Pinnock seriously neglects that fundamental factor of resistance.

## III

Pinnock, to say it once again, has his eye on those who are considering whether or not to accept the Christian faith and want to be assured that it would be rational for them to do so. And since Pinnock agrees that God asks us to believe only what is rational for us to believe, he tries to meet the challenge. But is the assumption correct? Does God in fact ask us to believe only what is rational to believe?

The Christian, in my judgment, is not entitled to deal with this question by dismissing the issue of rationality out of hand. Rationality is one of the things God asks of us. To say that it is rational for me to believe something is to say that I am *justified* in believing it. And to say that I am justified in believing it is to say that I am *permitted* to believe it. Further, to say that I am permitted to believe it is to say that believing it is *not in violation of the norms* that pertain to my believings—that my believing it does not represent any failure on my part to have governed my believings as I ought to have done.

Now surely the Christian agrees that we do have obligations with respect to our believings. It is not true that anything goes in our treatment of other human beings; neither is it true that anything goes in our believings. And as with moral obligations, so with intellectual obligations: ultimately these are grounded in our responsibility to God. The reason the Christian cannot dismiss the claims of rationality, then, is that these are God's claims on him. It is as shallow to suppose that God asks us in general to choose between Christ and rationality as it would be shallow to suppose that God asks us in general to choose between Christ and morality.

Nonetheless, I do not think we can conclude that God will never ask us to believe what would not be rational for us to believe. For intellectual obligations are only one among various types of obligations; and in specific cases they may well be overridden by obligations of other types. This is clear in simple cases. Sometimes I have to choose between taking my daughter boating and calculating my bank account with sufficient care for me to be fully justified in my belief as to the size of the balance; and in some such cases, I ought to choose the former. May it not be so in the matter of Christian belief as well? Suppose that a relatively unsophisticated believer listens to a powerful attack on Christianity and finds herself incapable of finding any flaw in the attack. Suppose that she talks to others, and that they too can find no flaw. May it not be then that she is no longer intellectually justified in accepting the faith—that she does so in violation of the evidence available to her? Nonetheless, I do not believe that she should give up the faith, and neither, I suspect, does Pinnock.

Such a situation can best be understood, I think, as a situation in which God has permitted the person to enter into a trial. The biblical witness makes clear that faith may be tried. Usually the trial is that of suffering. But may the trial not sometimes take the form of an intellectual trial in which we are asked to endure in the faith in spite of the fact that we find ourselves with adequate reason to give it up?

## IV

Many in the Reformed tradition would object to Pinnock's undertaking because, they would argue, there is in fact no point of contact, no common ground, between believer and unbeliever, and thus Pinnock's project cannot possibly succeed. Either he will surreptitiously grant something to the unbeliever that he should not grant, or the unbeliever will unwittingly grant something to Pinnock that he or she as an unbeliever should not grant.

I do not share this objection. When the believer tries to offer evidence to the unbeliever for the truth of Christianity, he tries to find beliefs that both of them believe and are justified in believing, and with respect to which Christianity is evident. I see no reason to suppose that this is in principle impossible. Believers and unbelievers do in fact share justified beliefs—many of them. And I see no reason to suppose that Christianity is never evident with respect to such shared beliefs.

Actually, whether or not there are *shared* justified beliefs is not actually relevant. What counts is simply whether the unbeliever has justified beliefs with respect to which Christianity is evident. Whether those justified beliefs are shared is not to the point. And if Christianity *is* evident with respect to the justified beliefs of some unbeliever, what could possibly be wrong with pointing this out to him or her?

Nonetheless, there are questions to be raised about Pinnock's procedure—or his understanding of it. The way in which the traditional dispute over common ground was conducted seems to me to have seriously misconceived the situation. One party assumed that there was no common ground between believer and unbeliever. The other party assumed that there *was* common ground. The truth is that, for any pair of believer and unbeliever, there will be shared justified beliefs; but the particular beliefs shared will differ from pair to pair. The common ground between a Barthian Christian and a positivist is very different from that between a liberal Christian and a Muslim.

What this means is that apologetics must always be person-specific. It must always be contextual. An apologetic satisfactory for all comers is impossible. Granted, as Pinnock observes, the New Testament writers gave reasons for the faith that was in them. But the reasons Peter gave on Pentecost were peculiarly relevant to Jews, and the reasons Paul gave in Athens were peculiarly relevant to Greeks— and neither of these sets of reasons is directly relevant to contemporary positivists.

Pinnock proposes to start solely from some items of perceptual knowledge. Presumably his reason for doing so is that he thinks these items are common to all— that everyone is justified in believing them. That is more than dubious. But in any case, even a hasty glance at his arguments will make clear that they are far indeed from all starting out solely from perceptual knowledge. In fact, what Pinnock does is construct an apologetic relevant to typical Western twentieth-century university students.

# V

I raise one last point. "We must," says Pinnock, "exercise critical judgment in the context of our beliefs, so that the faith we hold is reasonable." And presumably he is speaking to everyone here, not just to inquirers. Now if an unbeliever comes along and asks to be shown that it would be reasonable for him to accept the faith, and if one thinks it best to meet this request head-on rather than treating it "therapeutically," then one thing one might try doing is present evidence for the truth of Christianity, starting from things that it is already reasonable for him to believe. But where does that leave you and me, who are already believers? We also are enjoined to be reasonable in our beliefs, other things being equal. Must we also have evidential arguments? Starting from what? From sensory experience? And what about the simple believer in Uganda? Must she also, if she is to be justified in her belief, have evidential arguments of the Pinnockian sort?

It is crucial here to distinguish two situations, all too often confused. It is one thing, given a person's set of beliefs, to distinguish those that are rational from those that are not, and then to raise the question: What accounts for the rationality of those that are rational? It is quite another thing, when a person does not yet believe a certain thing, to answer his question whether it *would be* rational for him to believe it, by presenting him with evidence for its truth.

Deeply embedded in the Reformed tradition is the conviction that a person's belief that God exists may be a justified belief even though that person has not inferred that belief from others of his beliefs which provide good evidence for it. After all, not all the things we are justified in believing have been inferred from other beliefs. We have to start somewhere! And the Reformed tradition has insisted that the belief that God exists, that God is Creator, etc., may justifiably be found there in the foundation of our system of beliefs. In that sense, the Reformed tradition has been fideist, not evidentialist, in its impulse. It seems to me that that impulse is correct. It is not in general true that to be justified in believing in God one has to believe this on the basis of evidence provided by one's other beliefs. We are entitled to reason *from* our belief in God without first having reasoned *to* it.

But if fideism is true, then perhaps there is available another and quite different way of answering the inquirer than the way Pinnock pursues. Pinnock tries to show the inquirer that it would be rational for him to accept the faith by showing him that the faith is probable with respect to his justified beliefs. Perhaps it would be just as well or better to point out to some inquirers that justifiably believing in God does not always require holding that belief on the basis of arguments.

## Notes

1. Clark H. Pinnock, *Reason Enough: A Case for the Christian Faith* (Downers Grove, IL: InterVarsity Press, 1980).
2. Pinnock, *Reason Enough*, pp. 9–10.
3. Pinnock, *Reason Enough*, p. 10.
4. Pinnock, *Reason Enough*, p. 69.
5. Pinnock, *Reason Enough*, pp. 17–18.
6. Pinnock, *Reason Enough*, p. 13.
7. Pinnock, *Reason Enough*, p. 18.
8. Pinnock, *Reason Enough*, p. 121.
9. Pinnock, *Reason Enough*, p. 13.
10. Pinnock, *Reason Enough*, pp. 121–22.
11. Pinnock, *Reason Enough*, p. 17.

# 11

# Experience, Proper Basicality, and Belief in God

*Robert Pargetter*

## 1. Introduction

Theists often acknowledge that if their belief in the existence of God is to count as rational, it cannot be that the belief is justified by or inferred from some other belief or beliefs which have general, rational acceptance. That is, there appear to be no generally accepted beliefs which will in turn give a justification of theism.

One response to this has been to account for belief in God as a basic belief. Of course this in itself does not make the belief rational, for that would require that the belief is a properly basic belief. And if belief in God is to be properly basic, it has plausibly been argued, it would need to be a belief grounded in or warranted by experience, in a way similar to many of our perceptual beliefs.

The problem with such an account of the rationality of belief in God is that it involves views about rationality, and epistemology generally, which are far from being generally accepted and noncontroversial. So without some development of the notion of proper basicality, especially where basic beliefs are grounded in experience, it is difficult to assess whether belief in God can reasonably be construed as a properly basic belief.

This paper seeks to develop an adequate account of properly basic belief, particularly where such beliefs are grounded in experience, to allow an evaluation of the contention that the belief in God could be properly basic. But we shall try to keep this account of proper basicality compatible with as wide a range of epistemic views as is possible. We shall endeavor to restrict ourselves to very plausible and generally acceptable views about belief formation and rationality. Thus our evaluation of belief in God as a properly basic belief will be as independent as possible of particular epistemic theories.

## 2. Basic Belief Grounded in Experience

We shall consider those properly basic beliefs which are rational because they are grounded in experience.[1] They are *basic* because they are not justified by, warranted by, or inferred from any other belief; they are *properly* basic because they are nonetheless appropriately grounded or warranted. Their warrant or grounding is in the experience or experiences of the person for whom they are properly basic.

It is clear that people, and many other kinds of sentient creatures, have perception- and belief-forming mechanisms which respond to various external and internal stimuli. The response to such a stimulus typically involves both the experience and the formation of one or more beliefs. We commonly accept that the beliefs are caused by the experiences, but the actual mechanism need not concern us. We certainly have counterfactual dependence of the belief(s) on the experience, so we will do no harm in maintaining the causal connection.[2] We normally have no control on the formation of the belief(s) (the reason for the qualification shall be made clear in a moment). The warrant or grounds for the belief we take to be experience. It would *seem rational* for the person to hold the belief(s) *because* of the experience.

This is a description of a process of belief formation which we will assume, in what follows, is roughly accurate for people like us. What we shall first question is the contention that it gives rise to *rational* beliefs. Should we accept that when A obtains a belief by this mechanism, a mechanism which we shall call $S_A$, that the belief formed in such circumstances, or which A is at least disposed to form in such circumstances, is rational for A (in those circumstances, at that time). It may be that we should not assume that A's belief is rational simply because of its mode of formation—that the belief is formed by $S_A$ (or because $S_A$ disposes A to form the belief) may not be *sufficient* to make a belief rational for A. There is one clear case in which the lack of sufficiency is exposed. Suppose the experience produces the belief $p$ in A, but A already has the belief $q$, and beliefs $p$ and $q$ are inconsistent or in some sense incompatible. It would not be rational for A to believe *both* $p$ and $q$. Maybe the belief is not formed in these circumstances (this is the reason for the "normally" qualifier used earlier). Perhaps A is disposed to form the belief, but the existence of the belief $q$ prevents it from forming. Or perhaps the belief is formed, and A must then engage in a belief revision process—perhaps conscious, perhaps unconscious—which renders A's system of beliefs consistent and in other ways rational. Perhaps this adjustment can only take place when A discerns incompatibility and, in the interim, an inherent irrationality remains in A's system of beliefs. Whatever the details of the process, A may end up believing $p$ but not believing $q$, or vice versa, or perhaps not believing either. So there can be cases where a belief of A which is grounded in experience is not rational for A (or the belief that would have been so grounded would not have been rational had it been formed—for simplicity in what follows we will talk as though the belief is formed). We shall not here further speculate on the nature of the revision process, or for the moment speculate on the principles which should prevail if such a revision process itself is to be rational, though the latter matter is one to which we shall return. Let us agree that there are such principles; and if a previously held belief of A, $q$, prevails and the belief $p$ grounded in experience does not prevail, then in those circumstances belief $q$ is a *defeater* of the belief *p* for A. So *p* being a basic belief grounded in experience does not ensure proper basicality of *p* for A in circumstances C. This failure happens when A has a belief *q* which is rational for A in C and which for A in C is a *defeater* of *p*. Note that this can happen whether or not A still believes *q* after the revision process. Note also that *q* may itself be a first-order belief, or a second-order belief, that is a belief about the nature of the beliefs formed or of other beliefs held.

Consider an example. Suppose a hand is held in front of A's eyes. A has a certain visual experience and forms the belief "There is a hand in front of me." Prima facie, this is a rational belief—it is not warranted by any other belief; it is warranted by, or grounded in, the experience itself. The prima facie nature of the rationality status is revealed because the rationality can be overridden. But it requires to be overridden, otherwise the belief is rational. If A holds a belief such as "My visual experiences are unreliable in my present circumstances," then this belief could well be a defeater of the belief about the hand for A. A maintains the defeating belief, and rejects the belief (or doesn't actually form it) based on the visual experience. If A had some other contrary belief, perhaps itself grounded in experience, it may defeat the belief about the hand and also may itself be abandoned by A.

(There is a complication where A may have a *partial* defeater, a belief that results in the belief being accepted but with only moderate confidence. Such a defeater would often be second-order, say a belief about the reliability of a belief formed in this way in these circumstances. However, we shall omit consideration of this complication in what follows).

Suppose there is no defeater for a belief grounded in experience, for the person at the time in the relevant circumstances. Is being counterfactually dependent on experience, or being caused by experience and being grounded in experience, sufficient for rational acceptance of the belief? That is, is the lack of an appropriate defeater sufficient for the proper basicality of a basic belief grounded in experience?

It could be urged that there are at least two other considerations that must be met before a basic belief is rational, that is, before it is properly basic.[3] First, we are not isolated persons—we could look for corroboration from others. We perhaps need to look for agreement between competent members of our belief-sharing community before a belief grounded in experience should be considered properly basic for any person. Second, perhaps we should consider features of the system of beliefs as a whole which include those beliefs based on experience that are in question, and compare them with related "alternative" systems of beliefs for the person in the circumstances at the time. It may be that a belief grounded in experience is properly basic only if it is part of a system of beliefs which has appropriate characteristics.

Although, as we shall see, discussion of these two considerations cannot be carried out independently of each other, we shall (as far as possible) look at them in turn.

## 3. Agreement about Basic Beliefs

Person A is like most (if not all) of us. A has an internal mechanism which has among its functions to respond to certain experiential inputs, the typical response being that A obtains some particular belief (perhaps to some degree, but we will omit this complication). These experiential inputs, which are internal to A, are themselves generally caused by external stimuli.

So if we stick a pin into A, A has some pain experience which produces the belief in A "I have a pain," or "I am in pain," or "I pain." We will take it as an empirical fact that the belief produced in such a situation is usually of this form. It is not "I seem to have a pain" or "I feel as if I pain." We also will take it as an empirical fact about A, and all or nearly all of us generally, that such beliefs are not in any way inferred by A from some intermediate belief state.

The pain example involves A's belief about A's mental state, but such basic beliefs are not restricted to beliefs about the mental. In our earlier example, we held a hand in front of A, and $S_A$ produced in A the belief "There is a hand in front of me." It too is basic, not inferred from other beliefs, but is produced by and grounded in the experiential input.

The beliefs that A obtains in this way seem to be paradigms of rationality. They are basic, but they also seem properly basic, provided A does not have an appropriate defeater belief. Yet these beliefs are not generally self-evident or infallibly held or incorrigible.[4] Maybe there are beliefs A could hold, warranted by or grounded in her experiences, which would be incorrigible, etc., but they are *not* (as a matter of fact) the sorts of beliefs that A, like the rest of us, typically forms as the result of perceptual experience. The belief "It seems to me that there is a hand in front of me" may be incorrigible as there may never be a defeater for such a belief, but this is not the kind of belief typically formed as a result of the experience. In most circumstances, provided the person holds no relevant defeaters for the belief, the person will on having a hand held in front of her form the belief, grounded in that experience, "There is a hand in front of me." But what besides the lack of defeaters is required for such a belief, grounded in experience, to be rational?

It is plausible that we may judge a basic belief of A, where there are no relevant defeaters, as properly basic for A if it is grounded in A's experience and $S_A$ is *reliable* with experiences of *this kind*.[5] And this reliability in turn could be related to *agreement* about such experientially grounded beliefs between A and other persons when in similar circumstances, and under similar external stimuli. When we have such agreement we would accept that the mechanisms of A and the others are functionally similar in these circumstances, and we believe that they are reliable in these circumstances—that is, they have a disposition to produce true beliefs. For we accept that there is a genetic and evolutionary story for why we have these functionally similar mechanisms, linking their functional roles to the nature of the circumstances surrounding the organism.

But we in fact moderate the requirement for agreement and corroboration. While we might regard general agreement as good evidence for reliability, we do not *require* such agreement, and in fact there are cases where it is rational to accept beliefs where there is not, and could not be, corroboration. Not only in some circumstances is corroboration not required in order for the person to be rational in accepting those beliefs grounded in her experience; others could in some such circumstances rationally accept those beliefs on the testimony of that person. And similarly in some cases where there is no corroboration for beliefs of a particular *kind*.

Suppose A and B generally form very similar basic beliefs under very similar

input stimuli in very similar circumstances. That is, A and B receiving external
stimuli which are prima facie very similar results in A and B forming (basic) beliefs
which are very similar. Hold your hand in front of each, and each believes that there
is a hand in front of her. Stick a pin in each and each believes she is in pain. And so
on. We may postulate, reasonably, that the mechanisms $S_A$ and $S_B$ are at least functionally very similar.

But suppose just occasionally this doesn't happen. What are prima facie very
similar external stimuli fail to produce very similar beliefs. It may be that beliefs are
produced in each, but they are very different beliefs; or it may be that there is no
corresponding belief formed in one person at all. What should we say, and what
should A and B say, about these sorts of cases?

There are three kinds of response. One is to doubt that the external stimuli were
similar after all. Prima facie they were, but really they are not. A second response
is to doubt whether the similar stimuli have in fact produced the same experiential
input to each of the two mechanisms. That is, there is some difference between A
and B such that when they receive *this kind* of stimuli they do not have the same
experiences; their perception mechanisms are different *in this range,* so to speak.
The third response is to doubt that the belief-forming mechanisms are the same in
*this range;* that is, although they have very similar experiences, these do not lead in
*this kind of case* to the formation of similar (basic) beliefs. And of course we could
also use more complicated combinations of these.

A response of kind one is rational provided we can at least make a prima facie,
independent case that the stimuli are different. For the nature of the external stimuli
are supervenient on the natural (physical) properties of the person (at the time) and
the circumstances. And in making this response there is a rejection of any need to
deny rationality to either of A and B. If there is, plausibly, a relevant difference in
external stimuli, then there is no requirement for A and B to form similar beliefs.
So we cannot look to agreement between them in these kinds of circumstances to
decide which of A and B is rational in her beliefs, or to look to the lack of agreement
to tell against the proper basicality of either's basic beliefs grounded in their respective experiences.

A response of kind three requires accepting that there is a relevant difference
between $S_A$ and $S_B$, provided that B does not now have a defeater which A lacks.
The experiential elements are the same, but the resulting beliefs are not; either different beliefs are formed, or perhaps in one case no belief is formed. We would generally entertain such a hypothesis when one belief-forming mechanism seems unreliable in forming *any* belief based on experience. For the postulated fault is in the
move from experience to belief, not in the having of experiences of a particular
kind. But it is not out of the question to reasonably suggest that just occasionally
the mechanism goes wrong. If there is general agreement between A and others, but
not B and others, *and* we have a justified belief that this lack of agreement is due to
a fault in A's belief-forming mechanism, then this would give us grounds to believe
that we would not be rational to accept beliefs of the appropriate kind on B's testimony. The lack of agreement may give us, or A, in such circumstances, a justification for a defeater to accepting beliefs based on B's testimony, testimony which
in turn involves beliefs based on B's experience. It may even give such a justification

for B to accept such a defeater herself. But the reasonableness of such a response to lack of agreement with others should be in terms of a justified defeater, perhaps justified by the lack of agreement. It also requires a justified belief, however such justification is to be achieved, that the lack of agreement is due to a fault in A's belief-forming mechanism, for, as we shall see, if it is believed to be due to other factors, there may be a different response to the lack of agreement.

We are left then with responses of the second kind, and it is this kind of response that is most important for our interests. We respond to a lack of agreement in beliefs grounded in experience, by persons in apparently similar circumstances with apparently similar belief-forming mechanisms, by postulating that they have different experiences when they have stimuli of *this kind*. We shall attend to this case in a little more detail.

Suppose A and B taste a phenol-laced but otherwise tasteless food item. It could well be that A on the basis of this stimulus has a certain perceptual experience leading to the belief "This item is bitter," while B analogously arrives at "This item is tasteless," or maybe B doesn't form a belief at all. Or if an appropriately colored hand is put in front of each of A and B against a color-blind test background, A may as a result of the experiential input form the belief "There is a hand in front of me," while B may not form that belief.

With such cases we accept the similarity of external stimuli. What could we point to in order to explain (in a non–question-begging way) the difference? We believe rather that A and B have different perceptual mechanisms; they do not have the same experiences, and hence should not be expected to (and in fact it would be surprising if they did) form the same basic beliefs on the basis of the experiences.

What beliefs should A and B have in such cases? It seems that A rationally could believe that phenol is bitter, while B could rationally believe that phenol is tasteless. And this is reinforced when we find people at large divide into two groups. One plausible move is to relativize bitterness. It is rational for A to believe that phenol is bitter, for phenol is bitter to A, while it is not rational for B to believe that phenol is bitter, for phenol is tasteless to B. Phenol shows us that bitterness is a relational property between a tasteable item and a person (at a time). For an item to have bitterness is for that item to be able to produce the right experience in people, and the same item may have it for some people and lack it for others. Similarly the hand against the color-blind background.[6]

To deny that bitterness of items is really relational would require us to explain *why* A and B generally agree about experiences and form similar basic beliefs grounded in experience, and only disagree in these unusual cases; and why the population similarly divides into two groups. And to explain why we believe that we ought to be able to ultimately find out what is different about the two perceptual mechanisms that causes the different experiences, and to make sense of the possible unifying operation we may one day be able to give to A or B (to bring them into agreement).

But a move to relativize in such cases of lack of agreement is not the only strategy, and it is not always the best. If one person, say A, is unique (or one of a very small minority), we may not generally relativize the property. We might continue to believe items are either bitter or not, except that A can experience bitterness from some nonbitter items. We might take a similar approach if we think, for some reason, that $S_A$ is defective. W would not rationally believe that an item is bitter on testimony from A, for A is unreliable in these matters, and A may also come to believe that she is unreliable in matters of bitterness. Once A has this belief, it could well act as a defeater when A experiences bitterness. And A could well reject as not rational beliefs like "This item is bitter," formed in her by $S_A$ when she experiences the item's bitterness, and believe instead "This item seems bitter to me, but I am unreliable in such things."

Here is an example where the lack of agreement *may* lead A to deny that one of her basic beliefs (grounded in experience) is rational. There is in fact still an appropriate defeater for A, for A believes that $S_A$ is unreliable in some range. But it is not a defeater she needed to have at the time of the experience—she may obtain it later. At the time of the experience A's belief was properly basic, but later when she has the defeater the belief is not properly basic. A has had to revise her beliefs in order to maintain rationality.

We have suggested that before she obtained knowledge of the lack of corroboration, before the defeater was there, the belief was rational for A. But really should we require that she *needs* evidence that the mechanism is *reliable for the range,* enough evidence to make a belief to that effect rational, *before* the basic belief is properly basic?

There are two reasons to reject this suggestion. First, clearly inductive principles are involved in belief formation and such principles involve forming beliefs in new cases on the basis of past success, and every new case will be different in kind in some way from every other case we have dealt with in the past.[7] Hence we would never be in the position of knowing that our mechanism was reliable in *exactly* this kind of case.

Second, the "odd-bod" is not always wrong. In the hypothetical case where one person found phenol bitter, but she was unique in this experience, it seemed that the view of the community at large should prevail: the "odd-bod" should believe a defeater, and we should not accept her testimony as reliable in this area. The case where we think A is hallucinating, or where we believe that A is schizophrenic, are even more extreme examples. But sometimes the "odd-bod" prevails. We have varying precision in our perceptual mechanisms. We might all fail to have an auditory experience, except A has one in the same circumstances because A has the best hearing. Similarly with seeing, and the other senses. Not only should A claim proper basicality for her beliefs, despite lack of agreement with others, but in time the others will come to accept these beliefs on A's testimony. Undoubtedly A will eventually believe she has special perceptual skills, and this will explain why others rely on her; but she does not need this belief before her basic beliefs are properly basic. In fact she may be unable to rationally hold this belief about her skills if she needed to have previously justified each instance of such experience-grounded belief by corroboration.[8] We do need to say more about why A fails to get a defeater belief with the lack of corroboration, and why others come to believe that A has special perceptual skills. This is a matter we shall return to shortly. But it is important now to note that she does not always form defeaters in such circumstances, nor should she, nor should she require a belief about established reliability before any belief grounded in experience is properly basic.

A final note on cases where we think A and B have different experiences yet receive the same external stimuli in similar circumstances. There is an important supervenience here. We believe that if A and B had the same kind of perceptual experience then they would have formed the same belief, provided neither had a defeater for such a belief. That is, in cases of the kind where we believe that the external stimuli are the same but the experiences are different, we must accept the existence of some significant difference between the perceptual mechanism of A and B producing a difference in perceptual experience, and the difference in perceptual mechanism is, in principle at least, something we could in the future isolate and identify.

In summary then, agreement with others or corroboration cannot be laid down as a condition for rationality for beliefs grounded in experience, that is, as a necessary requirement for proper basicality. Lack of agreement *may* justify a person believing a proposition which acts as a defeater for such a belief or beliefs; but it may not. It *may* also give others grounds for defeaters which prevent them from accepting beliefs on the basis of testimony from those who in turn ground these beliefs in experience; but it also may not. In fact we *may* decide to accept such beliefs on the basis of their testimony *just because* we cannot ground these beliefs in our own experiences. We will need to sort out how such diversity is possible, and why such alternative responses can be rational. We will see that it relates to holistic features of systems of beliefs, and thus is connected with the other suggestion we noted earlier in seeking sufficiency for proper basicality. We now turn to this other suggestion.

## 4. Holistic Features of Systems of Beliefs

For rationality we have postulated that individual beliefs need to be justified by or warranted by other beliefs, or the beliefs need to be properly basic. But, prima facie, not all such *systems of beliefs* need be *equally* rational.

It is widely agreed that holistic requirements such as coherency, consistency, simplicity, and so on, may be required for the rationality of a system of beliefs.[9] Perhaps also systems which are appropriately dynamic, that are responsive to change and to the addition of new beliefs, and that eliminate apparent incoherences, are to be considered more rational than other systems which lack such features.

It may also be argued that we should look to more pragmatic elements in assessing systems of beliefs for rationality. Which system leads to a more useful, workable, viable, happy, etc., life? Which disposes the person to adapt to and survive in his or her environment, or perhaps in a range of possible environments? Which system of beliefs contributes most to the individuals's well-being?

Take the survival potential of a system of beliefs. It seems highly analogous to the dispositional property of fitness of a biological organism.

For an organism to be the fittest in a particular environment it must have a survival advantage over its competitors for life resources in that environment, and such survival is in terms of the action of natural laws and processes, generally relating to the individual obtaining the necessary resources required for the natural functions associated with existing and reproducing. And, of course, if the environment itself is showing variation, the fitness will take into account the ability to cope with the variation in such a varying environment. Fitness is a relational dispositional property, relating the organism to its environment. Fitness is supervenient on the phenotypical (morphological, psychological, and behavioral) features of the organism. It is the fittest organism in virtue of these features.[10]

The survival potential of a system of beliefs is supervenient on the beliefs and their internal relationships, and it is a relational property between the person with the beliefs and the circumstances in which the person is endeavoring to achieve physical, emotional, and psychological survival. It relates to the potential survival advantage that a person with the set of beliefs has in those circumstances. And the survival is in terms of the person remaining not only alive, but living as an autonomous and independent being. Surviving by having to be locked up in an institution doesn't count, just as an organism surviving in a zoo doesn't count for fitness. The survival advantage will also reflect the ability to adapt to the likely changes in the circumstances.

It seems that systems of beliefs, or at least persons with them, have holistic properties like survival potential, and most likely there are a number of such important holistic properties. They are not merely formal logical properties like consistency, but are more pragmatic and contingent in nature. It seems that such features are essentially linked to rationality, and are empirically discernable just by observing how individuals with those beliefs generally cope with and survive in the world, and are happy and autonomous individuals.

Let us agree then that there are these sorts of holistic properties of systems of beliefs, which we will call *holistic features for the rationality of a system of beliefs.* We need a lot more work to be done on such features before we will know all we need to know about them. And we here should not attach much significance to the suggested list of such features. Whether or not survival potential, for instance, has this close link with rationality is controversial. But it does seem noncontroversial' that there are such holistic features of rational systems of beliefs, and their existence is essential to fully explicate the notion of rationality that we need in epistemology. It might be argued that these are related to rationality of a different kind, for instance to practical rationality, whereas the relevant sense of rationality required for the purpose at hand is epistemic rationality. Those who have discussed the acceptance and rejection of scientific theories have long given up the viability of this distinction, and since the writings of Quine on holism it is now widely agreed that holistic considerations play an essential part in any adequate theory of (epistemic) rationality. Besides, the essential connection between rationality on the one hand, and coherency, explanatory power, survival potential, and so forth, on the other, requires that rationality is of the usual epistemic kind, for this connection only holds if we are concerned with how the system of beliefs relates to what is true.

For instance, survival potential will be a function of the successful predictions which follow from a system of beliefs, and the success of such predictions will at least in part be a function of what is actually the case, that is, the nature of the external world.

What needs to be noted is that these holistic features cannot be identified with any particular internal requirements on the beliefs that make up the system. Two different systems of beliefs could be equally rational even though their component beliefs and the internal relationships between them are very different. Perhaps there is a most rational belief system when truth and belief coincide, but once we move away from this, various systems of beliefs could be equally rational. This again is analogous to two organisms being equally fit in an environment with very different phenotypical bases for their fitness.

It seems that these holistic features for rationality may supply some of the answers to the problem raised for proper basicality of beliefs grounded in experience.

We saw earlier that a requirement for proper basicality for a belief grounded in experience is that there is no defeater for such a belief. It seems plausible to say that a sufficient requirement for proper basicality of such a belief is that there is no rationally held defeater *and* that the resulting belief system is at least as rational holistically as the belief system that would result if the basic belief was rejected. In fact, given the way resolution takes place when there is a defeater, the no defeater requirement may well be subsumed into the holistic requirement, but we can afford to be ambiguous on this matter.

Three comments on this contention. First, we should not expect a proof that this requirement is sufficient, but the claim of sufficiency must at least be plausible. The plausibility stems from the open-ended nature of the holistic requirements for the comparative rationality of some belief system. Yet the requirement does not degenerate because of its open-endedness, for such requirements have other general applications in epistemology, and relate to theory justification in science. Second, we can question the "at least as good as" requirement. Why not the requirement that the resulting system is better than the one that would result if the basic belief was rejected? Since basic beliefs are caused by the experience, it seems that we should minimize the conditions where they are rejected, or where revisions are required by a belief system which undermine the grounding of a belief by experience. The suggested sufficiency condition seems to give the minimum rejection of beliefs grounded in experience, and this is the strongest condition we should demand. Third, we now have the promised explanation as to when agreement in belief between persons in similar circumstances is important and when it is not. When the belief clearly gives us a better belief system, one which obviously has the desirable holistic features of rationality, and has them to a greater degree than the alternative or alternatives, then we can reject any requirement for agreement. Of course, if there is no agreement, the system of beliefs will be likely to include the belief "Others do not have this belief grounded in experience," and we require that even with this belief the system is still holistically as rational.

We now have what appears to be an adequate account of proper basicality for a belief grounded in experience. It is an account which gives guidance as to when others should accept such a belief on testimony, even though they themselves lack the experiential grounding for the beliefs. It will be when on accepting such a belief from another (on their testimony) they obtain a belief system which is at least as good as the alternative belief system which would have resulted by not accepting that belief.

It might be thought that in the case of testimony we do not need to minimize the acceptance criterion. Why not require in this case that the system is clearly better on holistic grounds? But testimony provides an experience, and the belief is formed by that experience as long as there is no defeater. For consistency then, *this* kind of experience—hearing what others say—should be treated in the same way as other experiences. Hence it seems we should maintain the same standard of holistic evaluation in the case of accepting a belief grounded in the experience of testimony (rather than by direct experience relating to the content of the belief).

A final point, though, is to note that the criterion is ambiguous. Survival potential, etc., will in general depend not only on what A believes, but also on what other persons surrounding A believe. What others believe about an individual who believes what A believes will in part determine the survival potential of what A believes. What assumptions do we make about the kind of community we take A to be in when evaluating the survival potential of what A believes? A strictly pragmatic answer would require that we take it that the others believe what they would believe if A does have the belief system in question. An alternative answer is to take the others to believe what they rationally should believe given A has the system of beliefs in question. However, the most principled answer is to note that rationality not only applies to particular beliefs (of a person), to particular persons themselves (in virtue of their system of beliefs), but also to communities of persons (each with a system of beliefs). We can look for analogous holistic features of rationality in communities. And it is in a rational community, thus defined, that we assess the rationality of a particular belief system. We will here be content to note this ambiguity, and assume its satisfactory resolution in the rest of our discussions.

## 5. Belief in God as a Properly Basic Belief

Luke Skywalker did not know about The Force until he met Obi-Won Kenobi. Obi-Won, a Jedi Knight, knew of The Force by direct experience. His belief was grounded in his feeling of The Force. Perhaps this had not always been the case— he had been trained by Yoda, the Jedi Master—and this is the sort of result such training can have. But Luke believed in The Force on the testimony of Obi-Won, a testimony he was rational to accept given the kind of system of beliefs this gave him. He was able to explain and make sense of so much he saw about him: the lives and powers of Obi-Won and Yoda, the struggle between the Emperor and the Rebels, the history of his own family. It gave him direction and survival potential, and he found a new meaning and purpose to life.

In time, with training as a Jedi Knight by Obi-Won and Yoda, Luke too could feel the power of The Force. He sensed disturbances in it, and gained knowledge and power directly from it. His belief then too was grounded in experience, and rationally so. There was no relevant defeater for such a belief for Luke, and his belief system, including such a basic belief, had all the required holistic features of rationality in a fairly rational community. Han Solo was a skeptic about The Force, but with time he also came to believe in it. He never experienced The Force, and his belief was always warranted by beliefs based on the testimony of others. But his resulting belief system was made more rational by accepting the beliefs based on the testimony of Luke, Obi-Won, and Princess Leia.[11]

Alvin Plantinga argues that many theists believe in God for reasons which seem to be of exactly the same kind of reasons as those which Luke Skywalker and Obi-Won Kenobi have for believing in The Force in our story. Their belief in God is caused by and grounded in experience, and is not inferred from nor does it gain warrant from other beliefs. Given there are no defeaters of this belief for them, their belief is *properly basic,* and thus is rational.[12]

Let us grant Plantinga's empirical claim, for clearly this is an accurate reconstruction of why many theists take their theism to be rational. Plantinga identifies such theism as being of a Calvinist tradition, but perhaps he underestimates how widely his reconstrual applies. This probably depends on some of the detailed points concerning the nature of the experience. Plantinga's list of experiences include being directly aware of God speaking to one, feeling a Divine disapproval, and the feelings of God's forgiveness, all such experiences being in the appropriate circumstances. He also mentions the possibility of humans having a disposition to believe in a supreme designer in circumstances where they are confronted with natural beauty or order. He notes that a belief in God may be inferential from such basic beliefs, but (rightly) notes that, for simplicity, it is harmless enough to treat belief in God itself as being properly basic.[13]

Some theists would claim that they do in fact experience the direct presence of God, and that the experience may range over a great diversity of circumstances, perhaps even over all circumstances, though the nature of the experience is plausibly not exactly the same in all circumstances. These experiences are not usually episodes of extreme religious or mystical experience, such as those reported by St. Teresa and St. John of the Cross, though it is not out of the question that some such episodes could be made compatible with this sort of justified theistic belief. But the kinds of experiences that John Hick has pointed to as giving an experiential basis for rational belief in God would certainly be taken as experiences which could ground properly basic theistic belief.[14]

There are three matters that we will address in considering the proper basicality of belief in God. First, the question as to whether there are defeaters for the theist for such a basic belief, and which the theist should rationally hold. Second, the significance and implication of the empirical fact that many persons do *not* have these experiences in very similar circumstances, and how this bears on the question of rational theistic belief both for those who do, and for those who do not, have the experiences. Third, the question as to whether consideration of holistic features of systems of beliefs relevant for rationality will lead to the proper basicality of belief in God.

## 5.1. Defeaters

Suppose A forms the belief, or is disposed to form the belief, that God exists, as a result of some experience in some particular circumstance. What could act as a defeater for such a belief for A?

Obviously it could be a belief about the circumstances. If it was in the circumstance of having tried a new drug, or having had doubtful scallops the night before, or some similar such circumstance, it seems that there is an obvious defeater which should prevent A from rationally accepting a belief grounded in an unusual experience. It is for this reason that the experiences of St. John of the Cross and other mystics are problematic. Their mode of preparation seems to be exactly right for producing hallucinations, and in such circumstances we should be cautious about their beliefs grounded in experience. We certainly have rational defeaters which may well prevent us accepting their beliefs on their testimony and it seems that they also ought to have, if rational, such defeaters.

But let us suppose that A's circumstances seem normal, and that there is a range of circumstances in which A's experiences are such that they lead, via the internal mechanism $S_A$, to the formation of a basic belief that there is a God, a belief that is grounded in those experiences. What then are the possible defeaters? Plantinga considers and (rightly) rejects the suggestion that there is a general sophisticated intellectual belief in the community that God does not exist which A should share with others, and which would act as a defeater for A for the basic belief that God exists.[15]

There are two worries about taking this belief as a defeater. First, why does A accept the defeater belief, that is, what would make it rational for A? Because others accept it. But this should only be a rational belief if it is justified on holistic grounds as part of the most rational system of beliefs for A, or because A has reasons which justify atheism. But what are these reasons, and are they *still* reasons given the experiences A now has had? This will again require further provision of rational reasons for atheism, or it leads us again to those holistic features relevant to assessing A's belief system and modifications to it. Second, suppose there is a potential defeater. There is the question of what belief defeats what belief. Does the defeater prevail, or does the new basic belief grounded in experience prevail? As there is a prima facie case that each is rational, the answer to this question will be determined by consideration of those holistic features of systems of beliefs.

Plantinga also considers an obvious defeater (perhaps related to the one just discussed). The belief A has, or ought to have, about the existence of evil. But this is not straightforwardly a defeater.[16] What is required is that A has the belief that there is evil which is unnecessary if God exists. Now it seems *that* belief is either question begging or plain unjustified. But allowing it for the moment, it is again a question of which belief defeats which, and this again is a matter that will require holistic consideration of the alternative belief systems.

A passing note on the belief that there is evil. What is surprising to many atheists is that this is not taken by many theists to even give a prima facie case against the existence of God. For some theists, this could be because they regard such a case as question begging.[17] But for those who widely (or even continuously) experience the presence of God, the experience of evil does not alleviate that experience of God. The nature of the experience could vary, but it does not need to take on a "Godless" nature. (Even Obi-Won Kenobi experienced disturbances in The Force when the power of The Dark Side was manifested, but the experience of The Force was not lost.)

It may be thought that we are sidestepping the obvious defeater. A had the experience, but many do not have such an experience in the same or very similar circumstances. Hence this lack of agreement or corroboration itself supplies A with a defeater. And certainly it might be thought to supply anyone who does not experience the presence of God with a defeater to accepting the belief on the grounds of A's testimony. This brings us to our second matter for consideration.

## 5.2. Variation in Experience

A experiences the presence of God, B does not, and the circumstances are as similar as we can make them. What are we to make of this?

We noted earlier that this does not necessarily provide the basis for a rational defeater for A, or for a belief that would prevent B and others from adopting A's belief which for A is grounded in experience, on the basis of A's testimony. We need to examine the details.

B is not having the same experiences as A in the circumstances, but A is not alone. There is at least a reasonably large group of theists who claim to have experiences of this kind, in a large range of circumstances. Hence the view that there is a malfunction in $S_A$ seems implausible. It also seems implausible seeing A (and the others) generally agree about experiences with most other people most of the time. It does not rule out the possibility [that] A and the others all have something wrong with their perception and belief-forming mechanisms. Or perhaps they have special perception abilities. But given there are no discernible differences in these mechanisms, it seems very unlikely. It is also implausible that there really are different external stimuli acting on A and B, unless God is only stimulating the perception mechanisms in A. Perhaps such stimuli are *internal,* which would explain why B and many others do not have the experiences.

But is it true that we have no reason to doubt the reliability of A's relevant perceptual mechanism $S_A$? For unlike the case of the perceptual experiences considered earlier, aren't we ignorant about the mechanism by which A has her theistic experiences? We may have no reason to doubt that A and B differ in their modular delivery mechanisms, the sensory organs, which are responsible for normal perceptual experiences, but why do we think that the same mechanisms are responsible for A's "God experiences," and if they are not, then isn't it the case that we know nothing about the mechanism in A which is responsible?

The reason for not doubting the reliability of the $S_A$ involved in the formation of A's basic theistic belief rests on two considerations. First, the similarity between A and B is not limited to mere similarity of the sensory organs, but includes general physical and neurological similarity. If there is a special mechanism in A, it would need to be nonphysical. Second, there is no reason to suppose the experiential input should not be by the normal sensory mechanisms. The fact that the beliefs formed are not simple perceptual beliefs does not require a special sensory input. The belief "There is a hand in front of me" is a belief about a hand, not about hand-like sensations. Similarly the belief "God is present" is a belief about God, not a belief about God-like sensations. Difference in beliefs does not require a corresponding difference in the kind of sensory input. Consider how mathematical beliefs might form after sensory input, yet no special mathematics sensory mechanism is required.

If A and B have similar, reliable, sensory mechanisms, how are we to account for the difference in the beliefs formed? It may be that A has an acquired skill or improved awareness required to have the perceptual experience. Musicians have such skills. Also, one can improve auditory and visual perception with training. Luke Skywalker was trained to feel The Force. Many theists claim to have developed the ability to directly experience God. Or it just may be left as unexplained why A and B differ in their experiences.

These brief discussions seem to demonstrate that variation in experience, that is, some people having the experiences while others do not, does not *in itself* constitute grounds for A adopting a defeater for a belief in God grounded in her direct experience. Maybe, on careful examination, particular details will warrant A accepting a defeater, but this should not be presumed without the provision of such details, and there is no reason in advance for A adopting a defeater on the basis of variation in experience. Thus if A is to be denied proper basicality for her belief in God grounded in experience, it must be because that belief leads to a system of beliefs which does not score well on a holistic evaluation of rationality as a system of beliefs.

What should be the attitude of B and others to A's testimony about her experiences? There is at least a prima facie plausibility to the claim that B should adopt A's belief. We have pointed out that A has generally been reliable in beliefs based on experience, and we know that some do have experiences which others do not which are the basis for rational beliefs. So providing B has no independent reasons for accepting defeaters for this belief of A, or independent reasons for not accepting A's belief on the basis of A's testimony, and providing there are no discernible features of A's internal mechanisms to suggest selective unreliability, there is a strong prima facie case that B ought to accept A's belief on the basis of A's testimony. There is, in fact, a problem in rejecting A's testimony. A's testimonies in the past have been reliable, and the testimony itself constitutes an experience for B which would in most circumstances effect a corresponding belief in B. Why not accept A's testimony—what is B's defeater for this?[18]

It is plausible that perhaps in time B too could gain this ability to directly perceive God—as Luke and Princess Leia learnt to feel The Force. Or maybe B will always be like Han Solo. But this is unimportant. What will determine whether B should accept A's testimony will be exactly the same as what will determine A's claim to proper basicality. It will depend on the holistic features that determine the rationality of B's, and A's, overall systems of beliefs.

## 5.3. Holistic Evaluation

A's claim for proper basicality for her belief in God, grounded as it is in her experience, will ultimately depend on the holistic evaluation of the system of beliefs that A has with this belief compared with that which she would have if she rejected this belief. Similarly with B and others concerning whether they should accept A's testimony, and accept A's belief as their own on that basis.

Note that A and B will never be the same again. Before the experience A has the belief that she can reliably base beliefs on her perceptual experience. If she now rejects the belief in the presence of God, she also has modified her belief in her own perceptual reliability. And if she accepts the belief as properly basic, her belief system is also radically different.

Similarly with B. B has the belief that A's testimony is reliable, and that she can accept beliefs on the basis of A's testimony. If now she rejects such testimony, then B's system of beliefs is still quite different, and it also would be very different if B accepts theistic belief on the basis of A's testimony.

What holistic evaluation comes to is to consider the survival potential, meaningfulness, usefulness, cohesiveness, explanatory potential, contribution to general well-being, and so forth, of the two competing systems of beliefs for each of A and B. And of course there is the contention, common among theists, that the theistic belief system is clearly advantageous in these regards. Many atheists deny this, but of course questions about futility are held to be particularly troublesome for the atheist.[19]

We shall not here consider this holistic evaluation in detail, for, as we noted earlier, it is not completely clear exactly which features are relevant, and there is no general agreement about how such an evaluation should be carried out. But it seems plausible that the required comparisons can be made, and the matter is, at least in principle, decideable.

Notice that this is independent of what B experiences. B may claim to have no experiences of God's presence, or even claim to experience God's nonexistence (whatever that kind of experience could be like). What is needed is the holistic evaluation of B's system of beliefs if B were to accept a belief grounded in A's testimony, and a comparison of this with the system formed if B were to reject A's testimony.

It is not new to argue for the rationality of belief in God on the grounds of the overall, holistic, rationality of various systems of beliefs which include theistic belief.[20] But that is not what is here being suggested. The suggestion is that theism for many may be a basic belief grounded in experience, and the proper basicality of such belief for any such person is established by the holistic rationality of the resulting overall belief system. Similarly theism for many others may be grounded in the experience of others' testimonies, others who have experienced God's existence, and the rationality of such resulting belief systems will again depend on holistic evaluation.

In summary, then, the claim of proper basicality for belief in God, grounded in experience, will depend ultimately on reliable persons having such experiences in circumstances which do not undermine their reliability, and for the resulting systems of beliefs to fare well on holistic evaluation for rationality. The rationality of those who do not share these experiences in accepting such beliefs on the basis of testimony, will similarly depend on the holistic evaluation for rationality of their resulting systems of beliefs.[21]

## Notes

1. A general discussion of such beliefs, and their relevance to belief in God, is given in Alvin Plantinga, "Is Belief in God Properly Basic?," *Nous* 15 (1981):41–53 (reprinted in Part III of this volume, pp. 133–41; all other citations are from this reprint), and in his "Rationality and Religious Belief," *Contemporary Philosophy of Religion,* eds. Steven M. Cahn and David Shatz (New York: Oxford University Press, 1982). More detailed discussions of the epistemic issue are in Roderick Chisholm, *Theory of Knowledge,* 2nd ed. (Englewood Cliffs, NJ: Prentice-Hall, 1977); and in his *The Problem of the Criterion* (Milwaukee: Marquette University Press, 1973). Also see Jonathan Dancy, *Introduction to Contemporary Epistemology* (Oxford, Engl.: Basil Blackwell, 1985). A more recent discussion of the particular issue is to be found in Robert Audi, "Direct Justification, Evidential Dependence, and Theistic Belief," in *Rationality, Religious Belief, and Moral Commitment,* eds. Robert Audi and William J. Wainwright (Ithaca, NY, and London: Cornell University Press, 1986).

2. The relationship between causation and counterfactual dependence is discussed in David Lewis, "Causation," *The Journal of Philosophy* 70 (1973).

3. Robert Audi, "Direct Justification," considers various suggestions of necessary conditions for proper basicality, but reaches no definite conclusions on such requirements. His suggestions cut across our discussions, but it would not seem that he raises additional plausible requirements.

4. See Plantinga, "Rationality and Religious Belief," and the discussion of this in Phillip Quinn, "In Search of the Foundations of Theism," *Faith and Philosophy* 2 (1985): 469–86. See also Alvin Plantinga, "The Foundations of Theism: A Reply," *Faith and Philosophy* 3 (1986): 298–313.

5. The relationship between rationality and reliability is discussed in Alvin Goldman, "What is Justified Belief?" in *Justification and Knowledge: New Studies in Epistemology,* ed. George S. Pappas (Dordrecht, Neth.: D. Reidel, 1979), though we shall not couch our discussion in his framework. See also his *Epistemology and Cognition* (Cambridge, MA: Harvard University Press, 1986).

6. See Frank Jackson and Robert Pargetter, "Objectivist's Guide to Subjectivism About Colour," *Revue Internationale de Philosophie 41e année* 160 (1987).

7. See a discussion of what differences matter in Frank Jackson and Robert Pargetter, "Confirmation and the Nomological," *Canadian Journal of Philosophy* 10 (1980): 415–28.

8. This kind of case seems to count against at least one of the suggested requirements for proper basicality discussed by Robert Audi, "Direct Justification."

9. These features came into prominence for analytical philosophers with W. V. O. Quine, "Two Dogmas of Empiricism," *Philosophy Review* 60 (1951): 20–43; and Quine and J. S. Ullian, *Web of Belief* (New York: Random House, 1970), though there is a long history to such matters, including the works of Hegel and his followers, and the pragmatists. More recent discussions include J. L. Pollock, *Knowledge and Justification* (Princeton, NJ: Princeton University Press, 1974); and L. Bonjour, "The Coherence Theory of Empirical Knowledge," *Philosophical Studies* 30 (1976): 281–312.

10. See Eliott Sober, *The Nature of Selection* (Cambridge MA: 1984); Robert Pargetter,

"Fitness," *Pacific Philosophical Quarterly* 68 (1987): 44–56; and Elizabeth Prior, Robert Pargetter, and Frank Jackson, "Three Theses About Dispositions," *American Philosophical Quarterly* 19 (1982): 251–58.

11. The popular *Star Wars* films and paperback books by George Lucas form the basis for this story.

12. See Plantinga, "Is Belief in God Properly Basic?," and "Reason and Belief in God." See also William P. Alston, "Religious Experience and Religious Belief," *Nous* 16 (1982): 3–12 (reprinted in Part IV of this volume, pp. 295–303).

13. See "Is Belief in God Properly Basic?," p. 138 above.

14. See the section of William P. Alston and Richard B. Brandt, *The Problems of Philosophy* (Boston: Allyn and Bacon, 1967) citing William James, "Are Men Ever Directly Aware of God?" and F. C. Happold, *Mysticism* (Harmondsworth, Middlesex [Engl.]: Pelican, 1963). Also see Chapter 7 of John Hick's *Arguments for the Existence of God* (New York: Macmillan, 1970). Hick's views can also be found in the paper by him in this volume, pp. 302–19.

15. The question of various defeaters is discussed in Phillip L. Quinn, "In Search of the Foundations of Theism," and also in Plantinga, "A Reply."

16. See Plantinga, "A Reply"; and Quinn, "In Search of Foundations."

17. See Robert Pargetter, "Evil as Evidence Against the Existence of God," *Mind* 85 (1976): 242–45; and "Evil as Evidence," *Sophia* 21 (1982): 11–15.

18. The inductive basis for such practices is discussed in Plantinga, "Is Belief in God Properly Basic?," p. 140 above, which follows the thinking of Chisholm, *Theory of Knowledge* and *The Problem of the Criterion*.

19. See, for example, the section "Flight from Meaninglessness" in A. K. Bierman and James A. Gould, *Philosophy for a New Generation* (New York: Macmillan, 1970); see also W. D. Joske, "Philosophy and the Meaning of Life," *Australasian Journal of Philosophy* 52 (1974): 93–104.

20. See Bierman and Gould, *Philosophy for a New Generation*; and W. D. Joske, "Philosophy and the Meaning of Life."

21. Robert Young, John Bigelow, William P. Alston, and other readers have given me useful comments on an earlier version of this paper.

# 12

# Belief in God Is Not Properly Basic

*Stewart C. Goetz*

## I

In this article I shall concern myself with the question: "Is some type of justification required in order for belief in God to be rational?" Many philosophers and theologians in the past would have responded affirmatively to this question. However, in our own day, there are those who maintain that natural theology in any form is not necessary. This is because of the rise of a different understanding of the nature of religious belief. Unlike what most people in the past thought, religious belief is not in any sense arrived at or inferred on the basis of other known propositions. On the contrary, belief in God is taken to be as basic as a person's belief in the existence of himself, of the chair in which he is sitting, or the past. The old view that there must be a justification of religious belief, whether known or unknown, is held to be mistaken. One of the most outspoken advocates of this view is Alvin Plantinga.[1] According to Plantinga the mature theist ought not to accept belief in God as a conclusion from other things he believes. Rather, he should accept it as basic, as a part of the bedrock of his noetic structure. "The mature theist *commits* himself to belief in God; this means that he accepts belief in God as basic."[2]

In what follows I would like to examine and question the arguments Plantinga uses to support the view that religious belief ought to be basic in a person's epistemological structure. I will argue that belief in God *ought* not to be considered as basic because it *cannot* be. Belief in God is not basic because it is inferred, and thus based on a more basic proposition held to be true by the person doing the believing. In short, I shall maintain that an inference is needed if belief in God is to be considered rational.

## II

According to Plantinga, both the traditional natural theologian's (e.g., Aquinas, Descartes, Locke, *et al.*) and the traditional nontheist's (W. K. Clifford is Plantin-

Reprinted from *Religious Studies* 19 (1983), by permission of Cambridge University Press. Notes edited.

ga's chief example) position with regard to belief in God is based on some form of epistemological evidentialism. The evidentialist claims that belief in God is "irrational or unreasonable or not rationally acceptable or intellectually irresponsible or noetically substandard" unless there are sufficient reasons for it.[3] Thus the evidentialist denies that belief in God is, in Plantinga's terms, "properly basic."[4] In an evidentialist epistemology a proposition *p* is properly basic for a person S if and only if *p* is not accepted on the basis of any other beliefs or propositions. Plantinga maintains that the evidentialist position is rooted in a foundationalist epistemology. Basic propositions, which form the foundational set F of a person's noetic structure, are propositions which are not inferred from other propositions. The propositions in F are supposed to compose the evidential set of propositions E such that a person's belief in God is rational if and only if it is evident with respect to E. What Plantinga wants to know is how a proposition gets into the set F and why it is wrong to think (as most people have thought) that a belief in God is itself in F. A person knows the propositions in the foundation set F of his noetic structure, but not in virtue of other propositions, and Plantinga wants to know why belief in God cannot be a member of F.

Plantinga argues that if the evidentialist is to support his view of religious belief he must produce some necessary and sufficient conditions of proper basicality and show that belief in God does not satisfy those conditions. People whom Plantinga terms "classical foundationalists" have traditionally held that a proposition *p* is properly basic for a person S if and only if *p* is either self-evident or incorrigible for S (modern foundationalism) or either self-evident or 'evident to the senses' for S (ancient and medieval foundationalism). Examples of self-evident propositions are

1. $2 + 1 = 3$,
2. No man is both married and unmarried,
3. Redness is distinct from greenness,

and

4. The whole is greater than the part.

An example of an incorrigible proposition is

5. I seem to see a red book.

Propositions that are evident to the senses are

6. There is an ashtray on my desk,

and

7. I am wearing shoes.

The outstanding characteristics of self-evident propositions are that they are necessary truths and are such that one simply sees them to be true upon grasping or understanding the meanings of their terms. Moreover, a self-evident proposition is person-relative; that is, what is self-evident to one person might not be to another. An incorrigible proposition is one which a person could neither mistakenly believe nor disbelieve. Propositions that are evident to the senses are known immediately and grounded in a use of one's senses.

According to Plantinga, the classical foundationalist's criterion for proper basicality is something like the following:

8. For any proposition A and person S, A is properly basic for S if and only if A is either incorrigible for S or self-evident to S, or evident to the senses for S.

Now how can a person know a proposition like (8) to be true? Certainly, says Plantinga, (8) is neither self-evident nor incorrigible. If it is not, it is not basic. How, then, can the classical foundationalist lay it down as a criterion for proper basicality? He cannot simply take it to be true. He might try to produce some argument for it from premises that are self-evident or incorrigible. But it is very difficult to see how he might do this. If he cannot, or until he does, there is no reason why anyone should accept (8) as true.

## III

I think Plantinga has posed a serious problem for the classical foundationalist. But as Plantinga himself tells us, classical foundationalism is not the only form of foundationalism. There is also a weak foundationalism.[5] In such a foundationalism, one requirement for a proposition being properly basic is that it not be inferred from or dependent upon another proposition or propositions. This is just what it means to be properly basic.[6] However, a problem apparently presents itself for weak foundationalism. Given that there are no criteria for proper basicality like those suggested by the classical foundationalist, apparently anyone can include anything in his basic noetic structure, despite what any opponent might say or think. Plantinga calls this the "Great Pumpkin objection."[7] In response to this objection he suggests an inductive procedure for arriving at criteria for proper basicality. Moreover, he correctly notes that one need not have a criterion before one can sensibly make any judgments about proper basicality. Even if I do not know of a satisfactory substitute for the criteria of the classical foundationalist,[8] I am still entitled to hold that certain propositions are or are not properly basic.

However, contrary to Plantinga, I want to maintain that belief in God is not properly basic. I will try to show that this is the case, not by proposing some criteria which any proposition must meet in order to be properly basic (which is what Plantinga says I must do), but by maintaining that there is another proposition which is properly basic and which is incompatible with belief in God being properly basic. Because of this incompatibility, one or the other cannot be properly basic, and I am contending that it is belief in God which is not so characterized.

## IV

Plantinga cites the following group of propositions as examples of those which the theist might consider to be properly basic:

9. God is speaking to me,
10. God has created all this,
11. God disapproves of what I have done,
12. God forgives me,

and

13. God is to be thanked and praised.

Now it is, says Plantinga, consistent with the truth of (9) to (13) to hold that the proposition

14. There is such a person as God

is neither properly basic nor taken as basic by those who believe in God. They might consider (9)–(13) as basic and believe in (14) on the basis of these. On this view it is not strictly correct to say that belief in God is properly basic.

Plantinga suggests that we compare this with our belief in perceptual objects. Here, too, he claims, it is a relatively specific proposition rather than its more general associate that is properly basic. That is, the proposition

15. There are trees,

which is to be similar to proposition (14), is based on its more foundational associate

16. I see a tree,

which is supposed to parallel propositions (9)–(13). Thus, because a proposition like (15) is not genuinely properly basic, yet we take it as true, we should accept proposition (14) as true since it is based on the genuinely basic propositions (9)–(13).

However, are propositions (9)–(13) parallel to proposition (16)? I do not think that they are precisely parallel. Proposition (16) explicitly states a fact involving my awareness of an object. If propositions (9)–(13) are to parallel (16) in the relevant respects they must be rephrased to include a phrase about my awareness of God. Thus, we will have:

9'. I am aware of God speaking to me,
10'. I am aware of God as having created all this,
11'. I am aware of God disapproving of what I have done,
12'. I am aware of God forgiving me,

and

13'. I am aware that I should thank and praise God.

Now, when I am aware of an entity of any kind I must be aware of some of its properties. When I see the tree I am aware of its position in relationship to me, and I am also aware of its color, that it is swaying in the breeze, etc. These properties enable me to individuate it. If I am aware of God I must also be aware of some of the properties that enable me to individuate him. In propositions (9)–(12) the properties of God of which Plantinga says I am aware involve certain of God's activities. (Proposition 13 does not state an activity of God but rather what my response to God should be because of the activities like those mentioned in 9–12.) In other words, God is personally active in revealing himself directly to me or by means of his activities in the world about me of which I am aware. Now Plantinga, being a theist, holds that God is a being with distinctive properties, and it is these that make God God and enable me to individuate him as God. For example, God is a necessary being, all-powerful, all-knowing, etc. Granted this concept of God, in what way can he reveal himself to me? Does he say "Stewart (or "Alvin"), I am God"? If he does, he is assuming that *prior* to his revealing himself I already know the meaning of the name "God," and that I associate certain individuating properties with it. Or does he say "Stewart, I forgive you" (proposition 12) or "Stewart, I disapprove of what you have done" (proposition 11) or "Stewart, I am to be thanked and praised" (proposition 13)? These means of self-revelation will also, I suggest, require the possession on my part of the concept of God prior to his revelatory acts to me. At minimum it will require that I think of him as a person. Moreover, in these cases the properties manifested in God's revealing himself will not be distinctive enough and thus will not enable me to individuate him. For example, in the case of the first two statements, the activities involved are not distinctive activities of God, but can be performed by any person I know. Thus I will not directly believe (which I must do if these propositions are properly basic) that it is God performing them (assuming that I have a knowledge of *only* these activities). It seems wrong, then, to consider propositions (9)–(13) as properly basic, for each involves the prior possession by me of some knowledge or beliefs about the person or concept of God.

In order to clarify this point, consider my wife and myself. On various occasions she says to me, "Stewart, I forgive you." In these situations I am able to know that it is my wife forgiving me because in addition to her saying "I forgive you," I know other properties of her that enable me to individuate her. She has a body which now is the only body two feet in front of my body, two feet to the left of the table which is on my right, etc. Compare this with Plantinga's example. He tells us that God forgives him. But how does Plantinga know that it is God forgiving him? I presume that other people also forgive him at different times. If God is an immaterial being without a body, Plantinga cannot fill out a description of what God looks like and where he is standing (as I can with my wife when she forgives me), a description which would display a sufficient knowledge of various properties of his that are individuating in nature. If there is a voice involved in this act of forgiveness how does Plantinga know that it is God's voice? Can Plantinga rely solely on the sound of the voice—it has the resonance of God's voice? Again, I do not think so, unless, on previous occasions, the sound of the voice has been associated with a set of individuating descriptions like those just mentioned regarding my wife. A voice in and of itself bears no self-authenticating marks of its owner. Thus, in Chapter 9 of the Acts of the Apostles Saul hears a voice and queries, "Who are you?" It turns out to be the voice of Christ (whom Trinitarians consider to be divine).

Now consider the case of my thanking and praising God. The activities of thanking and praising, considered in and of themselves, are done by me toward a vast number of persons and not just toward God. Thus not only will there have to be a reason for my giving the particular person involved the appropriate praise and thanks due to him, but I will also have to be able to individuate this person. Or consider proposition (9). How do I know that it is God speaking to me? As we have just seen, the saying of things like "I forgive you" or "I disapprove of what you have done" will not alone lead me to believe that it is God speaking to me. Why not, then, think that my dead uncle is speaking to me? Presumably, in Plantinga's case, he does not think that his dead uncle is speaking to him because the voice (if there is one) does not sound like his uncle's voice, the content of what is said could not have been known by his uncle, etc. However, reference to such factors as these involves an appeal to distinctive properties possessed by God and his dead uncle. In short, if God is to successfully reveal himself to me (or Plantinga) and, just as important, if I am to recognize him, I must know certain of his individuating properties that will ground my assent to his being God, and one or more of these properties will have to be manifested in the revelatory situation. For example, because I believe that God has the property of being a necessary being the manifestation of this property in a revelatory situation will ground my assent to the proposition that God is involved. Thus the Christian theist sees the resurrection of Jesus Christ as having the marks of God's presence because it was impossible to keep Christ in the grave. Or consider the following proposition:

17. I am aware that God will mutilate my wife and child for no good reason.

I doubt that Plantinga would regard this proposition as properly basic. But why not? In so far as it is a proposition about God it seems no different from propositions (9)–(14). I suggest that Plantinga would not regard proposition (17) as properly basic because he does not think that God would commit an act like that described in (17). But why does he believe that this is so? Must he not have a reason? Must not his rejection of (17) as properly basic be based on some prior knowledge of what God is like? I believe that a reasonable theist would answer affirmatively.[9] For the same reason I think a reasonable theist would not claim that propositions (9)–(14) are properly basic.

The question which I now want to consider is whether I can have a knowledge of God's properties which allow me to individuate him when he reveals himself to me, without having performed any type of *inference* to obtain a knowledge of these properties. If I cannot know these properties and recognize him without such an inference, then propositions like (9)–(13) cannot be properly basic. They will presuppose an inference of some form, an inference by means of which I obtain a knowledge of what God is like. If such an inference is performed, what might be its basis?

I think that if I (or Plantinga) am to believe or know that God exists and is related to me and the world in the ways Plantinga suggests, then I need to make certain inferences about God based upon a knowledge of myself. One thing that I know about myself is that I am contingent, that is, I know that (i) I exist but not necessarily (I am not a necessary being), and (ii) because of the truth of (i), my existence needs an explanation. By 'necessary being' I mean a being for which it is not possible that it not exist. For purposes at hand I shall understand a necessary being to be a factually necessary being (as opposed to a logically necessary being).

Now suppose, for the sake of argument, that I were God and thus a necessary being. What would I think of propositions like (9)–(14)? Could I accept them as properly basic? Clearly I could accept (14) as properly basic because of the fact that I myself was the person to whom the proposition was referring. (14) would be properly basic for me because I would know immediately that I possessed the property of being a necessary being. Propositions (9)–(13), however, would not be properly basic, unless I was speaking to myself, forgiving myself, etc. (And if I am God I cannot, for example, forgive myself, because I cannot sin.) Yet, Plantinga tells us that a proposition like (14) is based upon (9)–(13). It appears in this case that I have a properly basic proposition based upon nonproperly basic propositions, indeed, on propositions which are now not even true.

In other words, what is properly basic is, in Plantinga's words, person-relative. Without mentioning any beliefs about my own nature, merely claiming that propositions (9)–(14) are properly basic can lead to some strange and, I think, undesirable conclusions. To prevent those problems from arising I must include within my foundational noetic structure F some propositions about *myself*. I will need to include at least the following two propositions:

18.  I exist,

and

19.  I am a contingent being.

Proposition (19) is particularly important for it will prevent me from identifying myself with the being referred to in propositions (9)–(14). But if proposition (19) is properly basic, can propositions (9)–(14) likewise be properly basic?[10] I do not think so. I want to maintain that if proposition (19) is properly basic it automatically excludes (9)–(14) from that status because it entails and I infer from it propositions, at least one of which is either identical with or contradictory to (14). And if something is inferred it is not properly basic.

What propositions do I infer from proposition (19)? One is that

20.  A necessary being exists.[11]

Who or what is this necessary being? Consider proposition (19). I am a contingent being. To what does the term 'I' refer in this proposition? If I am a materialist I will think that it refers to my body. If I am a dualist I will think that it refers to an immaterial soul or mind.[12] Take the first alternative. If I am identical with my body it is possible for me to regard the ultimate components of my body as necessary beings. My existence will be contingent in the sense that it depends upon the collection and organization of the necessary beings composing it. Should this collection and organization break down I will cease to exist. In this sense I am *naturally* contingent.

A belief such as this will pose insuperable problems for Plantinga's claim that proposition (14) is properly basic. For Plantinga maintains that the God of (14) is the creator of the material universe (see proposition 10). The material universe in his view of things is contingent. But if I believe that I am contingent and that I am composed out of my body, and the ultimate material components of my body are necessary, then I cannot accept proposition 14 as properly basic. For (10) (and, consequently, 14), contradicts what I believe and have inferred from proposition (19).

Nevertheless, there is another alternative. I may again think that the term 'I' refers to my body and that I am thus composed out of material entities. This time, however, I think that the ultimate material particles composing my body are themselves contingent. Because they are contingent they must be caused to exist. Their cause or creator is a necessary being and their contingency is a *metaphysical* contingency. Now either the cause of these material particles is identical with the God of proposition (14), or it is not. If it is then I have inferred that the God of (14) exists and thus (14) cannot be properly basic. If it is not identical with the God of proposition (14) then I have again inferred a proposition which contradicts proposition (10). (For if this other being is the cause of all this, 10 cannot be true of God.) As a result I cannot accept (14) as properly basic.

If the foregoing reasoning is sound I ought not to accept belief in God as properly basic. Without knowing that proposition (19) truly describes the nature of my own self, I might both accept proposition (14) as properly basic and think that it is true of myself. This would be, at the least, severe megalomania. I must accept proposition (19) as properly basic in order to avoid this situation. But once I accept (19) as properly basic I cannot accept (14) as properly basic. And since I cannot accept it as properly basic, I ought not to accept it.

It should also be noted that the inference made on the basis of proposition (19) provides the solution for a problem noted earlier in this section. I pointed out there that in order for God to successfully reveal himself to me, I must have a working concept of God which will enable me to recognize him. If I am correct in my analysis of the role played by proposition (19) in my noetic structure, I do have such a concept of God.

One further comment is appropriate. In arguing for the proper basicality of religious belief, Plantinga has attempted to draw certain analogies between being aware of a tree (proposition 16) and being aware of God (proposition 14). I think that Plantinga has failed to notice that the two are different in a crucial respect. I am not aware that the tree exists in the same way that I am aware that a necessary being or beings exist. The difference stems from self-knowledge. I can know myself without inferring (or knowing) that any other contingent entity like the tree exists. I might be the only contingently existing being. But I cannot know myself without inferring that a necessary being exists, for in knowing myself I know that I am contingent. The existence of a contingent being implies the existence of a necessary being, but the existence of a contingent self need not imply the existence of another contingent being.

## V

I conclude that Plantinga is wrong in regarding belief in God as properly basic. One can only maintain that belief in God is properly basic by ignoring one's own contingency. I contend that anyone who believes in God must acknowledge his contingency and that his knowledge of his contingent nature enables him to infer the existence of a necessary being or beings. I do not claim that any person who believes in God will be able to explicate his knowledge of his contingency in philosophical terms like 'contingency' and 'necessity'. Most people acknowledge their contingency in terms of questions like "Why do I exist?" and "What will happen to me when I die?"

My argument against Plantinga rests upon talk of necessary and contingent beings. Some philosophers and theologians might feel uncomfortable with such talk. Plantinga should not, however, for few have done more in our day than he to reestablish the integrity of talk about essential and accidental properties and contingent and necessary beings. Of course someone might grant the legitimacy of such talk but argue that I am wrong to think that a proposition such as (19) is in the foundation set F of my noetic structure. I cannot, he might argue, know (19) immediately. This, however, I find incredible. As Arnauld wrote to Descartes, ". . . that I cannot proceed from myself positively and as it were from a cause I deem it to be so evident to the light of nature that its proof would be vain, a proving of the known by the less known."[14]

## Notes

1. Alvin Plantinga, "Is Belief in God Rational?," in *Rationality and Religious Belief,* ed. C. F. Delaney (Notre Dame, IN: University of Notre Dame Press, 1979), pp. 7–27; "Is Belief in God Properly Basic?," *Nous* 15 (1981): 41–51 (reprinted in this volume, pp. 133–41; all other citations are from this reprint); and "The Reformed Objection to Natural Theology," *Christian Scholars Review* 11 (1981): 187–98. My discussion of Plantinga's views rests upon these articles.

2. Plantinga, "Is Belief in God Rational?," p. 27.

3. Plantinga, "Is Belief in God Properly Basic?," p. 133 above.

4. It seems fair to assume that when Plantinga speaks of beliefs being properly basic he is using "belief" for what is believed, the propositional content, rather than any psychological state of belief.

5. Plantinga, "The Reformed Objection to Natural Theology," pp. 193, 194. Plantinga notes that many Reformed thinkers have endorsed weak foundationalism.

6. Plantinga, "Is Belief in God Properly Basic?," pp. 139ff. above.

7. Plantinga, "The Reformed Objection to Natural Theology," pp. 195–98; see also "Is Belief in God Properly Basic?," p. 139.

8. I doubt that there are any criteria for proper basicality. If there are, I am convinced that they will involve propositions about states or events of myself.

9. I have stated that if proposition (19) is properly basic, it excludes propositions (9)–(14) from that status. I have explicitly outlined how (19)'s being properly basic affects the status of (10) and thus (14). I think that the status of (10) has implications for the status of (11), (12), and (13). Take (13). Why is God to be thanked and praised? One of the reasons theists give is that God has created us. I am grateful to God because he has given me existence. But giving me existence is an activity encompassed by proposition (10). Thus (10) is related to (13).

10. Is proposition (19) properly basic like proposition (18)? It might be maintained that I can only know (19) is true subsequent to my knowing that (18) is true. For purposes of discussion, however, I will assume (19) is properly basic. If it is not it is still more basic than proposition (14).

11. "I apprehend there are very few cases in which we can, from principles that are contingent, deduce truths that are necessary. I can only recollect one instance of this kind—namely—that, from the existence of things contingent and mutable, we can infer the existence of an immutable and eternal cause of them" (see Thomas Reid, "Essays on the Intellectual Powers of Man," in *The Works of Thomas Reid,* 2 Vols., ed. Sir William Hamilton [Edinburgh: Maclachlan and Stewart, 1863], Essay VI, Chapter 5; Vol. 1, p. 442).

12. This is Plantinga's view. See his *The Nature of Necessity* (Oxford, Engl.: Clarendon Press, 1974), pp. 65–69.

13. For example, the theist might reject proposition (20) by making use of the concept of a contingent being. He could infer that a being who can create contingent beings is all-powerful. Because he is all-powerful he cannot perform an evil act, for he would have no reason for performing such an act. A person performs an evil act because he needs or wants something he cannot have or obtain through legitimate means, and the needs or wants provide the reasons for the act. But a being with the power to create things could never need or want anything it could not just create.

14. In *The Philosophical Works of Descartes,* 2 Vols., trans. E. S. Haldane and G.R.T. Ross (Cambridge, Engl.: Cambridge University Press, 1931), Vol. 2, pp. 88–89.

# Bibliography

Abraham, William J. "Philosophical Fideism," in his *An Introduction to the Philosophy of Religion.* Englewood Cliffs, NJ: Prentice-Hall, 1985.

Alston, William. "Plantinga's Epistemology of Religious Belief." In *Alvin Plantinga* (Profiles, Vol. 5), eds. James Tomberlin and Peter van Inwagen. Dordrecht, Neth.: D. Reidel, 1985.

———. "What's Wrong with Immediate Knowledge?" *Synthese* 55 (1983): 73–95.

Appleby, Peter C. "Reformed Epistemology, Rationality and Belief in God." *International Journal for Philosophy of Religion* 24 (1988): 129–41.

Askew, Richard. "On Fideism and Alvin Plantinga." *International Journal for Philosophy of Religion* 23 (1988): 3–16.

Audi, Robert. "Direct Justification, Evidential Dependence, and Theistic Belief," in *Rationality, Religious Belief, and Moral Commitment: New Essays in the Philosophy of Religion,* eds. Robert Audi and William J. Wainwright. Ithaca, NY: Cornell University Press, 1986.

Baber, H. E. Review of *Alvin Plantinga,* edited by James E. Tomberlin and Peter van Inwagen. *International Philosophical Quarterly* 26 (Sept. 1986): 301–3.

Basinger, David. "Discussion Article I: The Rationality of Belief in God: Some Clarifications." *New Scholasticism* 60 (1986): 163–85.

———. "Plantinga, Pluralism and Justified Belief." *Faith and Philosophy* 8 (1991): 67–80.

Beaty, Michael D., ed. *Christian Theism and the Problems of Philosophy.* Notre Dame, IN: University of Notre Dame Press, 1990.

Boyle, Joseph, J. Hubbard, and Thomas Sullivan. "The Reformed Objection to Natural Theology: A Catholic Perspective." *Christian Scholar's Review* 11 (1982): 199–211.

Brown, H. "Alvin Plantinga and Natural Theology." *International Journal for Philosophy of Religion* 30 (1991): 1–19.

Clark, Kelly James. *Return to Reason: A Critique of Enlightenment Evidentialism and a Defense of Reason and Belief in God.* Grand Rapids, MI: Eerdmans, 1990.

Clifford, William K. "The Ethics of Belief," in *Philosophy of Religion: An Anthology,* ed. Louis P. Pojman. Belmont, CA: Wadsworth, 1987.

Davis, John Jefferson. "Belief in Design as Properly Basic." *Trinity Journal* 8 (1987): 145–57.

Dowey, Edward. *The Knowledge of God in Calvin's Theology.* New York: Columbia University Press, 1952.

Echeverria, Edward J. "The Fate of Theism Revisited." *Thomist* 51 (1987): 632–57.

———. "Rationality and the Theory of Rationality." *Christian Scholar's Review* 15 (1986): 372–87.

Edwards, Paul. "Is Fideistic Theology Irrefutable?" *The Rationalist Annual* (1966).

Evans, C. Stephen. "Kierkegaard and Plantinga on Belief in God." *Faith and Philosophy* 5 (1988): 25–39.

Ferreira, M. Jamie. "Universal Criteria and the Autonomy of Religious Belief." *International Journal for Philosophy of Religion* 15 (1984): 3–12.

Flint, Thomas, ed. *Christian Philosophy*. Notre Dame, IN: University of Notre Dame Press, 1990.

Frame, John M. "The New Reformed Epistemology" (Appendix I), in his *The Doctrine of the Knowledge of God*. Phillipsburg, NJ: Presbyterian & Reformed, 1987.

Gowen, Julie. "Foundationalism and the Justification of Religious Belief." *Religious Studies* 19 (1983): 393–406.

Grigg, Richard. "The Crucial Disanalogies between Properly Basic Belief and Belief in God." *Religious Studies* 26 (1990): 389–401.

———. "Theism and Proper Basicality: A Response to Plantinga." *International Journal for Philosophy of Religion* 14 (1983): 123–27.

Gutting, Gary. "The Catholic and the Calvinist: A Dialogue on Faith and Reason." *Faith and Philosophy* 2 (1985): 236–56.

———. "Disagreement and the Need for Justification," in his *Religious Belief and Religious Skepticism*. Notre Dame, IN: University of Notre Dame Press, 1982.

Hanink, James G. "Some Questions about Proper Basicality." *Faith and Philosophy* 4 (1987): 13–25.

Hart, Hendrik Johan Van der Hoeven, and Nicholas Wolterstorff, eds. *Rationality in the Calvinian Tradition*. Lanham, MD: University Press of America, 1983.

Hasker, William. "On Justifying the Christian Practice." *New Scholasticism* 60 (Spring 1986): 129–44.

Hatcher, Donald. "Plantinga and Reformed Epistemology: A Critique." *Philosophy and Theology* 1 (1986): 84–95.

———. "Some Problems with Plantinga's Reformed Epistemology." *American Journal of Theology and Philosophy* 10 (1989): 21–31.

Hoitenga, Dewey J., Jr. *Faith and Reason from Plato to Plantinga: An Introduction to Reformed Epistemology*. Albany, NY: State University of New York Press, 1991.

Hughes, G. E. "Plantinga on the Rationality of God's Existence." *Philosophical Review* 79 (1970): 246–52.

Johnson, Bredo C. "Basic Theistic Belief." *Canadian Journal of Philosophy* 16 (1986): 455–64.

Kennedy, Leonard A., ed. *Thomistic Papers,* Vol. IV. Houston, TX: Center for Thomistic Studies, 1988.

Kenny, Anthony. *Faith and Reason*. New York: Columbia University Press, 1983.

Konyndyk, Kenneth. "Faith and Evidentialism," in *Rationality, Religious Belief, and Moral Commitment: New Essays in the Philosophy of Religion,* eds. Robert Audi and William J. Wainwright. Ithaca, NY: Cornell University Press, 1986.

Langtry, Bruce. "Properly Unargued Belief in God." *International Journal for Philosophy of Religion* 26 (1989): 129–54.

Malino, Jonathan. "Comments on Quinn." *Faith and Philosophy* 2 (1985): 487–92.

Martin, Michael. "Faith and Foundationalism," in his *Atheism: A Philosophical Justification*. Philadelphia: Temple University Press, 1990.

Mavrodes, George I. "Jerusalem and Athens Revisited," In *Faith and Rationality: Reason and Belief in God,* eds. Alvin Plantinga and Nicholas Wolterstorff. Notre Dame, IN: University of Notre Dame Press, 1983.

McCarthy, Gerald D., ed. *The Ethics of Belief Debate*. Dordrecht, Neth.: D. Reidel, 1983.

McLeod, Mark. "The Analogy Argument for the Proper Basicality of Belief in God." *International Journal for Philosophy of Religion* 21 (1987): 3–20.

Mitchell, Basil. "Two Approaches to the Philosophy of Religion," in *For God and Clarity,* eds. Jeffrey C. Eaton and Ann Loades. Allison Park, PA: Pickwick Publications, 1983.

Nash, Ronald H. *Faith and Reason: Searching for a Rational Faith.* Grand Rapids, MI: Zondervan, 1988.

Parker, Francis H. *Reason and Faith Revisited.* Milwaukee: Marquette University Press, 1971.

Parsons, Keith M. *God and the Burden of Proof.* Buffalo, NY: Prometheus Books, 1989.

Penelhum, Terence. *God and Skepticism.* Dordrecht, Neth.: D. Reidel, 1983.

Peterson, Michael L. Review of *Thomistic Papers,* Vol. IV, edited by Leonard A. Kennedy. *Faith and Philosophy* 8 (1991): 115–20.

Peterson, Michael, William Hasker, Bruce Reichenbach, and David Basinger. "Knowing God without Arguments: Does Theism Need a Basis?" in *Reason and Religious Belief: An Introduction to the Philosophy of Religion.* New York: Oxford University Press, 1991.

Phillips, D. Z. *Faith After Foundationalism.* London: Routledge & Kegan Paul, 1988.

———. "Grammarians and Guardians," in *The Grammar of the Heart: New Essays in Moral Philosophy and Theology,* ed. Richard H. Bell. San Francisco: Harper & Row, 1988.

Pinnock, Clark H. "Response by Clark Pinnock." *The Reformed Journal* 31 (April 1981): 25–26.

Plantinga, Alvin. "Advice to Christian Philosophers." *Faith and Philosophy* 1 (1984): 253–71.

———. "Coherentism and the Evidentialist Objection to Belief in God," in *Rationality, Religious Belief, and Moral Commitment,* eds. Robert Audi and William J. Wainwright. Ithaca, NY: Cornell University Press, 1986.

———. "Discussion Article II: Existence, Necessity, and God." *New Scholasticism* 50 (1976): 61–72.

———. "Epistemic Justification." *Nous* 20 (1986): 3–18.

———. "The Foundations of Theism: A Reply." *Faith and Philosophy* 3 (1986): 298–313.

———. *God and Other Minds: A Study of the Rational Justification of Belief in God.* Ithaca, NY: Cornell University Press, 1967.

———. "Is Belief in God Rational?" in *Rationality and Religious Belief,* ed. C. F. Delaney. Notre Dame, IN: University of Notre Dame Press, 1979.

———. "Is Theism Really a Miracle?" *Faith and Philosophy* 3 (1986): 109–34.

———. "Justification and Theism." *Faith and Philosophy* 4 (1987): 403–26.

———. *The Nature of Necessity.* Oxford, Engl.: Clarendon Press, 1974.

———. "Rationality and Religious Belief," in *Contemporary Philosophy of Religion,* eds. Steven M. Cahn and David Shatz. New York: Oxford University Press, 1982.

———. "On Reformed Epistemology." *The Reformed Journal* 32 (January 1982): 13–17.

———. "The Reformed Objection to Natural Theology." *Proceedings of the American Catholic Philosophical Association* 54 (1980): 49–63; also published in *Christian Scholar's Review* 11 (1982): 187–98.

———. "The Reformed Objection Revisited." *Christian Scholar's Review* 12 (1983): 57–61.

———. "Replies." In *Alvin Plantinga* (Profiles, Vol. 5), eds. James Tomberlin and Peter van Inwagen. Dordrecht, Neth.: D. Reidel, 1985.

———. "The Sceptic's Strategy," in *Faith and the Philosophers,* ed. John Hick. London: Macmillan, 1966.

———. "On Taking Belief in God as Basic," in *Religious Experience and Religious Belief: Essays in the Epistemology of Religion,* eds. Joseph Runzo and Craig K. Ihara. Lanham, MD: University Press of America, 1986.

———. *Warrant: The Current Debate.* New York: Oxford University Press, in press.

———. *Warrant and Proper Function.* New York: Oxford University Press, in press.

Plantinga, Alvin, and Nicholas Wolterstorff, eds. *Faith and Rationality: Reason and Belief in God.* Notre Dame, IN: University of Notre Dame Press, 1983.

Pojman, Louis P. *Religious Belief and the Will.* London: Routledge & Kegan Paul, 1989.

Purtill, Richard L. "Discussion Article I: Plantinga, Necessity, and God." *New Scholasticism* 50 (1976): 46–60.

Quinn, Philip L. "Epistemic Parity and Religious Argument," in *Philosophical Perspectives. 5: Philosophy of Religion, 1991,* ed. James E. Tomberlin. Atascadero, CA: Ridgeview Publishing Co., 1991.

———. "In Search of the Foundations of Theism." *Faith and Philosophy* 2 (1985): 469–86.

Robbins, J. Wesley. "Does the Existence of God Need Proof?" *Faith and Philosophy* 2 (1985): 272–86.

———. "Is Belief in God Properly Basic?" *International Journal for Philosophy of Religion* 14 (1983): 241–48.

Runzo, Joseph, "World-Views and the Epistemic Foundations of Theism." *Religious Studies* 25 (1989): 31–51.

Schubert, Frank D. "Is Ancestral Testimony Foundational Evidence for God's Existence?" *Religious Studies* 37 (1991): 499–510.

Sessions, William Lad. "Plantinga's Box." *Faith and Philosophy* 8 (1991): 51–66.

Stout, Jeffrey. *The Flight from Authority: Religion, Morality and the Quest for Autonomy.* Notre Dame, IN: University of Notre Dame Press, 1981.

Swinburne, Richard. "Rational Belief," in his *Faith and Reason.* Oxford, Engl.: Clarendon Press, 1981.

———. Review of *Faith and Rationality: Reason and Belief in God,* edited by Alvin Plantinga and Nicholas Wolterstorff. *Journal of Philosophy* 82 (1985): 46–53.

Tomberlin, James E. "Is Belief in God Justified?" *Journal of Philosophy* 67 (1970): 531–38.

———. Review of *Faith and Rationality: Reason and Belief in God,* edited by Alvin Plantinga and Nicholas Wolterstorff. *Nous* 20 (1986): 401–13.

Tomberlin, James E., and Peter van Inwagen, eds. *Alvin Plantinga* (Profiles, Vol. 5). Dordrecht, Neth.: D. Reidel, 1985.

Van Hook, Jay. "Knowledge, Belief, and Reformed Epistemology." *The Reformed Journal* 31 (July 1981): 12–17.

Vos, Arvin. *Aquinas, Calvin, and Contemporary Protestant Thought: A Critique of Protestant Views on the Thought of Thomas Aquinas.* Grand Rapids, MI: Eerdmans, 1985.

———. Review of *Rationality in the Calvinian Tradition,* edited by Hendrik Hart, Johan Van Der Hoeven, and Nicholas Wolterstorff. *Faith and Philosophy* 3 (1986): 324–28.

Wachthauser, Brice R., ed. *Hermeneutics and Modern Philosophy.* Albany, NY: State University of New York Press, 1986.

Westphal, Merold. Review of *Faith and Rationality: Reason and Belief in God,* edited by Alvin Plantinga and Nicholas Wolterstorff. *International Journal for Philosophy of Religion* 16 (1984): 183–84.

Williams, Michael. *Groundless Belief* (Library of Philosophy and Logic). New Haven, CT: Yale University Press, 1977.

Wisdo, David. "The Fragility of Faith: Toward a Critique of Reformed Epistemology." *Religious Studies* 24 (1988): 365–74.

Wolterstorff, Nicholas. "On Avoiding Historicism." *Philosophia Reformata* 45 (1980): 178–85.

———. "Calvin, John," in *Encyclopedia of Philosophy,* ed. Paul Edwards. New York: Macmillan, 1967.

———. "Can Belief in God Be Rational If It Has No Foundations?" in *Faith and Rationality: Reason and Belief in God,* eds. Alvin Plantinga and Nicholas Wolterstorff. Notre Dame, IN: University of Notre Dame Press, 1983.

———. "The Migration of the Theistic Arguments: From Natural Theology to Evidentialist Apologetics," in *Rationality, Religious Belief, and Moral Commitment: New Essays in the Philosophy of Religion,* eds. Robert Audi and William J. Wainwright. Ithaca, NY: Cornell University Press, 1986.

———. "Once More Evidentialism—This Time, Social." *Philosophical Topics* 16 (1988): 53–74.

———. *Reason within the Bounds of Religion,* 2nd ed. Grand Rapids, MI: Eerdmans, 1984.

———. "Thomas Reid and Rationality," in *Rationality in the Calvinian Tradition,* eds. Hendrik Hart, Johan Van der Hoeven, and Nicholas Wolterstorff. Lanham, MD: University Press of America, 1983.

Wykstra, Stephen. "Plantinga versus Evidentialism: Relocating the Issue." Paper presented at the Eastern Regional Meeting of the Society of Christian Philosophers, Notre Dame, IN, March 1984.

———. Review of *Faith and Rationality: Reason and Belief in God,* edited by Alvin Plantinga and Nicholas Wolterstorff. *Faith and Philosophy* 3 (1986): 206–13.

———. "Toward a Sensible Evidentialism: On the Notion of 'Needing Evidence'," in *Philosophy of Religion,* eds. William Rowe and William Wainwright. New York: Harcourt Brace Jovanovich, 1989.

Zagzebski, Linda, ed. *Rational Faith: Catholic Responses to Reformed Epistemology.* Notre Dame, IN: University of Notre Dame Press, in press.

———. "Recent Work in the Philosophy of Religion." *Philosophical Books* 31 (1990): 1–6.

Zeis, John. "A Critique of Plantinga's Theological Foundationalism." *International Journal for Philosophy of Religion* 28 (1990): 173–89.

# IV

# NATURAL THEOLOGY

# 13

# Philosophical and Scientific Pointers to
# *Creatio ex Nihilo*

## *William Lane Craig*

". . . The first question which should rightly be asked," wrote Gottfried Wilhelm Leibniz, is "Why is there something rather than nothing?"[1] Think about that for a moment. Why *does* anything exist at all, rather than nothing? Why does the universe, or matter, or anything at all exist, instead of just nothing?

Many great minds have been puzzled by this problem. For example, in his biography of the renowned philosopher Ludwig Wittgenstein, Norman Malcolm reports,

> . . . he said that he sometimes had a certain experience which could best be described by saying that 'when I have it, *I wonder at the existence of the world.* I am then inclined to use such phrases as "How extraordinary that anything should exist!" or "How extraordinary that the world should exist!" '[2]

Similarly, the Australian philosopher J.J.C. Smart has said, ". . . my mind often seems to reel under the immense significance this question has for me. That anything exists at all does seem to me a matter for the deepest awe."[3]

Why *does* something exist instead of nothing? Unless we are prepared to believe that the universe simply popped into existence uncaused out of nothing, then the answer must be: something exists because there is an eternal, uncaused being for which no further explanation is possible. But who or what is this eternal, uncaused being? Leibniz identified it with God. But many modern philosophers have identified it with the universe itself. Now this is exactly the position of the atheist: the universe itself is uncaused and eternal; as Russell remarks, ". . . the universe is just there, and that's all."[4] But are there reasons to think that the universe is not eternal and uncaused, that there is something more? I think that there are. For we can consider the universe by means of a series of logical alternatives:

Reprinted from *Journal of the American Scientific Affiliation* 32 (March 1980), by permission of the author, who revised the article for this collection. Notes edited.

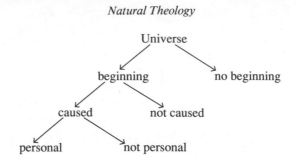

By proceeding through these alternatives, I think we can demonstrate that it is reasonable to believe that the universe is not eternal, but that it had a beginning and was caused by a personal being, and that therefore a personal Creator of the universe exists.

## Did the Universe Begin?

The first and most crucial step to be considered in this argument is the first: that the universe began to exist. There are four reasons why I think it is more reasonable to believe that the universe had a beginning. First, I shall expound two philosophical arguments and, second, two scientific confirmations.

### *The First Philosophical Argument:*

1. An actual infinite cannot exist.
2. A beginningless series of events in time is an actual infinite.
3. Therefore, a beginningless series of events in time cannot exist.

A collection of things is said to be actually infinite only if a part of it is equal to the whole of it. For example, which is greater? 1, 2, 3, . . . or 0, 1, 2, 3, . . . According to prevailing mathematical thought, the answer is that they are equivalent because they are both actually infinite. This seems strange because there is an extra number in one series that cannot be found in the other. But this only goes to show that in an actually infinite collection, a part of the collection is equal to the whole of the collection. For the same reason, mathematicians state that the series of even numbers is the same size as the series of all natural numbers, even though the series of all natural numbers contains all the even numbers plus an infinite number of odd numbers as well. So a collection is actually infinite if a part of it is equal to the whole of it.

Now the concept of an *actual* infinite needs to be sharply distinguished from the concept of a *potential* infinite. A potential infinite is a collection that is increasing without limit but is at all times finite. The concept of potential infinity usually comes into play when we add to or subtract from something without stopping. Thus, a finite distance may be said to contain a potentially infinite number of smaller finite distances. This does not mean that there actually are an infinite number of parts in a finite distance, but rather it means that one can keep on dividing endlessly. But one will never reach an "infinitieth" division. Infinity merely serves as the limit to which the process approaches. Thus, a potential infinite is not truly infinite—it is simply indefinite. It is at all points finite but always increasing.

To sharpen the distinction between an actual and a potential infinite, we can draw some comparisons between them. The concept of actual infinity is used in set theory to designate a set which has an actually infinite number of members in it. But the concept of potential infinity finds no place in set theory. This is because the members of a set must be definite, whereas a potential infinite is indefinite—it acquires new members as it grows. Thus, set theory has only either finite or actually infinite sets. The proper place for the concept of the potential infinite is found in mathematical analysis, as in infinitesimal calculus. There a process may be said to increase or diminish to infinity, in the sense that the process can be continued endlessly with infinity as its terminus.[5] The concept of actual infinity does not pertain in these operations because an infinite number of operations is never actually made. According to the great German mathematician David Hilbert, the chief difference between an actual and a potential infinite is that a potential infinite is always something growing toward a limit of infinity, while an actual infinite is a completed totality with an actually infinite number of things.[6] A good example contrasting these two types of infinity is the series of past, present, and future events. For if the universe is eternal, as the atheist claims, then there have occurred in the past an actually infinite number of events. But from any point in the series of events, the number of future (that is, subsequent) events is potentially infinite. Thus, if we pick 1845, the birth year of Georg Cantor, who discovered infinite sets, as our point of departure, we can see that past events constitute an actual infinity while future events constitute a potential infinity. This is because the past is realized and complete, whereas the future is never fully actualized, but is always finite and always increasing. In the following discussion, it is exceedingly important to keep the concepts of actual infinity and potential infinity distinct and not to confuse them.

A second clarification that I must make concerns the word "exist." When I say that an actual infinite cannot exist, I mean "exist in the real world" or "exist outside the mind." I am not in any way questioning the legitimacy of using the concept of actual infinity in the realm of mathematics, for this is a realm of thought only. What I am arguing is that an actual infinite cannot exist in the real world of stars and planets and rocks and men. What I will argue in no way threatens the use of the actual infinite as a concept in mathematics. But I do think it is absurd that an actual infinite could exist in the real world.

I think that probably the best way to show this is to use examples to illustrate the absurdities that would result if an actual infinite could exist in reality. For suppose we have a library that has an actually infinite number of books on its shelves. Imagine furthermore that there are only two colors, black and red, and these are placed on the shelves alternately: black, red, black, red, and so forth. Now if somebody told us that the number of black books and the number of red books is the same, we would probably not be too surprised. But would we believe someone who told us that the number of black books is the same as the number of black books *plus* red books? For in this latter collection there are all the black books plus an infinite number of red books as well. Or imagine there are three colors of books, or four, or five, or a hundred. Would you believe someone if he told you that there are as many books in a single color as there are in the whole collection? Or imagine that there are an infinite number of colors of books. You would probably think that there would be one book per color in the infinite collection. You would be wrong. If the collection is actually infinite then, according to mathematicians, there could be for each of the infinite colors an infinite number of books. So you would have an infinity of infinities. And yet it would still be true that if you took all the books of all the colors and added them together, you wouldn't have any more books than if you had taken just the books of a single color.

Suppose each book had a number printed on its spine. Because the collection is actually infinite, that means that *every possible number* is printed on some book. Now this means that we could not add another book to the library. For what number would we give to it? All the numbers have been used up! Thus, the new book could not have a number. But this is absurd, since objects in reality can be numbered. So *if* an infinite library could exist, it would be impossible to add another book to it. But this conclusion is obviously false, for all we have to do is tear out a page from each of the first hundred books, add a title page, stick them together, and put this new book on the shelf. It would be easy to add to the library. So the only answer must be that an actually infinite library could not exist.

But suppose we *could* add to the library. Suppose I put a book on the shelf. According to the mathematicians, the number of books in the whole collection is the same as before. But how can this be? If I put the book on the shelf, there is one more book in the collection. If I take it off the shelf, there is one less book. I can see myself add and remove the book. Am I really to believe that when I add the book there are no more books in the collection and when I remove it there are no less books? Suppose I add an infinity of books to the collection. Am I seriously to believe there are no more books in the collection than before? Suppose I add an infinity of infinities of books to the collection. Is there not now one single book more in the collection than before? I find this hard to believe.

But now let's reverse the process. Suppose we decide to loan out some of the books. Suppose we loan out book number 1. Isn't there now one less book in the collection? Suppose we loan out all the odd-numbered books. We have loaned out an infinite number of books, and yet mathematicians would say there are no less books in the collection. Now when we loaned out all these books, that left an awful lot of gaps on the shelves. Suppose we push all the books together again and close the gaps. All these gaps added together would add up to an infinite distance. But, according to mathematicians, after you pushed the books together, the shelves will still be full, the same as before you loaned any out! Now suppppose once more we loaned out every other book. There would still be no less books in the collection than before. And if we pushed all the books together again, the shelves would still be full. In fact, we could do this an infinite number of times, and there would never be one less book in the collection, and the shelves would always remain full. But suppose we loaned out book numbers 4, 5, 6, . . . out to infinity. At a single stroke, the collection would be virtually wiped out, the shelves emptied, and the infinite library reduced to finitude. And yet, we have removed exactly the same number of books this time as when we first loaned out all the odd numbered books! Can anybody believe such a library could exist in reality?

These examples serve to illustrate that *an actual infinate cannot exist* in the real world. Again I want to underline the fact that what I have argued in no way attempts to undermine the theoretical system bequeathed by Cantor to modern mathematics. Indeed, some of the most eager enthusiasts of trans-finite mathematics, such as David Hilbert, are only too ready to agree that the concept of an actual infinite is an idea only and has no relation to the real world.[7] So we can conclude the first step: an actual infinite cannot exist.

The second step is: *a beginningless series of events in time is an actual infinite.* By "event" I mean something that happens. Thus, this step is concerned with change, and it holds that if the series of past events or changes just goes back and back and never had a beginning, then, considered all together, these events constitute an actually infinite collection. Let me provide an example. Suppose we ask someone where a certain star came from. He replies that it came from an explosion in a star that existed before it. Suppose we ask again, where did that star come from? Well, it came from another star before it. And where did that star come from?— From another star before it; and so on and so on. This series of stars would be an example of a beginningless series of events in time. Now if the universe has existed forever, then the series of all past events taken together constitutes an actual infinite. This is because for every event in the past, there was an event before it. Thus, the series of past events would be infinite. Nor could it be potentially infinite only, for we have seen that the past is completed and actual; only the future can be described as a potential infinite. Therefore, it seems pretty obvious that a beginningless series of events in time is an actual infinite.

But that leads us to our conclusion: *therefore, a beginningless series of events in time cannot exist.* We have seen that an actual infinite cannot exist in reality. Since a beginningless series of events in time is an actual infinite, such a series cannot exist. That means the series of all past events must be finite and have a beginning. But because the universe *is* the series of all events, this means that the universe must have had a beginning.

Let me give a few examples to make the point clear. We have seen that if an actual infinite could exist in reality, it would be impossible to add to it. But the series of events in time is being added to every day. Or at least so it appears. If the series were actually infinite, then the number of events that have occurred up to the present moment is no greater than the number of events up to, say, 1789. In fact, you can pick any point in the past. The number of events that have occurred up to the present moment would be no greater than the number of events up to that point, no matter how long ago it might be.

Or take another example. Suppose Earth and Jupiter have been orbiting the sun from eternity. Suppose that it takes the Earth one year to complete one orbit, and that it takes Jupiter three years to complete one orbit. Thus, for every one orbit Jupiter completes, Earth completes three. Now here is the question: if they have been orbiting from eternity, which has completed more orbits? The answer is: they are equal. But this seems absurd, since the longer they went, the farther and farther Jupiter got behind, since every time Jupiter went around the sun once, Earth went around three times. How then could they possibly be equal?

Or, finally, suppose we meet a man who claims to have been counting from eternity, and now he is finishing: $-5, -4, -3, -2, -1, 0$. Now this is impossible.

For, we may ask, why didn't he finish counting yesterday or the day before or the year before? By then an infinity of time had already elapsed, so that he should have finished. The fact is, we could never find anyone completing such a task because at any previous point he would have already finished. But what this means is that there could never be a point in the past at which he finished counting. In fact, we could never find him counting at all. For he would have already finished. But if no matter how far back in time we go, we never find him counting, then it cannot be true that he has been counting from eternity. This shows once more that the series of past events cannot be beginningless. For if you could not count numbers from eternity, neither could you have events from eternity.

These examples underline the absurdity of a beginningless series of events in time. Because such a series is an actual infinite, and an actual infinite cannot exist, a beginningless series of events in time cannot exist. This means that the universe began to exist, which is the point that we set out to prove.

### The Second Philosophical Argument:

1. The series of events in time is a collection formed by adding one member after another.
2. A collection formed by adding one member after another cannot be actually infinite.
3. Therefore, the series of events in time cannot be actually infinite.

This argument does not argue that an actual infinite cannot exist. But it does argue that an actual infinite cannot come to exist by the members of a collection being added one after the other.

*The series of events in time is a collection formed by adding one member after another.* This point is pretty obvious. When we consider the collection of all past events, it is obvious that those events did not exist simultaneously—all at once—but they existed one after another in time: we have one event, then another after that, then another, then another, and so on. So when we talk about the collection of "all past events," we are talking about a collection that has been formed by adding one member after another.

The second step is the crucial one: *a collection formed by adding one member after another cannot be actually infinite.* Why? Because no matter how many members a person added to the collection, he could always add one more. Therefore, he would never arrive at infinity. Sometimes this is called the impossibility of counting to infinity. For no matter how many numbers you had counted, you could always count one more. You would never arrive at infinity. Or sometimes this is called the impossibility of traversing the infinite. For you could never cross an infinite distance. Imagine a man running up a flight of stairs. Suppose everytime his foot strikes the top step, another step appears above it. It is clear that the man could run forever, but he would never cross all the steps because you could always add one more step.

Now notice that this impossibility has nothing to do with the amount of time available. It is of the very nature of the infinite that it cannot be formed by adding one member after another, regardless of the amount of time available. Thus, the only way an infinite collection could come to exist in the real world would be by having all the members created simultaneously. For example, if our library of infinite books were to exist in the real world, it would have to be created instantaneously by God. God would say, "Let there be . . . !" and the library would come into existence all at once. But it would be impossible to form the library by adding one book at a time, for you would never arrive at infinity.

Therefore, our conclusion must be: *the series of events in time cannot be actually infinite.* Suppose there were, for example, an infinite number of days prior to today. Then today would never arrive. For it is impossible to cross an infinite number of days to reach today. But obviously, today has arrived. Therefore, we know that prior to today, there cannot have been an infinite number of days. That means that the number of days is finite and therefore the universe had a beginning. Contemporary philosophers have shown themselves to be impotent to refute this reasoning.[8] Thus, one of them asks,

> If an infinite series of events has preceded the present moment, how did we get to the present moment? How could we get to the present moment—where we obviously are now—if the present moment was preceded by an infinite series of events?[9]

Concluding that this difficulty has not been overcome and that the issue is still in dispute, Hospers passes on to another subject, leaving the argument unrefuted. Similarly, another philosopher comments rather weakly, "It is difficult to show exactly what is wrong with this argument," and with that remark moves on without further ado.[10]

Therefore, since the series of events in time is a collection formed by adding one member after another, and since such a collection cannot be actually infinite, the series of events in time cannot be actually infinite. And once more, since the universe is nothing else than the series of events, the universe must have had a beginning, which is precisely the point we wanted to prove.

## The First Scientific Confirmation: The Evidence from the Expansion of the Universe

Prior to the 1920s, scientists assumed that the universe as a whole was a stationary object. But in 1929 an astronomer named Edwin Hubble contended that this was not true. Hubble observed that the light from distant galaxies appeared to be redder than it should be. He explained this by proposing that the universe is expanding. Therefore, the light from the stars is affected since they are moving away from us. But this is the interesting part: Hubble not only showed that the universe is expanding, but that *it is expanding the same in all directions.* To get a picture of this, imagine a balloon with dots painted on it. As you blow up the balloon, the dots get further and further apart. Now those dots are just like the galaxies in space. Everything in the universe is expanding outward. Thus, the relations in the universe do not change, only the distances.

Now the staggering implication of this is that . . . at some point in the past, *the entire known universe was contracted down to a single point,* from which it has been expanding ever since. The farther back one goes in the past, the smaller the universe becomes, so that one finally reaches a point of *infinite density* from which the universe began to expand. That initial event has come to be known as the "big bang."

How long ago did the big bang occur? Only during the 1970s [did] accurate estimates become available. In a very important series of six articles published in 1974 and 1975, Allan Sandage and G. A. Tammann estimate that the big bang occurred about 15 billion years ago.[11] Therefore, according to the big bang model, the universe began to exist with a great explosion from a state of infinite density about 15 billion years ago. Four of the world's most prominent astronomers describe that event in these words:

> The universe began from a state of infinite density. Space and time were created in that event and so was all the matter in the universe. It is not meaningful to ask what happened before the big bang; it is somewhat like asking what is north of the north pole. Similarly, it is not sensible to ask where the big bang took place. The point-universe was not an object isolated in space; it was the entire universe, and so the only answer can be that the big bang happened everywhere.[12]

This event that marked the beginning of the universe becomes all the more amazing when one reflects on the fact that a state of "infinite density" is synonymous with "nothing." There can be no object that possesses infinite density, for if it had any size at all, it would not be *infinitely* dense. Therefore, as astronomer Fred Hoyle points out, the big bang theory requires the creation of matter from nothing. This is because as one goes back in time, he reaches a point at which, in Hoyle's words, the universe was "shrunk down to nothing at all."[13] Thus, what the big bang model requires is that the universe had a beginning and was created out of nothing.

Now some people are bothered with the idea that the universe began from nothing. This is too close to the Christian doctrine of creation to allow atheistic minds to be comfortable. But if one rejects the big bang model, he has apparently only two alternatives: the steady state model or the oscillating model. Let's examine each of these.

The steady-state model holds that the universe never had a beginning but has always existed in the same state. Ever since this model was first proposed in 1948, it has never been very convincing. According to S. L. Jaki, this theory never secured "a single piece of experimental verification."[14] It always seemed to be trying to explain away the facts rather than explain them. According to Jaki, the proponents of this model were actually motivated by "openly anti-theological, or rather anti-Christian motivations."[15] A second strike against this theory is the fact that a count of galaxies emitting radio waves indicates that there were once more radio sources in the past than there are today. Therefore, the universe is not in a steady state after all. But the real nails in the coffin for the steady state theory came in 1965, when A. A. Penzias and R. W. Wilson discovered that the entire universe is bathed with a background of microwave radiation. This radiation background indicates that the universe was once in a very hot and very dense state. In the steady-state model no such state could have existed, since the universe was supposed to be the same from eternity. Therefore, the steady-state model has been abandoned by virtually everyone. According to Ivan King, "The steady-state theory has now been laid to rest, as a result of clear-cut observations of how things have changed with time."[16]

But what of the oscillating model of the universe? John Gribbin describes this model,

> The biggest problem with the big bang theory of the origin of the universe is philo-sophical—perhaps even theological—what was there before the bang? This prob-lem alone was sufficient to give a great initial impetus to the steady-state theory, but with that theory now sadly in conflict with the observations, the best way round this initial difficulty is provided by a model in which the universe expands, collapses back again, and repeats the cycle indefinitely.[17]

According to this model, the universe is sort of like a spring, expanding and con-tracting from eternity. It is only in the last three or four years that this model has been discredited. The key question here is whether the universe is "open" or "closed." If it is "closed," then the expansion will reach a certain point, and then the force of gravity will pull everything together again. But if the universe is "open," then the expansion will never stop, but will just go on and on forever. Now clearly, if the universe is open, then the oscillating model is false. For if the universe is open, it will never contract again.

Scientific evidence seems to indicate that the universe is open. The crucial factor here is the density of the universe. Scientists have estimated that if there are more than about three hydrogen atoms per cubic meter on the average throughout the universe, then the universe would be closed. That may not sound like very much, but remember that most of the universe is just empty space. I shall not go into all the technicalities of how scientists measure the density of the universe,[18] but let me simply report their conclusions. According to the evidence, the universe would have to be at least ten times denser than it is for the universe to be closed.[19] There-fore, the universe is open by a wide margin. Let me share with you the conclusion of Alan Sandage: (1) the universe is open, (2) the expansion will not reverse, and (3) *the universe has happened only once* and the expansion will never stop.[20]

The evidence therefore appears to rule out the oscillating model, since it requires a closed universe. But just to drive the point home, let me add that the oscillating model of the universe is only a *theoretical* possibility, not a *real* possi-bility. As Dr. Tinsley of Yale observes, in oscillating models

> even though the mathematics *says* that the universe oscillates, there is no known physics to reverse the collapse and bounce back to a new expansion. The physics seems to say that those models start from the big bang, expand, collapse, then end.[21]

Hence, it would be impossible for the universe to be oscillating from eternity. Therefore, this model is doubly impossible.

## The Second Scientific Confirmation: The Evidence from Thermodynamics

According to the second law of thermodynamics, processes taking place in a closed system always tend toward a state of equilibrium. In other words, unless energy is constantly being fed into a system, the processes in the system will tend to run down and quit. For example, if I had a bottle that was a sealed vacuum inside, and I intro-duced into it some molecules of gas, the gas would spread itself out evenly inside the bottle. It is virtually impossible for the molecules to retreat, for example, into one corner of the bottle and remain. This is why when you walk into a room, the air in the room never separates suddenly into oxygen at one end and nitrogen at the other. It is also why when you step into your bath you may be confident that it will be pleasantly warm instead of frozen solid at one end and boiling at the other. It is clear that life would not be possible in a world in which the second law of thermodynamics did not operate.

Now our interest in the law is what happens when it is applied to the universe as a whole. The universe is a gigantic closed system, since it is everything there is and there is nothing outside it.[22] What this seems to imply then is that, given enough time, the universe and all its processes will run down and the entire universe will slowly grind to a halt. This is known as the heat death of the universe. Once the universe reaches this state, no further change is possible. The universe is dead.

There are two possible types of heat death for the universe. If the universe is "closed," then it will die a hot death. Tinsley describes such a state:

> If the average density of matter in the universe is great enough, the mutual gravitational attraction between bodies will eventually slow the expansion to a halt. The universe will then contract and collapse into a hot fireball. There is no known physical mechanism that could reverse a catastrophic big crunch. Apparently, if the universe becomes dense enough, it is in for a hot death.[23]

If the universe is closed, it is in for a fiery death from which it will never reemerge. But suppose, as is more likely, the universe is "open." Tinsley describes the final state of this universe:

> If the universe has a low density, its death will be cold. It will expand forever, at a slower and slower rate. Galaxies will turn all of their gas into stars, and the stars will burn out. Our own sun will become a cold, dead remnant, floating among the corpses of other stars in an increasingly isolated milky way.[24]

Eventually, equilibrium will prevail throughout, and the entire universe will reach its final state from which no change will occur.

Now the question that needs to be asked is this: If given enough time, the universe will reach heat death, then why is it not in a state of heat death now if it has existed forever, from eternity? If the universe did not begin to exist, then it should now be in a state of equilibrium. Its energy should be all used up. For example, I have a very loud wind-up alarm clock. If I hear that the clock is ticking—which is no problem, believe me—then I know that at some point in the recent past, it was wound up and has been running down since then. It is the same with the universe. Since it has not yet run down, this means, in the words of one baffled scientist, "In some way the universe must have been wound up."[25]

Some scientists have tried to escape this conclusion by arguing that the universe oscillates back and forth from eternity and so never reaches a final state of equilibrium. I have already observed that such a model of the universe is a physical impossibility. But suppose it were possible. The fact is that the thermodynamic properties of this model imply the very beginning of the universe that its proponents seek to avoid. For as several scientists have pointed out, each time the model universe expands it would expand a little further than before. Therefore, if you traced the expansions back in time they would get smaller and smaller and smaller. Therefore, in the words of one scientific team, "The multicycle model has an infinite future, but only a finite past."[26] As yet another writer points out, this implies that the oscillating model of the universe still requires an origin of the universe prior to the smallest cycle.[27]

Traditionally, two objections have been urged against the thermodynamic argument.[28] First, the argument does not work if the universe is infinite. I have two replies to this. (a) The universe is not, in fact, infinite. An actually spatially infinite universe would involve all the absurdities entailed in the existence of an actual infinite. But if space-time is torus-shaped, then the universe may be both open and finite. The objection is therefore irrelevant. (b) Even if the universe were infinite, it would still come to equilibrium. As one scientist explained in a letter to me, if every finite region of the universe came to equilibrium, then the whole universe would come to equilibrium.[29] This would be true even if it had an infinite number of finite regions. This is like saying that if every part of a fence is green, then the whole fence is green, even if there are an infinite number of pickets in the fence. Since every single finite region of the universe would suffer heat death, so would the whole universe. Therefore, the objection is unsound.

The second objection is that maybe the present state of the universe is just a fluctuation in an overall state of equilibrium. In other words, the present energy is like just the ripple on the surface of a still pond. But this objection loses all sense of proportion. Fluctuations are so tiny, they are important only in systems where you have a few atoms. In a universe at equilibrium, fluctuations would be imperceptible.[30] A chart showing fluctuations in such a universe would be simply a straight line. Therefore, since the present universe is in *dis*equilibrium, what are we to conclude? According to the English scientist P.C.W. Davies, the universe must have been created a finite time ago and is in the process of winding down.[31] He says the present disequilibrium cannot be a fluctuation from a prior state of equilibrium, because prior to this creation event the universe simply did not exist. Thus, Davies concludes, even though we may not like it, we must conclude that the universe's energy "was simply 'put in' at the creation as an initial condition."[32]

Thus, we have two philosophical arguments and two scientific confirmations of the point we set out to defend: the universe began to exist. In light of these four reasons, I think we are amply justified in affirming the first alternative of our first disjunction: *the universe had a beginning.*

## Was the Beginning Caused?

Having concluded that the evidence points to a beginning of the universe, let's now turn to our second set of alternatives: the beginning of the universe was either caused or not caused. I am not going to give a lengthy defense of the point that the beginning of the universe must have been caused. I do not think I need to. For probably no one in his right mind *sincerely* believes that the universe could pop into existence uncaused out of nothing. Even the famous skeptic David Hume admitted that it is preposterous to think anything could come into existence without a cause.[33] This is doubly true with regard to the entire universe. As the English philosopher C. D. Broad confessed, "I cannot really *believe in* anything beginning to exist without being caused by something else which existed before and up to the moment when the thing in question began to exist."[34] As still another philosopher has said, "It seems quite inconceivable that our universe could have sprung from an absolute void. If there is anything we find inconceivable it is that something could arise from nothing."[35] The old principle that "out of nothing, nothing comes" is so manifestly true that a sincere denial of this point is practically impossible.

This puts the atheist on the spot. For as Anthony Kenny explains, "A proponent of [the big bang] theory, at least if he is an atheist, must believe that the matter of the universe came from nothing and by nothing."[36] That is a pretty hard pill to swallow. In terms of sheer "believability," I find it intellectually easier to believe in a God who is the cause of the universe than in the universe's popping into existence uncaused out of nothing or in the universe's having existed for infinite time without a beginning. For me these last two positions are intellectually inconceivable, and it would take *more* faith for me to believe in them than to believe that God exists. But at any rate, we are not dependent upon just "believability," for we have already seen that both philosophical and empirical reasoning points to a beginning for the universe. So the alternatives are only two: either the universe was caused to exist or it sprang into existence wholly uncaused out of nothing about fifteen billion years ago. The first alternative is eminently more plausible.

It is interesting to examine the attitude of scientists toward the philosophical and theological implications of their own big bang model. It is evident that there are such implications, for as one scientist remarks, "The problem of the origin (of the universe) involves a certain metaphysical aspect which may be either appealing or revolting."[37] Unfortunately, the man of science is, as Albert Einstein once observed, "a poor philosopher."[38] For these implications seem either to escape or not to interest most scientists. Since no empirical information is available about what preceded the big bang, scientists simply ignore the issue. Thus, Hoyle, after explaining that the big bang model cannot inform us as to where the matter came from or why the big bang occurred, comments, "It is not usual in present day cosmological discussions to seek an answer to this question; the question and its answer are taken to be outside the range of scientific discussion."[39] But while this attitude may satisfy the scientist, it can never satisfy the philosopher. For as one scientist admits, the big bang model only *describes* the initial conditions of the universe, but it cannot *explain* them.[40] As yet another astronomer concludes, "So the question 'How was the matter created in the first place?' is left unanswered."[41] Thus, science begs off answering the really ultimate question of where the universe came from. Scientific evidence points to a beginning of the universe; as rigorous scientists we may stop there and bar further inquiry, but as thinking people must we not inquire further until we come to the cause of the beginning of the universe?

Either the universe was caused to exist or it just came into existence out of nothing by nothing. Scientists refuse to discuss the question; but philosophers admit that it is impossible to believe in something's coming to exist uncaused out of nothing. Therefore, I think that an unprejudiced inquirer will have to agree that the beginning of the universe was caused, which is the second point we set out to prove: *the universe was caused to exist.*

Now this is a truly remarkable conclusion. For this means that the universe was caused to exist by something beyond it and greater than it . . .

## Personal or Impersonal Creator?

I think there is good reason to believe that the cause of the universe is a personal creator. This is our third set of alternatives: *personal or not personal.*

The first event in the series of past events was, as we have seen, the beginning of the universe. Furthermore, we have argued that the event was caused. Now the question is: If the cause of the universe is eternal, then why isn't the universe also eternal, since it is the effect of the cause? Let me illustrate what I mean. Suppose we say the cause of water's freezing is the temperature's falling below 0 degrees. Whenever the temperature is below 0 degrees, the water is frozen. Therefore, if the temperature is always below 0 degrees, the water is always frozen. Once the cause is given, the effect must follow. So if the cause were there from eternity, the effect would also be there from eternity. If the temperature were below 0 degrees from eternity, then any water around would be frozen from eternity. But this seems to imply that if the cause of the universe existed from eternity then the universe would have to exist from eternity. And this we have seen to be false.

One might say that the cause came to exist just before the first event. But this will not work, for then the cause's coming into existence would be the first event, and we must ask all over again for its cause. But this cannot go on forever, for we have seen that a beginningless series of events cannot exist. So there must be an absolutely first event, before which there was no change, no previous event. We have seen that this first event was caused. But the question then is: How can a first event come to exist if the cause of that event is always there? Why isn't the effect as eternal as the cause? It seems to me that there is only one way out of this dilemma. That is to say that the cause of the universe is personal and chooses to create the universe in time. In this way God could exist changelessly from eternity, but choose to create the world in time. By "choose" I do not mean God changes his mind. I mean God intends from eternity to create a world in time. Thus, the cause is eternal, but the effect is not. God chooses from eternity to create a world with a beginning; therefore, a world with a beginning comes to exist. Hence, it seems to me that the only way a universe can come to exist is if a Personal Creator of the universe exists. And I think we are justified in calling a Personal Creator of the universe by the name "God."

I would just like to make a few concluding remarks on God's relationship to time. Many people say God is outside time. But this is not what the Bible says. According to James Barr, in his book *Biblical Words for Time,* the Bible does not make it clear whether God is eternal in the sense that he is outside time or whether he is eternal in the sense of being everlasting throughout all time.[42] Thus, the issue must be decided philosophically. It seems to me that prior to creation God is outside time, or rather there is no time at all. For time cannot exist unless there is change.

And prior to creation God would have to be changeless. Otherwise, you would get an infinite series of past events in God's life, and we have seen that such an infinite series is impossible. So God would be changeless and, hence, timeless prior to creation. I think that the doctrine of the Trinity can help us to understand this. Before creation, the Father, Son, and Holy Spirit existed in a perfect and changeless love relationship. God was not lonely before creation. In the tri-unity of his own being, he had full and perfect personal relationships. So what was God doing before creation? Someone has said, "He was preparing hell for those who pry into mysteries." Not at all! He was enjoying the fullness of divine personal relationships, with an eternal plan for the creation and salvation of human persons. The Bible says Christ "had been chosen by God before the creation of the world, and was revealed in these last days for your sake."[43] Nor was this plan decided on several eons ago. It is an eternal plan: The Bible says, "God did this according to his eternal purpose which he achieved through Christ Jesus our Lord."[44] Why did God do this? Not because he needed us, but simply out of his grace and love.

So in my opinion, God was timeless prior to creation, and He created time along with the world. From that point on God places Himself within time so that He can interact with the world He has created. And someday God will be done with this creation. The universe will not, in fact, suffer cold death, for God will have done with it by then. The Bible says,

> You, Lord, in the beginning created the earth,
> and with your own hands you made the heavens.
> They will all disappear, but you will remain;
>     they will all grow old like clothes.
> You will fold them up like a coat,
>     and they will be changed like clothes.
> But you are always the same,
>     and you will never grow old.[45]

We have thus concluded to a personal Creator of the universe, who exists changelessly and independently prior to creation, and in time subsequent to creation. This is the central idea of what theists mean by "God."

## Notes

1. G. W. Leibniz, "The Principles of Nature and of Grace, Based on Reason," in *Leibniz Selections,* ed. Philip P. Wiener, The Modern Student's Library (New York: Charles Scribner's Sons, 1951), p. 527.

2. Norman Malcolm, *Ludwig Wittgenstein: A Memoir* (London: Oxford University Press, 1958), p. 70.

3. J.J.C. Smart, "The Existence of God," *Church Quarterly Review* 156 (1955): 194.

4. Bertrand Russell and F. C. Copleston, "The Existence of God," in *The Existence of God* (Problems of Philosophy Series), ed. with an Introduction by John Hick (New York: Macmillan, 1964), pp. 174, 176.

5. See Abraham A. Fraenkel, *Abstract Set Theory,* 2nd rev. ed. (Amsterdam: North-Holland Publishing Co., 1961), pp. 5–6.

6. David Hilbert, "On the Infinite," in *Philosophy of Mathematics,* ed. with an Introduction by Paul Benacerraf and Hilary Putnam (Englewood Cliffs, NJ: Prentice-Hall, 1964), pp. 139, 141.

7. Hilbert, "On the Infinite," p. 151.

8. For an in-depth discussion of this see William Lane Craig, *The* Kalam *Cosmological Argument* (New York: Macmillan, 1979), App. 1 and 2.

9. John Hospers, *An Introduction to Philosophical Analysis,* 2nd ed. (London: Routledge & Kegan Paul, 1967), p. 434.

10. William L. Rowe, *The Cosmological Argument* (Princeton, NJ: Princeton University Press, 1975), p. 122.

11. Allan Sandage and G. A. Tammann, "Steps Toward the Hubble Constant. I-VI," *Astrophysical Journal* 190 (1974): 525–38; 191 (1974): 603–21; 194 (1974): 223–43, 559–68; 196 (1975): 313–28; 197 (1975): 265–80.

12. J. Richard Gott III, James E. Gunn, David N. Schramm, Beatrice M. Tinsley, "Will the Universe Expand Forever?," *Scientific American,* March 1976, p. 65. This article is a popular rewrite of their article, "An Unbound Universe?," *Astrophysical Journal* 194 (1974): 543–53.

13. Fred Hoyle, *Astronomy and Cosmology: A Modern Course* (San Francisco: W. H. Freeman, 1975), p. 658.

14. Stanley L. Jaki, *Science and Creation* (Edinburgh and London: Scottish Academic Press, 1974), p. 347.

15. Jacki, *Science and Creation,* p. 347.

16. Ivan R. King, *The Universe Unfolding* (San Francisco: W. H. Freeman, 1976), p. 462.

17. John Gribbin, "Oscillating Universe Bounces Back," *Nature* 259 (1976): 15.

18. See Gott, et al., "Will the Universe Expand Forever?," for a good synopsis.

19. J. Richard Gott III and Martin J. Rees, "A Theory of Galaxy Formation and Clustering," *Astronomy and Astrophysics* 45 (1975): 365–76; S. Michael Small, "The Scale of Galaxy Clustering and the Mean Matter Density of the Universe," *Monthly Notices of the Royal Astronomical Society* 172 (1975): 23p–26p.

20. Sandage and Tammann, "Steps Toward the Hubble Constant. VI," p. 276; Allan Sandage, "The Redshift Distance Relation. VIII," *Astrophysical Journal* 202 (1975): 563–82.

21. Beatrice M. Tinsley, personal letter.

22. In saying the universe is a closed system, I do not mean it is closed in the sense that its expansion will eventually contract. I rather mean that there is no energy being put into it. Thus, in the thermodynamic sense, the universe is closed, but in the sense of its density the universe is open. One must not confuse "open" and "closed" in thermodynamics with "open" and "closed" in expansion models.

23. Beatrice M. Tinsley, "From Big Bang to Eternity?," *Natural History Magazine,* October 1975, p. 103.

24. Tinsley, "From Big Bang to Eternity?," p. 185.

25. Richard Schlegel, "Time and Thermodynamics," in *The Voices of Time,* ed. J. T. Fraser (London: Penguin, 1968), p. 511.

26. I. D. Novikov and Ya. B. Zel'dovich, "Physical Processes Near Cosmological Singularities," *Annual Review of Astronomy and Astrophysics* 11 (1973): 401–2. See also P.C.W. Davies, *The Physics of Time Asymmetry* (London: Surrey University Press, 1974), p. 188. These findings are also confirmed by P. T. Landsberg and D. Park, "Entropy in an Oscillating Universe," *Proceedings of the Royal Society of London* A 346 (1975): 485–95.

27. Gribbin, "Oscillating Universe," p. 16.

28. R. G. Swinburne, *Space and Time* (London: Macmillan, 1968), p. 304; Adolf Grunbaum, *Philosophical Problems of Space and Time,* (Boston Studies in the Philosophy of Science), 2nd ed., Vol. 12 (Dordrecht, Neth., and Boston: D. Reidel Publishing, 1973), p. 262.

29. P.C.W. Davies, personal letter.

30. P. J. Zwart, *About Time* (Amsterdam and Oxford, Engl.: North Holland Publishing Co., 1976), pp. 117–19.

31. Davies, *Physics,* p. 104.

32. Davies, *Physics,* p. 104.

33. David Hume to John Stewart, February 1754, in *The Letters of David Hume,* Vol. 1, ed. J.Y.T. Greig (Oxford, Engl.: Clarendon Press, 1932), p. 187.

34. C. D. Broad, "Kant's Mathematical Antinomies," *Proceedings of the Aristotelian Society* 55 (1955): 10.

35. Zwart, *About Time,* p. 240.

36. Anthony Kenny, *The Five Ways: St. Thomas Aquinas' Proofs of God's Existence* (New York: Schocken Books, 1969), p. 66.

37. Hubert Reeves, Jean Audouze, William A. Fowler, and David N. Schramm, "On the Origin of Light Elements," *Astrophysical Journal* 179 (1973): 909–30.

38. Albert Einstein, *Out of My Later Years* (New York: Philosophical Library, 1950), p. 58.

39. Fred Hoyle, *Astronomy Today* (London: Heinemann, 1975), p. 166.

40. Adrian Webster, "The Cosmic Background Radiation," *Scientific American,* August 1974, p. 31.

41. J. V. Narlikar, "Singularity and Matter Creation in Cosmological Models," *Nature: Physical Science* 242 (1973): 136.

42. James Barr, *Biblical Words for Time* (London: SCM Press, 1962), pp. 80, 145–47.

43. I Peter 1:20. (TEV)

44. Ephesians 3:11. (TEV)

45. Hebrews 1:10–12. (TEV)

# 14

# The Argument from Design

## Richard Swinburne

The object of this paper[1] is to show that there are no valid formal objections to the argument from design, so long as the argument is articulated with sufficient care. In particular I wish to analyze Hume's attack on the argument in *Dialogues Concerning Natural Religion* and to show that none of the formal objections made therein by Philo have any validity against a carefully articulated version of the argument.

The argument from design is an argument from the order or regularity of things in the world to a god or, more precisely, a very powerful, free, nonembodied rational agent, who is responsible for that order. By a body I understand a part of the material Universe subject, at any rate partially, to an agent's direct control, to be contrasted with other parts not thus subject. An agent's body marks the limits to what he can directly control; he can only control other parts of the Universe by moving his body. An agent who could directly control any part of the Universe would not be embodied. Thus ghosts, if they existed, would be nonembodied agents, because there are no particular pieces of matter subject to their direct control, but any piece of matter may be so subject. I use the word 'design' in such a way that it is not analytic that if anything evinces design, an agent designed it, and so it becomes a synthetic question whether the design of the world shows the activity of a designer.

The argument, taken by itself, as was admitted in the *Dialogues* by Cleanthes, the proponent of the argument, does not show that the designer of the world is omnipotent, omniscient, totally good, etc. Nor does it show that he is the God of Abraham, Isaac, and Jacob. To make these points further arguments would be needed. The isolation of the argument from design from the web of Christian apologetic is perhaps a somewhat unnatural step, but necessary in order to analyze its structure. My claim is that the argument does not commit any formal fallacy, and by this I mean that it keeps to the canons of argument about matters of fact and does not violate any of them. It is, however, an argument by analogy. It argues from an analogy between the order of the world and the products of human art to a god

Reprinted from *Philosophy* 43 (1968), by permission of Cambridge University Press. Notes edited.

responsible for the former, in some ways similar to man who is responsible for the latter. And even if there are no formal fallacies in the argument, one unwilling to admit the conclusion might still claim that the analogy was too weak and remote for him to have to admit it, that the argument gave only negligible support to the conclusion which remained improbable. In defending the argument I will leave to the objector this way of escape from its conclusion.

I will begin by setting forward the argument from design in a more careful and precise way than Cleanthes did.

There are in the world two kinds of regularity or order, and all empirical instances of order are such because they evince one or other or both kinds of order. These are the regularities of copresence, or spatial order, and regularities of succession, or temporal order. Regularities of copresence are patterns of spatial order at some one instant of time. An example of a regularity of copresence would be a town with all its roads at right angles to each other, or a section of books in a library arranged in alphabetical order [by] author. Regularities of succession are simple patterns of behavior of objects, such as their behavior in accordance with the laws of nature—for example, Newton's law of gravitation, which holds universally to a very high degree of approximation, that all bodies attract each other with forces proportional to the product of their masses and inversely proportional to the square of their distance apart.

Many of the striking examples of order in the world evince an order which is due both to a regularity of copresence and to a regularity of succession. A working car consists of many parts so adjusted to each other that it follows the instructions of the driver delivered by his pulling and pushing a few levers and buttons and turning a wheel to take passengers whither he wishes. Its order arises because its parts are so arranged at some instant (regularity of copresence) that, the laws of nature being as they are (regularity of succession), it brings about the result neatly and efficiently. The order of living animals and plants likewise results from regularities of both types.

Men who marvel at the order of the world may marvel at either or both of the regularities of copresence and of succession. The men of the eighteenth century, that great century of "reasonable religion," were struck almost exclusively by the regularities of copresence. They marveled at the design and orderly operations of animals and plants; but since they largely took for granted the regularities of succession, what struck them about the animals and plants, as to a lesser extent about machines made by men, was the subtle and coherent arrangement of their millions of parts. Paley's *Natural Theology* dwells mainly on details of comparative anatomy, on eyes and ears and muscles and bones arranged with minute precision so as to operate with high efficiency, and Hume's Cleanthes produces the same kind of examples: "Consider, anatomise the eye, survey its structure and contrivance, and tell me from your own feeling, if the idea of a contriver does not immediately flow in upon you with a force like that of sensation."[2]

Those who argue from the existence of regularities of copresence other than those produced by men, to the existence of a god who produced them, are, however, in many respects on slippery ground when compared with those who rely for their premises on regularities of succession. We shall see several of these weaknesses later in considering Hume's objections to the argument, but it is worthwhile noting two of them at the outset. First, although the world contains many striking regularities of copresence (some few of which are due to human agency), it also contains many examples of spatial disorder. The uniform distribution of the galactic clusters is a marvellous example of spatial order, but the arrangement of trees in an African jungle is a marvellous example of spatial disorder. Although the proponent of the argument may then proceed to argue that in an important sense or from some point of view (e.g., utility to man) the order vastly exceeds the disorder, he has to argue for this in no way obvious proposition.

Second, the proponent of the argument runs the risk that the regularities of copresence may be explained in terms of something else by a normal scientific explanation[3] in a way that the regularities of succession could not possibly be. A scientist could show that a regularity of copresence R arose from an apparently disordered state D by means of the normal operation of the laws of nature. This would not entirely "explain away" the regularity of copresence, because the proponent of this argument from design might then argue that the apparently disordered state D really had a latent order, being the kind of state which, when the laws of nature operate, turns into a manifestly ordered one. So long as only few of the physically possible states of apparent disorder were states of latent order, the existence of many states of latent order would be an important contingent fact which could form a premise for an argument from design. But there is always the risk that scientists might show that most states of apparent disorder were states of latent order, that is, that if the world lasted long enough, considerable order must emerge from whichever of many initial states it began. If a scientist showed that, he would have explained by normal scientific explanation the existence of regularities of copresence in terms of something completely different. The eighteenth-century proponents of the argument from design did not suspect this danger and hence the devasting effect of Darwin's theory of evolution by natural selection on those who accepted their argument. For Darwin showed that the regularities of copresence of the animal and plant kingdoms had evolved by natural processes from an apparently disordered state and would have evolved equally from many other apparently disordered states. Whether all regularities of copresence can be fully explained in this kind of way no one yet knows, but the danger remains for the proponent of an argument from design of this kind that they can be.

However, those who argue from the operation of regularities of succession other than those produced by men, to the existence of a god who produces them, do not run into either of these difficulties. Regularities of succession (other than those produced by men), unlike regularities of copresence, are all-pervasive. Simple natural laws rule almost all successions of events. Nor can regularities of succession be given a normal scientific explanation in terms of something else. For the normal scientific explanation of the operation of a regularity of succession is in terms of the operation of a yet more general regularity of succession. Note, too, that a normal scientific explanation of the existence of regularities of copresence in terms of something different, if it can be provided, is explanation in terms of regularities of succession.

For these reasons the proponent of the argument from design does much better to rely for his premise more on regularities of succession. St. Thomas Aquinas, wiser than the men of the eighteenth century, did just this. He puts forward an argument from design as his fifth and last way to prove the existence of God, and gives his premise as follows:

> The fifth way is based on the guidedness of nature. An orderedness of actions to an end is observed in all bodies obeying natural laws, even when they lack awareness. For their behaviour hardly ever varies, and will practically always turn out well; which shows that they truly tend to a goal, and do not merely hit it by accident.[4]

If we ignore any value judgment in "practically always turn out well," St. Thomas' argument is an argument from regularities of succession.

The most satisfactory premise for the argument from design is, then, the operation of regularities of succession other than those produced by men, that is, the operation of natural laws. Almost all things almost always obey simple natural laws, and so behave in a strikingly regular way. Given the premise, what is our justification for proceeding to the conclusion, that a very powerful, free, nonembodied rational agent is responsible for their behaving in that way? The justification which Aquinas gives is that

> Nothing . . . that lacks awareness tends to a goal, except under the direction of someone with awareness and with understanding; the arrow, for example, requires an archer. Everything in nature, therefore, is directed to its goal by someone with understanding, and this we call "God."[5]

A similar argument has been given by many religious apologists since Aquinas, but clearly as it stands it is guilty of the grossest petitio principii. Certainly *some* things which tend to a goal, tend to a goal because of a direction imposed upon them by someone "with awareness and with understanding." Did not the archer place the arrow and pull the string in a certain way, the arrow would not tend to its goal. But whether *all* things which tend to a goal tend to a goal for this reason is the very question at issue, and that they do cannot be used as a premise to prove the conclusion. We must therefore reconstruct the argument in a more satisfactory way.

The structure of any plausible argument from design can only be that the existence of a god responsible for the order in the world is a hypothesis well confirmed on the basis of the evidence, viz., that contained in the premise which we have now stated, and better confirmed than any other hypothesis. I shall begin by showing that there can be no other possible explanation for the operation of natural laws than the activity of a god, and then see to what extent the hypothesis is well confirmed on the basis of the evidence.

Almost all phenomena can, as we have seen, be explained by a normal scientific explanation in terms of the operation of natural laws on preceding states. There is, however, one other way of explaining natural phenomena, and that is explaining in terms of the rational choice of a free agent. When a man marries Jane rather than Anne, becomes a solicitor rather than a barrister, kills rather than shows mercy after considering arguments in favor of each course, he brings about a state of the world by his free and rational choice. To all appearances this is an entirely different way whereby states of the world may come about than through the operation of laws of nature on preceding states. Someone may object that it is necessary that physiological or other scientific laws operate in order for the agent to bring about effects. My answer is that certainly it is necessary that such laws operate in order for effects brought about directly by the agent to have ulterior consequences. But unless there are some effects which the agent brings about directly without the operation of scientific laws acting on preceding physical states bringing them about, then these laws and states could fully explain the effects, and there would be no need to refer in explaining them to the rational choice of an agent. True, the apparent freedom and rationality of the human will *may* prove an illusion. Man may have no more option what to do than a machine and be guided by an argument no more than is a piece of iron. But this has never yet been shown and, in the absence of good philosophical and scientific argument to show it, I assume, what is apparent, that when a man acts by free and rational choice, his agency is the operation of a different kind of causality from that of scientific laws. The free choice of a rational agent is the only way of accounting for natural phenomena other than the way of normal scientific explanation, which is recognized as such by all men and has not been reduced to normal scientific explanation.

Almost all regularities of succession are due to the normal operation of scientific laws. But to say this is simply to say that these regularities are instances of more general regularities. The operation of the most fundamental regularities clearly cannot be given a normal scientific explanation. If their operation is to receive an explanation and not merely to be left as a brute fact, that explanation must therefore be in terms of the rational choice of a free agent. What, then, are grounds for adopting this hypothesis, given that it is the only possible one?

The grounds are that we can explain some few regularities of succession as produced by rational agents and that the other regularities cannot be explained except in this way. Among the typical products of a rational agent acting freely are regularities both of copresence and of succession. The alphabetical order of books on a library shelf is due to the activity of the librarian who chose to arrange them thus. The order of the cards of a pack by suits and seniority in each suit is due to the activity of the card player who arranged them thus. Among examples of regularities of succession produced by men are the notes of a song sung by a singer or the movements of a dancer's body when he performs a dance in time with the accompanying instrument. Hence, knowing that some regularities of succession have such a cause, we postulate that they all have. An agent produces the celestial harmony like a man who sings a song. But at this point an obvious difficulty arises. The regularities of succession, such as songs which are produced by men, are produced by agents of comparatively small power, whose bodies we can locate. If an agent is responsible for the operation of the laws of nature, he must act directly on the whole Universe, as we act directly on our bodies. Also, he must be of immense power and intelligence compared with men. Hence, he can only be somewhat similar to men having, like them, intelligence and freedom of choice, yet unlike them in the degree of these and in not possessing a body. For a body, as I have distinguished it earlier, is a part of the Universe subject to an agent's direct control, to be contrasted with other parts not thus subject. The fact that we are obliged to postulate on the basis of differences in the effects differences in the causes, men and the god, weakens the argument. How much it weakens it depends on how great these differences are.

Our argument thus proves to be an argument by analogy and to exemplify a pattern common in scientific inference. As are caused by Bs. A*s are similar to As. Therefore—given that there is no more satisfactory explanation of the existence of A*s—they are produced by B*s similar to Bs. B*s are postulated to be similar in all respects to Bs except insofar as shown otherwise, viz., except insofar as the dissimilarities between As and A*s force us to postulate a difference. A well-known scientific example of this type of inference is as follows. Certain pressures (As) on the walls of containers are produced by billiard balls (Bs) with certain motions. Similar pressures (A*s) are produced on the walls of containers which contain, not billiard balls, but gases. Therefore, since we have no better explanation of the existence of the pressures, gases consist of particles (B*s) similar to billiard balls except in certain respects, e.g., size. By similar arguments scientists have argued for the existence of many unobservables. Such an argument becomes weaker insofar as the properties which we are forced to attribute to the B*s because of the differences between the As and the A*s become different from those of the Bs. Nineteenth-century physicists postulated the existence of an elastic solid, the aether, to account for the propagation of light. But the way in which light was propagated turned out to have such differences (despite the similarities) from the way in which waves in solids are normally propagated that the physicists had to say that if there was an aether it had very many peculiar properties not possessed by normal liquids or solids. Hence, they concluded that the argument for its existence was very weak. The proponent of the argument from design stresses the similarities between the regularities of succession produced by man and those which are laws of nature, and so between men and the agent which he postulates as responsible for the laws of nature. The opponent of the argument stresses the dissimilarities. The degree of support which the conclusion obtains from the evidence depends on how great the similarities are.

The degree of support for the conclusion of an argument from analogy does not, however, depend merely on the similarities between the types of evidence, but on the degree to which the resulting theory makes explanation of empirical matters more simple and coherent. In the case of the argument from design, the conclusion has an enormous simplifying effect on explanations of empirical matters. For if the conclusion is true, if a very powerful nonembodied rational agent is responsible for the operation of the laws of nature, then normal scientific explanation would prove to be personal explanation. That is, explanation of some phenomenon in terms of the operation of a natural law would ultimately be an explanation in terms of the operation of an agent. Hence (given an initial arrangement of matter), the principles of explanation of phenomena would have been reduced from two to one. It is a basic principle of explanation that we should postulate as few as possible kinds of explanation. To take a more mundane example—if we have as possible alternatives to explain physical phenomena by the operation of two kinds of force, the electromagnetic and the gravitational, and to explain physical phenomena in terms of the operation of only one kind of force, the gravitational, we ought always—ceteris paribus—to prefer the latter alternative. Since, as we have seen, we are obliged, at any rate at present, to use explanation in terms of the free choice of a rational agent in explaining many empirical phenomena, then if the amount of similarity between the order in the Universe not produced by human agents and that produced by human agents makes it at all plausible to do so, we ought to postulate that an agent is responsible for the former as well as for the latter. So then, insofar as regularities of succession produced by the operation of natural laws are similar to those produced by human agents, to postulate that a rational agent is responsible for them would indeed provide a simple, unifying, and coherent explanation of natural phenomena. What is there against taking this step? Simply that celebrated principle of explanation—*entia non sunt multiplicanda praeter necessitatem*—"do not add a god to your ontology unless you have to." The issue turns on whether the evidence constitutes enough of a *necessitas* to compel us to multiply entities. Whether it does depends on how strong is the analogy between the regularities of succession produced by human agents and those produced by the operation of natural laws. I do not propose to assess the strength of the analogy, but only to claim that everything turns on it. I claim that the inference from natural laws to a god responsible for them is of a perfectly proper type for inference about matters of fact, and that the only issue is whether the evidence is strong enough to allow us to affirm that it is probable that the conclusion is true.

Now that I have reconstructed the argument from design in what is, I hope, a logically impeccable form, I turn to consider Hume's criticisms of it, and I shall argue that all his criticisms alleging formal fallacies in the argument do not apply to it in the form in which I have stated it. This, we shall see, is largely because the criticisms are bad criticisms of the argument in any form but also in small part because Hume directed his fire against that form of the argument which used as its premise the existence of regularities of copresence other than those produced by men, and did not appeal to the operation of regularities of succession. I shall begin by considering one general point which he makes only in the *Enquiry,* and then consider in turn all the objections which appear on the pages of the *Dialogues.*

1. The point which appears at the beginning of Hume's discussion of the argument in section XI of the *Enquiry* is a point which reveals the fundamental weakness of Hume's skeptical position. In discussing the argument, Hume puts forward as a general principle that "when we infer any particular cause from an effect, we must proportion the one to the other, and can never be allowed to ascribe to the cause any qualities but what are exactly sufficient to produce the effect."[6] Now it is true that Hume uses this principle mainly to show that we are not justified in inferring that the god responsible for the design of the Universe is totally good, omnipotent, and omniscient. I accept, as Cleanthes did, that the argument does not by itself lead to that conclusion. But Hume's use of the principle tends to cast doubt on the validity of the argument in the weaker form in which I am discussing it, for it seems to suggest that, although we may conclude that whatever produced the regularity of the world was a regularity-producing object, we cannot go further and conclude that it is an agent who acts by choice, etc., for this would be to suppose more than we need in order to account for the effect. It is, therefore, important to realize that the principle is clearly false on our normal understanding of what are the criteria of inference about empirical matters. For the universal adoption of this celebrated principle would lead to the abandonment of science. Any scientist who told us only that the cause of E had E-producing characteristics would not add an iota to our knowledge. Explanation of matters of fact consists in postulating on rea-

sonable grounds that the cause of an effect has certain characteristics other than those sufficient to produce the effect.

2. Two objections seem to be telescoped in the following passage of the *Dialogues*.

> When two *species* of objects have always been observed to be conjoined together, I can *infer* by custom the existence of one wherever I *see* the existence of the other; and this I call an argument from experience. But how this argument can have place where the objects, as in the present case, are single, individual, without parallel or specific resemblance, may be difficult to explain.[7]

One argument here seems to be that we can only infer from an observed A to an unobserved B when we have frequently observed As and Bs together, and that we cannot infer to a B unless we have actually observed other Bs. Hence we cannot infer from regularities of succession to an unobserved god on the analogy of the connection between observed regularities and human agents, unless we have observed at other times other gods. This argument, like the first, reveals Hume's inadequate appreciation of scientific method. As we saw in the scientific examples which I cited, a more developed science than Hume knew has taught us that when observed As have a relation R to observed Bs, it is often perfectly reasonable to postulate that observed A*s, similar to As have the same relation to unobserved and unobservable B*s similar to Bs.

3. The other objection which seems to be involved in the above passage is that we cannot reach conclusions about an object which is the only one of its kind, and, as the Universe is such an object, we cannot reach conclusions about the regularities characteristic of it as a whole.[8] But cosmologists are reaching very well-tested scientific conclusions about the Universe as a whole, as are physical anthropologists about the origins of our human race, even though it is the only human race of which we have knowledge and perhaps the only human race there is. The principle quoted in the objections is obviously wrong. There is no space here to analyze its errors in detail, but suffice it to point out that it becomes hopelessly confused by ignoring the fact that uniqueness is relative to description. Nothing describable is unique under all descriptions (the Universe is, like the solar system, a number of material bodies distributed in empty space), and everything describable is unique under some description.

4. The next argument which we meet in the *Dialogues* is that the postulated existence of a rational agent who produces the order of the world would itself need explaining. Picturing such an agent as a mind, and a mind as an arrangement of ideas, Hume phrases the objection as follows: "a mental world or Universe of ideas requires a cause as much as does a material world or Universe of objects."[9] Hume himself provides the obvious answer to this—that it is no objection to explaining X by Y that we cannot explain Y. But then he suggests that the Y, in this case the mind, is just as mysterious as the ordered Universe. Men never "thought it satisfactory to explain a particular effect by a particular cause which was no more to be accounted for than the effect itself."[10] On the contrary, scientists have always thought it reasonable to postulate entities merely to explain effects, so long as the postulated entities accounted simply and coherently for the characteristics of the effects. The existence of molecules with their characteristic behavior was "no more

to be accounted for" than observable phenomena, but the postulation of their existence gave a neat and simple explanation of a whole host of chemical and physical phenomena, and that was the justification for postulating their existence.

5. Next, Hume argues that if we are going to use the analogy of a human agent we ought to go the whole way and postulate that the god who gives order to the Universe is like men in many other respects. "Why not become a perfect anthropomorphite? Why not assert the deity or deities to be corporeal, and, to have eyes, a nose, mouths, ears, etc.?"[11] The argument from design is, as we have seen, an argument by analogy. All analogies break down somewhere; otherwise they would not be analogies. In saying that the relation of A to B is analogous to a relation of A* to a postulated B*, we do not claim that B* is in all respects like B, but only in such respects as to account for the existence of the relation, and also in other respects, except insofar as we have contrary evidence. For the activity of a god to account for the regularities, he must be free, rational, and very powerful. But it is not necessary that he, like men, should only be able to act on a limited part of the Universe, a body, and by acting on that control the rest of the Universe. And there is good reason to suppose that the god does not operate in this way. For, if his direct control was confined to a part of the Universe, scientific laws outside his control must operate to ensure that his actions have effects in the rest of the Universe. Hence the postulation of the existence of the god would not explain the operations of those laws: yet to explain the operation of all scientific laws was the point of postulating the existence of the god. The hypothesis that the god is not embodied thus explains more and explains more coherently than the hypothesis that he is embodied.[12] Hume's objection would, however, have weight against an argument from regularities of copresence which did not appeal to the operation of regularities of succession. For one could suppose an embodied god, just as well as a disembodied god, to have made the animal kingdom and then left it alone, as a man makes a machine, or, like a landscape gardener, to have laid out the galactic clusters. The explanatory force of such an hypothesis is as great as that of the hypothesis that a disembodied god did these things, and argument from analogy would suggest the hypothesis of an embodied god to be more probable. Incidentally, a god whose prior existence was shown by the existence of regularities of copresence might now be dead, but a god whose existence was shown by the present operation of regularities of succession could not be, since the existence of an agent is contemporaneous with the temporal regularities which he produces.

6. Hume urges: Why should we not postulate many gods to give order to the Universe, not merely one? "A great number of men join in building a house or a ship, in rearing a city, in framing a commonwealth, why may not several deities combine in framing a world?"[13] Hume again is aware of the obvious counterobjection to his suggestion: "To multiply causes without necessity is . . . contrary to true philosophy."[14] He claims, however, that the counterobjection does not apply here, because it is an open question whether there is a god with sufficient power to put the whole Universe in order. The principle, however, still applies, whether or not we have prior information that a being of sufficient power exists. When postulating entities, postulate as few as possible. Always suppose only one murderer, unless the evidence forces you to suppose a second. If there were more than one deity responsible for the order of the Universe, we should expect to see characteristic marks of

the handiwork of different deities in different parts of the Universe, just as we see different kinds of workmanship in the different houses of a city. We should expect to find an inverse square law of gravitation obeyed in one part of the universe, and in another part a law which was just short of being an inverse square law—without the difference being explicable in terms of a more general law. But it is enough to draw this absurd conclusion to see how ridiculous the Humean objection is.

7. Hume argues that there are in the Universe other things than rational agents which bestow order. "A tree bestows order and organisation on that tree which springs from it, without knowing the order; an animal in the same manner on its offspring."[15] It would therefore, Hume argues, be equally reasonable if we are arguing from analogy, to suppose the cause of the regularities in the world "to be something similar or analogous to generation or vegetation."[16] This suggestion makes perfectly good sense if it is the regularities of copresence which we are attempting to explain. But as analogous processes to explain regularities of succession, generation or vegetation will not do, because they only produce regularities of copresence—and those through the operation of regularities of succession outside their control. The seed only produces the plant because of the continued operation of the laws of biochemistry.

8. The last distinct objection which I can discover in the *Dialogues* is the following. Why should we not suppose, Hume urges, that this ordered Universe is a mere accident among the chance arrangements of eternal matter? In the course of eternity, matter arranges itself in all kinds of ways. We just happen to live in a period when it is characterized by order, and mistakenly conclude that matter is always ordered. Now, as Hume phrases this objection, it is directed against an argument from design which uses as its premise the existence of the regularities of copresence. "The continual motion of matter . . . in less than infinite transpositions must produce this economy or order, and by its very nature, that order, when once established, supports itself for many ages if not to eternity."[17] Hume thus relies here partly on chance and partly on the operation of regularities of succession (the preservation of order) to account for the existence of regularities of copresence. Insofar as it relies on regularities of succession to explain regularities of copresence, such an argument has, as we saw earlier, some plausibility. But insofar as it relies on chance, it does not, if the amount of order to be accounted for is very striking. An attempt to attribute the operation of regularities of succession to chance would not thus be very plausible. The claim would be that there are no laws of nature which always apply to matter. Matter evinces in the course of eternity all kinds of patterns of behavior; it is just chance that at the moment the states of the Universe are succeeding each other in a regular way. But if we say that it is chance that in 1960 matter is behaving in a regular way, our claim becomes less and less plausible as we find that in 1961 and 1962 and so on it continues to behave in a regular way. An appeal to chance to account for order becomes less and less plausible, the greater the order. We would be justified attributing a typewritten version of collected works of Shakespeare to the activity of monkeys typing eternally on eternal typewriters if we had some evidence of the existence of an infinite quantity of paper randomly covered with type, as well as the collected works. In the absence of any evidence that matter behaved irregularly at other temporal periods, we are not justified in attributing its present regular behavior to chance.

In addition to the objections which I have stated, the *Dialogues* contain a lengthy presentation of the argument that the existence of evil in the world shows that the god who made it and gave it order is not both totally good and omnipotent. But this does not affect the argument from design which, as Cleanthes admits, does not purport to show that the designer of the Universe does have these characteristics. The eight objections which I have stated are all the distinct objections to the argument from design which I can find in the *Enquiry* and in the *Dialogues,* which claim that in some formal respect the argument does not work. As well as claiming that the argument from design is deficient in some formal respect, Hume makes the point that the analogy of the order produced by men to the other order of the Universe is too remote for us to postulate similar causes.[18] I have argued earlier that if there is a weakness in the argument it is here that it is to be found. The only way to deal with this point would be to start drawing the parallels or stressing the dissimilarities, and these are perhaps tasks more appropriate for the preacher and the poet than for the philosopher. The philosopher will be content to have shown that, though perhaps weak, the argument has some force. How much force depends on the strength of the analogy.

## Notes

1. I am most grateful to Christopher Williams and to colleagues at Hull for their helpful criticisms of an earlier version of this paper.

2. David Hume, *Dialogues Concerning Natural Religion,* ed. H. D. Aiken (New York: Hafner, 1948), p. 28.

3. I understand by a "normal scientific explanation" one conforming to the pattern of deductive or statistical explanation utilized in paradigm empirical sciences such as physics and chemistry, elucidated in recent years by Hempel, Braithwaite, Popper, and others. Although there are many uncertain points about scientific explanation, those to which I appeal in the text are accepted by all philosophers of science.

4. St. Thomas Aquinas, *Summa Theologiae,* Ia, 2, 3, trans. Timothy McDermott, O.P. (London: Hafner, 1964.)

5. Aquinas, *Summa,* Ia, 2, 3.

6. David Hume, *An Enquiry Concerning Human Understanding,* 2nd ed., ed. L. A. Selby Bigge. 1902, p. 136.

7. Hume, *Dialogues,* p. 23.

8. For this argument see also *Enquiry,* p. 147f.

9. Hume, *Dialogues,* p. 33.

10. Hume, *Dialogues,* p. 36.

11. Hume, *Dialogues,* p. 40.

12. For the contrary view, see Michael Martin's essay reprinted in Part I of this volume.

13. Hume, *Dialogues,* p. 39.

14. Hume, *Dialogues,* p. 40.

15. Hume, *Dialogues,* p. 50.

16. Hume, *Dialogues,* p. 47.

17. Hume, *Dialogues,* p. 53.

18. See, for example, Hume, *Dialogues,* pp. 18 and 37.

# 15

# The Three-Stage Argument for the Existence of God

## *Dallas Willard*

. . . The case for the positive thesis of the existence of God . . . is not one which in one stroke, from one set of true premises, purports to establish or render plausible the existence of Jehovah, understood by Christians to also be the God and Father of our Lord Jesus Christ and referred to in Islam as "Allah." Rather, the plausibility of theism, as I shall henceforth simply refer to it, emerges in three stages. These stages are not three separate arguments or "ways," each of which, supposedly, bringing you to the *same* logical point. Three unsound arguments are not to be expected by their collective force to prove a conclusion which they cannot establish by themselves. Nor do the earlier stages establish conclusions which, in a straight-forward manner, serve as premises in the later stages. Instead, what is shown or evidentially supported in the earlier stages only determines a framework of possi-bilities within which the considerations of the later stages are carried on. For exam-ple, the first stage shows that there actually exists something which *might* be God in some more conventional sense.

What then, are the three stages? It is extremely hard to discuss the relevant issues without getting involved in many age-old entanglements that in fact have nothing to do with the case one is arguing. I shall, accordingly, avoid much of the traditional terminology in what follows and attempt to narrowly restrict myself to precisely those considerations upon which the evidence for theism, as I see it, depends. We begin with a *demonstration* that the physical or natural world recognized by com-mon sense and the "natural" sciences is not the only type of thing in existence: that there concretely exists, or at least has existed, something radically different from it in respects to be discussed. By a "demonstration" I mean a logical structure of prop-ositions where the premises are true and they logically imply or entail the conclu-sion when taken together.

## Stage One: The Physical World

The argument at stage one proceeds from *the nature and the existence of the physical*. Confusions, quibbles, and philosophical exercises—pointless and otherwise—aside, it is true that there is a physical world, and we do know that this is true. Further—although the nature of that world may ultimately be a profound mystery or turn out to have some deep kinship with what we call the mental or spiritual—there are some things about its general character which we also know to be true. One of these is: *However concrete physical reality is sectioned, the result will be a state of affairs which owes its being to something other than itself.*

This, I submit, is something which we know to be true of the general character of things in the physical world. (And, of course, anyone should feel free to submit a case of a physical state of which this proposition is *not* true.) Now it is, certainly, an extremely complex proposition, and, if we begin to take it apart, we will surely be led to many things we do not know and possibly do not even understand. But this proposition has that in common with nearly all of the truths which we know best, both in ordinary life and in science. One of the things which I hope might be clear at this point in humanity's intellectual development is that degree of simplicity or complexity in an object that has no automatic significance either for being or for knowledge. It should be equally clear that the inability to say *how* we know something does not imply that we do not know it—although it is always appropriate to raise the question of the "how" whenever someone claims to know something, and some appropriate kind of explanation is usually required.

Now any *general* understanding of the dependencies of physical states would require something like Aristotle's well-known four "causes." Restricting ourselves to the temporal order, however, we find, among other things, that every physical state, no matter how inclusive, has a necessary condition in some specific type of state which immediately precedes it in time and is fully existent prior to the emergence of the state which it conditions. This means that for any given state—for example, Voyager II being past Triton—all of the necessary conditions of that state must be over and done with *at* that state or *at* the event of which the state is the ontic residue. The series of "efficient" causes, to speak with Aristotle, is completed for any given event or state that obtains. *At* the state in question, we are not waiting for any of these causes to happen, to come into being.

Moreover, this completed set of causes is highly structured in time and in ontic dependence through relationships which are irreflexive, asymmetric, and transitive. Thus, no physical state is temporally or ontically prior to itself, and if one, *a,* is prior to another, *b, b* is not prior to *a.* Further, if *a* is prior to *b* and *b* to *c,* then *a* is prior to *c.* This rigorous structure of the past is eternally fixed, and it specifies a framework within which every event of coming into existence and ceasing to exist finds its place. Most importantly for present interests, since the series of causes for any given state is *completed,* it not only exhibits a rigorous structure as indicated, but that structure also has a first term. There is in it at least one "cause," one state of being, which does not derive its existence from something else. It is self-existent.

If this were not so, Voyager's passing Triton, or any other physical event or state, could not be realized, since that would require the actual completion of an infinite, an incompletable series of events. In simplest terms, its causes would never "get to" it. (As in a line of dominoes, if there is an infinite number of dominoes that must fall before domino *x* is struck, it will never be struck. The line of fallings will never get to it.) Since Voyager II *is* past Triton, there is a state of being upon which that state depends but which itself depends on nothing prior to it. Thus, concrete physical reality implicates a being radically different from itself: a being which, unlike any physical state, is self-existent.

This completes the *demonstration* in our first stage of theistic evidence. To sum up: the dependent character of all physical states, together with the completeness of the series of dependencies underlying the existence of any given physical state, logically implies at least one self-existent, and therefore nonphysical, state of being: a state of being, or an entity, radically different from those that make up the physical or "natural" world. It is demonstrably absurd that there should be a self-sufficient physical universe, if by that we mean an all-inclusive totality of entities and events of the familiar or scientific physical variety. Of course, we could, like Spinoza, prepare to treat the universe itself as having an essentially different type of being from the physical, but then we would be conceding our point.

It is common to hear in response to this argument the assertion that there just *cannot* be a self-existent being, but it is very uncommon to hear any very strong reason for the assertion. Professor Kai Nielsen, comments on the "incoherence" (once again) of a logically necessary individual, and I want to side with him in rejecting such a being. But I have said nothing so far about a logically necessary being. Only that, relative to the character of the physical world, it is logically necessary that there be something the existence of which does not derive from other things. So far as my argument goes, there is no reason why this should have to be a being logically necessary in itself—although, of course, I recognize there has been a lot of discussion about such a being in the history of our subject, and I do not discount that discussion as wholly pointless.

A more serious and perhaps more "common-sense" objection to my position, but one that is, I think, answerable, is contained in the child's question, "Mommy, where did God come from?" (He's just been told that God made trees and clouds, you know.) In our terminology: "Where did this self-existent being come from?" And the answer is that He (She, It) didn't come *from* anything because He didn't *come* at all.

One will have trouble with that answer only if one has already assimilated existence to *physical* existence. Then and only then does the perfectly general question, "Why is there something rather than nothing?" make sense—because it is assumed that the "something" refers only to the physical. Without that assimilation, the answer is, "Why shouldn't there be something—some existant or being?" And it turns out there is no good reason to suppose that everything that exists resembles physical existents in coming to be "from" something other than themselves. It should be pointed out that such a supposition, in any case, directly begs the question of God's existence—that is, it assumes that since all being is physical, there could be no spiritual reality such as God. For you certainly could not know that all reality is physical if the question of God's existence is yet to be decided. Efforts in the history of thought to tie the *concept* of being to that of the physical have proved resounding failures, it seems to me, although certain epistemological *programs*—for example, "Science is restricted to the physical (to physics and its derivatives), so 'knowledge' and therefore (!?!) being is restricted to the physical"—are still widely favored. The lack of a conceptual connection between being and the possibility of knowledge continues to plague such programs, as it has most philosophers from Hume and Kant to our time.

One has, I think, to go through a conceptual turnaround in general ontology somewhat like the one Newton executed for physics. Aristotelian physics made motion problematic and rest unproblematic. The question then was, "Why is there motion (here, or there, or at all) rather than rest?" Newton saw that motion was no more problematic than rest. What had to be explained was *change* from motion to rest, or conversely. Similarly, in general ontology one has to understand that existence is, in general, no more problematic than nonexistence. Existence isn't somehow "harder" or inherently less likely than nonexistence—unless, once again, we are obsessed with *physical* existents, which, because of their specific nature as dependent beings, *are* admittedly always more or less hanging on by the skin of their teeth and inevitably tending toward disintegration. (Aristotle, in his theory of motion, seems to have been obsessed with "forced" motion, such as donkeys pulling carts and persons hauling water out of a well.)

In fact, there are two interesting (by no means philosophically unproblematic) candidates other than God for the status of self-subsistent being or something similar: universals (Plato's "forms") and free human actions. With reference to universals, the question of origin in time does not arise, since they—as distinct from their exemplifications—are not temporally located at all, and since they lack any sort of adjacency or contiguity with other entities which would make sense of their being "produced" by them. Free actions also, it has been argued, involve at least an element of self-subsistence, lacking in their nature as free actions a sufficient, but not (at least on some accounts) necessary, condition.

Finally, it will be objected by some that, though the series of causes for any physical state is finite, the first physical event or state in the series could have come into existence without a cause—could have, in short, originated "from nothing." Many discussions today seem to treat the "Big Bang" in this way, though of course that would make it totally unlike any other "bang" of which we have any knowledge. "Big Bang" mysticism is primarily attractive, I think, just because "the bang" has stepped into a traditional role of God, which gives it a nimbus and seems to rule out the normal questions we would ask about any physical event. *That* "bang" is often treated as if it were not quite or not just a physical event, as indeed it could not be. But what then could it be? Enter "scientific mysticism." And we must at least point out that an eternally self-subsistent being is no more improbable than a self-subsistent event emerging from no cause. As C. S. Lewis pointed out, "An egg which came from no bird is no more 'natural' than a bird which had existed from all eternity."[1]

Now I am prepared to grant Hume's point that there is no logical contradiction in the supposition that something could come into existence without a cause. This, however, does not entail that Locke was wrong in his claim that "man knows by an intuitive certainty, that bare nothing can no more produce any real being, than it can be equal to two right angles."[2] There are, after all, general laws about how every type of physical state comes about. If we keep clearly before our minds that *any* "something" which comes into existence (including a however big "bang") will always be a completely specific type of thing, then we see that for that "something" to originate from nothing would be to violate the system of law which governs the origination of things of its type. To suppose that an apple, for example, could come into existence without any prior states upon which it depends for its existence is to simply reject all the laws we know to hold true of apple production. They are no longer laws. And it is not a matter of discovering further *conditions* under which apple-laws apply, for the hypothesis is one of no conditions whatever. The counter-intuitiveness of this is, I imagine, what Locke is referring to, and I certainly agree with him if it is. But even if it were neither self-contradictory nor counter-intuitive to suppose that something originated without a cause, the probability of it relative to our data would be exactly zero. There is, so far as I know, not a single case of a physical state or event being observed or otherwise known to originate "from nothing." And if anyone has observed such a thing, I am sure that our leading scientific journals and societies would like very much to hear about it. In fact, the idea is an entirely ad hoc hypothesis whose only 'merit' is avoidance of admission of a self-subsistent being—which it achieves precisely by claiming an entity of a type which in every other case is admitted to be dependent; to be, "just this once," itself self-subsistent.

Something which originates from nothing is precisely self-subsistent. It is dependent on nothing and exists in its own right. The editors of the Time-Life book *The Cosmos* gravely remark that "no one can say with certainty why the universe popped out of the void."[3] They, along with many sober cosmologists who ponder this question, seem oblivious to the fact that in the nature of the case there can be no *why* for its "popping out," since it is precisely the *void,* the "empty," out from which it popped. (There is nothing to be uncertain about.)

Of course there are many other points of interest and disagreement to be discussed with reference to my first stage argument. It doesn't prove that there is only one self-subsistent being. It doesn't show that the uncaused being or beings which lie at the foundation of the world-causal series still exist—though, certainly, we would like to know of any reason, beyond the mere empty logical possibility which might be offered, for them ceasing to exist. (Admittedly, their not being dependent and contingent in the sense of physical states and events does not immediately imply inability to dissipate themselves in some fashion.) Finally, this argument does not show that the self-subsistent first cause is a person.

All of this I cheerfully grant. Nevertheless, from the viewpoint of the atheist's enterprise, we now have an ontologically haunted universe. It is haunted by unnerving possibilities. If I am right, there has got to be something more than the physical or "natural" universe, and something obviously quite different in character—though also essentially related to it, for from this "something more" the physical universe ultimately derives. If this is established, it is not clear to me that very much of a point is left to atheism, which in the contemporary world surely draws most of its motivation from a desire to *tame* or *naturalize* reality, all hope of which is now lost. (Again: If I am right.) Of course many important points about the exact character of this "more and different" aspect of the universe are still left to be determined. In particular, religion as a human institution and certain kinds of gods, can be effectively attacked by the atheist. But the theist is concerned with this no less than the atheist, and perhaps even more so. Early Christians were sometimes called atheists by the Romans whose gods the Christians denied. Later, Christians called Spinoza an atheist. And so forth. But I think there is an obvious sense in which the atheist in the current, standard philosophical understanding can never feel comfortable in a universe which supplements the physical in the manner demonstrated by my first-stage argument. The *possibility* of there being a God, even in the full theistic sense, has now become significantly more substantial. There is an ontological "space" for it to be realized which just would not be there in a strictly physical universe.

## Stage Two: Design

The second stage in my development of the case for theism corresponds to what has traditionally been called the teleological argument, or the argument *to* design. The latter is the correct designation for what I take to be the essence of the point here. Many will be astonished at the suggestion that teleology actually has nothing at all essentially to do with the case, and has in fact only resulted in an incredible amount of confusion and arguing beside the point on both sides. Theists have, I believe, brought this upon themselves by fixing upon such striking cases of order as the human eye or the degree of inclination of the earth's axis in relation to the possibility of life on the planet. But, especially since the emergence of evolutionary theory, they in so doing open themselves up to massive and sophisticated, though often logically quite misguided, 'rebuttals'—every case of which purports to show how the cases fixed upon by the theist at least *could,* with *some* degree of probability, have originated, come into existence, by a lawlike process from a preexisting condition of the physical universe *without* assistance from what one recent practitioner of this routine smugly calls "a Great Spirit in the sky with a tidy mind and a sense of order" or "A blessed miracle of provident design."[4] The "rebutters," with almost no exceptions, quite conveniently manage to forget that evolution, whether cosmic or biological, *cannot—logically* cannot!—be a theory of ultimate origins of existence or order, precisely because its operation presupposes the *existence* of certain entities with specific potential behaviors and an *environment* of some specific kind that operates upon those entities in some specifically ordered fashion. It is characteristic of the thoughtlessness and ignorance which plagues the discussion of these issues that Darwin's book *On the Origin of Species by Means of Natural Selection* is often thought, by theists as well as anti-theists, to be an explanation of the origin of life and of living forms generally, when of course nothing was farther from Darwin's own mind. . . . Let us say quite generally then that *any sort of evolution of order of any kind will always presuppose preexisting order and preexisting entities governed by it.* It follows as a simple matter of logic that not all order evolved. Given the physical world—however much of evolution it may or may not contain—there is or was some order *in it* which did not evolve. However it may have originated (if it originated), *that* order did not evolve. We come here upon a logically insurpassable *limit* to what evolution, however it may be understood, can accomplish.

We should pause to notice that the order from which cosmic and biological evolution takes its rise must have been one of considerable power and complexity, since it provided the basis of cosmic and biological evolution. Evolution itself is a process that exhibits order of stunning dimensions, diachronic as well as synchronic, especially if given the scope customary among anti-theists. That specific type of structure found *in* evolution did not itself come about *through* evolution, any more than, as Liebniz pointed out, the laws of mechanics were instituted by the laws of mechanics. It is important to take note of this, because some partisans of evolution hold before us the image of being without order as that from which being with order emerged. Thus we find Dawkins, in the book mentioned above, discussing the non-random arrangement of pebbles of various sizes on an ocean beach. Clearly, the pebbles seem sorted and arranged. But, as he points out, this

> . . . arranging was really done by the blind forces of physics, in this case the action of waves. The waves . . . just energetically throw the pebbles around, and big pebbles and small pebbles respond differently to this treatment so they end up at different levels of the beach. A small amount of order has come out of disorder, and no mind planned it.[5]

Big Bang mysticism is, I find, usually accompanied by an "order out of chaos" mysticism.

After letting him enjoy a small moment of triumph, we can only say to this highly qualified scientist: "You gotta be kidding! No mind (directly) planned it, but nothing whatsoever 'has come out of disorder' in this case." Such an interaction of the waves and the pebbles is a perfectly orderly process, even if our comprehension of that order can only be statistically expressed. Moreover, *we* know for sure that *Dawkins himself* knows this. What afflicts him at this point can be very simply described: He is in the grip of the romanticism of evolution as a sweeping ontological principle, bearing in itself the mystical vision of an ultimate *Urgrund* of chaos and nothingness of itself, giving birth to the physical universe—which is all very fine *as* an aesthetic approach to the cosmos, and vaguely comforting. But it has nothing at all to do with "evidence of . . . a universe without design," as the dust jacket of his book suggests.

So at this second stage we have a challenge to offer the atheist which is similar to the one of the first stage. At the first stage we said that the probability, relative to our data, of something (in the physical universe, at least) originating from nothing was zero, and we invited the atheist to find one case of this actually happening, to raise the probability a bit above zero. Now we urge him to find one case of ordered being—or just being, for, whatever it is, it will certainly be ordered—originating from being without order.

Over against this challenge, we point out that the force, the power to convince, which most people seem to feel in the face of the existing physical order surrounding us undoubtedly comes from the simple fact that we all have experience—perhaps even a quite direct, first-hand experience—of order entering the physical world from minds, our minds as well as from those of others. Not as if the physical world were totally disordered before we produced our inventions. Of course it is not. We have no experience of *ex nihilo* creation, and the second stage of theistic evidence does not aim to establish such creation. But, to go back to Paley's classical example of finding a watch in the wilderness, we clearly know that the order that is in a watch first presented itself to the human mind without being present in physical reality, and only because of that did it later emerge within the physical world. We know that locomotives, bridges, and a huge number of other things exist in the physical world *because* the "design" for them previously existed in a mind. Some *person* designed them. Only the kind of skepticism that gives philosophy a deservedly bad name can suggest otherwise. That is why if we stepped on an apparently uninhabited planet and discovered what, to all appearance, was a branch of the May Company or Sears—or even a Coke bottle or a McDonald's hamburger wrapper—it would be both psychologically impossible as well as flatly irrational in the light of our available data to believe that they came into existence without a design and a mind "containing" that design. The extension of this conclusion to cover eyes, DNA structures, and solar systems, by appropriate modifications of premises, is only slightly less coercive.

That, surely, is why David Hume, in the "Introduction" to his *The Natural History of Religion,* states, "The whole frame of nature bespeaks an intelligent author; and no rational enquirer can, after serious reflection, suspend his belief a moment with regard to the primary principles of genuine Theism and Religion." And he puts in the mouth of Philo, at the end of his *Dialogues Concerning Natural Religion,* the somewhat more modestly formulated conclusion "*That the cause or causes of order in the universe probably bear some remote analogy to human intelligence.*" Now I am aware of the carefully weighted meaning which Hume assigned to these words, and, indeed, I accept them in that meaning as an adequate formulation of the results of my stage two. But it is necessary at the same time to insist that he really did mean what he did say in these two passages. (I take Philo to speak for him.) Hume was a minimal or stage-two theist. He believed that the physical universe rationally required a mind or mind-like being as its source, and for the reasons I have indicated above. His further views, to the effect that the world offers no rational support for the full-blown God of Christian theism, do not diminish this one bit.

We should occasionally think about the fact that all of the "great" philosophers—the ones which, up to very recently, all of the better graduate programs in philosophy thought you had to know something about before professional respectability could rest upon you (Plato, Aristotle, St. Augustine, St. Thomas, "St. Occam," Descartes, Spinoza, Liebniz, Locke, Berkely, Kant, and Hegel)—accepted either second-stage theism or (Spinoza, Kant, Hegel) something stronger. Kant, who along with Hume is generally credited among professional philosophers with destroying any possibility of significant theistic evidences, said that "belief in a God and in another world is so interwoven with my moral sentiment that as there is little danger of my losing the latter, there is equally little cause for fear that the former can ever be taken from me."[6] At the very least, he held, it is impossible to prove "that there is no such being and no such life."[7] His belief was that if the moral life is possible, there is "another world," the "intelligible world," which alone makes the moral life possible. And he indeed believed the moral life to be possible. So here is an argument which, to his own mind, secured the existence of a person-like transcendental being with *its* world. That it is in some sense a "moral argument" does not mean that it is not as logically serious as any other argument. Kant did not regard the moral world as nebulous or nonexistent in the contemporary manner.

Now I do not cite these great philosophers as authorities on the points here at issue, though it is about time that the actual role of authority in professional philosophy and in the intellectual world generally got a candid and thorough reexamination. (There's a whole lot of faking going on.) It is just that the general impression that philosophers—especially the "real" ones—are explicit or closet atheists, needs occasionally to be brought over against certain historical facts. And the often suggested idea that, if Aristotle or Descartes or Locke had only lived today, they too would have been atheists, needs to be faced with the challenge to point out exactly what it is that we now know or can do that would have modified the arguments upon which they based their theism. (I have even heard it suggested that these philosophers were just hypocrites and only seemed to accept theism from fear of their society!)

So what do we have at the second stage of theistic evidence? We have established that not all order is evolved, and that relative to our data, there is a probability of zero that order should emerge from chaos or from nothing into the physical world. In addition, we have experience of order emerging from minds (our minds) into the physical world. Under the limited conditions of human existence, we know what this is like and that it does happen.

Now what is the effect of all of this? Certainly no demonstration of God in the full theistic sense. But, similarly as with stage one, the possibility of there being such a God has become significantly more substantial. The existence of something significantly like Him has been given some plausibility, and the theist may now invite the atheist to show why the self-existent, mind-like entity of minimal theism—the God of the philosophers, shall we call Him—could not in reality be the same as the subject of praise and prayer and devotion in religion—the "God of Abraham, Isaac and Jacob." There is now a somewhat broader ontological "space" for the God of religion which would *not* be there in a universe without "design."

Once we are clear about this, we return to the more familiar cases associated with the "teleological" argument. . . . The intricate cases of adaptive order found about us in the world are said by the atheist to have resulted from trillions of tiny increments of order. ("We do the difficult immediately," the U.S. Marines say. "The impossible takes a little longer.") That *is* logically possible, once we free it, as discussed above, from the logical confusions and sweeping ontological pretensions which have encumbered the idea of evolution. On the other hand, once it becomes clear that order is not self-generating and all instances of it could not have originated from evolution, and in the light of the fact that order does (at least in some limited sense) upon some occasions actually enter the physical world from the mind, we would want to know exactly why—given all of this—we should rule out some fairly direct role of "larger minds," shall we say, in the production of eyeballs and planetary orbits. And the theist, for her part, must take seriously the question of "how" such a role is to be conceptualized—lacking interesting responses to which the whole idea of "creation science" must remain as vacuous as it is today. That is a tough assignment. But it may be that *human history,* the realm of action and personality, more readily exhibits a direct role of larger minds in the course of worldly events. And that brings us to the third stage of theistic evidences, as I understand them.

## Stage Three: The Course of Human Events

In this third stage we look at *the course of human events*—historical, social, and individual—*within the context of* a demonstrated extranaturalism (stage one) and of a quite plausible cosmic intellectualism (stage two). Thus human life is to be interpreted within the ontological space of the actualities, with their attendant possibilities, hewn out in stages one and two. Further things which we know about some minds (ours) and their creations at least put us in position to face the atheist with an urgent "Why not?" and to test the basis of any knowledge claims she may make about cosmic minds in relation to human history and experience. We know, most importantly, that human minds standardly create for a purpose, and that they retain an active interest in, feel intimately invested in, what they create—and all the more so the greater the originality or "creativity" involved. Intervention in human affairs by God need not, as in deism, be regarded as a sign of imperfection in the original creation. (Another factory recall?) Creation *might,* after all, be an ongoing affair with God, including what is usually called "redemption" in the language of theology. Intervention appropriately conducted could plausibly be seen as a loving will to communicate and to help, or to secure the purposes in creation, which is at least not radically foreign even to personality as we know it under human conditions. And, given all the preceding, we would like to know why the same *should not* be true of cosmic intelligence—all the while unequivocally conceding that we have not demonstrated it to be true or even strongly probable. While unexcluded possibilities do not imply truth or probability, they are nonetheless relevant to rationality.

More important in our third stage than these rather speculative extensions of minimal theism toward a more full-blown personal God is the examination of the actual course of human history and the actual contents of human experience to determine, as honestly and thoroughly as possible, what can and what cannot be understood in terms of "natural" events verifiable within objectively established methodologies of science. These methodologies are to be distinguished, as clearly as possible, from philosophical speculations about them, of course. But, to put it simply, we should always assume that particular events and experiences *might* be scientifically understood; and the theist should usually, if not always, give any benefit of any honest doubt to the naturalist in any particular question of fact (though, I think, not in matters of philosophical speculation). If there is anything to what the theist believes, we surely can afford to be generous.

But we must also be thorough, and we have every right to require the same of our atheist co-investigators and to ignore their objections if they refuse. Faith is not restricted to religious people, nor is blind prejudice and dogmatism. The atheist who can't be bothered to pay serious attention to the facts claimed for religious histories and religious experience is twin brother to the churchman who refused to look through Galileo's telescope because he *already knew* what was and was not to be seen. Of course the way is often paved for this in the life of the individual atheist by an equal prejudice and dogmatism on the theist side. Also, the (hopefully) sound argumentation laid out in stages one and two above may have been dismissed because it was presented as proving the existence of the God of religion, when it obviously does no such thing. Thus the individual atheist may recognize no context of possibilities within which the miraculous events of religious history and the experiences of sainthood and the devout can be taken seriously for the purposes of knowledge.

So I completely agree with Professor Kai Nielsen's comment . . . that the resurrection of Jesus from the dead, even if *he* stood by and saw it happen, "wouldn't show there was an infinite intelligible being."[8] He knows there are lots of weird things in the world, and, as he says, "It would be just that a very strange happening happened."[9] (So what else is new in a universe where nothing bangs big and order 'congeals' out of chaos?) Jesus himself, according to the record, agrees with us on this matter. In the story he told of Lazarus and the rich man (Luke 16), the self-indulged rich man asked Father Abraham to send Lazarus back to warn his brothers of their fate in Hades, saying that "if someone goes to them from the dead, they will repent!" But Abraham replied, "If they hear not Moses and the Prophets, neither will they be persuaded, though one rose from the dead" (vss. 30–31, KJV). (You can imagine the fine, witty actions and comments to be heard around the dinner table had Lazarus reappeared on the scene! Just think how Monty Python or Bill Cosby or Woody Allen would do it, and you've got it. Abraham didn't fall off the turnip truck.)

Jesus' approach to these matters was, I believe, expressed in His statement: "Ye believe in God, believe also in Me" (John 14:1, KJV). That's the right order. The religious ideas, history, and context in back of His life as an Israelite, *together with* his own teaching and action and character, provided for those who absorbed themselves in them something close to a *logical* demonstration, *not* of the existence of Jehovah, which was never in question for them, but of His specific nature. And *this* is third-stage work. It will have no epistemic weight whatsoever except within an appropriate historical context or within some other arrangement which for the individual settles the first- and second-stage questions. Of course, occasionally some people will just be overwhelmed by a historical or personal event. But a philosophically thoughtful person will never be convinced, much less someone operating from prejudice—even if she decides that she "had better give in to God"—unless she has found some intellectual satisfaction on stage-one and stage-two issues, which clearly the Bible for its part presumes is quite accessible and important (see Ps. 19; Rom. 1:19–20).

Historical events and individuals—real or imagined, rigorously reported or mythologically elaborated—do in fact provide the specific content for beliefs about the gods of religious devotion. But it is *always* a mistake—regretfully very common,

I'm afraid—to simply place the weight of proving the existence of God upon them, although they may always serve as appropriate points of challenge to dogmatic unbelief and although they in fact will lead some people to belief in God. It is the task of theistic evidences at stage three to subject these contents to appropriate rational tests to determine, so far as possible, the more specific nature of the mind-like causal ground of the physical universe. There is no reason whatsoever why recognized religious activities, such as prayer, ritual, and meditative practices, should not serve along with rational analysis, experimentation, and historical research to that end. In every domain, the subject matter ultimately must determine the suitability of the methods for its study.

My own conviction is that a properly worked out inference in terms of "the best explanation"—"best" in the full light of the results of stages one and two—will show it quite plausible that some extranatural mind or minds of roughly the full theistic variety are causally present in human events; that there is "a power working for righteousness," as Matthew Arnold called it, at work in human history and available for interaction with individuals under certain circumstances. The real force backing such a conclusion can never be felt in the abstract; it only comes from the patient, highly motivated examination and comparison of details, which simply can't be engaged in here—and really can't be done *for* another person. But, to nevertheless speak generally, the existence of the Jewish people and of the Christian church, when one goes into the fine texture of the history, personalities, thought, and experience which make them up, seems to me by far best explained by the existence of, roughly, the type of deity that Christians and Jews, among others, worship. I by no means suggest that God is responsible for everything in these traditions, nor do I restrict the action of God in history to them alone. Indeed, if He is the sort of being they themselves present Him as, then He is present with and makes Himself known to all peoples. Every religious culture and experience should be deeply respected—even if not adopted and even if regarded as mistaken in important respects. Christians above all *should* know of God's habit of turning up in the wrong company, where according to the official view He absolutely *could not* be. What further inferences are to be drawn from this is another matter: one which must be handled with the utmost care. But the partisan of one religion must extend the same generous openness and hopefulness to the practitiones of other religions as he would want them and the atheist to extend to himself. The rule, "Do unto others as you would have them do unto you," also extends to inquiry with others.

## A Concluding Word

I have attempted in these pages to clarify some points about the structure into which theistic evidences must be arranged if they are to be properly appreciated. Failure to understand the limitations and the interrelations of what I have called the "three stages" of theistic evidences seems to me a great hindrance both to philosophical treatment of the question of God's existence and to the individual's efforts to come to terms with what is, after all, a major issue in dealing with life. Given the very best possible exposition, theistic evidences never replace a choice as to what kind of universe we would have ours to be, and a personal adventure of trust, which involves living beyond what we can absolutely know. Nevertheless, I believe that the structure of evidence outlined—in spite of its far too simple discussions of the nature of the physical, causation, order, etc.—indicates that the basic doctrine of God present in the historically developed theisms of the major world religions is most likely true and is certainly capable of being rationally accepted. With that much secured, and yet mindful of the vast amount we do not know about that God, we here give the last word to Philo (Hume):

> . . . the most natural sentiment, which a well-disposed mind will feel on this occasion, is a longing desire and expectation, that heaven would be pleased to dissipate, at least alleviate, this profound ignorance, by affording some more particular revelation to mankind, and making discoveries of the nature, attributes, and operations of the divine object of our faith.

Possibly this prayer has already been answered.

# Notes

1. C. S. Lewis, *God in the Dock: Essays on Theology and Ethics,* ed. Walter Hooper (Grand Rapids, MI: Eerdmans, 1970), p. 211.

2. John Locke, *An Essay Concerning Human Understanding,* Book 4, Ch. 10.

3. Time-Life, *The Cosmos* (Alexandria, VA: Time-Life Books, 1989), p. 13.

4. Richard Dawkins, *The Blind Watchmaker: Why the Evidence of Evolution Reveals a Universe without Design* (New York: W. W. Norton, 1986), pp. 43–44.

5. Dawkins, p. 43.

6. Immanuel Kant, *Critique of Pure Reason,* B 857.

7. Kant, B 858.

8. Kai Nielsen, "An Atheist's Rebuttal," in J. P. Moreland and Kai Nielsen, *Does God Exist? The Great Debate* (Nashville, TN: Thomas Nelson, 1990), p. 64.

9. Nielsen, p. 64.

# 16

# Flavors, Colors, and God

## *Robert M. Adams*

In this essay I will be presenting, and defending, an argument for the existence of God. It will not be a knockdown proof that would suffice by itself to settle the issue in favor of theism; at best it will contribute to a cumulative case. Knockdown proofs are rare in metaphysics; and while the existence of God is much more than a metaphysical issue, it is that also, and is like other metaphysical questions in this respect. But even where there are no absolutely conclusive demonstrations, considerations for and against can still be found. We can look for theoretical advantages and disadvantages, as we may call them, of a metaphysical position. Theoretical advantages of theism can be found in the possibility of theological explanations of facts otherwise hard to explain.

The argument I will present is quite simple in a way, and not particularly original. It is a version of the argument from consciousness which was Locke's principal argument for theism,[1] and which has recently been so ably revived by Richard Swinburne as to claim a whole chapter of response in J. L. Mackie's apology for atheism.[2] Nonetheless, I think that it is still a neglected argument, and that some of its strengths can be brought out in new ways, first by placing it in a historical context, and second by concentrating on one particular aspect of consciousness.

## 1. The Question

Why do red things look the way they do (and not the way yellow things do)? And not less important, why do red things look today the way they looked yesterday? Why does sugar taste the way it does (and not the way salt does)? And not less important, why does sugar taste today the way it did yesterday? These are instances of a more general question, but to discuss it we will need a general term for such things as the look of red and the taste of sugar. The usual term is 'phenomenal qualia', or 'qualia' for short.

Philosophers have debated much about the nature of phenomenal qualia. Are they properties of the mind, or of states of mind, or of something else that might be called a "sense datum" or "idea"? I don't think we have to know, for present purposes. It is enough that we know that experiencing the appearance of something red, the appearance of something yellow, the taste of sugar, the taste of salt, the smell of a rose, the smell of hydrogen sulfide, are kinds of experiences that differ from each other in ways that cannot be analyzed in a definition, but with which most of us are vividly familiar. Kinds of experience that differ in those ways are, or are associated with, phenomenal qualia. (Some philosophers deny that there are any such things. I'm sure they are wrong. I will come to them in Section VI, but will ignore them for the time being, in the confidence that everyone will recognize what I am talking about.)

Now I can state my general question: Why are phenomenal qualia correlated as they are with physical qualities?

## II. The Obvious Attempt at a Scientific Explanation

One's first reaction to this question may be to think that the answer to it is well known and does not involve God. Red things look the way they do because they reflect red light (or more accurately, certain wavelengths of light) to our retinas, and that sort of light affects part of the retina, causing it to transmit certain electrical signals to the brain, setting up a certain pattern of electrical activity in the brain, which causes us to see red. Similarly sugar tastes the way it does because its chemical composition affects certain taste receptors in the tongue in such a way that they send electrical impulses to the brain that result in a certain pattern of electrical activity in the brain, which gives us the sensation of a sweet taste.

I assume that these scientific accounts are at least approximately true. The trouble with them is that they do not answer the question that I am asking. For suppose that the experience of seeing red is caused by brain state $R$, and the experience of seeing yellow by brain state $Y$ (both $R$ and $Y$ being patterns of electrical activity). This correlation of the appearance of red with $R$, and of the appearance of yellow with $Y$, is an example of precisely the sort of thing I am trying to explain. That is, it is an example of the correlation of phenomenal qualia with physical qualities or states. We have merely explained one mental/physical correlation in terms of another.

Why does $R$ cause me to see red? Why doesn't it cause me to see yellow—or to smell a foul odor? We do not imagine that $R$ is itself red, or $Y$ yellow. It is hard to conceive of any reason why a particular pattern of electrical activity would be naturally connected with the peculiar kind of experience that I call the appearance of red, rather than with that which I call the appearance of yellow. Indeed, it is hard to conceive of any reason why a pattern of electrical activity would be naturally connected with either of these appearances, rather than with no phenomenal qualia at all. Let us be clear that I am not denying that $R$ and $Y$ are in fact constantly *correlated* with the experience of red and yellow respectively. I am also not denying that $R$ and $Y$ *cause* me to experience red and yellow, respectively. What I want to know is why these relationships between brain states and phenomenal qualia obtain rather than others—and indeed why any such regular and constant relationships between things of these two types obtain at all.

The search for explanation does not normally stop with the discovery of a correlation. On the contrary, science mainly seeks to explain not particular events, but correlations and other general facts. If I want to find out why my car won't start this morning, I go to a mechanic, not a scientist. But I might go to a scientist to find out why water regularly boils at a lower temperature in Denver than in Los Angeles.

It is difficult, however, to see how science would even try to explain the correlation between phenomenal qualia and brain states (or whatever other physical states the qualia are most directly correlated with). For what science is geared up to do is to find laws governing physical states, described in terms of properties that are geometrical or electrical or at any rate quite different from phenomenal qualia. Whatever mechanisms of that sort we discover, the problem of why precisely these flavor experiences or color experiences should be associated with just those physical states will remain essentially the same.

## III. The Aristotelian Explanation

At this point we might be tempted to say that we cannot imagine what *any* explanation of the correlation of phenomenal qualia with physical states would look like; and that might lead us to suspect that the request for an explanation of it is misconceived. The history of Western thought comes to the aid of our imagination at this point, however, enabling us to see what a solution to our problem might look like. The first solution we will examine is surely false, but it does at least make sense enough to show that there is something here that in principle invites explanation.

It is part of the Aristotelianism that dominated Western thought in the later Middle Ages.[3] One difference between Aristotelianism and modern thought is this. We do not think there is any quality in physical objects that resembles the peculiar qualities or qualia that make the difference between experiencing red and yellow, or between the taste of sugar and salt. We believe that those experiences are caused by physical properties of bodies that are not at all like our phenomenal qualia. But the typical opinion of Aristotelian Scholastics was that phenomenal qualia are similar to, and produced by, physical qualities that we perceive in bodies by means of the qualia. There is a qualitative "form" in the sugar that is like the quality of the taste of sugar that makes it different from the taste of salt. The quality of the appearance of red that makes it different from the appearance of yellow resembles a form or quality that is present on the surface of a typical ripe apple.

On this Aristotelian view, the answer to the question, why phenomenal qualia are correlated with just those physical qualities with which they are in fact correlated, is straightforward. They are the same (or, at any rate, similar) qualities, present materially in the bodies that are perceived, and immaterially to the mind that perceives. This correlation is not arbitrary but natural, perhaps almost self-explanatory.

Of course it's not quite as simple as that. We want to know how the redness gets from the apple to the mind. Redness, Scholastics thought, exists on the surface of the apple as a qualitative "Form." Forms function as properties of things, but that is not their only role in Aristotelian theory; they are also causal agents. They operate by something like infection. Forms or qualities spread from things that have them to things that previously did not. Heat transfer provides a good case for this conception of causal interaction. If a heated rock is placed in cool water, the form of heat is imparted to the water from the rock; or, more precisely, the form of heat in the rock causes a new, similar form in the water.

Something like this happens in sensation, which is, after all, a causal process. If I place my hand in hot water, a sensible form of heat is transmitted from the water to my hand. From there it is transmitted through my body to the place at which it is made present to my mind as a feeling of warmth. In seeing red there is an additional complication, for the red surface of the apple is not in immediate contact with my body. For this reason vision requires a "medium," something transparent, like air, to which a form, typically called a "sensible species," of red is initially imparted and through which it is transmitted to my eye. From the medium the form of red enters the liquid in my eyeball; thence it is transmitted through my body to the appropriate place to become present to my mind. Thus I see red. The feature of this causal history that explains the connection between physical states and phenomenal qualia is that similar forms of red are present at every stage of the process: on the surface of the apple, in the medium, in the eyeball, and in or to the mind.

This theory is fantastic, you will object. Aren't these sensible species and media too bizarre to be taken seriously? That is my initial reaction too. But if we think about them carefully, trying to set aside the prejudices engendered by our own education, I believe we can see that in their own context these Aristotelian ideas are no more bizarre or incoherent or absurd than the quanta and quarks of modern physical theory. In fact there is something very common-sensical and directly experiential about the Aristotelian theory. Can't you *see* the "form" of whiteness on the surface of this piece of paper? Of course you are not accustomed to call it that, but doesn't the peculiar quality of whiteness known only by sight appear to you to lie on the surface of the page?

Nonetheless we have good reason to reject the Aristotelian account of these matters. Its rejection, in the early seventeenth century, was an important part of the beginning of modern science. Galileo wanted to develop a *mathematical* science of nature. "Philosophy," he wrote, meaning what we mean by 'science',

> is written in this grand book, the universe, which stands continually open to our gaze. . . . It is written in the language of mathematics, and its characters are triangles, circles, and other geometric figures without which it is humanly impossible to understand a single word of it.[4]

But the Aristotelian physics of qualities was relatively unamenable to mathematization. If we consider them purely in themselves, and as phenomenal qualia (or qualitatively identical with phenomenal qualia), leaving out of account everything we now know or believe about physical qualities that are correlated with them (such as wavelengths of light), the qualities of red and yellow, or (worse yet) the qualities of sweet and green, stand in no obvious or easily measured geometrical or arithmetical relationship to each other. This point will become important later in our argument. It was also a motive for rejecting the infection conception of causation and the idea that the whole diverse array of sensible qualities are causal agents in nature.

One well-known type of causation lent itself magnificently to mathematical treatment. *Mechanical* interactions, in which bodies affect each other by impact, by virtue of their motions and their mutual contact, can be described and explained in terms of sizes, shapes, and motions which can be treated geometrically and arithmetically. Galileo, Descartes, and other seventeenth-century natural philosophers proposed to reduce all causation in nature to purely mechanical interactions. That would make geometrical properties, plus motion and rest, the sole causally relevant properties of physical objects.

The mechanistic theory was applied to the action of physical objects on our sense organs, and of the sense organs on the central nervous system, as well as to other causal interactions in nature. Sight, for example, was explained in terms of mechanical action on the retina by light, conceived as either a stream of minute particles or pressure in a subtle circumambient fluid. From the retina, visual data were transmitted by mechanical operation of the nerves to the brain. There, notoriously, things got more complicated—but more of that later.

It follows from this theory that even if resemblances of our phenomenal qualia are in physical objects, they do not *cause* our sensations. But in fact the whole idea of such physical resemblances of the qualia was given up as explanatorily superfluous—and worse, as something for which no mechanical explanation could be given (and for other reasons that were found). Thus the Aristotelian explanation of the correlation between the qualia and physical states was relinquished.

The progress of modern science has vindicated the rejection of Aristotelianism. Our science is no longer mechanistic in the seventeenth-century sense. It admits electrical charge, for instance, alongside size and shape, as a causally relevant physical property. But it has no use for Aristotelian "forms," nor for any sort of physical resemblance of phenomenal qualia. The Aristotelian solution of our problem is no longer a live option. Even if we adopted a "common-sense realism" about flavors, colors, and other "secondary qualities," as some contemporary philosophers have proposed, we would not thereby revive the Aristotelian scheme of causal explanation; and we would still face the question of how to explain the correlation of flavors, colors, etc. (in the objects as well as in the mind), with the electromagnetic states that modern science seems to have discovered.

## IV. The Theological Alternative

In this rejection of Aristotelianism something interesting happened to those peculiar qualities we experience in seeing red and yellow and tasting sugar and salt. They were "kicked upstairs," as M. R. Ayers has put it, into the mind.[5] Galileo concluded that "tastes, odors, colors, and so on, are no more than mere names so far as the object in which we place them is concerned, and that they reside only in the consciousness."[6] Since the existence of the phenomenal qualia is so evident in sensation that it can hardly be denied, they are seen as features belonging exclusively to the mental realm, and absent from the physical. One of the ways in which the mind/body problem is more difficult for modern thought than for Aristotelianism is that there is for us no affinity between the mental and the physical with respect to these qualities and it becomes an unsolved problem again *why* phenomenal qualia are correlated as they seem to be with physical qualities.

How did early modern thinkers propose to explain this correlation? Theologically, for the most part. Descartes ascribed it to the arbitrary action of God, though he thought the mind/body relations that actually obtain had been designed by God with certain ends in view.

> The nature of man could indeed have been constituted by God in such a way that that same motion in the brain [which in fact causes me to feel a pain in my foot] would have presented whatever else you please to the mind. In particular, it could have displayed itself, insofar as it is in the brain, or insofar as it is in the foot, or in some place in between, or finally anything else whatever. But nothing else would have been as conducive to the preservation of the body.[7]

Locke dwells extensively on the need for theological explanation at this point:

> . . . the production of Sensation in us of Colours and Sounds, *etc.* by impulse and motion . . . being such, wherein we can discover no natural connexion with any *Ideas* we have, we cannot but ascribe them to the arbitrary Will and good Pleasure of the Wise Architect.[8]

> 'Tis evident that the bulk, figure, and motion of several Bodies about us, produce in us several Sensations, as of Colours, Sounds, Tastes, Smells, Pleasure and Pain, *etc.* These mechanical Affections of Bodies, having no affinity at all with those *Ideas,* they produce in us, (there being no conceivable connexion between any impulse of any sort of Body, and any perception of a Colour, or Smell, which we find in our Minds) we can have no distinct knowledge of such Operations beyond our Experience; and can reason no otherwise about them, than as effects produced by the appointment of an infinitely Wise Agent, which perfectly surpass our Comprehensions.[9]

The cautious Locke does not flatly assert that there cannot be a nontheological explanation; but he thinks a theological explanation is the only one that is accessible to us, and he seems quite prepared to embrace it.

This is in agreement with Locke's views about the relation of physical qualities to consciousness in general. He states, "Matter, *incogitative Matter* and Motion, whatever changes it might produce of Figure and Bulk, *could never produce Thought.*"[10] Motion, shape, and size cannot explain the existence of thought. Neither can the geometrical structure of a system of bits of matter, "For unthinking Particles of Matter, however put together, can have nothing thereby added to them, but a new relation of Position, which 'tis impossible should give thought and knowledge to them."[11]

The rejection of Aristotelianism thus left the most typical of early modern thinkers with a system of physical states of affairs and a system of mental states of affairs, utterly diverse from each other and correlated only by the will and power of God. The supernaturalism of this view of the world was not unnoticed in the seventeenth century, and was not unwelcome to most of the founders of modern thought. Aristotelianism in its less theological forms, on the other hand, offered the possibility of a more integrated naturalistic world view that would not need to appeal to voluntary acts of God to explain the interaction of corporeal and mental nature.

It was an audacious move to give up that possibility of integration by rejecting Aristotelianism and splitting the world into physical and mental states of affairs between which no natural connection could be seen. This has clearly been such a good move for the progress of science that we can hardly doubt that it has brought us closer to the truth. But we may wonder whether this step would have been taken in a culture in which theism was not taken more or less for granted, as it was in seventeenth-century Europe. Without a theological explanation of the correlation between phenomenal qualia and physical states, would it have seemed plausible to reject the Aristotelian doctrine of their affinity? At any rate, a theological explanation of the correlation was the main one that was offered; and I think it is the only promising one that has been proposed. It is a theoretical advantage of theism that it makes possible such an explanation.

A brief digression is in order before we conclude our historical survey. In this discussion of seventeenth-century thought I have focused on thinkers who were dualistic in their view of the relation between physical and mental states of affairs. There was of course also an important idealistic movement in early modern philosophy, represented by Leibniz and Berkeley—a movement to which I personally am very sympathetic. Idealism seems to solve our problem. Physical and mental states are correlated as they are because the physical states are constructed out of the mental ones. But this only accentuates another problem. Why do our perceptual states occur in the order in which they do? This cannot be explained in terms of the action of bodies, for bodies are constructed out of the very perceptual facts to be explained, according to the idealist. And it certainly is not plausible to regard it as sheer happenstance that our perceptions are such that we can regard them as representing an orderly world. Early modern idealists had recourse to a theological explanation at this point, and I do not think any other plausible explanation is available.[12] Idealism has at least as much need of God as dualism, and cannot offer an atheistic escape from the problem of phenomenal qualia.

## V. The Impossibility of Any Scientific Explanation

The hardest philosophical work in this paper has been reserved for the final two sections, in which I must deal with the two main objections to my argument. The first is an objection to my claim that there is no prospect of a plausible alternative to a theological explanation of the correlation between phenomenal qualia and physical states, and in particular to my claim that natural science cannot provide such an explanation.

Many people, including many theologians, are deeply prejudiced against any theistic argument based on a claim that science cannot explain something. Immensely (and rightly) impressed by the success of modern science in explaining the phenomena of nature, they judge it reasonable to assume that any remaining "gaps" in the scientific explanation of the world can in principle, and very likely will in fact, be filled by the continuing advance of science. A "god of the gaps," postulated to account for things that science cannot yet explain, seems to them a monarch of an inexorably dwindling realm, and doomed to be dethroned. Shouldn't the track record of science lead us to assume that there is a purely natural, nontheological explanation of the correlation of phenomenal qualia with physical states—an explanation that scientists can, and probably eventually will, discover?

What I have to make clear in opposition to this objection is that it is not just that science has not *yet* found an explanation for the correlation between qualia and physical states. Science is headed in the wrong direction for finding such an explanation, and it would be silly to expect science to turn in another direction.

Here it will be convenient to follow Richard Swinburne in distinguishing between two types of explanation. "Scientific explanation" is explanation in terms of laws of nature. "Personal explanation" is explanation in terms of the powers and intentional actions of voluntary agents.[13] If such a deep structural feature of at least the conscious part of nature as the correlation of phenomenal qualia with physical states is to be explained by the action of a voluntary agent, the agent will pretty well have to have such knowledge and power, and such a creative role, as to count as a deity. So, assuming that the only available types of explanation are the scientific and the personal, the alternatives to a theological explanation of this correlation will be to leave it a brute, unexplained fact (which seems pretty implausible), or else to explain it by a law of nature.

What would a law of nature have to look like in order to explain this correlation? Many seventeenth-century thinkers would have said the law would have to indicate a "perspicuous," intuitively intelligible connection between the phenomenal and physical states. It also seemed to them unlikely that there could be such a connection. That is part of what Locke was saying in the passages I quoted in Section IV. These views still seem rather plausible to me, and perhaps there is an echo of them in Swinburne's statement that "brain-states are such different things qualitatively from experiences, intentions, beliefs, etc. that a *natural* connection between them seems almost impossible."[14] But I will not insist on this line of argument, for perspicuity and intuitive satisfaction are widely distrusted as criteria of success in scientific explanation.

A more universally accepted requirement for adequacy of a scientific explanation of a correlation is that the law in terms of which it is explained must be more *general* than the correlation. The explanation will thus embed the correlation in a more comprehensive and powerful theory. In order to be general enough to explain the correlation, the law must correlate things that do or could occur more widely than the terms of the correlation to be explained. In this and other ways it must present a *simpler* view of the universe than we have with the correlation unexplained. And of course the explanation must not be circular: it must not presuppose any of the facts to be explained. These requirements will be enough for my argument.

For it seems impossible to obtain the requisite generality. Suppose again that $R$ and $Y$ are patterns of electrical activity in the brain that cause the phenomenal qualia of red and yellow, respectively. A more *general* law that explained these corre-lations would not mention $R$ or $Y$ or the specific qualia of red and yellow. It would be stated in terms of other, more general characteristics of physical and conscious states. But it would imply that a physical state whose description (in the more gen-eral terms) $R$ uniquely satisfies is correlated with a conscious state whose descrip-tion (in the more general terms) is uniquely satisfied by the phenomenal quale of red. Here we stumble on the first difficulty in the way of obtaining the desired gen-erality: Are there such general descriptions that are uniquely satisfied by the various phenomenal qualia?

I can think of two ways of trying to obtain descriptions of particular phenom-enal qualia in more general terms, on which a sufficiently general scientific law could operate. Neither will do the job. The first would be to try to analyze the qualia as structured complexes of a small number of simpler elements common to all or many of them. For example, it has been claimed that the phenomenal quale of orange is composed of qualia of red and yellow. Experimental evidence can be cited in support of this claim.[15] Perhaps the evidence could sustain an alternative inter-pretation; but the main point to be made here is that even if the phenomenal quale of orange can be constructed out of qualia of red and yellow, that will not go very far toward a solution of the problem. For the qualia, or phenomenal hues, of red and yellow are generally acknowledged to be simple rather than complex, and we still want an explanation of their correlation with physical states.

This objection might be avoided by a much more ambitious analysis of phe-nomenal qualia. Leibniz held that though we are unable to explain what red is, or what any other phenomenal quale is, except by exhibiting it, "yet it is certain that the concepts of these qualities are composite and can be analyzed, as is obvious since they have their causes."[16] His opinion seems to be that our perceptions of the so-called secondary qualities, such as colors, smells, and tastes, are confused per-ceptions of their physical causes, which on his mechanistic view are to be under-stood in terms of primary qualities, such as size, shape, position, and motion, of minute particles of matter. He argues for the analyzability of phenomenal qualia explicitly on the ground that it provides a solution to our problem.

> It is also the insensible parts of our sensible perceptions that make there to be a relationship between these perceptions of colors, warmths, and other sensible qual-ities and the movements in bodies that correspond to them; whereas the Cartesians, with our Author [Locke], penetrating as he is, conceive the perceptions that we have of these qualities as arbitrary—that is to say, as if God had given them to the soul according to his good pleasure without having regard to any essential relation-ship between these perceptions and their objects: an opinion that surprises me and seems rather unworthy of the wisdom of the author of things, who does nothing without harmony and without reason.[17]

On Leibniz's view there is a natural affinity between the phenomenal qualia and their physical causes, in that the former are representations (albeit confused) of the latter. There is an obvious similarity between Leibniz and Aristotelianism on this point. The natural affinity makes it easy to state a general law governing the cor-relation between the qualia and physical states (although Leibniz thinks it is indeed

God who gives the law effect). The general law is that each perceiving substance has perceptions representing the state of its organic body (and indirectly representing other things insofar as its body, as affected by them, represents them too).

But Leibniz's theory still is liable to the objection that many (at least) of the phenomenal qualia seem quite simple. Indeed, I think this objection is fatal to the theory. We can simply see and taste that the phenomenal qualia of red and sweet are quite different from any perception of sizes, shapes, and motions as such, and do not have the structure of such a perception. Perhaps if our sensory powers were more acute, we would perceive the shapes of sugar molecules instead of tasting their sweetness as we now do; and that might be in some sense a less "confused" perception than we actually have. But it would be qualitatively different from our present sensation of sweetness. It would not be the phenomenal quale whose actual correlation with sugar stimulation of the tongue we are trying to explain.

If the analysis of phenomenal qualia as complexes of simpler qualities cannot plausibly be carried far enough to solve our problem, there may be another way of trying to obtain identifying descriptions of the qualia in sufficiently general terms. If they cannot be broken up into more fundamental elements, it might still be possible to find patterns of resemblance among them that would enable us to arrange them on a scale and assign a unique numerical value to each phenomenal quale. Phenomenal pitches of sound, even if simple, can be ordered on a scale; and practiced persons with "perfect pitch" can assign quite definite proportionate values to the "distances" between pitches on the scale. Phenomenal hues of color, likewise, might be assigned real numbers according to their position in the spectrum. This suggests that our general, explanatory law could take the form of an algorithm for finding the numerical value of the corresponding phenomenal quale, given a numerical value determined by certain quantities in a physical state.

A law of this sort could presumably be put in the form,

$$\text{L: If } F(p) = S(q), \text{ then } p \text{ causes } q,$$

where $p$ ranges over suitable physical states of affairs, and $q$ over phenomenal qualia and perhaps over conscious states in general.[18] $F(p)$ will be a non–ad-hoc function from physical properties of $p$ to mathematical values, and $S(q)$ an independent, non–ad-hoc function from $q$ to mathematical values from the same range. It is convenient to think of these values as real numbers, but in principle they could be ordered n-tuples of real numbers; ordered triples might be required as values of $S(q)$, for example, in order to represent the relations of color qualia in hue, brightness, and saturation. The functions must be non–ad-hoc, or the law will not explain the phenomena, but merely restate them. And $F(p)$ and $S(q)$ must be mutually independent, in the sense that for a given $p$ and $q$, the values of $F$ and $S$ can in principle be determined without knowing whether $p$ and $q$ are correlated; otherwise the explanation would be circular.

Two difficulties confront this approach, one associated with $F(p)$ and the other with $S(q)$. We will begin with the former. In order for the law to have the requisite generality, $p$ must range over a sufficiently broad class of physical states of affairs. It will be easier to understand this in an example. Suppose we are trying to explain the correlation of phenomenal qualia with patterns of electrical discharge in the brain. In this case perhaps $p$ would range over all electrical discharges in the universe. If $p$ ranged only over those electrical discharges that occur in the brain, then a law in terms of $p$ would merely restate, and not explain, an important part of what is to be explained here. For we would still want to know why phenomenal qualia are correlated with electrical discharges in the brain, and not with others.

Let's assume that $F(p)$ is the voltage of $p$. That is not plausible, but it will provide a clear and simple initial illustration. Then the general law says that each mathematical value of $F(p)$—that is, each voltage—is equal to the mathematical value assigned by $S$ to a phenomenal quale, or perhaps some other conscious or mental state, that is caused by, and found in association with, electrical discharges of the corresponding voltage.

The objection that will occur immediately to most of us is that this implies that all the electrical discharges in the universe are associated with phenomenal qualia, or with other mental states, as our brain states are associated with them. What, we may ask, do the spark plugs in the engine feel, as we start a car? Could we make them see yellow by supplying them with the appropriate voltage? This is a sort of panpsychism. It could conceivably be true. But it surely has *no more* intrinsic plausibility than theism, and a lot less explanatory power.

Perhaps, however, this panpsychist result is due to the crudity of identifying $F(p)$ with voltage. Any plausible account of $F(p)$ will be much more complicated. Might we not be able to find an acceptable account on which the value of $F(p)$ would turn out to be zero for all values of $p$ that occur outside of central nervous systems? We could then interpret L as implying that if $F(p) = 0$, $p$ has no associated mental state. To assume that this could be done in a plausible, non—ad-hoc way would be issuing a very large promissory note; but let us grant it for the sake of argument, and pass on to the difficulty associated with $S(q)$, which seems to me decisive.

There is no plausible, non—ad-hoc way of associating phenomenal qualia in general (let alone conscious or mental states in general) with a range of mathematical values, independently of their empirically discovered correlations with physical states. The independence requirement is crucial here. Assuming that there is indeed a correlation between phenomenal qualia and physical states, and a mathematical function $F(p)$ that expresses the variation in physical states with which variation in qualia is found to be correlated, we could of course just assign to each phenomenal quale $q_i$ the value $F(p_i)$, where $p_i$ is the physical state with which $q_i$ is correlated. That would guarantee mathematical values to the qualia. But it would only *restate* the correlation of phenomenal and physical states; it would not *explain* it. For there would be a vicious circle in saying that $q_i$ is causally correlated with $p_i$ *because* $S(q_i) = F(p_i)$, when the only thing that attaches the value of $F(p_i)$ to $S(q_i)$ is the fact that $q_i$ is causally correlated with $p_i$. In order for $F(p) = S(q)$ to *explain* the correlation of physical states with phenomenal qualia, $S(q)$ must be a mathematical expression of a dimension (or structured system of dimensions) that can be discerned in the qualia independently of the physical states, just as voltage (for example) is a dimension of electrical discharges that can be discerned independently of associated qualia.

How would we find such an independent dimension or way of associating phenomenal qualia in general with a range of mathematical values? We began with the suggestion that phenomenal pitches and hues could be assigned real numbers on the basis of their position on the scale and the spectrum. But what is thus begun cannot be carried to completion. For the sake of argument, let us set aside any doubts about whether there are colors (some browns, perhaps) that have no phenomenally natural position in a "color space" mathematically ordered on the dimensions of hue, brightness, and saturation. Let us assume also that all the phenomenal qualia of sound can be assigned a phenomenally natural position in a "sound space" ordered on pitch, loudness, and perhaps one or more other dimensions. The chief difficulty with this strategy is that these orderings cannot be extended to the other sensory modalities, and are not naturally integrated with each other.

It is much harder, in the first place, to find such an ordering among the qualia of any of the other senses. Is there a spectrum of odors? Is there an objectively valid, phenomenally natural order in which the flavors of chocolate, anise, and hazelnut—or sweet, sour, bitter, and salty—should be placed? As for the sense of touch, the degrees of phenomenal warmth and cold can be arranged in scales; but is there any natural continuum on which we would arrange the feelings of a moderate warmth, a moderate coolness, and a gentle stroking of the skin—all of approximately equal strength and agreeableness—in such a way as to represent the qualitative differences among them?

The problem, moreover, does not end there. For even if we had, from a purely phenomenal point of view, a single uniquely valid spectrum for each sensory modality, we would still face the mind-boggling problem of finding a mathematical relationship between the qualia of the different modalities. And without such a relationship, our law of nature will not explain why certain brain states produce phenomenal qualia such as red, yellow, and blue, and others produce qualia such as sweet, sour, and salty.

This is a crucial point. There are certain structural analogies between the current "opponent process theory" of the physiology of color vision and the spectral ordering of hues.[19] This may provide some explanation of why the pattern of neuron firings in the central nervous system that is actually correlated with the perception of orange is naturally more suited to that correlation than to a correlation with the perception of red. But that does not contribute to an explanation of why the actual correlation obtains, unless we take it as given that this electrical process in the central nervous system is part of a process of vision of colors. But what explains that given? My desire for an explanation on this point, obviously, will not be satisfied by any account that deals only with the physical side of the correlation, telling us why these electrical events in the nervous system are responsive to differences in reflected light. What I want to know is why this or any other pattern of electrical discharges should be correlated with color qualia rather than with odor qualia, or with no qualia at all.

If a law of the form L is to explain this, it is required, at a minimum, that the function $S(q)$ should represent a phenomenally natural ordering of *all* phenomenal qualia. But is there a unique objectively valid spectrum in which all phenomenal qualia are ordered? Or at any rate a unique phenomenally natural order in which the taste of anise, perhaps, comes between blue and the smell of hydrogen sulfide? Surely not. There is no such comprehensive ordering that will generate a function $S(q)$ sufficiently nonarbitrary to serve as a suitable term in a plausible law of nature. The different sorts of phenomenal qualia are too diverse from each other for that.

Here we may recall that or.e important motive for kicking the phenomenal qualia out of the physical world and upstairs into the mind, in the seventeenth century, was that the qualia do not have the mathematical structures and relationships in terms of which the modern approach to science was setting out to interpret the physical world. Given the mathematical character of our science, the physical side of any general law correlating physical with phenomenal states must be expected to have a mathematical structure. But given that the system of phenomenal qualia does not have a similar mathematical structure, I do not see where we would find the common denominator between the phenomenal and the physical that such a law would require. This is what I had in mind in saying that science (for its own good and sufficient reasons) is headed in the wrong direction for finding an explanation of the correlation between phenomenal qualia and physical states.

## VI. Materialism

Some may think that the real objection to everything that I have been saying is that I have been ignoring materialism. Aristotelianism explained the correlation between phenomenal qualia and physical states by identifying them. Materialism, it might be suggested, can do the same, but in a different way. Whereas the Aristotelian postulated a (causally efficacious) qualitative identity of phenomenal and physical qualities, the materialist can solve the problem by identifying the phenomenal qualia with their correlated brain states. Surely no problem remains of explaining the "correlation," if the correlated states are identical![20]

It is important, however, to be clear about what is being identified with what. The mind with the brain? I don't believe in that identification, but I can accept it here for the sake of argument. It is enough (indeed, more than enough) for my argument to say that there are phenomenal qualia, and that even if they are properties of brains, they are distinct from the physical properties of brains (or of anything else). That is, they are distinct from the properties studied by physics, such as geometrical and electrical properties.

For as long as that distinction of properties remains, we can still ask why brains that have those physical qualities also have these phenomenal qualia. Why don't they have other phenomenal qualia instead, or none at all? This is essentially the same explanatory problem that we started with, and the materialist claim that it is brains that are the subject of the phenomenal qualia does nothing to solve it.

This is not a novel insight. Locke is careful to state his theistic argument from consciousness in terms of a demand for the explanation of mental *properties,* rather than substances (being notoriously cagey about committing himself as to the identity or duality of mental and material substances). And Swinburne is quite explicit that his version of the argument depends only on a dualism of properties—though he is personally willing to accept a dualism of substances.[21]

Although these classic formulations of the argument from consciousness are stated in terms of a dualism of properties, I think that even that is more than the argument requires. For suppose a materialist claims that $R$ and the phenomenal appearance of red are one and the same property of brains, identified as $R$ on the basis of its place in the physical system, and as the appearance of red on the basis of the way it seems to us when our brains have it. We can still ask why $R$ seems to us the way it does, rather than the way $Y$ (the physical brain state which "is" the appearance of yellow) does. This is quite recognizably our original question, and it remains unanswered. And if the materialist replies (implausibly, to my mind) that the "way" $R$ seems to us when our brains have it is identical with the physical property $R$ itself, but allows that when our brains have $R$ we have a "first-person" way of identifying it that is not available to others for "third-person" identification of $R$, then we can reinstate our problem as the question why this physical property is regularly identified from the first-person position in the way that it is, rather than in the way that the appearance of yellow is.

In order to block the theistic argument from qualia by providing a materialistic explanation of phenomenal/physical correlations, one would have to adopt a very radical materialism indeed, rejecting not only the dualism of substances, but also the dualism of properties, and even the distinction of first- and third-person aspects or ways of identifying the sensible qualities, as well as the notion of a way in which conscious states seem to us when we are in them, as opposed to their place in the physical scheme of things. Thus one would have to *eliminate* phenomenal qualia, or reduce them in a most extreme way to physical qualities. It seems to me that this sort of eliminationism or reductionism can be refuted by seeing red and yellow and tasting onions.

Of course I know there are eminent philosophers who espouse it. How can they believe it? Thomas Nagel has written that "the only motive [he] can see for accepting [such extreme] kinds of reductionism [of mental to physical properties] is a desire to make the mind-body problem go away. None of them has any intrinsic plausibility."[22] I agree with Nagel's judgment, but I would add that the desire to make the mind/body problem go away is not laughable. It is a motive that is highly relevant to the present discussion. David Armstrong, following J. J. C. Smart, has argued for a reduction of phenomenal qualia (as well as other mental properties) to physical qualities at least partly on the ground that if they are not reduced, we will be left with a mental/physical correlation that physical science probably cannot explain.[23] Armstrong makes no mention of a possible theological explanation of the correlation, but I think it is fair to say that a main motive of his reductionism, indicated in his argument, is a desire to obtain an integrated naturalistic view of the world. He wants a view that neither appeals to a supernatural explanation nor leaves a central correlation unexplained. In order to obtain this integrated naturalistic world view, he is prepared to deny what I take to be obvious facts about phenomenal qualia.

Theism seems a less desperate expedient. Perhaps, since the demise of Aristotelianism, the problem of phenomenal qualia is at least as intractable for naturalism as the problem of evil is for theism. It is interesting to note that "eliminative" solutions have been proposed for both problems: denying that there really are any phenomenal qualia or that there really is any evil, as the case may be. Eliminative optimism and eliminative materialism seem about equally implausible to me.[24]

# Notes

1. John Locke, *An Essay Concerning Human Understanding,* ed. Peter H. Nidditch (Oxford, Engl.: Clarendon Press, 1975), Bk. IV, Ch. x.

2. Richard Swinburne, *The Existence of God* (Oxford, Engl.: Clarendon Press, 1979), Ch. 9; J. L. Mackie, *The Miracle of Theism: Arguments for and Against the Existence of God* (Oxford, Engl.: Clarendon Press, 1982), Ch. 7. I have criticized Mackie's reply to Swinburne in a review of *The Miracle of Theism,* in *The Philosophical Review* 95 (1986): 309–16.

3. It should be emphasized that I am speaking here about Aristotelianism as it was understood in the later medieval and early modern periods, and not about Aristotle himself. My presentation abstracts from many disagreements within Aristotelianism about details of the theory of sensation, and would not fit all Scholastics equally well. For a clear account of an important period of the history of the Aristotelian theory, see Anneliese Maier, "Das Problem der 'species sensibiles in medio' und die neue Naturphilosophie des 14. Jahrhunderts," in her *Ausgehendes Mittelalter: Gesammelte Aufsätze zur Geistesgeschichte des 14. Jahrhunderts,* Vol. 2 (Rome: Edizioni di Storia e Letteratura, 1967), pp. 419–51.

4. Galileo Galilei, *The Assayer* (1623), trans. Stillman Drake, excerpted in *The Philosophy of the Sixteenth and Seventeenth Centuries,* ed. Richard H. Popkin (New York: Free Press, 1966), p. 65. I do not mean to imply that mathematization was as important to *all* seventeenth-century anti-Aristotelian physicists as it was to Galileo.

5. M. R. Ayers, "Mechanism, Superaddition, and the Proof of God's Existence in Locke's Essay," *The Philosophical Review* 90 (1981): 237. Ayers's statement applies specifically to Cudworth; what can be said about Locke, as Ayers points out, is somewhat more complicated.

6. Galileo, *The Assayer,* p. 65 in *The Philosophy of the Sixteenth and Seventeenth Centuries,* ed. Richard H. Popkin.

7. Bracketed words added. Sixth *Meditation,* in René Descartes, *Oeuvres Philosophiques,* Vol. 2, ed. F. Alquié (Paris: Garnier, 1967), p. 234. The references to the old standard edition and English translation are AT VII, 88/HR I, 197.

8. Locke, *Essay,* IV, iii, 29.

9. Locke, *Essay,* IV, iii, 28; cf. IV, iii, 6.

10. Locke, *Essay,* IV, x, 10.

11. Locke, *Essay,* IV, x, 16. I am here accepting the traditional reading of this passage, in conscious opposition to that of M. R. Ayers, "Mechanism, Superaddition, and the Proof of God's Existence," p. 245, which seems to me (uncharacteristically) forced. Ayers thinks that Locke is holding open the possibility that some sort of motion and mechanical operation of a system of matter might *be* its thought, and that 'however put together' here must be understood to mean 'however put together *by chance*'.

12. J. L. Mackie, in *The Miracle of Theism,* Ch. 4, recognizes that Berkeley's theism is crucial to the plausibility of his metaphysics at just this point, and sees that this is the basis of a serious Berkeleyan argument for theism. Mackie's defense against this theistic argument is also an attack on Berkeley's immaterialism.

13. Swinburne, *The Existence of God,* Ch. 2. Swinburne also proposes an alternative analysis of scientific explanation in terms of the powers and liabilities of bodies, but argues that it will commonly support versions of the same explanations as the analysis in terms of laws.

And to the extent that it is not equivalent, I cannot see that it is likely to help us beyond the point that we want explained, which is that bodies in certain physical states have the power, and liability, to give rise to certain phenomenal qualia.

14. Swinburne, *The Existence of God,* p. 171f.

15. See C. L. Hardin, "The Resemblances of Colors," *Philosophical Studies* 48 (1985): 35–47.

16. Leibniz, "Meditations on Knowledge, Truth, and Ideas," G IV, 422f. (*Die philosophischen Schriften von Gottfried Wilhelm Leibniz,* ed. C. I. Gerhard, Vol. IV [Berlin, 1880], p. 422f. A standard English translation is in Leibniz, *Philosophical Papers and Letters,* trans. and ed. L. E. Loemker, 2nd ed. [Dordrecht, Neth.: D. Reidel, 1969], p. 291.)

17. Leibniz, *New Essays Concerning Human Understanding,* Preface (G V, 49).

18. J. L. Mackie seems to think that naturalism requires something like this. Acknowledging that "it is hard to see how there can be an intelligible law connecting material structures, however we describe them, with experiential content," he says that the materialist or naturalist "has to assume that there is a fundamental law of nature which says that such content will arise whenever there is a material structure of a certain complicated sort, and that that content will vary in a certain systematic way with the material basis—a fundamental law, because the basic fact of occurrent awareness seems not to be analyzable into any simpler components, so that the law of its emergence could not be derived from a combination of more basic laws" (*The Miracle of Theism,* p. 127).

19. See C. L. Hardin, "A New Look at Color," *American Philosophical Quarterly* 21 (1984): 125–33.

20. An alternative materialist approach would use a strong conception of metaphysical necessity rather than identity. It would claim that each phenomenal state supervenes on its physical correlate by metaphysical necessity. The short answer to this is that it is not easier to see how these correlations could be metaphysically necessary than to see how they could be scientifically explained. If they were metaphysically necessary, there would surely have to be a reason why. And while there may in principle be grounds of metaphysical necessity that escape our understanding . . . , it is rather implausible to postulate them in the present case, given the apparent arbitrariness of the correlations. Grounds could of course be manufactured by stipulation, by defining the identity of the phenomenal qualia as depending on the identity of the physical processes that cause them; but this would commit the fallacy of *ignoratio elenchi* ("ignoring the stated issue"). For the term 'phenomenal qualia' was introduced specifically to signify qualities whose identity is completely determined by subjective experience. To stipulate that the identity of phenomenal qualia depends on the identity of physical processes is to change the subject and, in effect, to deny that there are any phenomenal qualia in the original sense. I will respond, below, to a straightforward form of such denial.

21. Swinburne, *The Existence of God,* pp. 164–66.

22. Thomas Nagel, *Mortal Questions* (Cambridge, Engl.: Cambridge University Press, 1979), p. 194.

23. D. M. Armstrong, *A Materialist Theory of the Mind* (London: Routledge & Kegan Paul, 1968), p. 50. Noting the mismatch, on which I have dwelt, between the complexity of physical processes and the apparent simplicity of phenomenal qualia, Armstrong states that the existence of "laws connecting these incredible physiological complexities with the relatively simple mental events . . . fits in very ill with the rest of the structure of science."

24. Discussions with Richard Healey and Terence Horgan, as well as written comments from George Pappas and Peter van Inwagen, have given rise to improvements in this paper. I am glad to express my gratitude, without burdening them with responsibility for anything I have said.

# 17

# The Irrelevance to Religion of Philosophic Proofs for the Existence of God

*Steven M. Cahn*

Philosophic proofs for the existence of God have a long and distinguished history. Almost every major Western philosopher has been seriously concerned with defending or refuting such proofs. Furthermore, many contemporary philosophers have exhibited keen interest in such proofs. A survey of the philosophical literature of the past decade reveals quite a concentration of work in this area.[1]

One might expect that religious believers would be vitally interested in discussions of this subject. One might suppose that when a proof of God's existence is presented and eloquently defended, believers would be most enthusiastic, and that when a proof is attacked and persuasively refuted, believers would be seriously disappointed. But this is not at all the case. Religious believers seem remarkably uninterested in philosophic proofs for the existence of God. They seem to consider discussion of such proofs as a sort of intellectual game which has no relevance to religious belief or activity. And this view is shared by proponents of both supernaturalist and naturalist varieties of religion. For example, Søren Kierkegaard, a foremost proponent of supernaturalist religion, remarked: "Whoever therefore attempts to demonstrate the existence of God . . . [is] an excellent subject for a comedy of the higher lunacy!"[2] The same essential point is made in a somewhat less flamboyant manner by Mordecai M. Kaplan, a foremost proponent of naturalist religion, who remarks that the "immense amount of mental effort to prove the existence of God . . . was in vain, since unbelievers seldom become believers as a result of logical arguments."[3]

In what follows, I wish to explain just why religious believers have so little interest in philosophic proofs for the existence of God. I wish to show that their lack of interest is entirely reasonable, and that whatever the philosophic relevance of such proofs, they have little or no relevance to religion.

The three classic proofs for the existence of God are the ontological, the cosmological, and the teleological. Each of these proofs is intended to prove something different. The ontological argument is intended to prove the existence (or necessary

Reprinted from the *American Philosophical Quarterly* 6 (1969), by permission of the editor. Notes edited.

existence) of the most perfect conceivable Being. The cosmological argument is intended to prove the existence of a necessary Being who is the Prime Mover or First Cause of the universe. The teleological argument is intended to prove the existence of an all-good designer and creator of the universe.

Suppose we assume, contrary to what most philosophers, I among them, believe, that all of these proofs are valid. Let us grant the necessary existence (whatever that might mean) of the most perfect conceivable Being, a Being who is all-good and is the designer and creator of the universe. What implications can be drawn from this fact which would be of relevance to human life? In other words, what difference would it make in men's lives if God existed?[4]

Perhaps some men would feel more secure in the knowledge that the universe had been planned by an all-good Being. Others, perhaps, would feel insecure, realizing the extent to which their very existence depended upon the will of this Being. In any case, most men, either out of fear or respect, would wish to act in accordance with the moral code advocated by this Being.

Note, however, that the proofs for the existence of God provide us with no hint whatever as to which actions God wishes us to perform, or what we ought to do so as to please or obey Him. We may affirm that God is all-good and yet have no way of knowing what the highest moral standards are. All we may be sure of is that whatever these standards may be, God always acts in accordance with them. One might assume that God would have implanted the correct moral standards in men's minds, but this seems doubtful in view of the wide variance in men's moral standards. Which of these numerous standards, if any, is the correct one is not known, and no appeal to a proof for the existence of God will cast the least light upon the matter.

For example, assuming that it can be proven that God exists, is murder immoral? One might argue that since God created man, it is immoral to murder, since it is immoral to destroy what God in His infinite wisdom and goodness has created. This argument, however, fails on several grounds. First, if God created man, He also created germs, viruses, disease-carrying rats, and man-eating sharks. Does it follow from the fact that God created these things that they ought not to be eliminated? Second, if God arranged for men to live, He also arranged for men to die. Does it follow from this that by committing murder we are assisting the work of God? Third, if God created man, He provided him with the mental and physical capacity to commit murder. Does it follow from this that God wishes men to commit murder? Clearly, the attempt to deduce moral precepts from the fact of God's existence is but another case of trying to do what Hume long ago pointed out to be logically impossible, viz., the deduction of normative judgments from factual premises. No such deduction is valid, and, thus, any moral principle is consistent with the existence of God.

The fact that the proofs of God's existence afford no means of distinguishing good from evil has the consequence that no man can be sure of how to obey God and do what is best in His eyes. One may hope that his actions are in accord with God's standards, but no test is available to check on this. Some seemingly good men suffer great ills, and some seemingly evil men achieve great happiness. Perhaps in a future life these things are rectified, but we have no way of ascertaining which men are ultimately rewarded and which are ultimately punished.

One can imagine that if a group of men believed in God's existence, they would be most anxious to learn His will, and consequently, they would tend to rely upon those individuals who claimed to know the will of God. Diviners, seers, and priests would be in a position of great influence. No doubt competition between them would be severe, for no man could be sure which of these oracles to believe. Assuming that God made no effort to reveal His will by granting one of these oracles truly superhuman powers (though, naturally, each oracle would claim that he possessed such powers), no man could distinguish the genuine prophet from the fraud.

It is clear that the situation I have described is paralleled by a stage in the actual development of religion. What men wanted at this stage was some way to find out the will of God. Individual prophets might gain a substantial following, but prophets died and their vital powers died with them. What was needed on practical grounds was a permanent record of God's will as revealed to His special prophet. And this need was eventually met by the writing of holy books, books in which God's will was revealed in a permanent fashion.

But there was more than one such book. Indeed, there were many such books. Which was to be believed? Which moral code was to be followed? Which prayers were to be recited? Which rituals were to be performed? Proofs for the existence of God are silent upon these crucial matters.

There is only one possible avenue to God's will. One must undergo a personal experience in which one senses the presence of God and apprehends which of the putative holy books is the genuine one. But it is most important not to be deceived in this experience. One must be absolutely certain that it is God whose presence one is experiencing and whose will one is apprehending. In other words, one must undergo a self-validating experience, one which carries its own guarantee of infallibility.

If one undergoes what he believes to be such an experience, he then is certain which holy book is the genuine one, and consequently he knows which actions, prayers, and rituals God wishes him to engage in. But notice that if he knows this, he has necessarily validated the existence of God, for unless he is absolutely certain that he has experienced God's presence, he cannot be sure that the message he has received is true. Thus, he has no further need for a proof of God's existence.

For one who does not undergo what he believes to be such a self-validating experience, several possibilities remain open. He may accept the validity of another person's self-validating experience. He thereby accepts the holy book which has been revealed as genuine, and he thereby also accepts the existence of God, since unless he believed that this other person had experienced the presence of God, he would not accept this person's opinion as to which is the genuine book.

It is possible, however, that one does not accept the validity of another person's supposedly self-validating experience. This may be due either to philosophical doubts concerning the logical possibility of such an experience[5] or simply to practical doubts that anyone has, in fact, ever undergone such an experience. In either case, adherence to a particular supernatural religion is unreasonable.

But having no adherence to a supernatural religion does not imply that one does not still face the serious moral dilemmas which are inherent in life. How are these dilemmas to be solved? To believe that God exists is of no avail, for one cannot learn His will. Therefore, one must use one's own judgment. But this need not be solely an individual effort. One may join others in a communal effort to propound and promulgate a moral code. Such a group may have its own distinctive prayers and rituals which emphasize various aspects of the group's beliefs. Such a naturalistic religious organization does not depend upon its members' belief in the existence of God, for such a belief is irrelevant to the religious aims and activities of the group.

Is it surprising then that proponents of both supernaturalist and naturalist religion are uninterested in philosophic proofs for the existence of God? Not at all. A supernaturalist believes in God because of a personal self-validating experience which has shown him (or someone he trusts) not only that God exists, but also what His will is. A philosophic proof of the existence of God is thus of no use to the supernaturalist. If the proof is shown to be valid, it merely confirms what he already knows on the much stronger evidence of personal experience. If the proof is shown to be invalid, it casts no doubt on a self-validating experience.

On the other hand, a naturalist believes either that no one has learned or that no one can learn the will of God. If, therefore, a proof for the existence of God is shown to be valid, this has no implications for the naturalist, for such a proof does not provide him with any information which he can utilize in his religious practice. If, on the contrary, a proof for the existence of God is shown to be invalid, this casts no doubt on the naturalist's religious views, since these views have been formulated independently of a belief in the existence of God.

Who, then, is concerned with philosophic proofs for the existence of God? First, there are those who believe that if such proofs are invalid, religion is thereby undermined. This is, as I have shown, a wholly erroneous view. Neither supernaturalist nor naturalist religion depends at all upon philosophic proofs for the existence of God. To attack religion on the grounds that it cannot provide a philosophic proof for the existence of God is an instance of *ignoratio elenchi.*

Second, there are those who believe that if the philosophic proofs for the existence of God are invalid, our moral commitments are necessarily undermined. This is also, as I have shown, a wholly erroneous view. It is, however, a common view, and one which underlies the so-called moral argument for the existence of God. According to this argument, it is only if one believes in the existence of God that one can reasonably commit oneself to respect the importance of moral values. This argument is invalid, however, for, as I have shown, belief in the existence of God is compatible with any and all positions on moral issues. It is only if one can learn the will of God that one can derive any moral implications from His existence.

Third, there are philosophers who discuss proofs for the existence of God because of the important philosophical issues which are brought to light and clarified in such discussions. So long as philosophers are aware of the purpose which their discussions serve, all is well and good. It is when philosophers and others use discussions of this sort as arguments for and against religion that they overstep their bounds. Religion may be rationally attacked or defended, but to refute philosophic proofs for the existence of God is not to attack religion, and to support philosophic proofs for the existence of God is not to defend religion.

## Notes

1. For a partial bibliography, see Robert C. Coburn's "Recent Work in Metaphysics," *American Philosophical Quarterly* 1 (1964): 218–20. Two comprehensive treatments of the subject are Wallace I. Matson's *The Existence of God* (Ithaca, NY: Cornell University Press, 1966) and Antony Flew's *God and Philosophy* (London: Hutchinson & Co., 1966).

2. Søren Kierkegaard, *Philosophical Fragments,* tr. David F. Swenson (Princeton, NJ: Princeton University Press, 1936), Ch. 3, p. 34.

3. Mordecai Kaplan, *The Future of the American Jew* (New York: The Macmillan Company, 1948), p. 171.

4. I am not concerned here with the implications of God's omniscience and omnipotence for man's free will. It is possible to interpret these divine attributes in such a way as not to entail the loss of man's free will, and for the purposes of this essay, I shall assume such an interpretation.

5. Such doubts are forcefully expressed in C. B. Martin's *Religious Belief* (Ithaca, NY: Cornell University Press, 1959), Ch. 5.

# Bibliography

Abraham, William J. *An Introduction to the Philosophy of Religion*. Englewood Cliffs, NJ: Prentice-Hall, 1985.

Adams, Robert Merrihew. "Moral Arguments for Theistic Beliefs," in *Rationality and Religious Belief,* ed. C. F. Delaney. Notre Dame, IN: University of Notre Dame Press, 1979.

Allen, Diogenes. *Christian Belief in a Postmodern World: The Full Wealth of Conviction*. Louiseville, KY: Westminster/John Knox Press, 1989.

Anderson, Douglas R. "Three Appeals in Pierce's Neglected Argument." *Transactions of the Charles S. Pierce Society* 26 (Summer 1990): 349–62.

Audi, Robert. "Direct Justification, Evidential Dependence, and Theistic Belief," in *Rationality, Religious Belief, and Moral Commitment: New Essays in the Philosophy of Religion,* eds. Robert Audi and William J. Wainwright. Ithaca, NY: Cornell University Press, 1986.

Baker, John Austin. *The Foolishness of God*. London: Darton, Longman & Todd, 1970.

Bambrough, Richard. *Reason, Truth and God*. London: Methuen, 1975.

Banner, Michael C. *The Justification of Science and the Rationality of Religious Belief*. Oxford, Engl.: Clarendon Press, 1990.

Bartel, Timothy W. "The Cosmological Argument and the Uniqueness of God." *International Journal for Philosophy of Religion* 13 (1982): 23–31.

Beards, Andrew. "Creator and Causality: A Critique of Pre-Critical Objections." *Thomist* (1989): 573–86.

Bertocci, Peter. *Introduction to the Philosophy of Religion*. New York: Prentice-Hall, 1951.

Bonansea, Bernardino M. *God and Atheism: A Philosophical Approach to the Problem of God*. Washington, DC: Catholic University Press of America, 1979.

———. "The Impossibility of Creation from Eternity According to St. Bonaventure." *Proceedings of the American Catholic Philosophical Association* 48 (1974): 121–35.

Bowker, John. "Did God Create This Universe?" in *The Sciences and Theology in the Twentieth Century,* ed. A. R. Peacocke. Notre Dame, IN: University of Notre Dame Press, 1981.

Braine, David. *The Reality of Time and the Existence of God: The Project of Proving God's Existence*. Oxford, Engl.: Clarendon Press, 1988.

Burrill, Donald R., ed. *The Cosmological Arguments: A Spectrum of Opinion*. Garden City, NY: Doubleday, 1967.

Burtola, F., and U. Curi, eds. *The Anthropic Principle—The Conditions for the Existence of Mankind in the Universe*. Cambridge, Engl.: Cambridge University Press, 1990.

Byrne, Peter. *Natural Religion and the Nature of Religion: The Legacy of Deism* (Routledge Religious Studies). London: Routledge, 1989.

Cartwright, Nancy. "Comments on Wesley Salmon's 'Science and Religion . . .'" *Philosophical Studies* 33 (1978): 178–83.

Casserly, J. V. Langmead. *Graceful Reason: The Contribution of Reason to Theology.* Greenwich, CT: Seabury Press, 1954.

Charlesworth, M. J. "Philosophy as the Handmaid of Religion," in his *Philosophy of Religion: The Historic Approaches.* London: Macmillan, 1972.

Clark, Kelly James. "Proofs of God's Existence." *Journal of Religion* 69 (1989): 59–84.

Clark, Robert E. D. *The Universe: Plan or Accident?* Grand Rapids, MI: Zondervan, 1949.

Cleobury, F. H. *A Return to Natural Theology.* London: James Clarke, 1967.

Conway, David A. "Concerning Infinite Chains, Infinite Trains and Borrowing a Typewriter." *International Journal for Philosophy of Religion* 14 (1983): 71–86.

———" 'It Would Have Happened Already': On One Argument for a First Cause." *Analysis* 44 (1984): 159–66.

Corner, Mark. *Does God Exist?* (Mind Matters Series). New York: St. Martin's Press, 1992.

Cosslett, Tess, ed. *Science and Religion in the Nineteenth Century.* New York: Cambridge University Press, 1984.

Craig, William Lane. "Barrow and Tipler on the Anthropic Principle vs. Divine Design." *British Journal for the Philosophy of Science* 39 (1988): 389–95.

———. *The Cosmological Argument from Plato to Leibniz.* London: Macmillan; New York: Barnes & Noble, 1980.

———. *The Existence of God and the Beginning of the Universe.* San Bernardino, CA: Here's Life, 1979.

———. "A Further Critique of Reichenbach's Cosmological Argument." *International Journal for Philosophy of Religion* 9 (1978): 53–60.

———. "God, Creation and Mr. Davies." *British Journal for the Philosophy of Science* 37 (1986): 163–75.

———. *The* Kalam *Cosmological Argument* (Library of Philosophy and Religion). London: Macmillan; New York: Harper & Row, 1979.

———. "The *Kalam* Cosmological Argument and the Hypothesis of a Quiescent Universe." *Faith and Philosophy* 8 (1991): 104–8.

———. "Professor Mackie on the *Kalam* Cosmological Argument." *Religious Studies* 20 (1984): 367–75.

———. "Theism and Big Bang Cosmology." *Australasian Journal of Philosophy* 69 (1991): 492–503.

———. "Time and Infinity." *International Philosophical Quarterly* 31 (1991): 387–401.

———. "Wallace Matson and the Crude Cosmological Argument." *Australasian Journal of Philosophy* 57 (1979): 163–70.

———. "What Place, Then, for a Creator?" *British Journal for the Philosophy of Science* 49 (1990): 473–91.

———, ed. "New Arguments for the Existence of God." *Truth* 3, Nos. 3 and 4 (1990).

Craighead, Houston. "The Cosmological Argument: Assessment of a Reassessment." *International Journal for Philosophy of Religion* 6 (1975): 117–24.

Creel, Richard E. "A Realistic Argument for Belief in the Existence of God." *International Journal for Philosophy of Religion* 10 (1979): 223–53.

Davidson, H. A. *Proofs for Eternity, Creation and the Existence of God in Medieval Islamic and Jewish Philosophy.* New York: Oxford University Press, 1987.

Davies, Brian. "Mackie on the Argument from Design." *New Blackfriars* (September 1983).

Davies, Paul. *God and the New Physics.* New York: Simon & Schuster, 1983.

Davis, Stephen T. "What Good Are Theistic Proofs?" in *Philosophy of Religion: An Anthology,* ed. Louis P. Pojman. Belmont, CA: Wadsworth, 1987.

Dejnozka, J. "Zeno's Paradoxes and the Cosmological Argument." *International Journal for Philosophy of Religion* 25 (1989): 65–81.

Devine, Philip E. *Relativism, Nihilism, and God.* Notre Dame, IN: University of Notre Dame Press, 1989.

Doore, Gary. "The Argument from Design: Some Better Reasons for Agreeing with Hume." *Religious Studies* 16 (1980): 145–61.

Dore, Clement. *Moral Scepticism.* New York: St. Martin's Press, 1991.

———. *Theism.* Dordrecht, Neth.: D. Reidel, 1984.

Drees, Willem B. *Beyond the Big Bang: Quantum Cosmologies and God.* La Salle, IL: Open Court, 1990.

Edwards, Paul. "A Critique of the Cosmological Argument." *The Rationalist Annual* (1959): 63–77.

Edwards, Rem B. *Reason and Religion.* New York: Harcourt Brace Jovanovich, 1972.

Eells, Ellery. "Quentin Smith on Infinity and the Past." *Philosophy of Science* 55 (1988): 453–55.

Emmet, Dorothy. *The Effectiveness of Causes.* London: Macmillan, 1984.

Ewing, A. C. *Value and Reality: The Philosophical Case for Theism.* London: Allen & Unwin, 1973.

Farrer, Austin. *Faith and Speculation.* New York: New York University Press, 1967.

———. *Finite and Infinite.* Westminster: Dacre Press, 1943.

Ferre, Frederick. *Basic Modern Philosophy of Religion.* New York: Charles Scribner, 1967.

Flew, Antony. *God and Philosophy.* London: Hutchinson, 1966.

Frank, Erich. *Philosophical Understanding and Religious Truth.* New York: Oxford University Press, 1966.

Freeman, Eugene, ed. "The Philosophic Proofs for God's Existence." *The Monist* 54, Nos. 2 and 3 (April 1970 and July 1970).

Gale, Richard M. *On the Nature and Existence of God.* Cambridge, Engl.: Cambridge University Press, 1991.

Geisler, Norman L. "The Missing Premise in the Cosmological Argument." *The Modern Schoolman* 56 (November 1978): 31–45.

Geisler, Norman L., and Winfried Corduan. *Philosophy of Religion,* 2nd ed. Grand Rapids, MI: Baker, 1988.

Geivett, R. Douglas. "The Possibility of Natural Theology," in his *Evil and the Evidence for God: The Challenge of John Hick's Theodicy.* Philadelphia: Temple University Press, in press.

Gerson, L. P. *God and Greek Philosophy: Studies in the Early History of Natural Theology* (Issues in Ancient Philosophy). London: Routledge & Kegan Paul, 1990.

———. "Two Criticisms of the Principle of Sufficient Reason." *International Journal for Philosophy of Religion* 21 (1987): 129–42.

Gibson, A. Boyce. *Theism and Empiricism.* New York: Schocken Books; London: SCM Press, 1970.

Gillespie, N. C. "Divine Design and the Industrial Revolution: William Paley's Abortive Attempt to Reform Natural Theology." *Isis* 81 (June 1990): 214–29.

Gilson, Etienne. *From Aristotle to Darwin and Back Again,* trans. John Lyon. Notre Dame, IN: University of Notre Dame Press, 1984.

Goetz, Stewart C. "Craig's *Kalam* Cosmological Argument." *Faith and Philosophy* 6 (1989): 99–102.

Gornall, T. *A Philosophy of God: The Elements of Natural Theology.* New York: Sheed & Ward, 1962.

Green, Ronald M. *Religious Reason: The Rational and Moral Basis of Religious Belief.* New York: Oxford University Press, 1978.

Grisez, Germain. *Beyond the New Theism: A Philosophy of Religion.* Notre Dame, IN: University of Notre Dame Press, 1975.

Hackett, Stuart C. *The Reconstruction of the Christian Revelation Claim: A Philosophical and Critical Apologetic.* Grand Rapids, MI: Baker, 1984.

———. *The Resurrection of Theism.* Chicago: Moody, 1957.

Hambourger, Robert. "The Argument from Design," in his *Intention and Intentionality: Essays in Honor of G. E. M. Anscombe.* Ithaca, NY: Cornell University Press, 1979.

Harrison, C. "Totalities and the Logic of First-Cause Arguments." *Philosophy and Phenomenological Research* 35 (1974–75): 1–19.

Hepburn, Ronald W. "From World to God." *Mind* 72 (1963): 40–50.

Herrera, R. A. "A Point of Departure for a Proof of God's Existence for Unsettled Times." *Philosophy Today* 30 (1986): 325–37.

Hick, John. *Arguments for the Existence of God.* New York: Herder & Herder, 1971.

———. *Faith and Knowledge,* 2nd ed. Ithaca, NY: Cornell University Press, 1966.

———. *Philosophy of Religion,* 3rd ed. Englewood Cliffs, NJ: Prentice-Hall, 1983.

Horigan, James. *Chance or Design?* New York: Philosophical Library, 1979.

Hudson, W. D. Review of *Faith and Reason,* by Richard Swinburne. *Religious Studies* 19 (1983): 93–96.

Hurlbutt, R. H. *Hume, Newton and the Design Argument.* Lincoln, NE: University of Nebraska Press, 1966.

Jack, Henry. "A Recent Attempt to Prove God's Existence." *Philosophy and Phenomenological Research* 25 (1965): 575–79.

Jaki, Stanley L. *Cosmos and Creator.* Edinburgh: Scottish Academic Press, 1980.

———. *God and the Cosmologists.* Edinburgh: Scottish Academic Press, 1989.

———. *The Road of Science and the Ways to God.* Chicago: University of Chicago Press, 1978.

———. *Science and Creation: From Eternal Cycles to an Oscillating Universe.* Edinburgh: Scottish Academic Press, 1974.

Jones, B. E., ed. *Earnest Enquirers After Truth: A Gifford Anthology (1888–1968).* London: Allen & Unwin, 1970.

Kennedy, Leonard A., ed. *Thomistic Papers,* Vol. IV. Houston, TX: Center for Thomistic Studies, 1988.

Kennick, W. E. "A New Way with the Five Ways." *Australasian Journal of Philosophy* 38 (1960): 225–33.

Kenny, Anthony. *The Five Ways: St. Thomas Aquinas' Proofs of God's Existence.* Notre Dame, IN: University of Notre Dame Press, 1969.

King-Farlow, J., and W. N. Christian. *Faith and the Life of Reason.* Dordrecht, Neth.: D. Reidel, 1972.

Konyndyk, Kenneth. "Faith and Evidentialism," in *Rationality, Religious Belief, and Moral Commitment: New Essays in the Philosophy of Religion,* eds. Robert Audi and William J. Wainwright. Ithaca, NY: Cornell University Press, 1986.

Kordig, C. R. "Falsifiability and the Cosmological Argument." *New Scholasticism* 46 (1972): 485–87.

Leftow, Brian. "A Leibnizian Cosmological Argument." *Philosophical Studies* 57 (1989): 135–55.

Leftow, C. R. "A Modal Cosmological Argument." *International Journal for Philosophy of Religion* 24 (1988): 159–88.

Leslie, John. "Anthropic Principle, World Ensemble, Design." *American Philosophical Quarterly* 19 (1982): 141–51.

———. "Efforts to Explain All Existence." *Mind* 87 (1978): 181–94.

———. "God and Scientific Verifiability." *Philosophy* 53 (1978): 71–79.

————. "Modern Cosmology and the Creation of Life," in *Evolution and Creation,* ed. Ernan McMullin. Notre Dame, IN: University of Notre Dame Press, 1985.

————. *Universes.* New York: Routledge & Kegan Paul, 1989.

————, ed. *Physical Cosmology and Philosophy.* New York: Macmillan, 1990.

Lewis, C. S. *Mere Christianity.* New York: Macmillan, 1943.

McCarthy, Gerald D., ed. *The Ethics of Belief Debate.* Dordrecht, Neth.: D. Reidel, 1983.

McInerny, Ralph. "Analogy and Foundationalism in Thomas Aquinas," in *Rationality, Religious Belief, and Moral Commitment: New Essays in the Philosophy of Religion,* eds. Robert Audi and William J. Wainwright. Ithaca, NY: Cornell University Press, 1986.

Mackay, Donald. *Science, Chance, and Providence.* New York: Oxford University Press, 1978.

Mackie, J. L. *The Miracle of Theism: Arguments for and against the Existence of God.* Oxford, Engl.: Clarendon Press, 1982.

McLeod, M. S. "Can Belief in God Be Confirmed?" *Religious Studies* 24 (1988): 311–23.

McPherson, Thomas. *The Argument from Design.* London: Macmillan, 1972.

————. "The Existence of God." *Mind* 59 (1950): 545–50.

————. *The Philosophy of Religion.* New York: Van Nostrand, 1965.

————. *Philosophy and Religious Belief.* London: Hutchinson, 1974.

Martin, Michael. *Atheism: A Philosophical Justification.* Philadelphia: Temple University Press, 1990.

————. "Does the Evidence Confirm Theism More Than Naturalism?" *International Journal for Philosophy of Religion* 16 (1984): 257–62.

————. "On a New Argument for the Existence of God." *International Journal for Philosophy of Religion* 28 (1990): 25–34.

————. "Swinburne's Inductive Cosmological Argument." *The Heythrop Journal* 27 (1986): 151–62.

Mascall, E. L. *He Who Is.* New York: Longmans, Green, 1954.

————. *The Openness of Being: Natural Theology for Today.* Philadelphia: Westminster Press, 1971.

Matson, Wallace I. *The Existence of God.* Ithaca, NY: Cornell University Press, 1965.

Matthews, Gareth. "Theology and Natural Theology." *Journal of Philosophy* 56 (1964): 99–108.

Mavrodes, George I. "Religion and the Queerness of Morality," in *Rationality, Religious Belief, and Moral Commitment: New Essays in the Philosophy of Religion,* eds. Robert Audi and William J. Wainwright. Ithaca, NY: Cornell University Press, 1986.

Mellor, D. H. "God and Probability." *Religious Studies* 5 (1969): 223–34.

Meynell, Hugo. *God and the World: The Coherence of Christian Theism.* London: SPCK, 1971.

————. "The Intelligibility of the Universe," in *Reason and Religion,* ed. Stuart C. Brown. Ithaca, NY: Cornell University Press, 1977.

————. *The Intelligible Universe: A Cosmological Argument.* London: Macmillan, 1982.

Miller, Barry. *From Existence to God: A Contemporary Philosophical Argument.* London: Routledge & Kegan Paul, in press.

Miller, Ed L. *God and Reason: A Historical Approach to Philosophical Theology.* New York: Macmillan, 1972.

————. *Questions That Matter: An Introduction to Philosophy.* New York: McGraw-Hill, 1984.

Mitchell, Basil. *How to Play Theological Ping Pong: Essays on Faith and Reason.* Grand Rapids: Eerdmans, 1991.

————. *The Justification of Religious Belief.* New York: Oxford University Press, 1981.

————. "Two Approaches to the Philosophy of Religion," in *For God and Clarity,* eds. Jeffrey C. Eaton and Ann Loades. Allison Park, PA: Pickwick Publications, 1983.

————, ed. *The Philosophy of Religion.* London: Oxford University Press, 1971.

Montefiore, Hugh. *The Probability of God.* London: SCM Press, 1985.

Moreland, J. P. *Scaling the Secular City.* Grand Rapids, MI: Baker, 1987.

Moreland, J. P., and Kai Nielsen. *Does God Exist? The Great Debate.* Nashville, TN: Thomas Nelson, 1990.

Munitz, Milton K. *The Mystery of Existence: An Essay in Philosophical Cosmology.* New York: Appleton-Century-Crofts, 1965.

————. *Space, Time, and Creation.* New York: Dover, 1981.

Narveson, Jan. "On a New Argument from Design." *Journal of Philosophy* 62 (1965): 223–29.

Nichols, Aidan, O. P. *A Grammar of Consent: The Existence of God in the Christian Tradition.* Notre Dame, IN: University of Notre Dame Press, 1991.

Oakes, R. A. "Is Probability Inapplicable—In-Principle—to the God-Hypothesis?" *The New Scholasticism* 44 (1970): 426–30.

Olding, Alan. *Modern Biology and Natural Theology.* London: Routledge & Kegan Paul, 1991.

Opey, G. "Craig, Mackie, and the *Kalam* Cosmological Argument." *Religious Studies* 27 (1991): 189–97.

Owen, H. P. *Christian Theism: A Study in Basic Principles.* Edinburgh: T. & T. Clark, 1984.

————. *The Moral Argument for Christian Theism.* London: Allen & Unwin, 1965.

Parsons, Keith M. *God and the Burden of Proof.* Buffalo, NY: Prometheus Books, 1989.

Pearl, Leon. "Hume's Criticism of the Argument from Design." *The Monist* 54 (1979): 270–84.

Penelhum, Terence. *Problems of Religious Knowledge* (Philosophy of Religion Series), ed. John Hick. New York: Herder & Herder, 1972.

Peterson, Michael, William Hasker, Bruce Reichenbach, and David Basinger. "Theistic Arguments: The Case for God's Existence," in their *Reason and Religious Belief: An Introduction to the Philosophy of Religion.* New York: Oxford University Press, 1991.

Plantinga, Alvin. *God, Freedom and Evil.* Grand Rapids, MI: Eerdmans, 1974.

————. "The Prospects for Natural Theology," in *Philosophical Perspectives. 5: Philosophy of Religion, 1991,* ed. James E. Tomberlin. Atascadero, CA: Ridgeview Publishing, 1991.

————. "The Reformed Objection to Natural Theology." *Proceedings of the American Catholic Philosophical Association* 54 (1980): 49–63; also published in *Christian Scholar's Review* 11 (1982): 187–98.

————. "The Reformed Objection Revisited." *Christian Scholar's Review* 12 (1983): 57–61.

————. *Warrant: The Current Debate.* New York: Oxford University Press, in press.

————. *Warrant and Proper Function.* New York: Oxford University Press, in press.

Prevost, Robert. *Probability and Theistic Explanation.* Oxford, Engl.: Clarendon Press, 1990.

Priest, Graham. "The Argument from Design." *Australasian Journal of Philosophy* 59 (1981): 422–31.

Prigogine, Ilya, and Isobelle Stengers. *Order Out of Chaos.* London: Heineman, 1984.

Purtill, Richard L. "The Current State of Arguments for the Existence of God." *Review and Expositor* 82 (1985): 521–33.

————. *Reason to Believe.* Grand Rapids, MI: Eerdmans, 1974.

————. *Thinking About Religion.* Englewood Cliffs, NJ: Prentice-Hall, 1978.

Reichenbach, Bruce R. *The Cosmological Argument: A Reassessment.* Springfield, IL: Charles C Thomas, 1972.

———. "The Cosmological Argument and the Causal Principle." *International Journal for Philosophy of Religion* 6 (1975): 185–90.

———. "Divine Necessity and the Cosmological Argument." *The Monist* 54 (July 1970): 401–15.

Rescher, Nicholas, ed. *Current Issues in Teleology.* Lanham, MD: University Press of America, 1986.

Richmond, James. *Faith and Rationality.* New York: J. B. Lippincott, 1966.

———. *Theology and Metaphysics.* New York: Schocken Books, 1971.

Ross, James F. *Philosophical Theology.* Indianapolis, IN: Bobbs-Merrill, 1969.

Rowe, William. *The Cosmological Argument.* Princeton, NJ: Princeton University Press, 1975.

———. Review of *Theism,* by Clement Dore. *Faith and Philosophy* 3 (1986): 202–6.

Salmon, Wesley C. "Religion and Science: A New Look at Hume's *Dialogues.*" *Philosophical Studies* 33 (1978): 143–76.

Schlesinger, George N. "The Availability of Evidence in Support of Religious Belief." *Faith and Philosophy* 1 (1984): 421–36.

———. *Religion and Scientific Method.* Dordrecht, Neth.: D. Reidel, 1982.

———. "Theism and Scientific Method," in his *Metaphysics: Methods and Problems.* Oxford, Engl.: Basil Blackwell, 1983.

Sheehan, Michael. *Apologetics and Catholic Doctrine.* Dublin, Ireland: M. H. Gill, 1962.

Shepard, John J. *Experience, Inference and God.* London: Macmillan; New York: Harper & Row, 1975.

Shields, George W. "Davies, Eternity and the Cosmological Argument." *International Journal for Philosophy of Religion* 21 (1987): 21–37.

Shutte, Augustine. "A New Argument for the Existence of God." *Modern Theology* 3 (1987): 157–77.

Sillem, Edward. *Ways of Thinking About God: Thomas Aquinas and the Modern Mind.* New York: Sheed & Ward, 1961.

Small, Robin. "Tristam Shandy's Last Page." *British Journal for the Philosophy of Science* 37 (1986): 213–16.

Smart, Ninian. "Criteria for Appraisal in Comparative Religion," in *God, Man and Religion,* ed. Keith E. Yandell. New York: McGraw-Hill, 1973; previously published as "Revelation, Reason and Religion," in *The Prospect for Metaphysics,* ed. Ian Ramsey (London: Allen & Unwin, 1956; New York: Philosophical Library, 1961).

Smith, Gerard. *Natural Theology.* New York: Macmillan, 1951.

Smith, John E. *Experience and God.* New York: Oxford University Press, 1968.

———. *Philosophy of Religion.* New York: Macmillan, 1965.

———. "The Present Status of Natural Theology." *Journal of Philosophy* 55 (1958): 925–35.

Smith, Quentin. "Atheism, Theism and Big Bang Cosmology." *Australasian Journal of Philosophy* 69 (1991): 48–66.

———. "Infinity and the Past." *Philosophy of Science* 54 (1987): 63–75.

———. "The Uncaused Beginning of the Universe." *Philosophy of Science* 55 (1988): 39–57.

Sorabji, Richard. *Time, Creation and the Continuum: Theories in Antiquity and the Early Middle Ages.* Ithaca, NY: Cornell University Press, 1983.

Stopes-Roe, Harry V. "The Intelligibility of the Universe," in *Reason and Religion,* ed. Stuart C. Brown. Ithaca, NY: Cornell University Press, 1977.

Swinburne, Richard. "The Argument from Design: A Defense." *Religious Studies* 8 (1972): 193–205.

———. "The Beginning of the Universe." *Proceedings of the Aristotelian Society* (Suppl.) 40 (1966): 125–38.

———. *The Existence of God.* Oxford, Engl.: Clarendon Press, 1979.

———. *Faith and Reason.* Oxford, Engl.: Clarendon Press, 1981.

———. "Mackie, Induction and God." *Religious Studies* 19 (1983): 385–91.

———. Reviews of *The Miracle of Theism,* by J. L. Mackie; *Faith and Rationality,* edited by Alvin Plantinga and Nicholas Wolterstorff, *Faith and Reason,* by Anthony Kenny; and *God and Skepticism,* by Terence Penelhum. *Journal of Philosophy* 82 (1985): 46–53.

———. Review of *Theism,* by Clement Dore. *Philosophical Books* 27 (1986): 191–92.

Sykes, Rod. "Soft Rationalism." *International Journal for Philosophy of Religion* 8 (1977): 51–66.

Taylor, A. E. *The Faith of a Moralist.* London: Macmillan, 1951.

Taylor, Richard. "God," in his *Metaphysics,* 3rd ed. Englewood Cliffs, NJ: Prentice-Hall, 1983.

Tennant, F. R. *Philosophical Theology. 2: The World, the Soul, and God.* Cambridge, Engl.: Cambridge University Press, 1956.

Thompson, Samuel M. *A Modern Philosophy of Religion.* Chicago: Henry Regnery, 1955.

Torrance, T. F. "The Problem of Natural Theology in the Thought of Karl Barth." *Religious Studies* 6 (1970): 121–35.

Trethowan, Dom Illtyd. "In Defense of Theism: A Reply to Professor Kai Nielsen." *Religious Studies* 2 (1966): 37–48.

Wainwright, William J. Review of *The Kalam Cosmological Argument,* by William Lane Craig. *Nous* 16 (1982): 328–34.

Wolfson, Harry Austryn. *The Kalam Arguments for Creation in Saadia, Averroes, Maimonides and St. Thomas.* New York: n.p., 1943.

———. "Patristic Arguments against the Eternity of the World." *Harvard Theological Review* 59 (1966): 354–67.

———. *The Philosophy of the Kalam.* Cambridge, MA: Harvard University Press, 1976.

———. *Repercussions of the Kalam in Jewish Philosophy.* Cambridge, MA: Harvard University Press, 1979.

Wolterstorff, Nicholas. "The Migration of the Theistic Arguments: From Natural Theology to Evidentialist Apologetics," in *Rationality, Religious Belief, and Moral Commitment,* eds. Robert Audi and William J. Wainwright. Ithaca, NY: Cornell University Press, 1986.

———. "Thomas Reid and Rationality," in *Rationality in the Calvinian Tradition,* eds. H. Hart, J. Van der Hoeven, and N. Wolterstorff. Lanham, MD: University Press of America, 1983.

Woods, George F. *Theological Explanation.* Welwyn, Engl.: J. Nisbet, 1958.

Yandell, Keith E. *Christianity and Philosophy.* Grand Rapids, MI: Eerdmans, 1984.

———. "Some Arguments for the Existence of God," in *Basic Issues in the Philosophy of Religion,* ed. Keith E. Yandell. Boston: Allyn & Bacon, 1971.

# V

# PRUDENTIAL ACCOUNTS
# OF RELIGIOUS BELIEF

# 18

## Pascalian Wagering

### *Thomas V. Morris*

> Either God is or he is not. But to which view shall we be inclined? Reason cannot
> decide this question. Infinite chaos separates us. At the far end of this infinite dis-
> tance, a coin is being spun which will come down heads or tails. How will you
> wager? Reason cannot make you choose either, reason cannot prove either wrong.

In this vivid and memorable passage, Blaise Pascal began to develop the famous
argument which has come to be known as "Pascal's Wager."[1] The Wager is widely
regarded as an argument for the rationality of belief in God which completely cir-
cumvents all considerations of proof or evidence that there is a God. Viewed as
such, it has both excited and aggravated philosophers for years. Some have
applauded it as a simple, down-to-earth, practical, and decisive line of reasoning
which avoids altogether the esoteric, mind-boggling intricacies and apparently
inevitable indecisiveness of the traditional theistic arguments that year after year
continue to be revised and reevaluated. They seem to share the view of Pascal himself who once wrote that

> The metaphysical proofs for the existence of God are so remote from human rea-
> soning and so involved that they make little impact, and, even if they did help some
> people, it would only be for the moment during which they watched the demon-
> stration, because an hour later they would be afraid they had made a mistake.[2]

Others have been exceedingly offended by the very idea of wagering on God in
hopes of obtaining infinite gain, and shocked by the suggestion that rational belief
can be established by wholly nonevidential, or nonepistemic means. Such philosophers have succeeded in raising an impressive number of objections to Pascal's
case, objections which in the eyes of many render the argument of the Wager a failure. In this essay, I propose to examine this common view of the Wager as intended
to secure the rationality of religious belief without any regard to purely epistemic
matters. I want to suggest that such a view involves a misunderstanding of the
Wager based on a neglect to take seriously an important feature of its original con-

---

Reprinted from the *Canadian Journal of Philosophy* 16 (1986), by permission of the author and
the editor. Notes edited.

text, manifested by those initial remarks which Pascal used to launch his argument, and from which this paper began. A proper understanding of the epistemic context within which the Wager was intended to be used can provide us with a way of answering a number of the most standard and imposing objections to this interesting argument.

**I**

In attempting to show on prudential grounds that everyone ought to be a theist, Wager enthusiasts often seek to maximize the rhetorical force of their argument by conceding almost everything to the epistemically reasonable atheist and then producing from his own premises their desired conclusion. The rhetoric of their presentation often develops like this. First, it is pointed out that rational gamblers seeking to maximize their gains over the long run bet in accordance with the highest mathematical expectation, where expectation is established with the formula

$$\text{(E) (Probability} \times \text{Payoff)} - \text{Cost} = \text{Expectation}$$

and is ranked for all possible bets in the contest or game situation. Then the confident Pascalian announces that in this life we are all in a forced betting situation in which the possible wagers are that there is a God and that there is no God. The situation is said to be forced in the sense that not acting as if there is a God—not praying, not seeking God's will for one's life, not being thankful to God—is considered to be the equivalent to acting as if there is no God, practically speaking.[3] So one either acts as if there is a God, thereby betting on God, or one does not so act, thereby betting there is no God. Which bet should a rational person make? To answer this question, we must make assignments to the expectation formula and compare outcomes for the bets of theism and atheism. And this is where the rhetorical flourishes come into play whose assumptions result in disaster for the argument.

Let atheism be assigned an extremely high probability, and theism accordingly a very low one, the modern-day Pascalian suggests. It will not matter, so long as neither value is 0 or 1. And so long as theism is even a possibility, it is claimed, its probability is greater than 0, however small, and atheism's is less than 1. Now consider the question of cost. What does it cost to be an atheist? The Pascalian is typically ready to concede that it costs nothing. For, remember, in betting situations the cost is figured under the presumption that the outcome is unknown. So atheism cannot be said here to cost the loss of eternal bliss. And further, any values of the religious life whose descriptions do not entail the existence of God, such as the aesthetic pleasures of liturgy, and the social fulfillment of religious community, are in principle available to atheists as well as theists, if they are sufficiently shrewd. Even the comfort of believing in an afterlife need not be the exclusive possession of theists. So even in this life atheism can be conceded to bear no cost. But religious belief, on the contrary, can be acknowledged to exact quite a cost from the believer. An adherent to typical theistic religions finds himself under all sorts of prohibitions and rules not recognized by the nonbeliever. So, the Pascalian is often quick to agree, the cost of betting on God is great.

Unlike standard betting situations, we have not to this point had determinate, precise assignments of probability and cost, but rather have contented ourselves with very general, comparative indications. According to the view of the Wager under consideration, this does not matter, however, since the values we must assign to the payoff variable will work in the formula for expectation in such a way as to render any precision with respect to the other variables irrelevant. Theism promises infinite, eternal reward. Atheism at best carries with it a promise of finite rewards—whatever pleasures in this life would have been prohibited to the theist. So the Pascalian claims.

Respective expectations of atheism and theism are then figured and ranked as follows. In the case of atheism, multiplying a very high probability by a great finite payoff, and subtracting no cost at all will yield at best a very large finite value. For theism, on the other hand, the product of an infinite payoff and any positive finite probability, however small, will yield an infinite expectation, regardless of how great a finite cost is subtracted. So theism has an infinitely higher expectation than atheism. Thus, the rational person seeking to maximize his gains in this betting situation ought to bet on God.

## II

Many objections have been raised against Pascal's Wager. I want to focus for a moment on those which I think to be particularly problematic for the sort of presentation of the Wager just elucidated. Let us refer to that development of the argument as the epistemically unconcerned version of the Wager, a version in which it does not matter what the precise epistemic status of theism or of atheism is, as long as neither is certainly true. Such a version is vulnerable to a number of objections.

First of all, many people who accept (E) as a formula appropriate for use in normal betting situations may hesitate or refuse to use it in this situation. For the conditions under which it is appropriately used may not obtain with respect to this quite unusual bet. In normal situations, for which the formula was constructed, possible payoffs are always finite in value. The insertion of an infinite value here so overrides considerations of probability and cost as to render them nearly irrelevant. Can (E) be expected to serve its ordinary function with such an extraordinary assignment to one of its variables?

Likewise, in normal betting situations there is usually a controlled range of divergence between probability values when the cost of some bet is high. And, again, it is in such situations that (E) has its appropriate application. Often, this feature of a betting situation is not perceived as being so important. And it need not be, so long as there is, as there usually is, a direct correlation and otherwise proper sort of relation between magnitude of cost and magnitude of probability. But in this version of the Wager, there is an inverse correlation between these factors. Under such conditions, degree of divergence between probabilities becomes a concern. The epistemically unconcerned version of the Wager purports to work regardless of the disparity between the probabilities of theism and atheism, even if, for example, there is only a one in a trillion chance, or less, of theism's being true. It can be rational to distrust the formula's application under such conditions. Further, there is some serious question about the use of probability assignments at all by this version of the Wager. It seems clear that the only interpretation of probability relevant and useable here is the subjective one; yet, how are even subjective probability assignments supposed to arise out of the mere insistence that theism is not demonstrably impossible? Its mere possibility need not be taken to endow it with any positive probability at all.

Third, (E) clearly functions to aid a rational gambler in maximizing his gains over the long run. And this it does, since long-run success is compatible with the losing of many individual bets along the way. Now, despite the fact that one often hears Pascalians insist on the formula's appropriateness in this case since "there is no longer run than eternity," it is clear that in the bet concerning God we do not have a situation of repetitive wagering, in which ultimate maximization of gain is compatible with numerous losses along the way. And so again it could be argued that conditions do not obtain in which the rational bettor is best guided by (E). But of course, if (E) is not used, this popular form of the Wager does not work.

A fourth objection to the Wager we must consider, one raised and developed by numerous critics in recent years, is the Many Claimants Objection, one which is often characterized as resulting from a partitioning problem. The Wager, it is said, partitions the variously possible bets on the issue of God inadequately, presenting us with only two options, theism and atheism, when in reality there are many, perhaps innumerably many. And this is much more than an easily correctable oversight. First of all, there are numerous different versions of theism extant, all vying for credence. For any which promises eternal bliss, and many do, (E) will yield an infinite expectation, as long as there is the slightest positive probability that it is true. And if mere possibility yields some positive probability, as the epistemically unconcerned version of the Wager alleges, matters are even worse. For if it is even logically possible that there exists a being who promises infinite eternal reward to all and only those who deny the existence of all other claimants to worship, including the Christian God, (E) yields a dilemma equivalent to a practical contradiction: a rational person both ought and ought not bet on, say, the Christian God. Further, as if this were not enough, not even will it be the case that some theism or other will be preferable to all forms of atheism. For consider the apparent logical possibility that there is no God and that by some weird law of nature there will be an infinite, eternally blissful afterlife for all and only those who in this life live as convinced atheists. On the basic assumptions of the epistemically unconcerned version of the Wager, the expectation associated with this form of atheism will also be infinite. Clearly, we have here a serious problem.[4]

Most recent commentators have seen one or more of these objections as decisive against the Wager, sufficient to show it to have no rational force. And this is, I think, a correct judgment with respect to the epistemically unconcerned version of the Wager. But it is neither the only version of a Wager-style argument nor, I believe, the sort of version we should attribute to Pascal. When the formula (E) is allowed to work on very low probability values, even those so low as to be approaching 0, and the positive probability of a bet is thought to be provided by the mere logical possibility of its outcome, a context is created in which the production of absurd results is unavoidable. But this is not the context of the original Wager.

It is almost anyone's guess as to what Pascal's planned defense of the Christian faith would have looked like in detail had he lived to complete it. One thing that is clear, though, is that it was not an epistemically unconcerned project. In fact, even a fairly casual reading of the *Pensées* will show that Pascal felt it important to try to defeat prima facie evidential considerations which could be held to count seriously against the truth of Christian beliefs, considerations such as, for example, the hidden-ness of God, and the rejection by most of his Jewish contemporaries of the Christian claim that Jesus was the long-awaited Messiah sent from God. Furthermore, although he engages in no natural theology at all, Pascal does marshal together quite a few considerations in favor of the reliability of the Bible and the trustworthiness of Christian claims. We have no reason to think that he intended his Wager argument to operate in complete isolation from any purely epistemic considerations. In fact quite the contrary is indicated even by the remarks with which he launched the argument. Recall the claim that "Reason cannot decide this question." If epistemic conditions were such that Christian theism could properly receive a very low assignment of subjective probability by any well-informed rational person, and its denial a correspondingly high value, it would not be the case that "reason cannot decide this question." I think we have here sufficient textual indication that the Wager argument was intended to work only for people who judge the theism Pascal had in mind and its denial to be in rough epistemic parity.

If reason cannot decide whether the Christian God exists or not, there cannot be a clear preponderance of purely epistemic considerations either way. Thus there cannot be a great disparity between the assigned probability values of theism and atheism. If it can be rational for a person to judge these positions to be in rough epistemic parity, it can be rational to dismiss altogether one objection to the Wager we considered, the one in which hesitation is expressed concerning the application of (E) to situations with greatly disparate probability values. The objection in this context becomes irrelevant.

Likewise, the hesitation to employ (E) with an infinite value for one of its variables is groundless unless there is reason to believe that allowing such a value assignment will have obviously absurd or unacceptable consequences. And a moment's consideration will show that the only problematic and absurd consequences of applying (E) with an infinite payoff value are displayed in the famous Many Claimants problem, a problem which as we have seen results only from the additional assumptions as well that (1) apparent logical possibility should be translated into some positive nonzero probability value, and (2) the Wager formula can and should be employed regardless of the probability disparity between possible bets. But if both these assumptions are rejected, the Many Claimants problem docs not arise, and the importation of an infinite value into (E) has no clearly problematic results.

So holding the Wager to be appropriate only under conditions of rough epistemic parity between Christian theism and its denial avoids altogether three otherwise interesting and worrisome objections. What about the fourth we considered? We do not have here a repetitive wagering situation in which short-term loss is compatible with long-term gain. There is only one bet; it is either won or lost. But if (E) is thought not to be relevant, how is a decision between theism and atheism to be made? If theism and atheism are in rough epistemic parity, no decision between them can be made on purely epistemic grounds. Some form of agnosticism would be the appropriate doxastic stance if no considerations other than purely epistemic ones could or should enter into such decisions. But, according to Pascal, this is betting against God. One's doxastic stance is a form of, and a function of, behavior which amounts, in the context, to the placing of a bet. And surely there are values other than purely epistemic values which are relevant in the placing of a bet. What sort of values? Just the ones which function in (E). So even though the wager concerning God is not only one episode in a repetitive wagering situation, there seems to be no good alternative to (E) to employ here when choosing one's bet. So given our restriction of the Wager argument to conditions of rough epistemic parity, this objection is neutralized as well.

This view of the wager is an improvement over the epistemically unconcerned version, then, in two respects. It seems to be more in line with Pascal's original intentions, and it is immune to certain difficult objections which plague the more contemporary version. But this version of the wager can have use for a rational person only if it can be reasonable to judge Christian theism and its denial to be in rough epistemic parity. Pascal seems to have thought this was possible. But others have offered reasons to think otherwise. So this is an issue which will merit some consideration.

## III

There are two possible ways in which theism and atheism can be in rough epistemic parity for a person. It seems possible for a person rationally to think that there is no positive evidence or any other epistemic ground for thinking that there is a God, nor any good evidence or other epistemic ground for thinking that there is not. Such a person might be aware of traditional arguments for both positions but find all of them flawed to such an extent that he reasonably judges none of them to endow either conclusion with any positive epistemic status. And he might lack any other purely epistemic consideration either way. For example, he could also lack any natural inclination to believe either way, and so find himself with neither a properly basic theistic belief nor a properly basic atheistic belief. Let us say that with respect to the issue of theism versus atheism, such a person would find himself in epistemically null conditions. The other way in which theism and atheism can be in rough epistemic parity for a person obtains when each is judged to have some positive epistemic status, but neither is more evident than, or clearly outweighs, the other. Let us say that a person who reasonably makes such a judgment is in epistemically ambiguous conditions regarding theism and atheism. Initially, it would seem that if either epistemically null, or epistemically ambiguous conditions can reasonably be thought sometimes to obtain, we have reason to believe that a version of the Wager requiring rough epistemic parity can be formulated as a potentially useful decision making device.

Both N. R. Hanson and Michael Scriven, however, have argued that it is impossible to be in epistemically null conditions with respect to any positive existence claim. In the posthumously published "What I Don't Believe," Hanson wrote: "When there is no good reason for thinking a claim to be true, *that* in itself is good reason for thinking the claim to be false"[5] and, accordingly, "a 'proof' of x's non-existence usually derives from the fact that there is no good reason for supposing that x *does* exist."[6] In the line with this, Scriven wrote in *Primary Philosophy* that: "The proper alternative, when there is no evidence, is not mere suspension of belief; it is disbelief."[7] Applying this to the question of theism, Scriven went on to say that, "Atheism is obligatory in the absence of any evidence for God's existence."[8] If epistemically null conditions could obtain for any proposition $p$ and its denial $-p$, then according to Hanson and Scriven, it seems, we would be forced to disbelieve $p$, thereby believing $-p$, and to disbelieve $-p$, thereby believing $p$. But this is absurd, so epistemically null conditions cannot obtain both for a proposition and its denial. The absence of a positive epistemic consideration in favor of $p$ will just be a positive epistemic consideration in favor of $-p$, and vice versa.

On close inspection of their arguments, however, it becomes clear that Hanson and Scriven are not concerned to make a completely general claim about the epistemic dynamics of just any sort of proposition whatsoever, but rather that they want to lay down a rule for the evaluation only of positive existence claims, propositions which assert that some sort of object exists. One feature of such propositions Hanson points out is this: it is possible in principle to gather conclusive evidence concerning any positive existential generalization; whereas, it is not possible in principle to gather such evidence for the denial of an unrestricted, positive existential, a proposition of the form of an unrestricted universal generalization. Hanson sees this asymmetry as setting the logical backdrop for what we can call the Hanson-Scriven Thesis:

> HST For any rational subject S and any positive existence claim P, if S is in possession of no good evidence or any other positive epistemic ground for thinking that P is true, then S ought to adopt the cognitive relation to P of denial.

Now of course, the evidential asymmetry between unrestricted positive and negative existentials does not entail or in any other way dictate the HST. But the intuitive force the HST has had for many philosophers need not be impugned in the least by this fact. For it just seems that in many ordinary situations we do govern our assent by something like it.

Suppose I am seated in my office, which is neither excessively large nor unusually cluttered. The proposition suddenly occurs to me that there is a large boa constrictor in the room. I make a quick but cautious, thorough inspection of the place. Suppose I find absolutely no trace of such an animal anywhere in the office. What is the most rational stance for me to take concerning the suddenly entertained proposition? Affirmation? Certainly not. Agnosticism? Surely this would be just as inappropriate. The only rational stance to take in absence of any evidence or any other positive epistemic consideration at all will be one of denial. And that judgment seems to accord perfectly with the HST. Any number of such examples from everyday life could be produced as well which seem to show that Hanson and Scriven have indeed captured in their thesis one of our ordinary principles for rational judgment. And if we are committed to such a principle, we are committed to refusing to allow the claim that epistemically null conditions concerning both theism and atheism can obtain for any rational subject. The absence of any evidence or any other positive epistemic consideration for theism will just count as providing a good, decisive consideration for atheism.

An ingenious rejoinder to Hanson and Scriven has been devised by Alvin Plantinga.[9] Plantinga asks us to consider the proposition

　　1. There is at least one human being that was not created by God.

Since it is, he suggests, a necessary truth about God (at least about the God of orthodox Christian theology) that

　　2. If God exists, then God has created all the human beings there are,

any set of epistemic considerations in favor of the truth of (1)—evidences, arguments, etc.—will have to contain an argument that there is no God. But suppose that

　　A. There is no good argument against God's existence.

Then we shall have in consequence no good argument for (1) and so, according to Hanson and Scriven, we must believe its denial:

　　1′. All human beings are created by God.

Now suppose also, Plantinga suggests, that

　　B. There is no good argument for God's existence,

a supposition which surely would be dear to the hearts of both Hanson and Scriven. Then when considering

　　3. There is a God

we find that we are obliged to believe its denial

　　3′. There is no God.

But then, Plantinga continues, assuming that

　　C. There are no good arguments for or against the existence of God,

the Hanson-Scriven view forces us to believe

　　4. There is no God and all human beings are created by him,

which is awkward and embarassing enough for anyone, but which also, along with the obvious truths that

5. Some human beings exist

and that

6. No human being was created by God unless God exists

entails a contradiction. And certainly, no principle which produces this sort of absurdity is worthy of rational acceptance.

But, of course, we can well imagine that Hanson and Scriven would reply that this attempted refutation of their principle just begs the question against them. For on their principle, assumption (C) could never be true. The absence of any good argument *for* the existence of God would just itself provide us with a good argument *against* the existence of God. The epistemically null situation portrayed by (C) could not obtain. So this argument against the principle espoused by Hanson and Scriven cannot after all show it to be unacceptable.

Is there anything wrong with their principle? It has stood for years in the literature, unrefuted, and apparently endorsed by many philosophers. Further, it has the apparent backing of common intuitions about the proper governance of our assent, as illustrated by the story of the boa constrictor. However, it is easy to show that such backing is apparent only for the specific HST formulation we are considering and which is necessary for blocking the possibility of epistemically null conditions obtaining for both theism and atheism.

Circumstances in which the lack of any positive epistemic considerations (evidence, etc.) for some positive existence claim P rationally oblige a subject S to deny P rather than to withhold on it are those in which S reasonably believes he is in *good epistemic position* with respect to P, where being in good epistemic position relative to a proposition is understood in such a way that any subject S is in good epistemic position relative to P if and only if (1) P is such that if it were true, there would exist positive epistemic considerations indicating or manifesting its truth, and (2) S is such that if there existed such considerations, he would, or most likely would, possess them. When I have completed my search for the boa, I am in good epistemic position to assess the claim that such a thing exists in my office. *In that position,* and only in that position, lack of any positive epistemic consideration for the claim amounts to as decisive a consideration against the claim as one could want. It is only when a person reasonably believes himself to be in good epistemic position for assessing an existence claim that an absence of any evidence or other positive epistemic consideration for it can warrant and require his denial of the claim.

So the HST should be revised to read something like

> HST′   For any rational subject S and any positive existence claim P, if S rationally believes himself to be in good epistemic position relative to P, and S is in possession of no good evidence or any other positive epistemic ground for thinking that P is true, then S ought to adopt the cognitive relation to P of denial.

Suppose that someone believes there to be no positive epistemic support for theism. Can he also believe there to be no such support for atheism? Can he rationally judge himself to be in epistemically null conditions regarding both claims? According to the HST', he can so long as he is rationally unsure whether he is in a good epistemic position relative to theism, or rationally believes himself not to be in such a position.

A rational person lacking any positive epistemic considerations can certainly be agnostic about his epistemic position on theism. For suppose he thinks there to be no good evidence or any other positive epistemic consideration either way. Either the Christian God exists or he does not. If the Christian God exists, any failure to have positive considerations of this (any lack of evidence, or of a natural inclination to believe, etc.) may be due to the noetic effects of sin. And on the other hand, if there is no such being, a failure to see that there is not may be due to low-grade effects of a deep psychological need not to know. In either case, one who lacks evidence or other positive considerations would not be in good epistemic position, having his cognitive abilities clouded in one way or another. Realizing these possibilities can rationally warrant agnosticism with respect to one's epistemic position on this issue.[10] And that condition is sufficient for one's rationally judging the situation to be epistemically null, and on purely epistemic grounds withholding on both theism and atheism. HST' does not require otherwise.

Any perceived condition of epistemic parity between a proposition and its denial can be expressed in a subjective probability assignment of ½ to each option. And for anyone in a condition of epistemic nullity with respect to Christian theism and its denial who is willing to register this with a probability estimation (a function of expectations) of "50/50," Pascal's wager can be formulated to suggest prudential reasons for venturing in behavior beyond the agnosticism which only epistemic considerations alone would require.

But of course, as I have indicated earlier, Pascal did not believe that any well-informed inquirer would find himself in epistemically null conditions concerning Christian theism and its denial. So on this count it might seem unimportant to have argued the possibility of such conditions obtaining with respect to these alternatives. Furthermore, anyone willing to assign a subjective probability assignment to these two alternatives of ½ each, despite being bereft of any positive epistemic consideration for either, seems clearly to be adopting the procedure of assigning positive probability values on the ground of logical possibility alone, a policy which I have suggested is unwise, and has been partly responsible for actually weakening the reasoning of the Wager. So on its own, it is not so important to have established, against the contentions of Hanson and Scriven, the possibility of epistemically null conditions obtaining here. What is important is seeing how an HST-style principle requiring denial under conditions of no positive grounds for an existence claim must be qualified. For such a principle could be reformulated quite naturally and easily for circumstances in which the epistemic considerations relevant to such a proposition (distinct from any arising from the application of such a principle itself) were ambiguous, or counterbalanced in such a way that there existed no sufficient consideration for the purely epistemic endorsement of the proposition. Such an extension of the original HST might be thought to be in full accord with the basic intent of its proponents. And such a principle could be taken to rule out the possibility that any rational, well-informed inquirer be in epistemically ambiguous conditions with respect to any positive existence claim and its denial. But this is precisely what Pascal envisioned to be possible in the case of Christian theism and its denial. Once we have seen how the original HST must be qualified in such a way that it allows epistemically null conditions to obtain here, it surely will require no separate argument to see how a properly qualified version will allow the possibility of conditions of epistemic ambiguity. And surely, many people confess to finding themselves in just such conditions on the issue of Pascal's concern, seeing some reason to think Christian theism to be true, some reason to think it false. This perspective is very naturally reflected by such subjective probability assessments as "roughly 50/50." In any situation of rough epistemic parity the famous and much maligned Principle of Indifference can even be produced to yield a probability assignment of exactly ½ for each of the two competitors.[11] If it is rational for anyone to make such an assignment as a reflection of his subjective doxastic state, it is reasonable, so far, to think that Pascal's Wager has a context of rational application.

## IV

It seems to have been Pascal's conviction that a person's epistemic condition with respect to theism and atheism is a function of his attitudes, desires, and other commitments, and that in turn these are a function of the sorts of patterns of behavior he liked to call "habit." It is a dangerous illusion to think of our epistemic capacities as existing and operating independently of the other features of our lives. The person who loves God, according to Pascal, is able to see that everything is created by him (781). The person with contrary passions is bereft of this perspicacity. It was Pascal's view that there exists evidence for the truth of Christian theism which exceeds, or at least equals, evidence to the contrary (835). But he was convinced that it is a person's passional state which will determine how he sees the evidence, and what he does on the basis of it.

The enjoinder to wager on God is the recommendation, on prudential grounds, to adopt a Christian form of life to the extent that one is able. Pascal thought that an entry into that sort of life pattern would have a long-term and cumulative effect on a person's attitudes, desires, and epistemic state. As contrary passions were bridled and finally put aside, he was convinced that anyone who formerly was incapable of seeing or knowing God would attain this capacity, and only with the onset of such a capacity could true faith come.

It is not an assumption of the Wager that God will reward a person for a deliberate, calculated charade of belief undertaken and maintained on grounds of the grossest self-interest. So the famous objection of William James, who was offended by such an assumption, misses the point. There is no doubt that the argument as constructed by Pascal appeals to self-interest. But its intent and goal is to induce a wager whose outcome will yield true faith, an attitudinal state in which self-interest takes its rightful and subordinate place as a behavior motivation. Furthermore, the Wager need not be formulated as an appeal to self-interest at all. It can be presented as an appeal to altruism. One then bets on God so that one will be in a proper position nonhypocritically to urge others to do so, thereby potentially providing them with the greatest amount of good one possibly could.

Likewise, other moral objections to the Wager are easily defeated. James found it morally offensive that God would reward those who want reward. Terence Penelhum apparently has found it repugnant that God would punish anyone who did not otherwise believe for failing to following such a course of attempted aggrandizement.[12] Both James and Penelhum impose a conception of the eternal economy on the argument which it in no way requires and then object to their own creations. In particular, they have what we may call an inappropriately externalist conception of afterlife. One reads Pascal's original Wager passage in vain for the language of rewards and punishment. He does not there portray God at all as either granting or withholding benefits in accordance with how people bet. It seems on the contrary that a more internalist conception of eternal beatitude can both accord with Pascal's own Wager presentation and serve to neutralize the James and Penelhum type of objection. One's state after bodily death is then viewed as being in proper moral and spiritual continuity with one's earthly existence. Those who have hungered and thirsted after righteousness are satisfied. Those who have not, are not. Now, it might appear odd to characterize all those who align themselves with the Christian God as those who hunger and thirst after righteousness. In particular this may seem an inappropriate description of those who are, on Pascalian grounds, wagering on God. However, as indicated already, this is the sort of mind-set meant to eventuate from the particular wagering behavior recommended. Further, the infinite "payoff" as characterized in the Christian tradition, if delineated carefully enough, just may not appeal to a person with no taste for moral and spiritual good. For the heaven of Pascal is not the heaven of, say, popular Islam. It is not an infinite expansion of sensual delights. In fact, it is the sort of infinite bliss which will be attractive only to those with at least a latent capacity to exemplify the attitude characterized biblically as a hunger and thirst for righteousness. And only such as these are, in the theology of Christian theism, able to commune with God at all.

It is not my intent here to defend Pascal's Wager against all extant criticism, although I think it eminently more defensible than most recent commentators have allowed. My primary aim has been merely to suggest that when we attend carefully to some important clues in Pascal's text, we can see that the sort of argument he intended is immune to numerous potent objections which have been raised against contemporary versions of the argument differing in important respects from his own. When these objections have been cleared away, it becomes possible to consider more seriously other philosophical and religious questions raised by the whole idea of Pascalian Wagering.

## Notes

1. Blaise Pascal, *Pensées,* trans. A. J. Krailsheimer (Harmondsworth, Middlesex [Engl.]: Penguin Books, 1966), p. 150

2. Pascal, p. 86, pensée 190; hereafter citations from the *Pensées* will all be from the edition cited above, and will be given by the pensée numbering therein adopted.

3. Such a claim has been made or implied by many theists in different contexts. Recently, for example, Peter Geach has written: "Now for those who believe in an Almightly God, a

man's every act is an act either of obeying or of ignoring or of defying that God . . ." ("The Moral Law and the Law of God," in *Divine Commands and Morality*, ed. Paul Helm [Oxford, Engl.: Oxford University Press, 1980], p. 173). It is easy to see how ignoring and defying God could be categorized together as acting as if there is no God.

4. One of the best recent explications of this sort of problem is Michael Martin's essay, "Pascal's Wager as an Argument for Not Believing in God," *Religious Studies* 19 (1983): 57–64.

5. From N. R. Hanson, *What I Do Not Believe and Other Essays*, ed. Stephen Toulmin and Harry Woolf (Dordrecht, Neth.: D. Reidel, 1972), p. 323. I have explored the views of Hanson and Scriven in "Agnosticism," *Analysis* 45 (1985): 219–24, from which the present section derives some of its points.

6. Hanson, p. 310. (Eds.: For another statement of the thesis presented by Hanson and Scriven, see the Antony Flew article, "The Presumption of Atheism," reprinted in Part I of this volume, pp. 19–32.)

7. Michael Scriven, *Primary Philosophy* (New York: McGraw-Hill, 1966), p. 103.

8. Scriven, p. 103.

9. The argument is presented in his major paper, "Reason and Belief in God," in *Faith and Rationality*, ed. A. Plantinga and N. Wolterstorff (Notre Dame, IN: The University of Notre Dame Press, 1983), pp. 27–29.

10. I lay out a different ground for rational doubt here than in "Agnosticism."

11. The Principle of Indifference has recently received impressive defense at the hands of George N. Schlesinger. See his book *The Intelligibility of Nature* (Aberdeen: Aberdeen University Press, 1985).

12. Terence Penelhum, *Religion and Rationality* (New York: Random House, 1971), pp. 211–19.

# 19

# You Bet Your Life: Pascal's Wager Defended

*William G. Lycan*
*and George N. Schlesinger*

Pascal's famous Wager is often mentioned in introductory philosophy classes and very occasionally addressed in the professional literature, but never favorably on the whole. It is considered an amusing bonbon and an entertaining early (mis)application of decision theory, but it is hardly thought convincing or even intellectually respectable. We maintain, to the contrary, that the Wager is seriously defensible and that the stock objections to it can be answered, even if there are more sophisticated criticisms to be made of Pascal's argument. We are inclined to think that the Wager is rational, and we propose to defend it here.

## I. The Original Argument

We shall concentrate on the standard expected-utility version of the Wager.[1] Pascal supposed that the relevant partition was ("God exists," "God does not exist"), and, at least for the sake of argument, that its members are equiprobable, since

> [r]eason can decide nothing here. There is an infinite chaos which separates us. A game is being played at the extremity of this infinite distance where heads or tails will turn up. What will you wager?[2]

The relevant *choices* are to believe in God and adopt a reverent and devout lifestyle, or not to believe and to behave however one otherwise would.[3] Since the Christian God, at least, promises eternal joy and blissful union with Himself to those who do truly believe, and damnation (on some accounts eternal torment) to those who have heard but do not believe, the expected payoffs are as follows:

|        | God exists | God doesn't exist |
|--------|:----------:|:-----------------:|
| Believe | $\infty$ | $-20$ |
| Don't | $-\infty$ | $20$ |

The two nonfinite payoffs represent (respectively) the eternal joy granted to the believer if God does exist, and the infinite suffering one will undergo if God exists and one chooses not to believe in Him. " $-20$" somewhat arbitrarily represents the inconvenience of living a devout and continent life when one doesn't have to, and "20" represents the fun one would have if totally released from religious hang-ups. (We assume for the moment that sin is fun; if not, so much the better for Pascal's argument.) The expected utility (EU) of theism is thus $.5(\infty) + .5(-20) = \infty$; the EU of agnosticism or atheism is $.5(-\infty) + .5(20) = -\infty$.[4] According to Pascal, this doesn't even leave room for discussion; one would have to be demented to pass up such an offer. Whatever inconveniences may attend the devout and unpolluted life, they pale beside the hope of eternal joy and the fear of damnation.

Pascal is not, of course, arguing for the existence of God; he affects to think that no such argument can be given and that the balance of evidence favors agnosticism. He is contending that despite the epistemic irrationality of theism, if you like, it is *prudentially* rational—i.e., in one's interest—to believe in God regardless of the balance of evidence.[5]


## II. Misguided Objections

Just to get a better feel for the Wager, let us very quickly run through a few preliminary objections, before coming to the two which we consider serious.

(i) "But my beliefs are not under my control; if I don't believe, then I can't believe, any more than I can believe there to be a live swordfish in front of me just because someone offers me $1,000 if I can get myself to believe that." *Reply:* In the long run, most people's beliefs *are* under their control; as Pascal himself emphasized, behavior therapy is remarkably effective even upon intellectuals. Start going to church and observing its rituals; associate with intelligent and congenial religious people; stop reading philosophy and associating with cynics and logical positivists. To quote William James's pungent paraphrase of Pascal,[6] "Go then and take holy water, and have masses said; belief will come and stupefy your scruples." It may be that some people, of an indefatigably analytical and uncredulous temperament, simply cannot let themselves neglect the evidence and acquiesce in faith, just as some people simply cannot let themselves be hypnotized. But this is no reflection on the prudential rationality of the Wager; many people are psychologically incapable of doing what is demonstrably in their interest and known by them to be in their interest.[7]

(ii) "The Wager is cynical and mercenary; God wouldn't reward a 'believer' who makes it." *Reply:* Of course He wouldn't, just like that. Pascal's claim is rather that our interest lies in leaving our cynicism behind and eventually *becoming* believers, if we can. There is no particular reason to think that God would punish a truly sincere and devout believer just because of the historical origins of his or her belief. People are reportedly saved as a result of deathbed conversions, even after lives of the most appalling corruption, if their new belief is sincere and authentic.

(iii) "Pascal is wrong in conjecturing that the probability of theism is as high as .5. It isn't; it's minuscule." *Reply:* That doesn't matter; even if the probability of theism is .001, the expected payoffs are still infinite. "All right, then, the probability is *zero.* I'm *certain* there is no God." *Reply:* How certain? And on what grounds? We would need to see a very convincing argument that no God of even roughly the traditional sort *could* exist, and it would have to be better than most philosophical arguments. (How many philosophical arguments do we know that confer probability *1* on their conclusions??)

(iv) "But if I bet on theism and in fact there is no God, my life will have been based on a lie." *Reply:* But if one bets on atheism and in fact there is a God, one's life will have been based on a lie. (And one's *after*life will be based on the worm that dieth not and the fire that is not quenched.) "But Pascal is telling us, brazenly, to form a firm belief that is unsupported by evidence and may even go directly against the evidence. That is an epistemic vice, the shirking of an epistemic obligation. As a professional philosopher I couldn't live with myself knowing I had done that." *Reply:* Epistemic obligation is not moral obligation. No one suffers if (in this sort of case) one violates an epistemic norm.[8] No one could possibly care except (a) academic philosophers, (b) self-righteous textbook slaves, and (c) God Himself. As history abundantly shows, the first two of these may safely be ignored; the third is ultimately to be counted on Pascal's side (see the reply to objection [ii]). What does an epistemic peccadillo matter, compared to infinite joy or damnation?

(v) "What do you mean, '−20'? I *love* sin! And we're not talking about just a few Sunday mornings here, but proposing to bet an entire lifestyle." *Reply:* Does anyone *really* love sin so much as to be *rationally and without* AKRASIA willing to risk eternal damnation for it? That cannot be true of many people. Indeed (to make a slightly different point), a survey would probably show that religious people are on the average happier and more satisfied with their lives than are nonreligious people[9] (whether this happiness is *opiate* in some objectionable sense is a vexed question, resting on mixed empirical issues and philosophical concerns). How bad could a devout life be, compared to the (possible) alternative?

Actually, we are forced to agree, the devout life *could* be very bad indeed. The strictly correct answer to our rhetorical question leads directly to the first of the two objections to Pascal's argument that we are inclined to take more seriously. (After addressing it, we will turn to the second, viz., the celebrated Many Gods problem.)

## III. The Two Serious Objections

We need not dwell on the potential intolerability of time-consuming weekly devotions and of even more frequent abstinence from sin; for many leading religions, including Christianity and particularly Islam, require potentially far more: specifically, *martyrdom.* If political conditions are inimical, you or I might be faced with the choice of denying our faith or being put very horribly to death. Now, even if we grant that a few Sunday mornings and even a fully reverent Christian lifestyle of the 1980s are an eminently good bet *sub specie aeternitatis,* what if we were suddenly faced with real martyrdom? Would Pascal counsel beheading for anyone in Thomas More's position? Should we be willing, *just in virtue of making the Wager,* to be cast into the Coliseum and wait patiently for the biggest lion?

A first and sensible reply would be that most of us who are reading this paper have excellent (though hardly conclusive) grounds for thinking that we will never in fact be called upon to martyr ourselves; and if so, then the Wager remains reasonable at least *for us* until such time as we are presented with ominous new contrary evidence. But this is too simple. For in order to attain the *genuinely* religious life, as is required for salvation, we must achieve a condition in which we *would* gladly martyr ourselves if called upon to do so, even though we could not rationally want this in our present agnostic state. Could it possibly be reasonable for us, now, in our *present* circumstances and state of mind, to embark on a procedure that we fully intend will brainwash us into accepting a potentially disastrous course of action?—Is this any more rational than (for money) taking a pill that will make us into suicidal depressives or lunatic daredevils?

Yes, of course it is. The expected payoff is still infinite. For death, even horrible and very painful death, is still only finitely disutile. There are fates worse than death, as is evidenced by the plain fact that countless human beings *have* willingly and not irrationally chosen death before dishonor, death rather than drastic indignity, death to save a loved one, death in service of a cherished cause, or the like. In that sense one's life is one's own, and is available as a stake among other stakes in a gamble, though such a gamble must be a desperate one.

If this is right, then our instinctive recoil from martyrdom is just that—instinctive recoil. Of course we shrink from violent death, and of course the prospect of immediate rending and shredding would very likely cause us (quickly) to rethink the Wager. But this does nothing *argumentatively* to show that the Wager is not still in fact rational. At best it shows that visceral fear drives out sound argument, and we knew that anyway. If Pascal's argument works at all, it works in the face of martyrdom, and one cannot show the falsity of this latter conditional's antecedent by simply assuming that of its consequent; one must find an independent objection to the Wager.

Let us turn at last to the Many Gods problem.[10] Pascal assumes a very specific sort of god—roughly a Christian god who rewards His own partisans with infinite bliss and who perhaps sentences opponents and even neutrals to damnation of one truly awful sort or another.[11] But logical space contains countless possible gods of very different natures—all infinite, if you like—and if we can know nothing of infinitude then we cannot have reason to prefer any one of these gods to another. Unfortunately, their respective expected payoffs are diverse and conflicting: What if instead of the Christian God there is a Baal, a Moloch, a Wotan, or a Zeus, who prepares a particularly nasty fate for devout Christians? What if there is a very shy and reclusive god who does not want to be believed in and who enforces this desire by damning all believers to eternal torment? Etc., etc. Pascal assumed that *his* God has a .5 probability of existing, but this is grossly presumptuous in the face of all the other gods who cannot be ruled out a priori. Either Pascal's Christian God must take His place equiprobably alongside the indefinitely many other possible deities, in which case the probability of His existence is negligible, or Pascal's argument could be reiterated for every other god who offers infinite payoffs, in which case it proves too much and leads directly to contradiction due to incompatibly jealous gods.

## IV. A First Answer to the Many Gods Objection

A natural response is to say that for one reason or another all the various possible gods are *not* equiprobable.[12] Intuitively, it is far more likely that the Christian God, the God of the Jews, or Allah exists, than that there is a vindictively shy god or a god who rewards all and only those who do not shave themselves or a god who wears pink bow ties that light up. For here, we believe, empirical evidence is relevant to a certain extent.[13] There is *some* empirical reason for thinking that the Christian God or the God of Israel—or even Allah—exists, in the form of partially checkable scriptures, historical reports (made by ostensibly intelligent and impartial observers) of divine manifestations, and the like, even if this evidence is pathetically far from convincing; while there is simply no reason of any sort for thinking that there is a reclusive god or a divine rewarder of non–self-shaving or whatever. (We also think that the ability of a particular religion to attract and sustain millions of adherents over thousands of years is epistemically a mark in its favor, even if a very weak one.[14] More strongly, we suggest that on empirical grounds Pascal might justify, with fairly high probability, a conditional premise of the form "If there is any god at all, there is a god of type *G*," where '*G*' is replaced by some complex disjunction of conjunctions of traits of the deities of all the world's great religions. If this conditional premise is granted and if sufficiently many of the disjuncts have the infinite-payoff feature, then EUs are still on the side of accepting the disjunction [assuming one can manage it].)

There are still two powerful objections to this initial response. First, how are we to choose between the gods of the major religions? Why should we believe in the Christian God rather than Yahweh? (These deities may well be considered identical by theorists, but their worship is not; they respectively require incompatible conduct.) For that matter, why should we believe in either of those rather than in Allah, or in one or more of the Hindu gods? There are probably more Muslims and more Hindus than there are genuinely religious Christians or Jews, so consensus is of no help in the present regard.

Here some fine-tuning is in order, though we cannot pursue the question in any detail. (i) Empirical indications are still germane. If one looks carefully, one may find that history provides more respectable evidence (however imperfect) for one of the major gods than for another. (ii) One must attend to the details of the respective payoffs; other things being equal, one should go for the deity that offers the more attractive afterlife and/or the nastiest form of damnation. (More on this shortly.) (iii) Given the facts taken account of in (i) and (ii), one must try for the lowest common denominator in terms of tolerance; that is, one must keep one's faith as ecumenical as one dares. Some gods are more jealous than others, of course; some deny salvation to any but the adherents of some crackpot sect, while others grant it to anyone who has led the right sort of life and had an appropriately respectful attitude toward something or other. So, overall, one must balance considerations (i), (ii), and (iii) against each other for each particular case and see how the resulting EUs come out. This is a very tricky but not completely unfeasible bit of comparison shopping. Of course, we may get it wrong and back the wrong god. In fact, given the multiplicity of major deities and the narrow tolerances involved in our attempt at judicious ecumenism, we *probably will* get it wrong. But a significant chance of infinite success offset by a greater chance of infinite failure is still better odds than *no* chance of success supplemented by a *still* greater chance of failure.

A second objection to our initial line is that when nonfinite payoffs are at stake, finite probabilities simply do not matter. If the reclusive god, for example, offers infinite bliss to those who deny him and eternal torture to his worshippers, then (so long as the probability of his existence is not a flat *zero,* which it is not) the EU of belief in him is itself still infinite and so equal to that of belief in the Christian God despite the far greater probability of the latter.

Our first reply to this is that if EUs are *equal,* then by Bayesian principles it doesn't matter what one does and one may follow one's inclinations. Moreover, so long as prudence does not rule on the matter, one would do best on *epistemically* rational grounds to go with the probabilities, and side with one's best traditional bet rather than with a crackpot or made-up god. Indeed, in this case we think a person should be rationally faulted for failing to prefer an objectively more probable god, so long as EUs are equal.[15]

This response is complemented by our second general answer to the Many Gods Objection, to which we now turn.

## V. Lemma for a Second Answer to the Many Gods Objection: St. Anselm on the Divine Attributes

Some people may see no empirical ground for distinguishing the probabilities of the various rival theistic hypotheses, and may find no other reason for preferring any one possible supernatural being to the others. Even so, it seems reasonable for such people to employ a further, common methodological principle, universally applied in more mundane situations which present us with indefinitely large choices among down-to-earth empirical hypotheses.

In science, underdetermination of theory is rife: when we can find one hypothesis accounting for a particular body of observational data (no matter how large), then we are invariably able to produce indefinitely many alternative and competing hypotheses, each capable of accounting for the same body of data. For cxample, if an expression $y = f(x)$ explains such and such a large set of experimental results we have just obtained, then necessarily these same results could equally have been accommodated by $y = f(x) + g(z)$, where $g(z) = 0$ for all observations made prior to now. The two equations (actually infinitely many, according to varying versions of $g[z]$) are of course equivalent with respect to all past observations, and so the observations cannot adjudicate between them; but they make different predictions as regards future observations, and so there is a genuine question as to which we should rationally adopt. As everyone knows, we escape such indecision by using the principle of simplicity, and choose the simplest of all such hypotheses.[16]

For the case of theistic hypotheses, we suppose that one postulate is simpler than another if its statement requires fewer nonadventitious predicates (a predicate is adventitious if it is just *made up* by the theologian, in the manner of 'grue,' to abbreviate a longer complex expression). Now, St. Anselm called our attention to the very remarkable predicate "absolutely perfect," which is theologically unique in that it implies all the other predicates traditionally ascribed to God.[17] In proclaiming the existence of an absolutely perfect or "greatest possible" being, the theist offers a complete description of the deity thus postulated. The theist's brief statement, that his object of worship necessarily exemplifies a maximally consistent set of great-making properties, enables one to determine for any property P whether the putative being does or does not possess P: if having P contributes to the excellence of a thing that does have P, then an absolutely perfect being has P; otherwise the being does not have P. (If there are evaluatively *neutral* properties that a divine being could exemplify, these presumably do not affect the rationality of our choice. We shall say a bit more below on the question of neutral properties.)

By contrast, a statement of the existence of any deity other than the absolutely perfect being will inevitably be more complex. For example: although there is a very considerable body of ancient Greek literature regarding Zeus, we are still far from having a complete description of Zeus's character. We are informed that Zeus, who weighs the lives of men and informs the Fates of his decisions, can nevertheless change his mind; but we have no notion of *just* how unsteadfast he is and in what ways. He is sometimes described as being asleep, but we have no idea how many hours of sleep he gets per day. We know he is not omnipotent, but we are given no detail here. And so on.

No one would suggest that Zeus constitutes the simplest alternative to Anselmian theism. But someone might be attracted by the hypothesis that there is a deity who is almost perfect except in such and such a respect, say, except for falling short of being 100 percent just. The trouble is that that characterization provides incomplete information; we would need some further specification of the precise ways in which that god may be unjust.

Here again there are two obvious objections. First, one may question the sweeping assumption that it is within the power of a single nonadventitious predicate to contain a full description of all the divine attributes. After all, for some property P it is hardly obvious whether P adds to or subtracts from the excellence of its possessor. For example, we usually assume that *omniscience* is a perfection or at least an admirable quality. Yet someone might argue that a being whose knowledge is forever incomplete and who constantly, nobly seeks to increase it—who never ceases from inquiry and learning—is more to be admired (and certainly more to be emulated) than one for whom the concepts of seeking and inquiry do not even make sense. A more familiar example might be that of *timelessness*. Theologians have insisted throughout the ages that a being who exists in time is therefore in some important sense limited or circumscribed; so they have thought it necessary to release God from temporal confinement and place Him above or beyond time.[18]

However, some philosophers have recently maintained the contrary—that divine majesty requires temporality. E.g., J. R. Lucas writes: "To say that God is outside time, as many theologians do, is to deny, in effect, that God is a person."[19] So it seems that the application of the predicate "absolutely perfect" does not settle the temporal (or atemporal) nature of God.

A defender of Anselm can reply that the problem is merely epistemic. The objector's two examples show only that it is not always *obvious* whether the possession of a property P is an advantage or a liability, not that there is no fact of the matter. We might even go further and contend that it is always *knowable* whether P confers positive or negative value; perhaps careful, thorough analysis would inevitably reveal that in light of the various value judgments to which we are already committed, coherence requires our ascribing such and such a determinate value to P. Be that as it may, both parties to the dispute assume that the temporality question is one of fact, that temporality either is excluded or is required by the notion of absolute perfection.[20]

The second objection we anticipate is that the scientific principle of simplicity keys on laws rather than on entities, in that when we are confronted with infinitely many competing scientific hypotheses—paradigmatically in curve-fitting exercises—the alternatives do not differ in their existential claims, but rather presuppose the same set of phenomena and differ only in the laws they posit as governing those phenomena. For example, upon experimenting with freely falling bodies near the earth's surface, Galileo found that all the results satisfied $s = \frac{1}{2}gt^2$. The equation $s = \frac{1}{2}gt^2 + f(z)$ accommodates his results just as completely and must be considered as a competitor; but all parties are in full agreement concerning the existence of all the particulars relevant to the phenomena under investigation. In Pascal's case, by contrast, the dispute is precisely over which particular to postulate as the source of the great reward we may anticipate—not over which of a set of regularities obtains. Moreover, while it is intuitively obvious (if difficult to spell out) that putative laws of nature may be compared with respect to simplicity, it is quite possible to deny altogether the appropriateness of gauging the relative "simplicity" of two supernatural beings, or indeed of any two *particulars*; it makes moderately good sense to ascribe a degree of simplicity to a law which is represented by a mathematical expression, since the degree can be measured by the number of terms the expression contains, the powers of its variables, and other well marked and quantifiable features, but beings, individuals, are not capable of such representation.

To this we respond that a particular being or individual can be *posited* only under a description, and descriptions can be compared with respect to simplicity if predicates can. And if predicates *cannot* be compared with respect to simplicity, it is hard to see how laws themselves can; thus we see no contrast in comparability between hypothesized laws and posited particulars.[21]

## VI. Our Second Response to the Wager

The respective choices we face when confronted, on the one hand, with Galileo's equation and all its rivals, and on the other with our array of possible superbeings, are basically similar. For the nature of every particular is manifested in the laws it obeys; if the law governing the free fall of heavy objects near the earth's surface were other than Galileo's, then either the earth or some heavy objects would be different objects from what we now believe them to be. Thus in science as in theology, we may describe our problem as an uncertainty regarding the *kinds of particulars* we should postulate.

It also seems, therefore, that distinct individuals may be compared with respect to their simplicity. We may say that one individual is simpler than another if its properties can be described by simpler statements, that is, if its behavior can be described by simpler laws.

If we are realists enough to regard acceptable scientific hypotheses as presumed to be literally true, then it is also not unreasonable to select the Anselmian hypothesis rather than any of its many rival theologies. A staunch scientific realist thinks of the principle of simplicity not merely as an aesthetic consideration or a measure of short-term convenience, but as providing the best chance that we shall make the correct choice when faced with an infinite array of equally well-confirmed hypotheses. Reason recommends that we employ the same principle in our theological context.[22]

Our second approach to the Many Gods problem is of course troubled by the Problem of Evil: the Anselmian hypothesis of an absolutely perfect superbeing is not obviously compatible with the amount and variety of suffering we know the world to contain. We shall not suggest any particular theodicy here, but only point out that for purposes of Pascal's Wager there need only be some nonnegligible chance that an adequate theodicy exists; the Wager is still prudentially rational if we can assign a nonzero probability to the hope that the Problem of Evil admits of solution.

## VII. A Third Answer to the Many Gods Objection

A deeper and more authentic approach would take into account the special nature of the reward on which one is bid to wager. First, we are to realize that what Pascal is urging is for the gambler to set his eyes upon a prize of a sort entirely different from the "poisonous pleasures" Pascal advises him to abandon. The gratification to be pursued by the religious seeker is not something extrinsic to the devout life, but an organic outgrowth of it. It does not differ in kind from the seeking, as if one were to be handed a new IBM color-graphics monitor as a prize for having won the Carrboro marathon, but is the natural fruit of one's way of life. Theists in every age have anticipated the dissolving of their narrow selves in the ecstasy of a God-centered life here on earth and, more to Pascal's point, their eventual smooth translation into a disembodied existence in holy felicity—an eternal love of the divine. A human being becomes capable of this kind of love only after he or she has grasped the idea of God. Maimonides puts it as follows:

> What is the proper love of God? It is the love of the Lord with a great and very strong love so that one's soul shall be tied to the love of the Lord, and one should be continually enraptured by it, like a love-sick individual, whose mind is at no time free from his passion for a particular woman, the thought of her filling his heart at all

times, when sitting down or rising up, even when he is eating or drinking. Still more intense should be the love of God in the hearts of those who love Him.[23]

According to classical theologians, one who has spent one's life as a passionate servant of the Lord will have developed and perfected one's soul adequately to have acquired the capacity to partake in the transmundane bliss that awaits in the afterlife. The suitably groomed soul, when released from its earthly fetters, will bask in the radiance of the divine presence and delight in the adoring communion with a loving God (if this is a multiply mixed metaphor, it doesn't matter).

It is appropriate at this point to comment again upon objection (ii) considered in Section II above, the complaint that because of its calculating and mercenary character, the Wager is both morally repugnant and inefficacious, and incompatible with the spirit of any genuine religion. Many people would recoil from a wagerer just as they would from a hypocrite who went out of his way to brighten the mood of an enfeebled (but wealthy) elderly person for no loftier reason than to increase his chance of being mentioned in that person's will. Such misgivings could not easily be dismissed if Pascal had had in mind a pie-in-the-sky, anthropocentric sort of heaven such as that which Heinrich Heine sardonically claimed to be reserved for the righteous. According to Heine's mouth-watering description, Heaven is a place where roast geese fly around with gravy boats in their bills and there are brooks of boullion and champagne and everyone revels in eternal feasting and carousing. It would and should be hard to admire anyone who pursued a godly, righteous, and sober life mainly in the hope of gaining admission to that kind of paradise. But we are considering the Wager in the context of an infinitely more exalted afterlife. Suppose that we have always had great admiration for Smith because of the noteworthy humanitarian works he has performed, and that lately we have heard of further truly heroic acts of benevolence on his part that make his previous accomplishments pale into insignificance. Then we should hardly be condemned for making efforts to discover more information concerning Smith's further laudable deeds— even if we are fully conscious of the sentiments of Thomas Carlyle, who wrote, "Does not every true man feel that he is himself made higher by doing reverence to what is really above him?"[24] Most people would find our conduct neither ignoble nor stupid, even if our efforts to discover the grounds of Smith's greatly intensified worthiness were done explicitly for the sake of feeling ourselves made higher by doing reverence to a more exalted personage.

Let us return for a moment to the notion of expected utility. Rationality requires that when faced with a number of choices one is to bet on the hypothesis having the highest EU. In the special case in which the various outcomes are equiprobable, one's choice is then determined by the magnitudes of the respective payoffs. In Pascal's situation, then, where D ranges over possible deities: the degree of justified inclination to embark on a process leading to worshipping D = the probability that D exists $\times$ the magnitude of religious fulfillment to be gained by worshipping D provided D does exist. And when $D_1$, $D_2$, . . . are equiprobable, the degree of justified inclination and the rationality of one's choice must be determined by the second factor on the right-hand side.

It is the crux of our problem that for more than one deity there is an eternal and hence infinite payoff. Still, the very nature of the sublime gratification the believer aspires to ensures that its quality will vary with the character of the deity he or she bets on. When Carlyle spoke of the self-enhancement resulting from doing reverence to what is above oneself, he had in mind an entirely worldly context. But when the object of one's homage is a divine being, the uplift is immeasurably greater. Pascal wagered on the ecstasy to be derived from exalting a supereminent being and basking in its radiance, and naturally, the more glorious and sublime the being, the greater that worshipful ecstasy would be. Thus, Pascal's argument leads us to maximize religious benefit by positing that superbeing which is the very most worthy of worship, viz., the absolutely perfect being, which we take to be the God of Judeo-Christian theism and of some other, non-Western religions as well, minus some of the tendentious if traditional special features ascribed to Him by sectarian practitioners of those religions.[25]

## VIII. Conclusion

If one does not already incline toward theism, or perhaps even if one does so incline, there is still a temptation—a powerful one—to refuse to take the Wager seriously. How, again, can one listen to all this stuff about grooming one's soul, absolute perfection, infinite ecstasy, and the like, if one (as things are) *simply does not* believe in any god and regards theism of any sort as being on an equal epistemic footing with belief in the Easter Bunny?

To this we say: consider the arguments fairly. We maintain that the *standard* and ubiquitous intuitive rejection of the Wager by philosophers is grounded in a confused conflation of the objections we have already addressed, particularly: the feeling that one could not do anything about one's beliefs even if one tried, the feeling that theism has probability zero, and the feeling that any failure to proportion one's belief to the evidence is a shameful if secret vice. But once these various misgivings have been separated and cast explicitly in the form of objections, they are seen to have little rational force.[26] If one wishes to decline the Wager one will have to think of more subtle criticisms than those which have appeared in the literature to date.

We do not claim that our case is conclusive, or that the Wager is now dictated by reason. We do contend that at the present stage of investigation Pascal's argument is unrefuted and not unreasonable.

Let us pray.

## Notes

1. In "The Logic of Pascal's Wager," *American Philosophical Quarterly* 9 (1972): 186–92. Ian Hacking distinguishes the "equal probabilities" version of the argument from a simpler "dominance" version and from a mixed "dominating expectation" version. He also provides a fascinating account of the historical context and of the early reactions to Pascal's "Infini-rien."

2. Blaise Pascal, "The Wager," reprinted in *Reason and Responsibility,* 7th ed., ed. Joel Feinberg (Belmont, CA: Wadsworth, 1989), pp. 80–82.

3. Of course there are degrees of belief in between, including a significant range of agnosticism. The possibility of metaphysical agnosticism accompanied by a selflessly beneficent— even saintly—life is a piquant one, and much debated by some major religions, but we shall neglect it here.

4. Again, agnostics and atheists might not in fact be treated the same, depending on one's idea of God's jealousy, but we pass over this theological tangle.

5. The distinctness of these two notions of "rationality" should be obvious enough. The second seems not epistemic at all; but for that matter cost-benefit considerations have recently begun to enter into traditional epistemology in a disconcerting way: see Lycan, "Epistemic Value," *Synthese* 64 (1985): 137–64; and Hilary Kornblith, "Justified Belief and Epistemically Responsible Action," *Philosophical Review* 92 (1983): 33–48.

6. William James, "The Will to Believe," in *The Will to Believe and Other Essays* (New York: Dover Press, 1956), p. 6.

7. Someone experiences an ominous medical symptom, and does not—cannot—go to the doctor because he is paralyzed with fear. He ends up dead. Someone else does not—cannot—make Pascal's Wager because he is paralyzed with textbook rationality. He ends up dead. Permanently.

8. Indeed, if Pascal is right in conjecturing that the probabilities are even, one may not even *be* violating any norm; it is arguable that when probabilities are even, one may believe as one likes. On this issue, see K. Lehrer, R. Roelofs and M. Swain, "Reason and Evidence: An Unsolved Problem," *Ratio* 9 (1967): 33–48; and George Mavrodes, "Belief, Proportionality, and Probability," in *Reason and Decision* (*Bowling Green Studies in Applied Philosophy*), *Vol. III,* ed. Michael Bradie and Kenneth Sayre (1981). Mavrodes's article is the most trenchant examination we know of the thesis that one ought always to "proportion one's belief to the evidence."

9. Actual demographic surveys do show at least that religious people fare better with respect to divorce, suicide, and other indicators of troubled personal lives.

10. See Hacking, "The Logic of Pascal's Wager," p. 190; Cargile, "Pascal's Wager," *Philosophy* 41 (1966): 255 (reprinted in this volume, pp. 283–89; see especially p. 287—all further citations are from this reprint); Stich, "The Recombinant DNA Debate," *Philosophy and Public Affairs* 7 (1978): 187–205.

11. There was nothing dialectically suspect about this at the time; Pascal was writing specifically for fellow Christians whose faith was wavering, stagnant, or lapsed.

12. Cargile briefly considers this option, but dismisses it without much ado and goes on to press the negligible-probability version of the Many Gods objection ("Pascal's Wager," pp. 287–88). Our own responses to that objection work, we believe, against Cargile's version in particular.

13. See Schlesinger, *Religion and Scientific Method* (Dordrecht, Neth.: D. Reidel, 1977), in which the empiricalness of theistic hypotheses is emphasized.

14. One might wish to join Peirce, and more recently D. M. Armstrong, in seeing consensus as a mark of epistemic probity, though the epistemic value attaches more properly to methods of producing belief than to beliefs themselves.

15. It still may be protested (as it has been by Cargile in correspondence and by Michael Resnik in conversation) that the very idea of an infinite EU is still intrinsically problematic. In the St. Petersburg paradox, for example, a game is constructed which affords an infinite expected payoff in money but which no even faintly sensible person would pay more than a moderate amount of money to play. Cf. R. D. Luce and H. Raiffa, *Games and Decisions* (New York: John Wiley & Sons, 1957, p. 20). We cannot take up the paradox in any detail

here, but we are inclined to follow Bernoulli himself in ascribing it to the declining marginal value of money. If the game were recast in terms of some intrinsic value, such as happiness, *and if the infinite payoff were made possible to obtain* (which presumably requires eternal life), then it does not seem to us unreasonable to pay an arbitrarily large amount to play it (unless one in some way *knows* that one will not win).

16. For a defense of appeals to simplicity against various skeptical objections, see Schlesinger, "Induction and Parsimony," *American Philosophical Quarterly* 8 (1971): 179–85; Lycan, "Occam's Razor," *Metaphilosophy* 6 (1975): 223–37; and Lycan, "Epistemic Value."

17. This simple idea has not received nearly the attention it deserves.

18. This seems particularly reasonable if one supposes that time is nomologically, even metaphysically intertwined with space and with matter-energy, in such a way that time is inextricably part of the physical world and so part of *creation.*

19. J. R. Lucas, *A Treatise on Time and Space* (London: Methuen, 1973), p. 300.

20. There is of course the possibility that timelessness is evaluatively neutral and that two beings identical in every respect save that one is timeless while the other is not cannot differ in degree of excellence. If true this would refute Anselm's thesis, since the property of absolute perfection would not then determine the temporal nature of its possessor. Anselmian theology must presuppose that every property P that is a candidate for ascription to a divine being must either enhance or diminish the excellence of its instances; there cannot exist any neutral divine attribute. Though a fairly strong thesis, this does not seem unreasonable to us.

21. For that matter, it is by no means obvious that the questions of *the kinds of particulars that constitute the furniture of the universe* and *the laws that govern those particulars* are fundamentally different, or that the two notions of "initial conditions" and the "laws of nature" are truly separate and independent. In order to describe the initial conditions prevailing at $t_0$ one must give a full characterization of every particular existing at $t_0$, and we cannot fully have described a particular until we have listed all the properties in virtue of which that particular belongs to its particular kind, which in turn requires listing all the fundamental physical laws it obeys.

22. A further if small advantage of the Anselmian conception of God is that it answers to the feelings of many people that some version of the Ontological Argument is plausible. We do not share that feeling ourselves, but many excellent philosophers have manifested it; and unless the absolutely perfect being is the god of choice, the Ontological Argument is simply and obviously a nonstarter—no one would even think of trying to prove the existence of Zeus, or of Baal, by Anselmian means.

23. Maimonides, *Mishneh Torah,* Hilkhot Teshuvah X.

24. Thomas Carlyle, *On Heroes, Hero-Worship and the Heroic in History* (London: J. Fraser, 1841), p. 1.

25. For a loosely related argument and a limning of the connection between Pascal's Wager and Kierkegaard's "leap of faith," see Robert Merrihew Adams, "Kierkegaard's Arguments Against Objective Reasoning in Religion," *Monist* 60 (1977): 228–43.

26. Oddly, the Many Gods problem, which is surely the most powerful philosophical objection to the Wager, does not play a significant role in people's immediate intuitive revulsion; most people do not even think of it.

# 20

# Pascal's Wager

## *James Cargile*

**A.** Pascal's statement of his wager argument[1,2] is couched in terms of the theory of probability and the theory of games, and the exposition is unclear and unnecessarily complicated. The following is a "creative" reformulation of the argument designed to avoid *some* of the objections which have been or might be raised against the original.

**B.** *Premises:*

1. "If there is a God, we are incapable of knowing either what he is, or whether he exists" (Pascal). And further, we have no way of knowing that God does not exist.
2. If you perform religious rites with enthusiasm, and never question the claims of some religion, you will come to be devoutly religious. "Go then and take holy water, and have masses said; belief will come and stupefy your scruples" (William James' version[3] of a remark by Pascal).
3. If you are devoutly religious—Christian, Jew, Moslem, Hindu, polytheist, etc.—and there is a God, then he will send you to heaven when you die.

*Conclusion:* Solely on grounds of rational self-interest, you should participate in religious rites, refrain from skeptical thoughts, etc.

*Proof:* Consider the following case. A very rich man who is fond of jazz promises that in two years, he is going to toss an unbiased coin. If it lands heads, he will give each devoted jazz fan a million dollars. If it lands tails, he won't do anything. Every Sunday for the next two years, a one-hour jazz concert is scheduled. It is known to be highly likely that if you attend these concerts religiously, and avoid listening to classical music, you will become a devoted jazz fan.

This case is clearly analogous to the situation of the man who is reflecting as to whether or not he should take up religious observances. And in either case the answer is obvious: you had better start listening uncritically to a lot of jazz. You may return to classical music as a millionaire, and you may get to heaven and not have to listen to sermons any more.

Reprinted from *Philosophy* 41 (1966), by permission of Cambridge University Press. Notes edited.

It may be objected that the person who "wagers" by attending concerts loses, if he loses, only two years of classical music, while the person who "wagers" by participating in religious rites and avoiding skeptical thoughts loses, if he loses, the only chance for thinking he will ever have. But after all, what is thinking? You have only to pass up philosophical quibbling which everyone knows is silly anyway. You can keep your mind exercised on mathematics or formal logic or approved scientific topics. Concession to religion needn't be much, even when you strive for real faith. Look what subtle reasoners even fanatics can be!

It may be objected that God may save atheists and agnostics as well as religious people. And the rich man *might* give a million dollars to a lover of classical music— but why depend on *kindness* when you can get a *contract* (or rather, a *covenant*)?

Someone might plan to delay attending the concerts until the second year so as to get in as much classical music as possible. Similarly, someone might plan to follow the advice of Pascal's argument in forty years, after enjoying his skepticism as long as he can. But if the rich man announces that he *may* exclude people who are not jazz fans from his offer if they delay attending the concerts, it would obviously be foolish to delay. And if you plan to delay religious observance, you may not live that long. It is foolish to be even a little careless with an opportunity for infinite gain.

**C.** This argument is designed to convince an open-minded agnostic acting out of rational self-interest that he ought to take up religious practices in the hope of becoming religious. Pascal has other arguments which will then be brought forward to bring the newly won religious sympathizer into Pascal's own particular church, but the Wager argument is not one of these. William James (loc. cit.) criticizes Pascal's argument on the grounds that it would not convert a Moslem to Catholicism. But it wasn't intended to. James has probably been misled by Pascal's comment about holy water and masses. But this needn't occur in the presentation of the Wager argument; the point which the reference to holy water and masses is designed to illustrate could be made just as well with respect to Moslem rituals. The argument is aimed at convincing skeptics, whose coolness about their prospects for immortality horrifies Pascal, that they should become *involved* on the side of those committed to belief in immortality.

James also criticizes Pascal's argument as immoral, and says indignantly, "We feel that a faith in masses and holy water adopted wilfully after such a mechanical calculation would lack the inner soul of faith's reality: and if we were ourselves in the place of the Deity, we should probably take particular pleasure in cutting off believers of this pattern from their infinite reward." It seems that James is overlooking the fact that "*believers* of this pattern" are going to be just the same as other believers. Their belief isn't *sustained* by the argument, nor is it acquired by simply deciding to believe—James rightly regards the idea of "believing by our volition" as "simply silly"—rather, their faith is acquired as a result of actions which they were persuaded by the argument to perform. Once belief comes, the believer may genuinely despise his old skeptical self and shudder to think that such considerations as self-interest ever moved him. He may sincerely perform acts of faith, with no thought of his ultimate reward. A cynic may decide that the most convenient arrangement is a deathbed conversion; but if he is really converted, no one will despise this cynicism more than he.

Since James says that he is presenting Pascal's words "translated freely," it seems fair to protest against his representing Pascal as saying that "any finite loss is reasonable, even a certain one is reasonable, if there is but the possibility of infinite gain." Pascal's exposition is unclear, but he doesn't make such a mistake as this. James also presents the choice as one between belief and unbelief, which is probably one reason why he considers the argument immoral. But Pascal doesn't put it as a choice between belief and unbelief. He speaks obscurely of "risking your life," where he seems to be asking, not that you believe, but that you observe religious rites and abstain from criticism in the hope of being led to belief.

James also presents Pascal's argument as starting with the claim that human reason can't tell us what to do and ending with the claim that a certain course is obviously the reasonable one. This is especially reprehensible when presented as a translation. Jean Mesnard makes the same mistake in paraphrasing Pascal's argument,[4] apparently with approval, as starting with the claim that "reason cannot determine our choice" and ending with "Our reason therefore commands us to bet on the existence of God!" Pascal actually starts by saying that reason cannot settle the question as to whether or not there *is* a God, and concludes by saying that reason does clearly advise us to "*bet*" that there is a God—which for Pascal means being religious or sincerely trying to become so.

**D.** Various presentations of the Wager argument defend it against the charge that it is an immoral argument. But no presentation I know of notices that the argument, which is presented as an appeal to a self-interested, rational skeptic who is completely uncommitted,[5] is simply invalid, because no such person could accept the premises.

Premise (1) might not be acceptable to an agnostic because it considers only the possibility of a transcendent God. The agnostic might think that investigation of occult phenomena *could* answer the God question, though of course only an affirmative answer would be so obtainable. Still, the skeptic would certainly admit that the God question is pretty much up in the air. So with "could not know" changed to "do not know," premise (1) would be acceptable to a skeptic.

The skeptic might doubt that he is the sort of person of whom the factual claim of premise (2) is true. But he would probably admit that there are measures sufficient to bring him into a religious frame of mind, even if the measures required were somewhat more severe than are needed by the average man. So he might accept premise (2) while still preserving his title as a skeptic or agnostic.

However, no self-respecting skeptic could accept premise (3). For one thing, if he accepts premise (1) as stated, that is, accepts that if there is a God, then "we are incapable of knowing what he is," then he cannot consistently agree with premise (3) that one thing we can be sure of about the possible owner-operator of the universe is that he is the sort of being who will send religious people to heaven. And premise (1) apart, why should not the neutral skeptic think it just as likely that God will save atheists and agnostics as that he will save believers? He might hope that it is more likely, either purely for his own sake, or on moral grounds.

The fact that, say, Christianity or Mohammedanism *promise* their adherents an infinite reward, while, say, dialectical materialism does not, cannot be produced as a good reason for a neutral adopting one of the former positions rather than the latter. The argument, "If you become devoutly religious, and religion is right about there being a God, then you will get an infinite reward," is just invalid. It would be all right to argue, "If you become devoutly religious, and religion is right about there being a God and religion is right about one claim it makes about his character, then you will get an infinite reward." But with these premises, there are no longer just the two possibilities, "Religion is right about there being a God or it isn't right about there being a God." There are three possibilities: religion is right about there being a God and right about his character; or religion is right about there being a God and wrong about his character; or religion is wrong about there being a God.

**E.** However, an attempt might be made to reinstate the Wager argument in spite of the observations in (D), as follows:

Either (a) there is a god who will send only religious people to heaven or (b) there is not. To be religious is to wager for (a). To fail to be religious is to wager for (b). We can't settle the question whether (a) or (b) is the case, at least not at present. But (a) is clearly vastly better than (b). With (a), infinite bliss is *guaranteed,* while with (b) we are still in the miserable human condition of facing death with no assurance as to what lies beyond. So (a) is clearly the best wager.

This arrangement does indeed appeal to a self-interested, *uncommitted* skeptic—it does not *presuppose* anything about the nature of god—the assumption about the nature of god is explicit in the argument. A skeptic might accept this argument and still deserve the title of "skeptic," but he would not deserve the title of "clear thinker."

The argument just presented is formally similar to the following:

Either (a) there is a god who will send you to heaven only if you commit a painful ritual suicide within an hour of first reading this, or (b) there is not. We cannot settle the question whether (a) or (b) is the case; or it is at least not settled yet. But (a) is vastly preferable to (b), since in situation (a) infinite bliss is *guaranteed,* while in (b) we are left in the usual miserable human condition. So we should wager for (a) by performing the suicidal ritual.

It might be objected that we can be sure that there is not a god who will send us to heaven only if we commit suicide but we can't be sure that there is not a god who will send us to heaven only if we are religious. However, a skeptic would demand proof for this.

Both the foregoing arguments might gain plausibility through confusing possibility with probability. Certainly Pascal's application of probability theory could be severely criticized. However, my purpose has not been to criticize this aspect of the argument, but only to point out that the argument cannot stand as an appeal to someone who subscribes to no religious presuppositions.

**F.** Though my criticism of Pascal's argument has not been based on attacking his use of probability theory, it may be worth noting that if his use of probability theory were right, probability theory would be in a bad way.

Pascal uses a certain method from probability theory for calculating whether a given bet is a good one, to support his argument. The method is as follows: given a bet on whether or not an event E will happen, you multiply the probability of E by the odds offered (with the largest number in the odds, if there is one, in the numerator). If this product exceeds one, and you are getting the high end of the odds, then the bet is a good one for you no matter how low the probability of E may be.

The limitations of this method are well-known, and Pascal's application of it creates a situation somewhat like the Petersburg Paradox.[6] But I think we need not go as far as the Petersburg Paradox to criticize Pascal's application of this method. It is enough to observe that in applying the method, Pascal takes for granted that the hypothesis that there is a God has some nonzero probability.

The only support Pascal could have for this is the so-called "Principle of Indifference," the fallaciousness of which is well-known,[7] Pascal assumes that if a proposition is logically possible and not known to be false, then it has some nonzero probability. But the propositional function, "There exists a God who prefers contemplating the real number x more than any other activity," provides us with a set of mutually incompatible propositions, each of which is logically and epistemically possible, such that there could not be a nonzero probability for each member of the set. Even if this "propositional function" is rejected as nonsense, such a function as "There are $n$ rabbits in the universe" would provide a set of mutually incompatible propositions, infinitely many of which would be both logically and epistemically possible. They could all be assigned probability numbers, e.g., from the series ½, ¼, ⅛, . . . , but such an assignment would be absurd.

G. Of course, there remains the argument that if you become devoutly religious (and not a Calvinist!) you will *think* that you are going to get an infinite reward, and this is pleasanter than not thinking so. Whether Pascal would have stooped to this is a question outside the scope of the present essay.

H. It must be emphasized that my criticisms have not been intended to suggest that religious belief is unreasonable. It is one thing to hold that reason directs us to be religious, quite another to hold that it is (perfectly) reasonable to be religious.

Even in this connection, it is not the belief in an infinite gain which makes it reasonable to be religious. I may get the idea into my head that setting fire to the bus station will get me into heaven, but this belief does not make it *reasonable* for me to perform this religious act. *How I got the belief* would be crucial in determining whether the religious act of setting fire to the bus station is reasonable.

For example, if someone were dressed as an angel in a very convincing way, and lowered by an invisible wire to hang in front of me as I was climbing a cliff where I had every reason to think no one else was present, and this "angel" told me to burn the bus station, and I did, and the judge found out about the prank, and found out how diabolically convincing it had been, he might well dismiss my case, calling my action reasonable. Or again, if a heavenly host actually appeared to me and to all mankind, and promised us all eternal bliss if I burn down the bus station, my fellow men might consider me irrational to refuse.

On the other hand, if I were talked into burning the bus station by some sleazy prophet, my religious observance might well be called irrational.

I. There remains one way of reconstruing the Wager argument so as to make the preceding criticisms inapplicable. It might be observed that many professed skeptics have lingering tendencies to believe in some religion, and that proposing a wager is an effective way to exploit these tendencies to bring them back into the fold.

Thus a lapsed Christian might feel that there is a 1/100 chance that Christianity is right, while assigning no likelihood at all to the claims of other religions. Furthermore, he may be sure that if Christianity is right, then however ordinary sinners and believers in other religions may fare, hard-boiled atheists will fare very badly indeed. For such a person as this, the wager might be thought to exert a powerful attraction to return to active Christianity.

However, this doesn't seem to be true in actual practice, and there are good reasons why this should be so. For one thing, if someone is a hard-boiled atheist, he won't assign any positive probability to Christian claims about God. And if he isn't a hard-boiled atheist and does assign a positive probability to Christian claims, he is likely to imagine the Christian God as too nice to be stingy with rewards for people in his category, so the Wager won't lead him to change his schedule.

Furthermore, lingering religiosity is not in itself enough to make the Wager appetizing. It has to be lingering religiosity which the agent will express in a positive probability estimate, or otherwise the Wager won't get started. And many people who have superstitious tendencies would still not attach any positive probability to these superstitions.

And finally, even when someone does attach a positive probability to some religion's god-claims (and to no other's), the Wager argument is not sure to bind him. Let us very roughly distinguish between objective and subjective theories of probability by noting that on an objective theory, it is not necessary that someone's judgment of a probability have any connection with his wagering behavior; while on a subjective view, given the person's value scheme, his wagering behavior is essential to determining his probability judgments. Then on the objective view, even given a positive probability estimate for some religion and a definite preference for heaven, being willing to make the wager doesn't follow and it is even a vexed question (at least) to show that wager-reluctance in such circumstances would even be less than reasonable. And on the subjective view, the probability estimate won't be of much use in persuading the agent to wager, considering that willingness to wager was an essential feature in determining the probability estimate.

## Notes

1. *Pascal's Pensees,* bilingual ed., trans. H. F. Stewart (New York: Modern Library, 1947).

2. Georges Brunet, in *Le Pari de Pascal,* pp. 62–63, points out that Pascal was not the originator of the Wager argument. Other writings on the background of Pascal's argument are A. Ducas, *Le Pari de Pascal,* and M. J. Orcibal, "Le Fragment Infini-Rien et ses Sources," in *Blaise Pascal, L'Homme et L'Oeuvre,* (Paris, 1956), Sec. V.

3. William James, *The Will to Believe* (New York, 1897), pp. 5–6.

4. Jean Mesnard, *Pascal, His Life and Works,* trans. G. S. Fraser (London: Harvill Press, 1952), pp. 156–57.

5. M. L. Goldmann ("Le Pari, est-il Ecrit 'Pour le Libertin'?" in *Blaise Pascal: L'Homme et L'Oeuvre,* Sec. IV) argues that the argument is not for the skeptic who is *satisfied* with this world, but is rather for the man who is conscious of the miserable human condition. It is

certainly consistent for a self-interested, rational skeptic to feel unhappy with man's lot. But even if he has the appropriate human longings, the rational skeptic must find Pascal's argument invalid.

6. See, for example, Harald Cramer, *The Elements of Probability Theory* (New York: Wiley, 1955), p. 95; or William Feller, *Introduction to Probability Theory and its Applications* (New York: Wiley, 1957), pp. 199–201.

7. See William Kneale, *Probability and Induction* (Oxford, Engl.: Clarendon Press, 1949), pp. 184–85.

# Bibliography

Adams, Robert Merrihew. "Kierkegaard's Arguments Against Objective Reasoning in Religion." *The Monist* 60 (1977): 228–43.

——. "The Virtue of Faith," in his *The Virtue of Faith and Other Essays in Philosophical Theology.* New York: Oxford University Press, 1987.

Allen, Diogenes. *Christian Belief in a Postmodern World: The Full Wealth of Conviction.* Louiseville, KY: Westminster/John Knox Press, 1989.

Audi, Robert. "Faith, Belief, and Rationality," in *Philosophical Perspectives. 5: Philosophy of Religion, 1991,* ed. James E. Tomberlin. Atascadero, CA: Ridgeview Publishing, 1991.

Britton, Karl. *Philosophy and the Meaning of Life.* London: Cambridge University Press, 1969.

Collinge, William J. "The Return of Religious Community Life to Rationality in Augustine." *Faith and Philosophy* 5 (1988): 242–53.

Creel, Richard E. "Philosophy's Bowl of Pottage: Reflections on the Value of Faith." *Faith and Philosophy* 1 (1984): 230–35.

Dalton, Peter C. "Pascal's Wager: The First Argument." *International Journal for Philosophy of Religion* 7 (1976): 346–68.

——. "Pascal's Wager: The Second Argument." *Southern Journal of Philosophy* 13 (1975): 31–46.

Davis, Stephen T. "Pascal on Self-Caused Belief." *Religious Studies* 27 (1991): 27–37.

Duff, Anthony. "Pascal's Wager and Infinite Utilities." *Analysis* 46 (1986): 107–9.

Emmanuel, Steven M. "Kierkegaard's Pragmatist Faith." *Philosophy and Phenomenological Research* 51 (1991): 279–302.

Flew, Antony. *God and Philosophy.* London: Hutchinson, 1966.

——. "Is Pascal's Wager the Only Safe Bet?" *The Rationalist Annual* (1960): 21–25.

Fontinell, Eugene. *Self, God, and Immortality: A Jamesian Investigation.* Philadelphia: Temple University Press, 1986.

Gale, Richard M. "Pragmatism Versus Mysticism: The Divided Self of William James," in *Philosophical Perspectives. 5: Philosophy of Religion, 1991,* ed. James E. Tomberlin. Atascadero, CA: Ridgeview Publishing, 1991.

——. "William James and the Ethics of Belief." *American Philosophical Quarterly* 17 (1980): 1–14.

Hacking, Ian. "The Logic of Pascal's Wager." *American Philosophical Quarterly* 9 (1972): 186–92.

Holyer, Robert. "Scepticism, Evidentialism, and the Parity Argument: A Pascalian Perspective." *Religious Studies* 25 (1989): 191–208.

James, William. *The Will to Believe and Other Essays.* New York: Dover Books, 1956.

Jantzen, Grace M. " 'Religion' Reviewed," *Heythrop Journal* 26 (1985): 14–25.

Jordan, Jeff. "Duff and the Wager." *Analysis* 51 (1991): 174–76.

———. "The Many-Gods Objection and Pascal's Wager." *International Philosophical Quarterly* 31 (1991): 309–17.

Kaufmann, Walter. *Critique of Religion and Philosophy.* Princeton, NJ: Princeton University Press, 1958.

Keller, James. "Reflections on the Value of Knowledge: A Reply to Creel." *Faith and Philosophy* 2 (1985): 191–94.

Kolakowski, Leszek. *Religion.* London: Fontana, 1982.

Krailscheimer, Alban. *Pascal.* New York: Hill & Wang, 1980.

Kreeft, Peter J. *Heaven: The Heart's Deepest Longing.* San Francisco: Harper & Row, 1980.

———. *Love Is Stronger Than Death.* San Francisco: Harper & Row, 1979.

Landsberg, P. T. "Gambling on God." *Mind* 80 (1971): 100–104.

Levinson, H. S. *The Religious Investigations of William James.* Chapel Hill, NC: University of North Carolina Press, 1981.

Mackie, J. L. "Belief without Reason," in his *The Miracle of Theism: Arguments for and against the Existence of God.* Oxford, Engl.: Clarendon Press, 1982.

Martin, Michael. "Beneficial Arguments for God," in his *Atheism: A Philosophical Justification.* Philadelphia: Temple University Press, 1990.

———. "On Four Critiques of Pascal's Wager." *Sophia* 14 (1975): 1–11.

———. "Pascal's Wager as an Argument for Not Believing in God." *Religious Studies* 19 (1983): 57–64.

Mavrodes, George I. "Intellectual Profit in Clifford and James," in *The Ethics of Belief Debate* (American Academy of Religion Series, No. 14), ed. Gerald D. McCarthy. Atlanta, GA: Scholars Press, 1986.

Muyskens, James L. *The Sufficiency of Hope: The Conceptual Foundations of Religion.* Philadelphia: Temple University Press, 1979.

———. "What is Virtuous About Faith?" *Faith and Philosophy* 2 (1985): 43–52.

Natoli, Charles M. "The Role of the Wager in Pascal's Apologetics." *New Scholasticism* 57 (1983): 98–106.

Newman, Jay. "Popular Pragmatism and Religious Belief." *International Journal for Philosophy of Religion* 8 (1977): 94–110.

Nicholl, Larimore Reid. "Pascal's Wager: The Bet Is Off." *Philosophy and Phenomenological Research* 39 (1978): 274–80.

O'Connell, Robert. *William James on the Courage to Believe.* New York: Fordham University Press, 1984.

Opey, G. "On Rescher on Pascal's Wager." *International Journal for Philosophy of Religion* 30 (1991): 159–68.

Penelhum, Terence. *God and Skepticism.* Dordrecht, Neth.: D. Reidel, 1983.

Pojman, Louis P. "Belief and Will." *Religious Studies* 14 (1978): 1–14.

———. "Faith without Belief." *Faith and Philosophy* 3 (1986): 157–76.

———. *Religious Belief and the Will.* New York: Routledge & Kegan Paul, 1986.

Rescher, Nicholas. *Methodological Pragmatism.* New York: New York University Press, 1977.

———. *Pascal's Wager: A Study of Practical Reasoning in Philosophical Theology.* Notre Dame, IN: University of Notre Dame Press, 1985.

Resnick, Lawrence. "Evidence, Utility, and God." *Analysis* 31 (1971): 87–90.

Ross, James F. "Believing for Profit," in *The Ethics of Belief Debate* (American Academy of Religion Series, No. 14), ed. Gerald D. McCarthy. Atlanta, GA: Scholars Press, 1986.

Runzo, Joseph. "World-Views and the Epistemic Foundations of Theism." *Religious Studies* 25 (1989): 31–51.

Ryan, J. K. "The Wager in Pascal and Others." *New Scholasticism* 19 (1945): 233–50.

Schlesinger, George N. *New Perspectives on Old-time Religion.* Oxford, Engl.: Oxford University Press, 1988.

———. *Religion and Scientific Method.* Dordrecht, Neth.: D. Reidel, 1982.

Schwarz, Stephen D. "Faith, Doubt and Pascal's Wager." *Center Journal* 3 (1984): 29–58.

Scriven, Michael. *Primary Philosophy.* New York: McGraw-Hill, 1966.

Singer, Marcus G. "The Pragmatic Use of Language and the Will to Believe." *American Philosophical Quarterly* 8 (1971): 24–34.

Swinburne, Richard. "The Christian Wager." *Religious Studies* 4 (1969): 217–28.

———. *Faith and Reason.* Oxford, Engl.: Clarendon Press, 1981.

Topliss, Patricia. *The Rhetoric of Pascal: A Study of His Art of Persuasion in the* Provinciales *and the* Pensees. Leicester, Engl.: Leicester University Press, 1966.

Turner, Merle. "Deciding for God: The Baysian Support of Pascal's Wager." *Philosophy and Phenomenological Research* 29 (1968): 84–90.

Vanden Burgt, Robert. "William James on Man's Creativity in the Religious Universe." *Philosophy Today* 15 (Winter 1971): 292–301.

Westphal, Merold. "Religion as Means and as End," in his *God, Guilt, and Death: An Existential Phenomenology of Religion.* Bloomington, IN: Indiana University Press, 1984.

Wolterstorff, Nicholas. Review of *Religious Belief and the Will,* by Louis P. Pojman. *Faith and Philosophy* 8 (1991): 120–23.

# VI

# RATIONAL BELIEF AND RELIGIOUS EXPERIENCE

.

# 21

# Religious Experience and Religious Belief

*William P. Alston*

## I

Can religious experience provide any ground or basis for religious belief? Can it serve to justify religious belief, or make it rational? This paper will differ from many others in the literature by virtue of looking at this question in the light of basic epistemological issues. Throughout we will be comparing the epistemology of religious experience with the epistemology of sense experience.

We must distinguish between experience directly, and indirectly, justifying a belief. It indirectly justifies belief $B_1$ when it justifies some other beliefs, which in turn justify $B_1$. Thus I have learned indirectly from experience that Beaujolais wine is fruity, because I have learned from experience that this, that, and the other bottle of Beaujolais is fruity, and these propositions support the generalization. Experience will directly justify a belief when the justification does not go through other beliefs in this way. Thus, if I am justified, just by virtue of having the visual experiences I am now having, in taking what I am experiencing to be a typewriter situated directly in front of me, then the belief that there is a typewriter directly in front of me is directly justified by that experience.

We find claims to both direct and indirect justification of religious beliefs by religious experience. Where someone believes that her new way of relating herself to the world after her conversion is to be explained by the Holy Spirit imparting supernatural graces to her, she supposes her belief *that the Holy Spirit imparts graces to her* to be directly justified by her experience. What she directly learns from experience is that she sees and reacts to things differently; this is then taken as a reason for supposing that the Holy Spirit is imparting graces to her. When, on the other hand, someone takes himself to be experiencing the presence of God, he thinks that his experience justifies him in supposing that God is *what* he is experiencing. Thus, he supposes himself to be directly justified by his experience in believing God to be present to him.

In this paper I will confine myself to the question of whether religious experience can provide direct justification for religious belief. This has implications for the class of experiences we shall be considering. In the widest sense 'religious expe-

---

Reprinted from *Nous* 16 (1982), by permission of the author and the editor.

rience' ranges over any experiences one has in connection with one's religious life, including any joys, fears, or longings one has in a religious context. But here I am concerned with experiences that could be taken to *directly* justify religious beliefs, i.e., experiences that give rise to a religious belief and that the subject takes to involve a direct awareness of what the religious belief is about. To further focus the discussion, let's confine ourselves to beliefs to the effect that God, as conceived in theistic religions, is doing something that is directed to the subject of the experience—that God is speaking to him, strengthening him, enlightening him, giving him courage, guiding him, sustaining him in being, or just being present to him. Call these "M-beliefs" ('M' for 'manifestation').

Note that our question concerns what might be termed a general "epistemic practice," the accepting of M-beliefs on the basis of experience, rather than some particular belief of that sort.[1] I hold that practices, or habits, of belief formation are the primary subject of justification and that particular beliefs are justified only by issuing from a practice (or the activation of a habit) that is justified. The following discussion of concepts of justification will provide grounds for that judgment.

Whether M-beliefs can be directly justified by experience depends, inter alia, on what it is to be justified in a belief. So let us take a look at that.

First, the justification about which we are asking is an "epistemic" rather than a "moral" or "prudential" justification. Suppose one should hold that the practice in question is justified because it makes us feel good. Even if this is true in a sense, it has no bearing on epistemic justification. But why not? What makes a justification *epistemic?* Epistemic justification, as the name implies, has something to do with knowledge, or, more broadly, with the aim at attaining truth and avoiding falsity. At a first approximation, I am justified in believing that $p$ when, from the point of view of that aim, there is something O.K., all right, to be approved, about that fact that I believe that $p$. But when we come to spell this out further, we find that a fundamental distinction must be drawn between two different ways of being in an epistemically commendable position.

On the one hand there is what we may call a "normative" concept of epistemic justification $(J_n)$, "normative" because it has to do with how we stand vis-à-vis norms that specify our intellectual obligations, obligations that attach to one qua cognitive subject, qua truth seeker. Stated most generally, $J_n$ consists in one's not having violated one's intellectual obligations. We have to say "not having violated" rather than "having fulfilled" because in all normative spheres, *being justified* is a negative status; it amounts to one's behavior not being in violation of the norms. If belief is under direct voluntary control, we may think of intellectual obligations as attaching directly to believing. Thus one might be obliged to refrain from believing in the absence of adequate evidence. But if, as it seems to me, belief is not, in general, under voluntary control, obligations cannot attach directly to believing. However, I do have voluntary control over moves that can influence a particular belief formation, e.g., looking for more evidence, and moves that can affect my general belief-forming habits or tendencies, e.g., training myself to be more critical of testimony. If we think of intellectual obligations as attaching to activities that are designed to influence belief formation, we may say that a certain epistemic practice is normatively justified, provided it is not the case that the practitioner would not have engaged in it had he satisfied intellectual obligations to engage in activities designed to inhibit it. In other words, the practice is justified if and only if the practitioner did not fail to satisfy an obligation to inhibit it.

However, epistemologists also frequently use the term 'justified' in such a way that it has to do not with how the subject stands vis-à-vis obligations, but rather with the strength of her epistemic position in believing that $p$, with how likely it is that a belief of that sort acquired or held in that way is true. To say that a practice is justified in this, as I shall say, "evaluative" sense ($J_e$) is to say that beliefs acquired in accordance with that practice, in the sorts of circumstances in which human beings typically find themselves, are generally true.[2] Thus we might say that a practice is $J_e$ if and only if it is reliable.[3]

One further complication in the notion of $J_n$ remains to be canvassed. What is our highest reasonable aspiration for being $J_n$ in accepting a belief on the basis of experience? Being $J_n$ no matter what else is the case? A brief consideration of sense perception would suggest a negative answer. I may be justified in believing that there is a tree in front of me by virtue of the fact that I am currently having a certain kind of sense experience, but this will be true only in "favorable circumstances." If I am confronted with a complicated arrangement of mirrors, I may not be justified in believing that there is an oak tree in front of me, even though it looks for all the world as if there is. Again, it may look for all the world as if water is running uphill, but the general improbability of this greatly diminishes the justification the corresponding belief receives from that experience.

What this shows is that the justification provided by one's experience is only defeasibly so. It is inherently liable to be overriden, diminished, or cancelled by stronger considerations to the contrary. Thus the justification of beliefs about the physical environment that is provided by sense experience is a defeasible or, as we might say, prima facie justification. By virtue of having the experience, the subject is in a position such that she will be adequately justified in the belief *unless* there are strong enough reasons to the contrary.

It would seem that direct experiential justification for M-beliefs is also, at most, prima facie. Beliefs about the nature and ways of God are often used to override M-beliefs, particularly beliefs concerning communications from God. If I report that God told me to kill all phenomenologists, fellow Christians will, no doubt, dismiss the report on the grounds that God would not give me any such injunction as that. I shall take it that both sensory experience and religious experience provide, at most, prima facie justification.

One implication of this stand is that a particular experiential epistemic practice will have to include some way of identifying defeaters. Different theistic religions, even different branches of the same religion, will differ in this regard, e.g., with respect to what sacred books, what traditions, what doctrines are taken to provide defeaters. We also find difference of this kind in perceptual practice. For example, with the progress of science new defeaters are added to the repertoire. Epistemic practices can, of course, be individuated with varying degrees of detail. To fix our thoughts with regard to the central problem of this paper, let's think of a "Christian epistemic practice" (CP) that takes its defeaters from the Bible, the classic creeds, and certain elements of tradition. There will be differences between subsegments of the community of practitioners so defined, but there will be enough commonality to make it a useful construct. My foil to CP, the practice of forming beliefs about the physical environment on the basis of sense-experience, I shall call "perceptual practice" (PP).

Actually, it will prove most convenient to think of each of our practices as involving not only the formation of beliefs on the basis of experience, but also the retention of these beliefs in memory, the formation of rationally self-evident beliefs, and various kinds of reasoning on the basis of all this. CP will be the richer complex, since it will include the formation of perceptual beliefs in the usual way,[4] while PP will not be thought of as including the distinctive experiential practice of CP.

One final preliminary note. $J_n$ is relative to a particular person's situation. If practice $P_1$ is quite unreliable, I may still be $J_n$ in engaging in it either because I have no way of realizing its unreliability or because I am unable to disengage myself; while you, suffering from neither of these disabilities, are not $J_n$. When we ask whether a given practice is $J_n$, we shall be thinking about some normal, reasonably well-informed, contemporary member of our society.

## II

Let's make use of all this in tackling the question as to whether one can be justified in CP and in PP. Beginning with $J_n$, we will first have to determine more precisely what one's intellectual obligations are vis-à-vis epistemic practices. Since our basic cognitive aim is to come into possession of as much truth as possible and to avoid false beliefs, it would seem that one's basic intellectual obligation vis-à-vis practices of belief formation would be to do what one can (or, at least, do as much as could reasonably be expected of one) to see to it that these practices are as *reliable* as possible.[5] But this still leaves us with an option between a stronger and a weaker view as to this obligation. According to the stronger demand one is obliged to refrain (or try to refrain) from engaging in a practice unless one has adequate reasons for supposing it to be reliable. In the absence of sufficient reasons for considering the practice reliable, it is not justified. Practices are guilty until proved innocent. While on the more latitudinarian view one is justified in engaging in a practice provided one does not have sufficient reasons for regarding it to be unreliable. Practices are innocent until proved guilty. Let's take $J_{ns}$ as an abbreviation for 'justified in the normative sense on the stronger requirement', and '$J_{nw}$' as an abbreviation for 'justified in the normative sense on the weaker requirement.'

Now consider whether Mr. Everyman is $J_{nw}$ in engaging in PP. It would seem so. Except for those who, like Parmenides and Bradley, have argued that there are ineradicable inconsistencies in the conceptual scheme involved in PP, philosophers have not supposed that we can show that sense perception is not a reliable guide to our immediate surroundings. Skeptics about PP have generally confined themselves to arguing that we can't show that perception is reliable; i.e., they have argued that PP is not $J_{ns}$. I shall assume without further ado that PP is $J_{nw}$.

$J_{ns}$ and $J_e$ can be considered together. Although a practice may actually be reliable without my having adequate reasons for supposing so, and vice versa, still in considering whether a given practice is reliable, we will be seeking to determine whether there *are* adequate reasons for supposing it reliable, that is whether Everyman *could* be possessed of such reasons. And if we hold, as we shall, that there are no such reasons, the question of whether they are possessed by one or another subject does not arise.

I believe that there are no adequate noncircular reasons for the reliability of PP but I will not be able to argue that point here. If I had a general argument I would unveil it, but, so far as I can see, this thesis is susceptible only of inductive support, by unmasking each pretender in turn. And since this issue has been in the forefront of the Western philosophical consciousness for several centuries, there have been many pretenders. I do not have time even for criticism of a few representative samples. Instead I will simply assume that PP is not $J_{ns}$, and then consider what bearing this widely shared view has on the epistemic status of CP.

If $J_{nw}$ is the most we can have for perceptual practice, then if CP is also $J_{nw}$ it will be in at least as strong an epistemic position as the former. (I shall assume without argument that CP can no more be noncircularly shown to be reliable than can PP.) And CP will be $J_{nw}$ for S, provided S has no significant reasons for regarding it as unreliable. Are there any such reasons? What might they be? Well, for one thing, the practice might yield a system that is ineradically internally inconsistent. (I am not speaking of isolated and remediable inconsistencies that continually pop up in every area of thought and experience.) For another, it might yield results that come into ineradicable conflict with the results of other practices to which we are more firmly committed. Perhaps some fundamentalist Christians are engaged in an epistemic practice that can be ruled out on such grounds as these. But I shall take it as obvious that one *can* objectify certain stretches of one's experience, or indeed the whole of one's experience, in Christian terms without running into such difficulties.

## III

One may grant everything I have said up to this point and still feel reluctant to allow that CP is $J_{nw}$. CP does differ from PP in important ways, and it may be thought that some of these differences will affect their relative epistemic status. The following features of PP, which it does not share with CP, have been thought to have this kind of bearing.

1. Within PP there are standard ways of checking the accuracy of any particular perceptual belief.
2. By engaging in PP we can discover regularities in the behavior of the objects putatively observed, and on this basis we can, to a certain extent, effectively predict the course of events.
3. Capacity for PP, and practice of it, is found universally among normal adult human beings.
4. All normal adult human beings, whatever their culture, use basically the same conceptual scheme in objectifying their sense experience.

If CP includes PP as a proper part, as I ruled on above, how can it lack these features? What I mean is that there is no analogue of these features for that distinctive part of CP by virtue of which it goes beyond PP. The extra element of CP does not enable us to discover extra regularities, e.g., in the behavior of God, or increase our predictive powers. M-beliefs are not subject to interpersonal check in the same way as perceptual beliefs. The practice of forming M-beliefs on the basis of experience is not engaged in by all normal adults. And so on.

Before coming to grips with the alleged epistemic bearing of these differences, I want to make two preliminary points. *First,* we have to engage in PP to determine that this practice has features (1)–(4), and that CP lacks them. Apart from observation, we have no way of knowing that, e.g., while all cultures agree in their way of cognizing the physical environment they differ in their ways of cognizing the divine, or that PP puts us in a position to predict while CP doesn't. It might be thought that this is loading the dice in favor of my opponent. If we are to use PP, rather than some neutral source, to determine what features it has, shouldn't the same courtesy of self-assessment be accorded CP? Why should *it* be judged on the basis of what we learn about it from another practice, while that other practice is allowed to grade itself? To be sure, this is a serious issue only if answers to these questions *are* forthcoming from CP that differ from those we arrive at by engaging in PP. Fortunately, I can avoid getting involved in these issues by ruling that what I am interested in here is how CP looks from the standpoint of PP. The person I am primarily concerned to address is one who, like all the rest of us, engages in PP, and who, like all of us except for a few outlandish philosophers, regards it as justified. My aim is to show this person that, on his own grounds, CP enjoys basically the same epistemic status as PP. Hence it is consonant with my purposes to allow PP to determine the facts of the matter with respect to both practices. *Second,* I could quibble over whether the contrast is as sharp as is alleged. Questions can be raised about both sides of the putative divide. On the PP side, is it really true that all cultures have objectified sense experience in the same way? Many anthropologists have thought not. And what about the idea that all *normal* adult human beings engage in the same perceptual practice? Aren't we loading the dice by taking participation in what we regard as standard perceptual practice as our basic criterion for normality? On the CP side, is it really the case that this practice reveals no regularities to us, or only that they are very different from regularities in the physical world? What about the point that God is faithful to His promises? Or that the pure in heart will see God? However, I believe that when all legitimate quibbles have been duly registered there will still be very significant differences between the two practices in these respects. So rather than contesting the factual allegations, I will concentrate on the de jure issue as to what bearing these differences have on epistemic status.

How could the lack of (1)–(4) prevent CP from being $J_{nw}$? Only by providing an adequate ground for a judgment of unreliability. And why suppose that? Of course, the lack of these features implies that we lack certain reasons we might conceivably have had for regarding CP as reliable. If we could ascertain that PP has those features, without using PP to do so, that would provide us with strong reasons for judging PP to be reliable. And the parallel possibility is lacking for CP. This shows that we cannot have *certain* reasons for taking CP to be reliable, but it doesn't follow that we have reasons for unreliability. That would follow only if we could also premise that a practice is reliable *only if* (as well as *if*) it has (1)–(4). And why suppose that?

My position is that it is a kind of parochialism that makes the lack of (1)–(4) appear to betoken untrustworthiness. The reality CP claims to put us in touch with is conceived to be vastly different from the physical environment. Why should the sorts of procedures required to put us in effective cognitive touch with this reality not be equally different? Why suppose that the distinctive features of PP set an appropriate standard for the cognitive approach to God? I shall sketch out a possible state of affairs in which CP is quite trustworthy while lacking (1)–(4), and then suggest that we have no reason to suppose that this state of affairs does not obtain.

Suppose, then, that

A. God is too different from created beings, too "wholly other," for us to be able to grasp any regularities in His behavior.

Suppose further that

B. for the same reason we can only attain the faintest, sketchiest, and most insecure grasp of what God is like.

Finally, suppose that

C. God has decreed that a human being will be aware of His presence in any clear and unmistakable fashion only when certain special and difficult conditions are satisfied.

If all this is the case, then it is the reverse of surprising that CP should lack (1)–(4) even if it does involve a genuine experience of God. It would lack (1)–(2) because of (A). It is quite understandable that it should lack (4) because of (B). If our cognitive powers are not fitted to frame an adequate conception of God, it is not at all surprising that there should be wide variation in attempts to do so. This is what typically happens in science when investigators are grappling with a phenomenon no one really understands. A variety of models, analogues, metaphors, hypotheses, hunches are propounded, and it is impossible to secure universal agreement. (3) is missing because of (C). If very difficult conditions are set, it is not surprising that few are chosen. Now it is compatible with (A)–(C) that

D. religious experience should, in general, constitute a genuine awareness of the divine,

and that

E. although any particular articulation of such an experience might be mistaken to a greater or lesser extent, indeed even though all such articulations might miss the mark to some extent, still such judgments will, for the most part, contain some measure of truth; they, or many of them, will constitute a useful approximation of the truth;

and that

F. God's designs contain provision for correction and refinement, for increasing the accuracy of the beliefs derived from religious experience. Perhaps as one grows in the spiritual life one's spiritual sight becomes more accurate and more discriminating; perhaps some special revelation is vouchsafed under certain conditions; and there are many other conceivable possibilities.

If something like all this were the case, then CP would be trustworthy even though it lacks features (1)–(4). This is a conceivable way in which CP would constitute a road to the truth, while differing from PP in respects (1)–(4). Therefore unless we have adequate reason for supposing that no such combination of circumstances obtains, we are not warranted in taking the lack of (1)–(4) to be an adequate reason for a judgment of untrustworthiness.

Moreover it is not just that the (A)–(C) constitute a bare possibility. In the practice of CP we seem to learn that this is the way things are. As for (A) and (B) it is the common teaching of all the higher religions that God is of a radically different order of being from finite substances and, therefore, that we cannot expect to attain the grasp of His nature and His doings that we have of worldly objects. As for (C), it is a basic theme in Christianity, and in other religions as well, that one finds God within one's experience, to any considerable degree, only as one progresses in the spiritual life. God is not available for *voyeurs*. Awareness of God, and understanding of His nature and His will for us, is not a purely cognitive achievement; it requires the involvement of the whole person; it takes a practical commitment and a practice of the life of the spirit, as well as the exercise of cognitive faculties.

Of course these results that we are using to defend CP are derived from that same practice. But in view of the fact that the favorable features of PP, (1)–(4), are themselves ascertained by engaging in PP, our opponent is hardly in a position to fault us on this score. However, I have not forgotten that I announced it as my aim to show that even one who engaged only in PP should recognize that CP is $J_{nw}$. For this purpose, I ignore what we learn in CP and revert to the point that my opponent has no basis for ruling out the conjoint state of affairs (A)–(F), hence has no basis for taking the lack of (1)–(4) to show CP to be untrustworthy, and hence has no reason for denying that CP is $J_{nw}$.

I conclude that CP has basically the same epistemic status as PP and that no one who subscribes to the former is in any position to cavil at the latter.

## Notes

1. Alternatively, we might say that it concerns the acceptability of a certain general epistemic principle: M-beliefs can be directly justified by experience; but since people seldom formulate and appeal to such principles, we will be staying closer to our subject matter if we think in terms of the practices, rather than in terms of the principles, implicitly imbedded therein.

2. And not just that the practice has a good track record up to now; rather, it is a law-like truth that beliefs formed in accordance with that practice, in those kinds of circumstances, are at least likely to be true.

This formulation can be weakened in various ways, without violating the spirit of the conception. If we want to allow that perceptual beliefs about the physical environment are, by and large, justified in this evaluative sense, while admitting that they may all be somewhat off the mark, we can weaken 'truth' to 'closely approximating the truth', and further require the practice to include procedures for progressively correcting and refining these first approximations.

3. If we go the route of the last footnote, we may want to substitute some such term as 'trustworthy'. I shall freely interchange these terms in this paper.

4. Without this the practitioners of CP could hardly appeal to what is written in some sacred book.

5. Note that, even though the normative and evaluative senses of justification are non-equivalent extensionally as well as intensionally, the above point indicates a crucial conceptual connection between the two senses. Roughly speaking, to be normatively justified is to have done as much as could be reasonably expected of one to see to it that one is evaluatively justified.

# 22

# The Rationality of Religious Belief

## John Hick

It is as reasonable for those who experience their lives as being lived in the presence of God, to believe in the reality of God, as for all of us to form beliefs about our environment on the basis of our experience of it.

## I. Identifying the Question

. . . Religious belief does not properly depend upon inference from evidences discovered in the structure of the universe or in the course of human experience—for such evidences are always theoretically ambiguous—but upon unconsciously interpreting the impacts of the environment in such a way that it is consciously experienced as having the kind of meaning articulated in religious language. In interpreting in this way the believer is making a basic cognitive choice and thereby running a risk: the risk of being very importantly mistaken. For in proceeding in this way one is living "by faith" and not "by sight." Under the influence of one of the great religious figures and/or traditions one is interpreting and experiencing one's situation in a way which will ultimately prove to be either appropriate or inappropriate. If inappropriate, we are being profoundly deluded. If appropriate, we shall have so interpreted our situation that the picture of it in terms of which we live is in basic conformity with its actual character. In either case we have made a cognitive choice which has some of the characteristics of a wager.

To treat religious belief in this way, as expressing a cognitive choice, has been a relatively modern development. Alasdair MacIntyre points out that Pascal was the first Western theist to see the universe as religiously ambiguous and atheism as accordingly a serious option; and likewise the first to formulate a religious response to this situation.[1] This response was the calculation that (given Pascal's concept of God) the risk run by not believing is considerably greater than that run by believing; and therefore that it is prudent, and in that sense reasonable, to believe.[2] I want to replace the rationality of this kind of calculation of risks with the rationality, on the part of those who experience 'the presence of God', of accepting that experience as basically veridical. Pascal was however, in my view, importantly right in seeing that the justification of theistic belief does not consist in an argument moving directly to the conclusion that God exists but rather in an argument for the rationality of so believing despite the fact that this cannot be proved or shown to be in any objective sense more probable than not. The appropriate form of reasoning seeks to establish the reasonableness of religious persons trusting and proceeding to live on the basis of their own religious experience and, through it, of the wider stream of such experience in which they participate.

The relationship between experience and belief has been much debated in recent work in the philosophy of religion. This discussion has focused upon specifically theistic belief and I shall be discussing it here in these terms. However, as I shall indicate at the end of the [paper], essentially the same considerations apply to the nontheistic forms of religious experience and belief.

I am going to argue, then, that it is rational to believe in the reality of God. More precisely, by taking account of differences between different people, and also between the cognitive situations of the same person at different times, the thesis elaborates itself as follows: it has been rational for some people in the past, it is rational for some people now, and it will presumably in the future be rational for yet other people to believe in the reality of God. For what it is reasonable for a given person at a given time to believe depends in large part upon what we may call, in the cybernetic sense, his or her information or cognitive input. And the input that is most centrally relevant in this case is religious experience. Here I have in mind particularly the fact that people report their being conscious of existing in God's presence and of living in a personal relationship of mutual awareness with God; and being conscious of their life as part of a vast teleological process whose character as a whole gives meaning to what is presently taking place.

That modifications of human consciousness described in these terms have occurred and do occur can, I think, safely be affirmed as noncontroversial. But from the point of view of epistemology the modifications of consciousness constituting our apparently perceptual experience are of importantly different kinds. In addition to true perceptions there are misperceptions (as, for example, when I mistake a leaf on a bough for a bird sitting on the bough), illusions (for example, the illusion that the straight stick in water is bent), and hallucinations (if, for example, I "see" a person before me when there is no person physically present). If I am misled by any of these forms of perceptual error, I am then deluded. In each case the delusion consists in a mistaken implicit belief about the cause of the experience: believing that it was caused by a bird on the bough, by an actually bent stick, by a physical body near me. Applying this concept of delusion to the realm of religious experience, we have to ask whether those who assume that their 'experience of living in God's presence' is caused (in however complexly mediated a way) by their being in God's presence are believing truly or are, on the contrary, under a delusion. We can express the two opposed possibilities slightly loosely by saying that, according to one, the 'experience of being in God's presence' is a genuine, whilst, according to the other, it is a delusory experience.

We shall not, however, be asking directly whether A's 'experience of existing in the presence of God' *is* genuine (for that would require us to know first, independently of this and all other such experiences, and as a matter of established public knowledge, whether God does indeed exist and was present to A), but rather whether it is rational for A to trust his or her experience as veridical and to behave on the basis of it; and also, as an important secondary question, whether it is rational for others to believe in the reality of God on the basis of A's report. It is thus evident that as we proceed to speak in this [paper] of the rationality of belief in God, the reference is to the rationality of the believing, not of what is believed. A proposition believed can be true or false: it is the believing of it that is rational or irrational. (The content of the belief is, however, relevant to the rationality or otherwise of someone's believing it: see pp. 310–11 below.)

## II. Theistic Belief as a Foundational Natural Belief

Our ordinary daily activity presupposes a general trust in the veridical character of perceptual experience. For whilst we are aware that we are sometimes subject to illusions, hallucinations, and misperceptions of various kinds, this awareness presupposes a general trust in the main bulk and normal run of our apparently cognitive experience. It is only on the basis of this trust that we can have reason to distrust particular moments of it which fail to cohere with the rest. We are here up against something that is for us foundational. We have to rely on our experience in general; for in order to go on living we must continually act, and we can have no reason to do so in one way rather than another except on the assumption that we inhabit the world that is apparently disclosed to us by our senses.

And yet, as has often been pointed out,[3] Western philosophy from Descartes to Hume has shown by default that we cannot prove the existence of an external world. None of the philosophical arguments that have been advanced has proved generally convincing; and all the empirical evidences that might be taken as confirming our ordinary belief in the reality of the perceived world—such as the fact that the belief works successfully both in daily life and in the sciences—are circular, presupposing the reality of that world. We thus come to rest in something like the "natural belief" that Hume—according to Norman Kemp Smith's interpretation,[4] in contrast to the older reading of Hume as a systematic skeptic—adumbrated. Kai Nielsen, referring to these basic givens, speaks of "framework beliefs."[5] That is to say, we are so constituted that we cannot help believing and living in terms of the objective reality of the perceived world. We may be able to suspend our conviction during brief moments of philosophical enthusiasm; but natural belief in "the existence of body"[6] will soon reassert itself. As that eminently sensible philosopher Thomas Reid wrote, "a man may as soon, by reasoning, pull the moon out of her orbit, as destroy the belief in the objects of sense."[7] This seems to be a given circumstance that we can only accept.

Now although Hume himself resisted such a move it would clearly be possible to offer a parallel account of religious belief. Penelhum calls this the Parity Argument.[8] It grants that it is no more possible to prove the existence of God than the existence of a material world but claims that theistic belief arises, like perceptual belief, from a natural response of the human mind to its experiences. All that we can say of a form of natural belief, whether perceptual, moral, or religious, is that it occurs and seems to be firmly embedded in our human nature.

> We cannot explain how we are conscious of sensory phenomena as constituting an objective physical environment; we just find ourselves interpreting the data of our experience in this way. We are aware that we live in a real world, though we cannot prove by any logical formula that it *is* a real world. Likewise we cannot explain how we know ourselves to be responsible beings subject to moral obligations; we just find ourselves interpreting our social experience in this way. In each case we discover and live in terms of a particular aspect of our environment through an appropriate act of interpretation; and having come to live in terms of it we neither require nor can conceive of any further validation of its reality. The same is true of the apprehension of God. The theistic believer cannot explain *how* she knows the divine presence to be mediated through her human experience. She just finds herself interpreting her experience in this way. She lives in the presence of God, though she is unable to prove by any dialectical process that God exists.[9]

This seems to me to be correct. But nevertheless it is by no means the end of the story. A full account of our cognitive situation must be considerably more complex. For within the basic epistemological similarity between perceptual and religious experience-and-belief there are important dissimilarities, which we must now note and ponder.

## III. Trusting Our Experience

We have seen that we normally live on the basis of trust in the veridical character of our experience. We thus operate in ordinary life upon what Richard Swinburne calls the principle of credulity. That is, "what one seems to perceive is probably so. How things seem to be is good grounds for a belief about how things are."[10] This does not, however, apply indiscriminately to any and every "seeming." That things seem to be thus and thus is not an indefeasible reason for believing that they are indeed so. It is a good reason only if there are no countervailing considerations, or only to the degree that remains after such considerations have been fully and fairly taken into account. The general principle on which we operate is that it is rational to regard our apparently perceptual experiences as veridical except when we have reason to doubt their veridicality. Such reasons may be of one or other of two kinds. First, we may be aware of positive circumstances which could well cause us to be deluded in this case; and second, without our knowing of any specific deluding causes, nevertheless the experience may be so fleeting and discontinuous with the rest of our experience, and/or its implications so dissonant with our existing body of belief, that it is reasonable for us to regard it as delusory, or at least to withhold positive acceptance of it as a genuine 'experience of *x*.'

As an example of the first kind of circumstance, if after I have consumed a considerable amount of alcohol the floor seems to me to be heaving up and down and the walls to be wobbling back and forth, my knowledge of the effects of alcohol on the nervous system would properly make me doubt (whether at the time or later) the physical reality of the heaving and wobbling. As an example of the second kind, if when apparently awake, alert, and in good health I have the experience for a split second of "seeing" a flying saucer, which the very next moment is not to be seen, I probably ought to dismiss the experience as due to some kind of malfunctioning of my perceptual machinery.

Returning now to the safer territory of normal experience, we can adopt the general principle that in the absence of adequate grounds for doubt it is rational to trust our putative experience of an external world that is apparently impinging upon us. This reflects our basic operative conception of what it is to be in cognitive touch with our environment. And to believe, without any positive reason, that that which persistently appears within our experience has no objective existence, or to fail to adjust our beliefs about our environment in accordance with our seeming experience of it, would border upon insanity. Let us then look at the operation of this principle in the case with which we are concerned here, namely the claim to have experienced the presence of God.

I want to focus attention initially on the great souls or mahatmas whose experience lies at the origin of the theistic traditions. Among these I shall refer particularly to Jesus, as the one through whom my own consciousness of God has been largely formed. The New Testament records show, I believe, that Jesus was vividly aware of "living in the unseen presence of God" as "abba," father. God, as personal loving will, was as real to him as his neighbors or as the hills and rivers and lake of Galilee. The heavenly father was not for him a mere concept or a hypothetical entity, but an experienced living reality; and the supposition that there is no heavenly father would doubtless have seemed as absurd to him, as incapable of being taken seriously, as the supposition that a human being with whom he was talking did not exist. And so let us ask: Is it rational for *such* persons, experiencing on this level of intensity, to believe and indeed to claim to know, on the basis of their own experience, that God is real?

The question at the moment is not what *we* should make of Jesus' sense of the present reality of God, but what Jesus himself, as a rational human being, could properly believe on the basis of his own powerful religious experience. And I suggest that we can only say that for such a person, 'experiencing the presence of God' in this way, it was entirely rational to believe that God is real; and indeed that it would have been irrational on his part not to. For unless we trust our own experience we can have no reason to believe anything about the nature, or indeed the existence, of the universe in which we find ourselves. We are so made that we live, and can only live, on the basis of our experience and on the assumption that it is generally cognitive (though perhaps in complexly mediated ways) of reality transcending our own consciousness. Indeed, what we designate as sanity consists in acting on the basis of our putatively cognitive experience as a whole. We cannot go beyond that; for there is no "beyond" to go to, since any further datum of which we may become aware will then form part of our total experience. And if some aspect of it is sufficiently intrusive or persistent, and generally coherent with the rest, to reject it would in effect be to doubt our own sanity and would amount to a kind of cognitive suicide. One who has a powerful and continuous sense of existing in the presence of

God *ought,* therefore, to be convinced that God exists. Accordingly, the religious person, experiencing life in terms of the divine presence, is rationally entitled to believe what he or she experiences to be the case—namely that God is real, or exists.[11]

But having said this one must immediately add certain essential qualifications. The first is that however psychologically coercive an 'experience of existing in God's presence' might be, it would be entirely put out of court by our arrival, along some other route, at the knowledge or the well-grounded belief that there is no God. This would be the case if we could see that the concept of deity is self-contradictory and thus incapable of being instantiated. Some have argued that this is the case; but the concept has, to my mind, been sufficiently defended in the course of the modern debate for it to be reasonable to proceed on the assumption that it is logically viable;[12] and I shall accordingly do so. It has also been argued that there are strong negative evidences which effectively rule out the possibility of divine existence; but I have argued . . . that these are not decisive and that, on the contrary, the universe is religiously ambiguous.[13]

Nevertheless we still cannot be happy to say that *all* religious and quasi-religious experiences without exception provide a good grounding for beliefs. There are errors and delusions in other spheres, and we must expect there to be such in religion also. Indeed, almost everyone will agree that this is in fact the case. The skeptic dismisses the entire realm of religious experience as delusory; but even believers regard some forms, other than their own, as delusory. Most of us, for example, are confident that Jim Jones, who induced some nine hundred of his followers to commit suicide with him at Jonestown, Guyana, in 1978, was religiously deluded. Or suppose that someone experiences life in terms of influences from extragalactic intelligences who control their minds by invisible thought rays; or experiences life in some other way that most of us regard as perverse or crazy? What are we to say about such aberrations? And indeed, what are we to say about the rationality of beliefs held on the basis of modes of experience in very different cultures from our own, and particularly in earlier epochs in which different ways of understanding and perceiving the world gave rise to different beliefs—such as belief in good and evil spirits, in witchcraft, astrology, and alchemy?

We meet a problem of this kind when pointing, as I have done, to paradigm cases of religious experience occurring within prescientific cultures. Jesus himself, for example, not only experienced his life as being lived in the presence of God but also experienced certain diseases (such as, possibly, epilepsy) as cases of demon possession (Mark 1:23–26). He may in addition have experienced temptation as the work of Satan, and the success of his disciples in their healing and preaching mission as the defeat of Satan—though it is also possible that the biblical accounts of Jesus' temptation in the wilderness (Mark 1:12) and of his seeing "Satan fall like lightning from heaven" (Luke 10:18) are intended as midrash and metaphor rather than as literal reports. But we should in any case distinguish between the New Testament notion of Satan as the supremely evil spirit, opposing God's purposes, and demons as relatively low-level spirits which may invade human beings, causing physical illness or mental insanity. The first idea, although certainly out of tune with modern Western culture, is not ruled out by any positive scientific knowledge.

The possibility of disembodied minds continues to be a matter of perennial debate; and if there are such minds it is possible that there are evil (as also good) nonhuman spirits and among them a supremely evil one. Disease-causing demons, on the other hand, do conflict with modern medical accounts of the etiology of disease. It is therefore belief in demons, rather than in the devil, that raises the problem we are considering. Such a belief, held by Jesus in first-century Palestine, is for us part of the general question of the rationality of the beliefs of prescientific cultures; but it also creates a special problem for the argument that Jesus' belief in the reality of God was well-founded because based on his own experience: For must we not then say the same of his belief in demon possession?

Let us separate out the two questions: (a) whether it may have been rational for the participants of prescientific cultures to have held beliefs which we today have reason to think false; and (b), if we answer that question affirmatively, whether it may be rational for us to hold those same beliefs on the ground that it was rational for the participants of another culture to hold them. As to the first question, the whole course of this discussion points to the conclusion that it *is* rational for people to believe what their experience leads them to believe. Therefore it was rational for people in the ancient world to believe that the earth is flat; it may well have been rational for some peoples in the ancient world to believe that disease and death are the result of hostile witchcraft; and it may well have been rational for Palestinian Jews of the first century CE, including Jesus, to have accepted a demonic diagnosis for certain diseases. It was, in general, as rational for them to have believed what they believed about these matters as for ourselves today to believe what we believe about them.

But the more important and difficult question is whether it is rational for *us* to adopt beliefs on the grounds that someone else, in another culture, reasonably held them. Whether we judge it proper to adopt another person's beliefs, held on the basis of [his or her] own experience—be that person a great religious leader or an ordinary participant in another culture—will properly depend upon further questions concerning the content of those beliefs. Generally it can only be rational for us to hold a belief on the basis of someone else's experience if the belief is compatible with our other beliefs, supported as they are by the general body of our own experience. Everything that we know or think that we know, and every critical resource that we have, is potentially relevant in screening candidates for belief as coherent or incoherent and plausible or implausible. And it may very well be that the acceptance of witchcraft, astrology, or alchemy, or the existence of extragalactic intelligences controlling our minds by thought rays, or the demonic causation of disease, fails to cohere with what we believe on the basis of our experience as a whole and, in particular, with our contemporary scientific beliefs. In that case, although we may recognize that people of other cultures have reasonably held these beliefs, nevertheless we shall not feel obliged to hold them ourselves; indeed, we may on the contrary feel obliged to reject them.

How does all this apply to the religious case? It means that a rational person will only be open to accepting others' religious experience reports as veridical, and indeed will only trust his or her own religious experience, if the beliefs to which they point are such as one judges *may* be true.[14] Thus the existence of God must be held to be possible—and not merely a bare logical possibility, but an *important* possibility—if the 'experience of living in God's presence' is to be taken seriously. This is where natural theology comes into its own. Its office is not to prove the existence of God, or even to show it to be probable, but to establish both the possibility of divine existence and the importance (that is, the explanatory power) of this possibility. I believe that reason *can* ascertain both that there *may* be a God and that this is a genuinely important possibility. In that case theistic religious experience has to be taken seriously. But whether reports of experiences of astrological influences and so on are to be taken seriously depends upon a corresponding rational scrutiny of the content of the knowledge-claims to which they give rise.

But is there not an inconsistency in accepting as veridical Jesus' 'experience of God's presence' whilst rejecting as delusory his 'experience of disease-causing demons'—or indeed his 'experience of the sun moving round the earth'? There seems to me to be no difficulty in principle in the thought that a person may be correctly experiencing some aspects of reality while falsely experiencing others. Indeed, this is so common a situation that we have to accept it as endemic to our human condition. And if we regard the great religious figures as human, and therefore as historically and culturally conditioned, we may expect them to be part of this cognitively checkered history. Why then should we not accept Jesus' 'experience of the presence of God' as genuine, because it evokes a confirming echo within our own experience, and yet regard his way of experiencing disease, and the relation between the earth and the sun, as erroneous because they clash with our modern medical and astronomical knowledge?

## IV. Complications

It will be evident that this is not an argument for, still less a proof of, the existence of God. It must not be mistaken for an argument from religious experience to God as its cause. . . . If we simply take a description of some moment of religious experience and ask, "Who or what but God could have caused such an experience?" there may be many answers. Conceivably it was caused by the experiencer's superego, or by a need for cosmic reassurance in face of danger or of the death of a loved one, or by the pressure of one's group, or even by a drug. But I have been suggesting that we should turn from experiences, considered as events whose cause we can seek, to consider the situation of the experiencer, and ask what such a person should rationally think and believe on the basis of his or her own experience. Thus, as I indicated at the beginning, what we are concerned with here is not directly an argument for divine existence but rather for the rationality of believing in the existence of God on the basis of theistic religious experience.[15] In William Alston's terminology, we are concerned with the justification of a doxastic practice, namely, the practice of forming beliefs on the basis of religious experience; or, as he also puts it, of using a particular conceptual scheme, namely, a theological one, to specify what we are encountering in religious experience.[16] Having posed the question in this way, we are, I have suggested, led to conclude that in the absence of any positive reason to distrust one's experience—and the mere fact that in this religiously ambiguous universe a different, naturalistic epistemic practice is also possible does not constitute such a reason—it is rational, sane, reasonable for those whose religious experience strongly leads them to do so to believe wholeheartedly in the reality of God.

This, then, I suggest, is the way in which belief in the existence of God is to be
justified. It is justified in basically the same way as our beliefs about "what there is
and how things are" in our total environment: namely, by the impact of that environment upon us, our consciousness of which is our experience of it. In order for it
to be rational for us to believe in the reality of entities which are ostensibly given in
our experience, whether directly (as when we experience what is before us as a chair)
or indirectly (as when we experience our lives as being lived in the unseen presence
of God), two conditions have to be fulfilled. One is that we have responsibly judged
(or reasonably assumed) it to be possible for such an entity to exist. The other is that
it seems to be given in our experience in a powerful, persistent, and intrusive way
which demands belief in its reality. When someone believes in the existence of God
on the basis of compelling religious experience, his or her belief is accordingly a case
of rational or reasonable or well-founded belief.

On this basis we must acknowledge that such persons as Moses, Jesus, St. Paul,
St. Francis, Martin Luther, Catherine of Genoa, Julian of Norwich, Muhammad,
al-Hallaj, Ramanuja, Guru Nanak, and Ramakrishna have been entitled as rational
persons to believe that God exists. But what about more ordinary believers who do
not enjoy the same overwhelmingly powerful forms of religious experience? Does
this line of thought point to any justification for belief in the reality of God on their
part?

Persons, if such there be, who never experience religiously in any degree whatever cannot have the same justification for belief as those who do. They might possibly, however, be so impressed by the moral and spiritual fruits of faith in the lives
of the saints as to be drawn to share, at least tentatively, the latter's beliefs—in
which case it would, I think, be proper to count their being impressed in this way
as itself a secondary kind of religious experience. Or again, very commonly, people
may hold religious beliefs, in spite of participating only minimally in any form of
religious experience, because they have accepted without question what they were
brought up to believe. If what they have thus accepted at second-hand is in fact true
(or is a viable symbolic representation of the truth), they are thus far in a fortunate
position. But still their hold upon this truth is very different from that of the first-
hand believer, because it is always vulnerable to the kind of skeptical challenge from
which any inhabitant of the modern world is increasingly unlikely to be isolated.

However, the more common case is probably that of the ordinary believer who
does have at least some remote echo or analogue within his or her own experience
of the much more momentous experience of the great religious figures. This echo
may not be at all dramatic or memorable. It may merely be a moment of greatly
intensified meaning in the midst of a church, synagogue, or mosque service, or in
private prayer, or when reading the scriptures or telling a rosary. Or, on a higher
level of significance, it may be the sense of a transcendent reality and goodness being
disclosed to us at one of the deep points of human experience, love or birth or death;
or through the insistent pressure of an ideal, leading to practical commitment

against some social evil or for the realization of some communal good; or in an awareness, when gazing up into the starry night, of the mysterious immensity of space around us; or again, in the presence of mountain or lake, forest or ocean, of

> A presence that disturbs me with the joy
> Of elevated thoughts; a sense sublime,
> Of something far more deeply interfused,
> Whose dwelling is the light of setting suns,
> And the round ocean and the living air,
> And the blue sky, and in the mind of man;
> A motion and a spirit, that impels
> All thinking things, all objects of all thought,
> And rolls through all things
>
> (Wordsworth, "Lines composed a few miles
>               above Tintern Abbey")

Such "peak experiences" can include very small and barely perceptible mole-hills within the humdrum spiritual life of most of us as well as the mountaintop experiences that startle and tend to be recorded. But if, within this continuum, one experiences one's own life religiously, even only occasionally and to some slight extent, this makes it both possible and reasonable to be so impressed by the reports of the mahatmas that one's own experience is supported by their much more massive awareness of the transcendent. One's belief is not *as* deeply or solidly grounded as theirs. But I would suggest that it is well enough grounded for it to be reasonable for us to proceed in faith in the footsteps of a great religious leader, anticipating the full confirmation which our faith will ultimately receive if it does indeed correspond with reality.

## V. The Problem of Criteria

At this point, however, another complication occurs. William Rowe has argued that a valid principle of credulity must not only require that A has an experience which seems to be of *x,* and that A has no positive reason to think that this experience is delusory, but also that A's belief that there is no such reason is itself an *informed* belief. In other words, A must know what sorts of circumstances would render the putative 'experience of *x*' suspect and must also know that these circumstances do not in fact obtain. If one lacks this further knowledge, one's belief that *x* exists will not, according to him, be properly rational. For rational belief requires a critical attitude in which we do not simply believe whatever *seems* to be so, but test and probe and insist upon seeking and taking account of all relevant consider-ations.[17]

In general, Rowe's additional criterion would seem to be an appropriate one. He now proceeds to apply it to theistic belief, claiming that in this case we do not know what all the possible causes of delusion are. We do not know, for example, what purely natural circumstances might have caused Jesus to have his intense, continuous, and coherent 'experience of the presence of God'. And since Jesus cannot have known this either, it was not rational for him to believe in God on the basis of his own experience. Nor, on the same principle, can it ever be rational for anyone else to hold beliefs on the basis of [his or her] own or anyone else's religious experience.

In order to isolate the basic issue raised by this challenge, we must distinguish between what we may call the general and the specific religious convictions concerning religious experience. The general religious conviction is that such experience is not as such and as a whole delusory, not in toto a high-level hallucination of religious individuals and communities. But this does not entail that religious awareness always constitutes, simply and without qualification, cognition of the divine. On the contrary, it is compatible with the view that this range of experience, whilst constituting our human consciousness of a transcendent divine reality, takes a great variety of concrete forms developed within the different historical traditions. It is in that case neither a pure undistorted consciousness of the divine, nor merely a human projection, but rather the range of differing ways in which the infinite divine reality has in fact been apprehended by finite and imperfect human beings.

Under the umbrella of this basic religious conviction there are more specific convictions formed within the particular historic traditions and tested by criteria established within them. Thus a sense of the presence of Christ would, on the face of it, be good currency within Christianity, as a sense of the presence of Krishna would be within the Vaishnavite tradition of India, but not vice versa. Again, among the subdivisions of Christianity, a vision of the Blessed Virgin Mary could count as a notable divine revelation within the Roman Catholic Church but might well be puzzling and even disturbing if it occurred within, say, the Southern Baptist, the Presbyterian, or the Quaker bodies. Again, each of the great traditions fully recognizes the possibility of error. In medieval Christendom it was accepted that the devil can sometimes cause people to have delusory religious experiences, so that it was important to be able to distinguish between true and false visions, auditions, senses of the divine presence, and so on.[18] St. Teresa of Avila, for example, was much concerned about the authenticity of her own mystical experiences. One of the main criteria that she and the church used was conformity with the scriptures. She says that,

> as far as I can see and learn by experience, the soul must be convinced that a thing comes from God only if it is in conformity with Holy Scripture; if it were to diverge from that in the very least, I think I should be incomparably more firmly convinced that it came from the devil than I previously was that it came from God, however sure I might have felt of this.[19]

And at an earlier stage, before the scriptural canon was formed, St. Paul had written that "no one can be speaking under the influence of the Holy Spirit and say 'Curse Jesus', and on the other hand, no one can say 'Jesus is Lord' unless he is under the influence of the Holy Spirit" (I Cor. 12:3).

Another, less tradition-specific, test has been provided by the spiritual and moral consequences in the experiencer's life. Thus, referring to the effects upon her of her visions of Jesus, St. Teresa says, all who knew me were well aware how my soul had changed: my confessor himself testified to this, for the difference was very great in every respect, and no fancy, but such as all could clearly see. As I had previously been so wicked, I concluded, I could not believe that, if the devil were doing this to delude me and drag me down to hell, he would make use of means which so completely defeated their own ends by taking away my vices and making me virtuous and strong; for it was quite clear to me that these experiences had immediately made me a different person.[20]

Another example in Christian mystical literature of the use of this criterion comes in St. John of the Cross's *Ascent of Mount Carmel* (Book II, Ch. 24), where he describes the effect of divinely caused visions as "quiet, illumination, joy like that of glory, sweetness, purity and love, humility and inclination or elevation of the spirit in God."[21] This criterion connects with one taught by Jesus himself concerning false prophets who were to come in the future. He is reported as saying, "You will be able to tell them by their fruits. Can people pick grapes from thorns, or figs from thistles?" (Matt. 7:16). Again, St. Paul listed as authenticating fruits of the Spirit, "love, joy, peace, patience, kindness, goodness, trustfulness, gentleness and self-control" (Gal. 5:22). This kind of moral criterion, applied to the outward effects in peoples' lives of their inner religious experiences and beliefs, is probably used more or less universally, at least within the large sphere of the great world faiths.

But, it may well be said, these are only human criteria for what people within this or that tradition have decided to *count* as an experience of the divine. We do not know that they indicate that a religious experience actually *is* an experience of the divine. For the general possibility remains that apparently cognitive religious experience, as such and in toto, is delusory. Indeed, it will be said, this is more than a mere logical possibility. For various naturalistic theories have been offered to explain why and how people seem to 'experience God' even though no God exists to be experienced. There are well-known psychological theories depicting theistic ideas and experiences as projections of the human mind, powered by our desire for assurance and comfort in a threatening world. Again, there are well-known sociological theories which claim that a religious sense has been instilled into us in the process of socialization as a means whereby the individual is led to serve the interests either of the group as a whole or of the governing class. And there are various other kinds and combinations of naturalistic analyses of religion.

These are all, necessarily, speculative analyses and have all been subjected to powerful criticisms. . . . They have proved convincing to some and unconvincing to others—though even when finally unconvincing they can nevertheless be seen as correctly indicating the presence of elements of human projection and cultural conditioning within the various forms of religious experience. But when we take the naturalistic theories as total explanations, excluding any divine impact triggering a culturally conditioned religious apperception, it is, I think, clear that both their acceptance and their rejection arise out of a prior commitment. . . . [F]rom our present standpoint, the universe is religiously ambiguous. Alternative total views confront one another, one interpreting religious data naturalistically and the other religiously. Each may in principle be complete, leaving no data unaccounted for; and the acceptance of either arises from a basic cognitive choice or act of faith. Once the choice has been made, and whilst it is operative, the alternative global view is reduced to a bare logical possibility. This is the status both of the various naturalistic theories of religion from the point of view of one who trusts one's own religious experience, and likewise of theistic theories from the point of view of one who is committed to a naturalistic interpretation.

## VI. The Right to Believe

The question then is whether the possibility, in a religiously ambiguous universe, that religious experience as a whole is illusory renders it irrational for those who participate in a form of such experience to believe in the reality of the divine. I think not; and my reason for so thinking is analogous to that classically expressed by William James in his famous essay, "The Will to Believe."[22] As James later recognized, this ought to have been called "The Right to Believe."[23] For its thesis, when we omit various subsidiary excursions, concerns our right to choose how to proceed within an ambiguous situation in which the choice is unavoidable and yet of momentous importance to ourselves. The universe as it confronts us is ambivalent, in that we can construe it either religiously or naturalistically; but when one option has been adopted it constitutes one's life a religious, or a naturalistic, response to reality. Such a response is ultimately true or false according as it conforms or fails to conform to the actual nature of things. However, there can at this stage be no confirmation of the final appropriateness of either response. Further, if the religious response is correct, it may be that it is only by living it out that one can progressively relate oneself to and thus be changed by the divine reality. On the other hand, if the naturalistic interpretation is correct, the religious option can only lead us further into error and delusion. Thus we run an unavoidable risk.

What is at stake is our relationship to reality. The possible gain is that of living in terms of reality and the possible loss is that of living in delusion. James argues that in such a situation it is entirely rational to follow the prompting of what he called our "passional" or "willing" nature. The weakness of his position, as he himself presents it, is that it would authorize us to believe anything that we may have a strong enough propensity to believe, providing the evidence concerning it is inconclusive. If we would *like* some unprovable proposition to be true, then, given that the option is for us a live, momentous, and forced one, James's argument would justify us in believing it. But this virtually amounts to a license for wishful thinking.[24] I suggest, however, that we can retain James's central insight, whilst avoiding this unacceptable consequence, if we substitute compelling religious experience for the mere desire to believe an unproved and undisproved proposition. James's basic argument then becomes an argument for our right to trust our own religious experience and to be prompted by it to trust that of the great religious figures. Thus, if in the existing situation of theoretic ambiguity a person experiences life religiously, or participates in a community whose life is based upon this mode of experience, he or she is rationally entitled to trust that experience and to proceed to believe and to live on the basis of it.

There is, then, on the one hand an "experience of existing in the presence of

God," which may be approved as authentic by the criteria of the individual's tradition. Such experience constitutes a good prima facie ground for religious belief. But on the other hand, there is the possibility that this entire realm of experience may be in toto illusory. I suggest that in these circumstances it is wholly reasonable for the religious person to trust his or her own experience and the larger stream of religious experience of which it is a part. Such a person will, if a philosopher, be conscious of the ever-present theoretical possibility that it is delusory; but will, I suggest, rightly feel that it would be irrational to base life upon this theoretic possibility. Why should one forego entry into a larger universe of meaning, which claims and seems to represent the actual structure of reality, simply because there is always the general possibility of delusion?

I have been presenting an argument for the rationality of belief in God on the part of one who experiences his or her life as being lived in the unseen divine presence. But it is evident that essentially the same argument could be formulated for nontheistic experience and belief. Thus, those who report the advaitic experience of oneness with Brahman, or who experience in the ego-less state of Nirvana the reality of the eternal Buddha-nature, or who are conscious of the "emptiness" of all things as their fullness of "wondrous being," are entitled to base their belief-systems on those forms of experience. . . .

# Notes

1. See Alasdair MacIntyre and Paul Ricoeur, *The Religious Significance of Atheism* (New York: Columbia University Press, 1969), pp. 12–13.

2. See Blaise Pascal, *Pensées,* ed. Leon Brunschvicg, trans. W. F. Trutter (London and New York: J. M. Dent and E. P. Dutton, 1932), No. 233. See also the articles on Pascal's Wager in Part V of this Volume, pp. 255–89.

3. E.g., William Temple, *Nature, Man and God* (London: MacMillan, 1934), Ch. 3; and, more recently, William Alston, "Christian Experience and Christian Belief," and Alvin Plantinga, "Reason and Belief in God," both in *Faith and Rationality,* ed. Alvin Plantinga and Nicholas Wolterstorff (Notre Dame and London: Notre Dame University Press, 1983); and Terence Penelhum, *God and Skepticism* (Dordrecht, Neth.: D. Reidel, 1983).

4. See Norman Kemp Smith, *The Philosophy of David Hume* (London: Macmillan, 1941).

5. Kai Nielsen, "Religion and Groundless Believing," in *Religious Experience and Religious Belief,* ed. Joseph Runzo and Craig K. Ihara (New York and London: University Press of America, 1986), p. 23f.

6. David Hume, *A Treatise of Human Nature,* trans. L. A. Selby-Bigge (London: Oxford University Press, 1968), p. 187.

7. Thomas Reid, *Essays on the Intellectual Powers of Man* [1785], John Bell Facsimile ed. (Edinburgh: Scholar Press), p. 274.

8. See Penelhum, *God and Skepticism,* Chs. 6 and 7.

9. John Hick, *Faith and Knowledge,* 2nd ed. (London: Macmillan, 1987), p. 132. (The argument is discussed critically by J. Wesley Robbins in "John Hick on Religious Experience and Perception," *International Journal for Philosophy of Religion* 5 [1974]: 272–86.) This notion of the fundamental character of beliefs based upon our experience, including religious experience, is related to, although not identical with, Alvin's Plantinga's much discussed con-

cept of "proper basicality" (Plantinga, "Reason and Belief in God"; and "On Taking Belief in God as Basic," in Runzo and Ihara, *Religious Experience and Belief;* see also Plantinga's paper "Is Belief in God Properly Basic?" in Part III of this volume, pp. 133–41). This is the view that belief in God is a belief that can be held, not on the basis of evidence, but as basic in its own right, a belief in holding which the believer is not violating any valid epistemological rules. At times Plantinga speaks of properly basic beliefs as ones which the believer has a "natural tendency" to believe (see Plantinga, "Reason and Belief in God," p. 78). This would surely be much too broad and permissive. However, Plantinga also says that properly basic beliefs, although not derived from evidence, do have grounds: for example, the experience of "seeing a tree" is generally a good justifying ground for the basic belief that I am seeing a tree. If religious experience is recognized as the parallel justifying ground of religious beliefs, then Plantinga's argument and the argument of this [paper] virtually coincide.

10. Richard Swinburne, *The Existence of God* (Oxford, Engl.: Clarendon Press; New York: Oxford University Press, 1979), p. 254, and *The Evolution of the Soul* (Oxford, Engl.: Clarendon Press, 1986), pp. 11–13. (See Richard Swinburne's paper in Part IV of this volume, pp. 201–11.)

11. Others who have argued along analogous lines include C. D. Broad, "Arguments for the Existence of God—I," *The Journal of Theological Studies* 40 (January 1939), and "Arguments for the Existence of God—II," *The Journal of Theological Studies,* 40 (April 1939); Alvin Plantinga, *God and Other Minds* (Ithaca, NY: Cornell University Press, 1967); Swinburne, *The Existence of God,* Ch. 13; Alston, "Christian Experience and Christian Belief"; J. A. Taber, "The Philosophical Evaluation of Religious Experience," *International Journal for Philosophy of Religion* 19, 1–2 (1986). I have myself previously argued in this way in *Faith and Knowledge,* and in *Arguments for the Existence of God* (London: Macmillan, 1970).

12. See, e.g., on the negative side, Anthony Kenny, *The God of the Philosophers* (Oxford, Engl.: Clarendon Press, 1979); and, on the positive side, Richard Swinburne, *The Coherence of Theism* (Oxford, Engl.: Clarendon Press, 1977); Keith Ward, *The Concept of God* (Oxford, Engl.: Basil Blackwell, 1974); and Stephen T. Davis, *Logic and the Nature of God* (London: Macmillan, 1983).

13. See John Hick, *An Interpretation of Religion* (London: Macmillan; New Haven, CT: Yale University Press, 1989), Ch. 7.

14. Sometimes, however, there appear to have occurred powerfully invasive experiences, setting up new beliefs that were not compatible with much of the individual's previous belief-system and indeed that required its wholesale reconstruction. These are dramatic conversion experiences, such as that of Muhammad when he first began to receive the Qur'anic revelation, or that of St. Paul on the road to Damascus. However, in accordance with the principle of a cognitive freedom which is proportioned to the value of the aspect of reality being cognized and in accordance also with plausible psychological analyses of conversion, it seems likely that even these apparently sudden and unexpected experiences were "threshold" phenomena in which a new awareness that had gradually been growing in the unconscious suddenly spills over into consciousness. (See, e.g., William James, *The Varieties of Religious Experience* [London: Collins, 1960], p. 236.)

15. It should be noted that much of the contemporary philosophical discussion of religious experience deals with the different question whether it provides the basis for a valid inference to divine existence; e.g., C. B. Martin, *Religious Belief* (Ithaca, NY: Cornell University Press, 1959); Wallace Matson, *The Existence of God* (Ithaca, NY: Cornell University Press, 1965), Pt. 1; T. R. Miles, *Religious Experience* (London and New York: Macmillan, 1972); Michael Goulder and John Hick, *Why Believe in God?* (London: SCM Press, 1983); R. W. Clark, "The Evidential Value of Religious Experience," *International Journal for Philosophy of Religion* 16 (1984): 189–202; J. William Forgie, "Mystical Experience and the Argument from Agreement," *International Journal for Philosophy of Religion* 17 (1985): 97–113.

16. Alston, "Christian Experience and Christian Belief," pp. 108–9. Alston is discussing beliefs about manifestations of God ("M-beliefs") rather than the more basic belief that there is a God to be manifested; but these M-beliefs entail that God exists, and the same argument is also relevant to that more basic belief. (See William Alston's paper in Part VI of this volume, pp. 295–303.)

17. See William Rowe, "Religious Experience and the Principle of Credulity," *International Journal for Philosophy of Religion* 13 (1982): 90–91. For different responses to Rowe from the one developed here, see Jonathon L. Kvanvig, "Credulism," *International Journal for Philosophy of Religion* 16 (1984): 101–10; and Peter Losin, "Experience of God and the Principle of Credulity: A Reply to Rowe," *Faith and Philosophy* 4 (1987): 59–70.

18. See, e.g., St. John of the Cross, *Ascent of Mount Carmel,* trans. E. Allison Peers (Garden City, NY: Doubleday, 1958), pp. 324–26.

19. St. Teresa of Avila, *Autobiography,* trans. E. Allison Peers (Garden City, NY: Doubleday, 1960), p. 239.

20. St. Teresa of Avila, p. 265.

21. St. John of the Cross, *Ascent,* p. 308.

22. See William James, *The Will to Believe and Other Essays* (New York and London: Longmans, Green, 1905).

23. See William James, *The Letters of William James,* Vol. 2 (London: Longmans, Green, 1920), p. 207.

24. I have developed this criticism more fully in *Faith and Knowledge,* Ch. 2. For a more sympathetic response to James's argument, see *Faith, Skepticism and Evidence,* ed. Stephen T. Davis (Lewisburg, PA: Bucknell University Press, 1978).

# 23

# Three Models of Faith

## *James Kellenberger*

## I

Philosophy of religion traditionally has been concerned with the coherence and rationality of religious belief. This concern is not only deeply rooted in Western religious thought, but, most would agree, it has been and continues to be a justifiable concern. Far from this concern being the property of the detractors of religion, it has been pursued by those sympathetic to religion as avidly as by those hostile to religion. Yet there have been others who have criticized this focus on religion for, among other things, making religious belief into belief in the existence of God or, less narrowly, propositional belief. And their criticism, too, is justifiable. The perspective that focuses on the coherence and rationality of religious belief is in danger of identifying it with a belief structure or making it theoretical in a way that it is not. Such a perspective never quite seems to get to the life of religious faith. Consequently it is unenlightening about the nature of religious belief, and it does not help us at all to appraise whether faith can take different forms.

It is not the purpose of this paper to challenge the legitimacy of a philosophical pursuit of the coherence and rationality of religious belief: that legitimacy we concede. Instead, in what follows we shall look at the grammatical area of religion just referred to, an area undiscovered by such a pursuit: the forms of faith. As we shall find, there are indeed different models of religious faith which are distinct from one another, though each is a type of faith in the full sense. We shall examine three. One is a faith-form evident in the Bible itself, particularly in the Old Testament. Two may appropriately be called existential.

Our primary task will be to bring into relief these three models of faith. As a part of this task, we shall explore how each relates to the requirements of rationality. Not all, as we shall see, bear the same relationship to the demands of rationality. We shall also, in Section III, try to identify what unifies the three faith-forms and makes each a type of faith in God. Then, in the last section, we shall look at what has been called "devout skepticism" in comparison with the models of faith we have discussed.

## II

Two 'truths' have struck thinkers regarding the nature of faith, or rather, the nature of religion's committed faith. One is that faith requires certainty on the part of the believer. The other is that serious faith requires uncertainty. The first 'truth' was recognized by Kierkegaard in *Fear and Trembling*. For Kierkegaard in *Fear and Trembling,* Abraham, the paradigmatic knight of faith, bore witness to his faith in God and his faith that Isaac would not be lost to him precisely because he did not doubt. Abraham believed with fear and trembling, with passion and dread—but he did not doubt. If he had, his faith would have failed and Abraham would not be the exemplar of faith. Thus Kierkegaard, in *Fear and Trembling.*[1]

The second 'truth' also has had its adherents. Belief in God, Miguel de Unamuno says, necessitates passion, anguish of mind, doubt, uncertainty, and even despair. Otherwise belief is not in God, but merely in the idea of God.[2] That is, otherwise, Unamuno is saying, belief is not *in* God, but is an intellectual and indifferent propositional belief *that* God exists. Unamuno was influenced by Kierkegaard. The Kierkegaard of the *Concluding Unscientific Postscript* defines faith as "An objective uncertainty held fast in an appropriation process of the most passionate inwardness."[3] In this work, then, he too sees faith as being in what is *uncertain* and, like Unamuno, he seems to see the commitment of faith itself as deriving from a passionate acceptance of what is uncertain. Clearly, very much in the life of a believer hinges on which view is correct: on the one hand certainty is required for depth of commitment, on the other hand certainty renders commitment impossible.

Some might try to resolve the problem by citing the distinction between *felt certainty* and *certainty of the matter*. This is the valid distinction between the certainty expressed by "*I* am certain that P" and the certainty indicated by "*It* is certain that P" (where P is some proposition). The first is the certainty or conviction a person has or feels; the second is the certainty that attaches to the matter at hand.[4] The two are related but not identical. One can consistently affirm that another is certain while affirming that the matter is uncertain ("He is sure that P, but in fact it's doubtful"); and one can admit that one oneself was certain while affirming that the matter was uncertain ("I was sure that P, but I shouldn't have been, for it was wholly in doubt").

However, this distinction does not help us resolve the problem we have encountered. It does not because we cannot sever these two kinds of certainty one from the other in the way such a resolution would presuppose. While, as we just saw, one can affirm another's certainty and the matter's uncertainty, or affirm one's own past certainty and the matter's uncertainty, still one cannot affirm one's *present* certainty and the matter's uncertainty or the matter's certainty and one's *present* uncertainty. One cannot because in affirming one's certainty one implies that the matter is certain and in affirming the matter's certainty one implies that one is certain. Neither "I am certain that P, but it is doubtful" nor "I am not certain that P, but it is indeed certain" makes much sense; both have contradictory implications. Yet it would be precisely this last sort of utterance that we would have to put into the mouth of the believer. We would have to make Abraham say "I am certain that God is good and Isaac will live, but it is not certain" or, alternatively, "I am not certain that God is good and Isaac will live, but it is indeed certain." Kierkegaard, in the *Concluding Unscientific Postscript,* says that faith is a passionate acceptance of an "objective uncertainty," and his perhaps suggests that he would attribute to Abraham "subjective certainty" and give him the first alternative ("I am certain, but it is uncertain"). But, in fact, for an emotionally and intellectually coherent faith neither alternative will do. And, fortunately, we need resort to neither.

Each of the two 'truths' that together form the problem before us has a basis in the nature of faith, I suggest. Each reflects a recognition of the importance of commitment to faith. The first 'truth', that faith is certain, sees that to allow what is fervently believed may be false, to express doubt, is to admit a failure of faith, and is a failure of commitment. The second 'truth', that faith is uncertain, sees that the less the evidence, and the less the certainty, the greater the "leap" required. The notion of the "leap of faith" is Kierkegaardian. If faith requires risk, as Kierkegaard said it does,[5] that risk need not be the risk-that-one-is-wrong, that one's belief is false. However, while it need not be, it can be; and when it is, the leap of faith is a leap over an evidential gap. Such is the conception of faith in the *Concluding Unscientific Postscript,* as opposed to that of *Fear and Trembling.*

In fact there are two models of faith before us. One 'truth' holds for one model, and the other 'truth' holds for the other. One 'truth' holds for the Biblical model of faith, and the other 'truth' holds for a particular existential model of faith. The Biblical model of faith is exemplified by the faith of Job and Abraham. Job thought of himself as living in the presence of God. He was certain of this and felt that he was surrounded by the signs of God's goodness in his daily life—in the sustenance of his life and in the prospering of his fields and in all that was given to him. Even when Job was made to suffer, and could not understand God's way, he did not doubt His goodness and was certain that the God he believed in had not forsaken him. What we should note here is that if he had doubted, it would have been a failure of his faith. The commitment of Job's faith requires his certainty. In this respect, as in others, Kierkegaard's characterization of Abraham's faith in *Fear and Trembling* holds for Job's faith and for the Biblical model itself.

On the other hand, there is an existential model of faith, one that might be called the Absurd model and which seems to accord with Kierkegaard's thinking in the *Concluding Unscientific Postscript.* Here the believer starts out in doubt and strives to maintain his faith in the face of his own doubts. Unlike Job, he is not aware of God's presence in the world about him. At best the world is silent. At worst the existence of evil speaks against there being a God. But yet the Absurd believer (as such a believer might be called) believes. If Job's affirmation of faith is, "I know my Redeemer liveth!" the existential affirmation is, "It cannot be, all reason is against it; yet I believe!" Job's faith requires certainty, and the existentialist's faith requires uncertainty. Neither, it should be noted, requires one sort of certainty and one sort of uncertainty. Job is certain and sees the matter as certain; the Absurd believer is neither certain nor sees the matter as certain.[6]

So far, then, we have identified two distinct models of faith. Job and Abraham are Biblical believers: they are certain that there is a God and certain of their relationship to God. Absurd believers, on the other hand, embrace with existential passion what they perceive as 'objectively uncertain'. However, Absurd faith is not the only existential model of faith contrasting with Biblical faith. If we reflect briefly on the role of choice in having faith we quickly discover a second existential model of faith.

For the Biblical believer Job, God's presence was certain, for it was manifested all about him. As a consequence, so far as Biblical faith is concerned, faith is not a matter of choosing to believe. One does not choose to believe what is certain and proclaimed on every side: one chooses to believe only what is not established as certain as one sees it. At the same time Job was not forced to believe what he did not want to believe. In what might approximate the language of the Job-like believer, it was given to Job to be aware of God and to believe in Him. As long as Job is the paradigmatic believer, faith is not something that is chosen.[7]

But this is not to say that no faith is chosen. Believers, according to the Absurd model, believe in God but believe against all reason. They believe, in Kierkegaard's phrase, "by virtue of the absurd."[8] Absurd believers believe by overcoming their doubt and uncertainty by an act of will.[9] They choose to believe, and do believe, in the face of their own doubts and in the face of no evidence and even negative evidence against there being a God. They strive to believe and succeed. The very heart of Absurd faith is this striving in the face of uncertainty. But what if the effort to believe were unsuccessful? This is just the case with Paradoxical faith, the second model of existential faith.

With the Paradox model believers do not have faith; yet they try with every fiber to believe, and so affirm the faith they do not have. Their cry of faith is: "I cannot believe. God have mercy upon me!" Unamuno's story, "Saint Manuel Bueno, Martyr," has as its protagonist such a Paradoxical believer. At any rate, the story and Don Manuel are open to this construction. Don Manuel is the priest in a small Spanish village, Valverde de Lucerna. He is well loved by those in the village and known as a saintly man. Yet, while he helps others to believe, he himself cannot believe. He falls silent when he reaches the last verse of the Creed, although this is unnoticed in the village. He trembles when he gives Communion, but this too is unnoticed. Because his life is selfless, his secret—that he cannot believe—goes undetected. Here the believer chooses to believe, and tries to believe, but cannot. His faith is his striving to believe.

For Unamuno, true faith is 'agonic' faith. It suffers in doubt; yet its very strength is born from its struggle with the "gimlet of doubt."[10] In the *Tragic Sense of Life,* in a passage referred to earlier and which we shall now quote in full, Unamuno said, "Those who believe that they believe in God, but without any passion in their heart, without anguish of mind, without uncertainty, without doubt, without an element of despair even in their consolation, believe only in the God-Idea, not in God Himself."[11] The elements of this description are met by Absurd and Paradoxical believers. They have passion, anguish, uncertainty, doubt, and, for Unamuno, even despair. But Biblical believers would fail to be believers in God according to Unamuno's test, for while they have passion and anguish, they have no doubt or uncertainty. Kierkegaard says of Abraham that if he had doubted, he would not have had faith, and of course this is right—as far as the Biblical model goes. (Or at any rate, his faith would have been lessened if he had doubted.) For Job and Abraham their commitment of faith is tied to their certainty and what they deem to be their knowledge.

And now we can see why the relationship between the existential models of faith and the issue of rationality is not the same as the relationship between the Biblical model and that issue. Absurd and Paradoxical faith are held against all reason. They are, then, frankly and assertively irrational—irrational in the sense that they are not grounded in support and shun support. But these models of faith provide an internal justification for their irrationality; for them, the passion of faith's commitment is proportionate to the uncertainty of what is believed. Thus, for these models, we must choose between support for what we would believe and belief, that is, faith. We can have one but not both. And, of course, the Kierkegaard of the *Concluding Unscientific Postscript* and Unamuno do not hesitate to accept faith's passionate commitment. If to do so they must hold an irrational faith, then so be it. At least their irrationality is not that of investigative deficiency but rather a consciously chosen condition internally necessary to their faith.

Biblical faith is another matter. Biblical believers are certain and regard what they believe as certain. They with perfect consistency are prepared to say, "I know my Redeemer liveth." But such certainty and such knowledge, or asserted knowledge, require support or grounding, as the existential models do not. The Biblical model must give some place to a grounding for the certainty it makes essential to faith. Thus, it is no accident that Job and Abraham exemplify this model of faith. The paradigms of this form of faith are Biblical figures who lived in the midst of personal religious experience, who regarded themselves as living in an individual relationship with God, communing daily with the living God of the Psalms, who, in their own eyes, could not but have been aware of the God who supported their lives. Those who conform to, or give a place to, the Biblical model of faith traditionally, and perhaps of necessity, give a place to religious experience. For religious experience—some kind of religious experience—traditionally is the ground for the certainty of Biblical faith.

# III

We find, then, three recognizable, distinct models of faith. Each is distinguishable from the others, and the existential forms, classed together, are distinguishable from the Biblical model. Moreover, let us observe, each of the three is distinguishable from holding a theoretical belief. Unamuno, following Kierkegaard, draws our attention to an essential difference: passion. Passion, or better, passionate commitment to the object of faith, has a central and essential place in faith. But passion is out of place in holding a theoretical belief. There one should try to hold one's belief with a conviction proportioned to the available evidence, and one should investigate to see what the evidence is before believing at all. With theoretical belief the issue is open, and the proper attitude is a measured tentativeness. But tentativeness, so far as faith goes, is a failure of commitment. It is, at any rate, for these three models of faith. Here, I believe, is a good part of the reason why many feel that a focus on the coherence and rationality of religious belief tends to mislead us about the nature of faith: it obscures the place of commitment by making religious belief into a kind of theory.

Is passion, or passionate commitment, what unifies these three faith-forms as types of faith? Surely each exhibits this feature, and, I suspect, whatever other faith-forms may be discoverable will as well. But styles of belief other than faith exhibit this feature (for instance—borrowing an example from Kierkegaard—Don Quixote's obsessive belief). Consequently, we shall have to look further for a unifying feature of faith.

The, or one, unifying feature of faith, I suggest, is *trust.* The place of certainty in faith is ambiguous, and as a consequence the place of an experiential grounding is also ambiguous. But the place of trust, I shall argue, is not ambiguous. Even though there may be, and are, different models of faith, all models of faith necessarily include trust. Why is this so?

The first thing to appreciate is that religious belief, as Norman Malcolm has pointed out, is *belief in* God and not *belief that* God exists.[12] Or, more accurately (going beyond Malcolm), *belief in* God is not *merely belief that* God exists, just as it is not *merely* a set of several *beliefs that* about God. And this is so even though *belief in* God presupposes a *belief that* there is the God in whom one believes. Indeed, certainty and lack of certainty in religious belief relate to the *belief that* there is a God or some other *belief that* about God. But such beliefs are not isolated; they are internal to *belief in* God.

Now, as *belief in God,* religious belief necessarily involves an affective state, Malcolm says. We can see that this is so by tracing in the distinction between *belief that* and *belief in simpliciter. Belief that* is belief that a proposition is true. *Belief in* is belief in something, primarily a person, although by extension also a policy or a principle, such as following the law. *Belief that* is different from *belief in* in two significant ways. First, the objects of belief are different: for *belief that* the object is a proposition, for *belief in* it is primarily a person. Second, while a *belief that* may be indifferently held, a *belief in* must be affective. One might believe that Jupiter has nine moons and not care much about it, but if a wife believes in her husband she necessarily is not indifferent toward him.

Of course, sometimes the English locution "believe in" is used to affirm a *belief that.* When individuals say that they believe in witches, most likely they are not expressing their affection for witches but affirming that there are witches. Usually the context makes such expressions unambiguous, but not always. And it is possible to trade on the ambiguity, as Coleridge once did. When Coleridge was asked if he believed in ghosts, he replied that no, he did not—for he knew them too well! The fact that a logical *belief that* can be given the grammatical expression of a *belief in,* of course, does not vitiate the distinction. Rather, this fact requires the distinction.

Malcolm, then, is quite clear, and clearly right, that religious belief, as belief *in*

God, necessarily involves an affective state. But Malcolm thinks that the attitude involved in belief in God can vary from reverential love to rebellious rejection. Belief in a person, he thinks, connotes trust, but belief in God might involve, instead of trust, fear, awe, dread, dismay, resentment, or even hatred. If Malcolm means *faith* in God, I believe that he is mistaken on this point and that we can see he is by reflecting on the religious rebellion of Ivan Karamazov in Dostoyevsky's novel.

Was Ivan, after all, a kind of religious believer, as Malcolm would have it? D. Z. Phillips agrees with Malcolm that he was. The rebel, Phillips suggests, knows the religious story from the inside but is not captivated by it. He knows the story and rejects it. He defies God, but he does not deny that there is a God, Phillips would say, following Camus.[13] And, in fact, after recounting to Alyosha the catalogue of evils done to children and before telling him the action of his poem, "The Grand Inquisitor," Ivan says, "It is not God that I do not accept, Alyosha. I merely most respectfully return him (my) ticket (of admission)."[14] Indeed, then, Ivan does not deny that there is a God. Rather, he rejects Him as unworthy of worship given His universe.

Ivan sends back his ticket in moral indignation. Clearly, Ivan does not trust in God. But just as clearly, we should agree with Malcolm and Phillips, he still believes in God. As Phillips says, even the rebel who hates God must believe in God, for whom does he hate if it is not God?[15] However, let us be as clear as we can about the nature of such a belief as Ivan's. Ivan rebels against God, and perhaps hates this God who allows the atrocities he recounts to Alyosha. He believes in God, then, at least in the sense that he believes that there is a God, for he must believe that there is the God whom he defies and hates. And, moreover, since he defies God, his belief is not indifferent. To say all of this, however, is not yet to say that he believes in God in the sense that stands opposed to believing that there is a God. Why not? Because "belief in" is ambiguous in the way that we noted. It can designate, in certain contexts, a *belief that* or it can designate a logical *belief in,* in which case it is a synonym for "faith in." Given only Ivan's belief that there is a God, we are allowed to say that Ivan believes in God—we are allowed to use the "believes in" locution—just as we are allowed to speak of someone's belief in witches or ghosts: the ambiguity of "believes in" allows us to do so. But, as Coleridge was aware, a belief in ghosts, in the sense of a belief that there are ghosts, even when conjoined with a fearful respect for ghosts, does not come to belief in ghosts in the other sense. Accordingly, though it be true that Ivan believes in God, and even has an affective belief in God, his belief is not therefore the *belief in* that internally requires an affective state. It is not, that is to say, therefore a form of *faith in* God. Perhaps we should recall the secret of Ivan's Grand Inquisitor. His secret, forced from Ivan by Alyosha, is that in the crucial sense he, the Grand Inquisitor, does not believe in God—despite his affective response. That is, he has no faith in God. And perhaps we should recall the character of Alyosha's own trial of faith after the death of Father Zossima. In his crisis Alyosha says to Rakitin, echoing his brother's rejection of God, that he has not taken up arms against God, he simply does not accept His world. Alyosha continues to believe that there is a God, and he continues to have an affective response to God and His world. But these cannot be sufficient for the presence of faith. If they were, there would be no trial of Alyosha's faith.

I suspect that Malcolm thinks any affective attitude, or any of a wide range, will do for religious belief in God because he focuses on *belief in* and not *faith in.* "Faith in" lacks the ambiguity of "belief in." While a belief in God might come to a belief that there is a God plus rebellion or hate, faith in God never will, for it is essentially tied to trust. In fact, 'trust' is a synonym, or near synonym, for "faith in." In a secular context, one way to demonstrate that one no longer has faith in a person is to show that one no longer trusts him or her, whether regarding a specific matter or in general. (Indeed, is it not *the* way?) And in a religious setting believers show their lack of faith in God by not trusting in Him. It is not accidental that Abraham's trial of faith, like Alyosha's, is a trial of trust. Martin Buber was confident that faith in God, as embodied in the stories of the Old Testament, is essentially trust. Buber thought that there are two and only two types of faith. One is *emuhah,* or *faith in,* and the other is *pistis,* or *faith that.*[16] The first, for Buber, arises in early Judaism, the second in Pauline and Hellenistic Christianity. The first is the faith-form of Israel and the original Christian community close to Jesus, where faith is essentially trust in an encountered Presence. The second is the faith-form of Hellenistic Christianity, toward which Hellenistic Judaism tended, where faith becomes faith that certain doctrines are the truth. Buber rightly thought that both, in their secular forms, "can be understood from the simple data of our lives." We need only consult our own experience to see that one kind of faith, faith in another, *is* trust of that other.

If I am right, "faith in," as opposed to "belief in," includes trust in its very meaning. They are synonyms, or nearly are. And we can see that this is so by reminding ourselves of what necessarily shows a person's lack of faith in another, or in God, namely, a lack of trust. If Buber is right, we can confirm that *faith in* is by its nature trust by looking at the "simple data" of our faith relationships to others. Either way we come to see that *faith in* is trust, or necessarily involves trust. Thus, all models of religious faith, as models of *faith* in God, as opposed to *belief* in God in Malcolm's or Phillips's sense, will necessarily give a place to trust. And, as models of faith *in God,* they will necessarily give a place to trust *in God.* Trust, then, is the, or one, unifying feature of faith, and trust in God is a unifying feature of the different models of religious faith in God, even though, as we have seen, different models of faith can vary in the place they give to certainty and its foundation.

## IV

So far we have discussed three models of religious faith, their interrelationships, their relationships to the issue of rationality, and their unifying feature of trust. But now let us ask if there are other models of religious faith. More precisely, let us ask if what came to be called "devout skepticism" is a form of religious faith, as some have argued.

Francis Bacon, in his essay on atheism, wrote that "a little philosophy inclineth man's mind to atheism, but depth in philosophy bringeth men's minds about to religion." By the mid-nineteenth century, however, it was thought that an even greater depth in philosophy would bring us one turn more to the suspended judgment of honest doubt. David Hume in the eighteenth century had said that "to be a philosophical skeptic is, in a man of letters, the first and most essential step towards being a sound, believing Christian."[17] It remained for the nineteenth century to make doubt itself a surrogate for faith, if not indeed a kind of faith. For so it came to be regarded by Tennyson, who wrote the lines that best capture the thought:

> There lives more faith in honest doubt,
> Believe me, than in half the creeds.[18]

The ideal here is that of the devout skeptic, who rejects or holds back from traditional religion, not because he is shallow or immoral, but because on ethical grounds he will not believe where the truth is not clear.[19] He is acquainted with the Bible and knows the naturalistic interpretation which it can be given, and he knows Hume's criticisms of miracles. And also he has come to know the various forms of religion too well to accept any one of them as his own.

The devout skeptic will not accept the religion of his fathers as a convention to be outwardly assumed or something to be piously mouthed while not lived. In this he is like Kierkegaard. For this is essentially a reaction against habitual belief. Kierkegaard saw inwardness as what was missing. The devout skeptic concludes that honesty requires doubt, and doubt requires the suspension of belief. But the devout skeptic is as passionate in his skepticism as Kierkegaard is in his inwardness. Furthermore, while he is an agnostic, he is not an antireligious agnostic. Antireligious agnostics are disposed to reject religious belief but do not feel justified in unequivocally denying God's existence; they are like those skeptics who are hostile to religion and do not want to be convinced. The devout skeptic, however, may be a religious agnostic disposed to believe.[20] Even so, despite sympathy and a concern to believe, his honesty requires doubt and that he not believe. Several nineteenth century figures exemplify this ideal, among them Matthew Arnold and Henry Sidgwick, as well as Tennyson.

We have quoted two lines from Tennyson's *In Memoriam.* One thing Tennyson is saying in this poem is that it is wrong to see doubt as evil. Doubt is not to be denied as sinful, but faced, measured, and dealt with; for only this honest facing of doubt will create an enduring faith.[21] But, beyond this, Tennyson is also saying, in accordance with the lines we quoted, that the best faith in an uncertain universe *is* honest doubt, as opposed to an unexamined acceptance of a creed or belief. It is true that Tennyson himself longs to believe: he wishes to "faintly trust the larger hope"—and we should note here the role of trust, the affective core of faith. But Tennyson had come to see nature as "red in tooth and claw," as denying the law of love.[22] Try as he would he could not deny this perception. Here, then, is the "honest doubt" that Tennyson recognized and sought to resolve. As for T. H. Huxley, Tennyson's contemporary, the processes of nature were at odds with the principles of ethics. The universe was not silent: it spoke against the presence of a God of love.

At one point in *In Memoriam,* Tennyson apparently finds his doubt answered, not by the wonder of the world or the design of its elements or an argument, but by the feelings of his heart. However, as soon as he allows such a resolution, he reasserts his doubt. Tennyson of course was not unaware of the sway of feelings and felt the force of his own. But in accordance with his own devout skepticism, he would not allow his feelings to usurp his reason, or his deeply felt wishes to overrule the doubt he could not honestly deny.[23]

Devout skeptics and existential believers are alike in that both have doubts and both face their doubts. However, they are utterly different in the ways that they treat their doubts. Existential believers seek to overcome their doubts by willing to believe despite their force. Devout skeptics seek to resolve their doubts and honestly to lay them to rest. For existential faith, the pitch and commitment of faith are in proportion to the doubt of the believer. Absurd believers are out upon the seventy thousand fathoms and yet believe. If they knew—and had no doubts to overcome—faith would be impossible. This, however, is not the picture of faith held by devout skeptics. For existential believers, the authenticity of their faith is a function of their inwardness and passion, which in turn require the objective uncertainty of what they believe. For devout skeptics, the integrity of their faith is a function of their intellectual honesty in believing or not believing. Their cry of faith, if they have one, is, "I affirm my integrity and believe as what I have seen of the truth allows." Devout skeptics may wish to believe, but they will believe only after they have honestly laid to rest their doubts. They prefer honest doubt to dishonest belief, not only as a matter of the ethics of belief, but also as a matter of what would be most fitting in the eyes of God.[24]

For Kierkegaard, at one point in the *Fragments,* if one truly wants to believe, then one can and must overcome doubt by a "free act" of will. For, he argues, doubt itself is an "act of will" and can only be overcome by a corresponding free act of will.[25] What Kierkegaard fails to observe is that doubt will be an act of will, or better, willful, only when the doubt does not arise from a subject which is itself doubtful. It may well be that the Greek skeptic he cites, who doubted the obvious, doubted, as Kierkegaard says, "not by virtue of his knowledge (or lack of knowledge), but by an act of will." He, as it were, had to "work himself up" into a state of doubt. However, Kierkegaard—the Kierkegaard of the *Fragments*—would be right regarding religious doubt and overcoming it only if religious doubt did not arise from the doubtfulness of God's existence and presence, but rather from a willful denial of the obvious. And this, the devout skeptic would maintain, is not the case.

On the other side, there are Biblical believers, who in other ways are like but also unlike the devout skeptic. They, like the devout skeptic, welcome a faith that is supported and, consequently, they may be more understanding of the desire to have an honest, supported faith. But they find God's presence all about them. There is an abundance of evidence in their eyes. For them, their experience of God speaks fully and conclusively of God's presence. There is a story of an agnostic philosopher, recounted by H. H. Price, to whom the question was put: "What would you say if God himself suddenly appeared among us in this room?" The philosopher, it is said, replied, " 'God', I should say, 'why did you make evidence for your existence so inadequate?' "[26] But the evidence is not inadequate, the Biblical believer would say. It speaks as loudly as the evidence for one's own life. It is only that, for one reason or another, many of us are blind to it all in its significance as assurance of God's presence.

In the background here is the issue of self-deception. Have religious doubters willfully deceived themselves into doubting God's presence? Or do religious doubters face a silent universe, or one that speaks against there being a God, to which the only honest response is one of doubt, even though there may be a desire to believe? Or might it be that God's presence is evident and inescapable to a Job, while others, though not self-deceived, are in their age blind to what Job could not but see?

In any case, there are ways of expelling doubt that devout skeptics will not countenance. They, of course, will not simply choose to believe in spite of their doubts, but also they will not give over to their feelings, nor will they employ psychological devices to lessen the force of their doubts. To resolve religious doubts, it may be said, one need not search for intellectual certainty nor submit to authority; one needs rather to hunger and thirst for righteousness and to be aware of a deep sense of personal infirmity. If one does this, then, deeply wishing and trying out faith in one's life, one will find all doubts answered.[27] But such a maneuver as this, to the mind of the devout skeptic, plays loose with the truth. And devout skeptics would have similar problems with Pascal's belief-creating measures. Pascal's advice to the unbeliever who felt forced not to believe because "I am so made that I cannot believe" was that he should behave as if he believed, taking holy water, having masses said, and so on, in order that he might be brought to belief.[28] The devout skeptic would hardly give such advice as this, nor would he give the advice, "Believe first and then you will see." All such devices fail to address doubts honestly. Either they require uncritically indulging an inclination or wish to believe, or they require believing (or trying to) before doubts are adequately resolved.

Similarly, devout skeptics are not inclined to set aside their doubts and take up religious belief for pragmatic reasons. They may concede, as James Leuba maintained, that the common religious impulse is to use God for the attainment of desires, not to know Him.[29] They may even allow that persons can, with success, consciously undertake to believe for pragmatic reasons: to relieve a fear of damnation, say, or to ease a sense of sin, or simply to conform. However, they will not try to precipitate faith in themselves by such means. Reasons of this sort only help one believe in spite of one's doubts. They can help one overcome doubt, but they cannot offer an honest resolution of doubt. For that matter, such an overcoming of doubt as this would be as distasteful to Kierkegaard as it is to the devout skeptic: it is as far from existential striving as it is from rational resolution.[30] And, too, while the devout skeptic and the Biblical believer may not agree on the epistemological import of Job's religious experience, they can agree that experience of God's presence does not comprise merely a pragmatic reason for believing.

Of course, it might be said that even though a person's faith were induced by pragmatic reasons, it itself, once gained, would not be a pragmatic state—which is what Terence Penelhum says in defense of Pascal's wager.[31] This may be true. If so, the induced faith once alive would gain a life of its own, as it were. But it would have to do so in spite of the reasons for its inception. And, in any case, the devout skeptic's honest doubts, which are about the truth of religious belief and not its attainability or usefulness, would not have been resolved.

Perhaps, however, the devout skeptic would have fewer problems with an approach suggested by H. H. Price. Price, too, is aware that serious believers can feel the need to have good reasons for their faith. He raises such a concern in connection with one for whom it would be acute, namely, a believer who is also a philosopher.[32] As a believer he cannot help believing in God and is thankful that he does. But as a philosopher he recognizes a duty to hold beliefs favored by the available evidence and is concerned about an apparent lack of good reasons for his religious belief. Price's philosopher, while remaining a religious believer, would wish also to be a "rational believer" in a certain definite sense of that term. He would wish to hold only beliefs that are supported by good reasons that he can present to others, and would wait for such reasons before believing. But he has no adequate reasons for his religious belief. At bottom, the issue for the rational believer (whether he believes already or not) and for the devout skeptic is the same: the issue of finding good reasons. The rational believer would find honest support for the belief he already holds or would hold. The devout skeptic would honestly resolve his doubts before he believes.

A way open to the rational believer to find such reasons, Price suggests, is to test "the Theistic hypothesis."[33] It is a way equally open to the devout skeptic. For Price, to test the Theistic hypothesis it is not necessary to believe already, and still less is it necessary to believe with conviction. Nor is it necessary to trust in God or in anything else. One need not have the conviction that the procedures to be undertaken will work. One need only think that they are worth trying. Granted, to test the Theistic hypothesis, one must have an "interest" in "the basic propositions of Theistic religion," which are "that there is a God who created the world, and that he loves each one of us." However, such an interest need only be sufficient for a certain effort in trying out the testing procedure. It need not amount to a prior acceptance. Price's model throughout is the empirical testing of a hypothesis.

The procedure to be followed in testing the Theistic hypothesis involves meditative and devotional practices. These include privately fixing one's thoughts on the theistic propositions and taking up the practice of prayer. Of course, the "praying" involved will be that of an agnostic and will have the character of a "devotional experiment." The tester of the Theistic hypothesis is to conduct the imaginative exercise of "taking up the role" of a religious person: not in order to precipitate belief, as Pascal would have one do, but to test the religious hypothesis, so that belief may be justified.

There are problems here, to be sure. For one thing, Price's Theistic hypothesis shifts. It starts out involving the proposition that there is a God but ends up as the proposition that if one takes up the role of a religious person, then one oneself will become a changed person and begin to have new experiences—quite a different hypothesis. For another thing, Price's devotional hypothesis, if it retains a reference to God, strains the logic of hypothesis confirmation. For, regarding such a hypothesis, no data emerge that will meet a confirming condition clear to all other investigators, and the experiment cannot be replicated by the disinterested, short of changing their lives. Still, Price shows us that the tradition of the devout skeptic and the rational believer who honestly seek reasons for their belief remains alive.

However, one might ask, is there any real *religious* use for such a devotional hypothesis and its pursuit? For one thing, does it not involve assuming that tentative attitude we earlier found to be antithetical to faith? Of course, it may be granted that there could be a person, like Levin in Tolstoy's *Anna Karenina,* who does not believe, who cannot quite believe that there is a God, but who prays the agnostic's prayer or tries to. But, again, given the logic of hypothesis confirmation, it is wholly dubious that such a practice can confirm a "God hypothesis." Furthermore, it is doubtful what the religious import of the confirmation of an objectively persued God hypothesis would be. Is it to result in a living faith, in which case it is a unique hypothesis, or might one confirm such a hypothesis and, like Malcolm's atheist,[34] end up 'knowing' that there is a God but not believing in God? Nevertheless, it might be said, such a practice can indirectly result in a truly religious faith, as in the case of Levin, and, moreover, it can open avenues to religious experience, which, in its turn, may provide a supportive ground for religious belief, even if not as data confirming a hypothesis.

As we have seen, the tradition of the devout skeptic merges with that of the rational believer, the believer who strives to believe in accordance with good reasons that can be articulated and presented to others. In this combined tradition, devout skeptics and believers *are* prepared to hold a tentative religious belief. They endeavor to hold all their beliefs with a firmness proportionate to the weight of their evidence, and until there is support they try to withhold belief. They know the claims of a Job or Abraham and their sense of the living presence of God. But their standards of evidence are not Job's and Abraham's, nor are they those of St. Bernard of Clairvaux or St. Bonaventura. They are not averse to drawing a close analogy between hypotheses and religious belief, and they are prepared to examine and debate the foundations of their belief. In fact, they may see this as a duty. In the present day, among those who are in this combined tradition or see it as the proper tradition of religious belief, following Hume if not Tennyson, are John King-Farlow, William Christensen, Paul Edwards, Terence Penelhum, Kai Nielsen, and many others.[35]

Do devout skeptics, who honestly doubt and seek to resolve their doubts through pursuing a devotional hypothesis, have religious faith, a type of religious faith? Like those Kierkegaard saw as having no faith, they seek safeguards and approach belief in God tentatively. But they do so for the sake of the honesty of their belief, not to lessen the risk they must take. Like Kierkegaard, devout skeptics refuse to go along with the members of Christendom who accept the belief of their fathers simply because they were born to it. Like Kierkegaard, they seek an individual relationship to God, if there is a God. Again, like the Kierkegaard of the *Fragments* and the *Concluding Unscientific Postscript,* they feel that they must face and contend with their doubts. But, unlike Kierkegaard, they feel that they must resolve their doubts, not "overcome" them. It, of course, is important that devout skeptics' doubts be honest doubts. For the honesty of the belief they would have requires that the doubts that prevent their belief be honest.

Do devout skeptics have faith, then, if their doubts are honest? Like believers, they strive to maintain their belief-attitude and not to capitulate to the pressures of conformity. Their effort is to retain the integrity of their lack of belief until they can honestly accept the faith of their fathers. Their motive is to have a worthy faith, even though they are skeptical and as yet do not believe. But their motive to have a worthy faith is not itself belief. Devout skeptics are not like Paradoxical believers, who, by striving to believe, affirm the faith they cannot attain. If devout skeptics have faith, it is not by virtue of a striving to believe.

Could devout skeptics be said to have faith by virtue of a core of belief they do hold? Tennyson and others did have a core of positive belief relating to God, or at least to the Unknown. In *In Memoriam* there is a reference to what "no man understands" reaching out of the darkness through nature, and Henry Sidgwick speaks of this as the "minimum of faith."[36] The idea that 'supreme reality' is unknown and even incomprehensible is, of course, found in various mystical traditions. But this idea was abroad in the nineteenth century. William James in his *Varieties* speaks in such terms of the "more" with which human beings feel connected in religious experience. On its hither side, this "more" is just the subconscious, but it is James's "over-belief," he says, that on its far side is "the supreme reality," beyond our understanding, which nevertheless affects our lives.[37]

Does such a belief come to faith in God? The conception of the object of belief, the Unknown, remains amorphous. But, it can be argued, a rigorous and true concept of God is not an absolute requirement for faith in God. Here, I believe, Kierkegaard would come to the defense of the devout skeptic.[38] However, the connections between such a belief and religious practice become tenuous, if they are not severed altogether. The roles of prayer, worship, and seeking to conform to the Divine will are not clear at all.

The final, essential question relates to trust: Is there trust in the Unknown on the part of the devout skeptic? James correctly perceives the necessity for religion—or, more accurately, for religious faith—of trust in the "larger power" that confronts humanity as the unknown.[39] But Tennyson's doubts, we will recall, arose precisely at the juncture of trust. He could not see the God of nature to be a God of love. Though he wanted to, he could not, in reason, trust in the Creator of the universe; and hence, as a devout skeptic, he could not affirm trust in God. If we take Tennyson to define the type, the devout skeptic will doubt God's goodness and lack in trust. Accordingly, if devout skeptics can be said to have a kind of faith, it must be by merit of the honesty and integrity of their belief-attitude, not by merit of the trust they do not have. Their "faith," if they can be said to have faith, is not faith *in* God, with its trust in God, but an epistemic pledge that devout skeptics deem to be fitting in the eyes of the only God they would believe in. However, in no way are devout skeptics that sort of skeptic who theoretically criticizes Judeo-Christian faith from the outside. Like Ivan Karamazov, they have confronted faith and the problem of trust. Their skepticism, as much as Ivan's rebellion, stands within the religious tradition of the Judeo-Christian heritage in tension and in dialogue with religious faith.

## Notes

1. Søren Kierkegaard, *Fear and Trembling*, and *The Sickness unto Death*, trans. Walter Lowrie (Princeton, NJ: Princeton University Press, 1968), pp. 22ff., esp. 36–37.

2. Miguel de Unamuno, *Tragic Sense of Life*, trans. J. F. Flitch (New York: Dover, 1954), p. 193.

3. Søren Kierkegaard, *Concluding Unscientific Postscript*, trans. David F. Swenson and Walter Lowrie (Princeton, NJ: Princeton University Press, 1941), p. 182.

4. This is the distinction cited by Richard Robinson between the "certainty of persons" and the "certainty of propositions," in "The Concept of Knowledge," *Mind* 80 (1971): 22.

5. Kierkegaard, *Concluding Unscientific Postscript*, p. 182.

6. For a longer discussion of the relationship of certainty to faith, and of both to religious knowledge, see my "Problems of Faith," *The Canadian Journal of Philosophy* 6 (1976): 431–33.

7. For a discussion of the ways *belief* and *awareness* are related to choice, see my "God and Mystery," *American Philosophical Quarterly* 11 (1974): 99–101. And cf. H. D. Lewis, *Our Experience of God* (London: George Allen & Unwin Ltd.; New York: The Macmillan Company, 1959), pp. 54–55.

8. Believing "by virtue of the absurd" is a notion we find in *Fear and Trembling,* where it is applied to Abraham's faith. Applied to Abraham's faith, its meaning would have to be consistent with Abraham's being certain that, and it being certain that, what he believes is true. But such is not the case here in its application to the Absurd model.

9. Søren Kierkegaard, *Philosophical Fragments,* trans. David Swenson, rev. Howard V. Hong (Princeton, NJ: Princeton University Press, 1962), pp. 102–3.

10. Miguel de Unamuno, "What is Truth?" *The Agony of Christianity and Essays on Faith,* trans. Anthony Kerrigan (Princeton, NJ: Princeton University Press, 1974), p. 175 and passim.

11. Unamuno, *Tragic Sense of Life,* p. 193.

12. Norman Malcolm, "Is it a Religious Belief That 'God Exists'?" in *Faith and the Philosophers,* ed. John Hick (London: Macmillan; New York: St. Martin's Press, 1964), pp. 106–7. (See the article by Malcolm reprinted in this volume, pp. 92–103.)

13. D. Z. Phillips, "Philosophy, Theology and the Reality of God," and "Faith, Scepticism, and Religious Understanding," *Faith and Philosophical Enquiry* (New York: Schocken Books, 1971), pp. 12 and 30 (reprinted in Part II of this volume, pp. 81–91; all further citations are from this reprint). Cf. Albert Camus in *The Rebel,* in a passage quoted by Phillips: "The rebel defies more than he denies. Originally, at least, he does not deny God, he simply talks to Him as an equal. But it is not a polite dialogue. It is a polemic animated by the desire to conquer."

14. Fyodor Dostoyevsky, *The Brothers Karamazov,* trans. David Magarshack (Baltimore, MD: Penguin Books, 1958), "Rebellion," I, p. 287.

15. See Phillips, "Faith, Skepticism, and Religious Understanding," *Faith and Philosophical Enquiry,* pp. 89–91 above.

16. Martin Buber, *Two Types of Faith,* trans. Norman P. Goldhawk (New York: Harper & Row, 1961), pp. 7, 11, 33–34, 170, and passim.

17. David Hume, *Dialogues Concerning Natural Religion,* Part XII.

18. *In Memoriam,* XCVI, 11, 1995–96.

19. See Basil Willey, *Nineteenth-Century Studies* (New York: Columbia University Press, 1949), p. 221.

20. Cf. Thomas McPherson, *Philosophy and Religious Belief* (London: Hutchinson University Library, 1974), pp. 22–23.

21. *In Memoriam,* XCVI.

22. *In Memoriam,* LV and LVI. See Basil Willey, *More Nineteenth-Century Studies* (New York: Columbia University Press, 1956), p. 91.

23. See Sec. CXXIV of *In Memoriam.*

24. Cf. Paul Edwards, "Kierkegaard and the 'Truth' of Christianity," *Philosophy* 46 (1971): 98.

25. Kierkegaard, *Philosophical Fragments,* pp. 102–3.

26. H. H. Price, "Faith and Belief," in *Faith and the Philosophers,* ed. John Hick, pp. 19–20.

27. Cf. Basil Willey on Coleridge's views on the first step in spiritual experience and finding in the Bible "copious sources of truth" (*Nineteenth Century Studies,* p. 41).

28. Blaise Pascal, *Pensées,* trans. J. M. Cohen (Baltimore, MD: Penguin Books, 1961), p.

158. Pascal gives the advice to one who has already accepted his wager argument but still feels unable to believe. (See Part V of this volume for a related discussion of Pascal's view.)

29. James H. Leuba, "The Contents of Religious Consciousness," *The Monist* 11 (1901): 571–72.

30. It would, I think, be contrary to Kierkegaard's entire thrust to make belief easier by arraying pragmatic reasons for believing: doing so would remove the possibility of offense that he says Christianity requires. True, in the *Concluding Unscientific Postscript,* Kierkegaard speaks of one's eternal happiness as the "interest" of faith. But his concern is not to lessen the offense; he says that his purpose is to make it difficult to become a Christian, though not more difficult than it is (*Concluding Unscientific Postscript,* p. 495).

31. Terence Penelhum, *Problems of Religious Knowledge* (New York: Herder and Herder, 1972), pp. 156–57.

32. Price, "Faith and Belief," p. 16.

33. See H. H. Price, *Belief* (London: George Allen & Unwin; New York: Humanities Press, 1969), pp. 481–88. This volume consists of Price's 1960 Gifford Lectures. In the presentation of Price's views I have drawn from this work and his "Faith and Belief."

34. Norman Malcolm, in a well-known article, tries to show that the ontological argument in one form is sound. At the end of the article, however, he raises the possibility that someone might follow the argument as a "piece of logic," become convinced that God's existence cannot coherently be denied, and yet remain an "atheist"—that is, one without religious faith in God. "Anselm's Ontological Arguments," reprinted in *The Existence of God,* ed. John Hick (New York: The Macmillan Company; Londen: Collier-Macmillan, 1964), p. 67.

35. See John King-Farlow and William Christensen, *Faith and the Life of Reason* (Dordrecht, Neth.: D. Reidel, 1972); Paul Edwards "Kierkegaard and the 'Truth' of Christianity"; Terence Penelhum, *Problems of Religious Knowledge,* esp. pp. 146–48; and Kai Nielsen, *Scepticism* (London: Macmillan; New York: St. Martin's Press, 1973).

36. *In Memoriam,* CXXIV. And see Willey, *More Nineteenth-Century Studies,* p. 103, for Sidgwick's comment.

37. William James, *The Varieties of Religious Experience* (New York: The Modern Library, 1902), pp. 502 and 505–7.

38. When Kierkegaard compares an idol worshipper, who with a false concept of God prays "with the entire passion of the infinite," to a member of Christendom, who prays with a "false spirit" even though he has the "true conception of God," Kierkegaard implies that it is the idol worshipper who has the "most truth" (*Concluding Unscientific Postscript,* pp. 179–80).

39. James, *The Varieties of Religious Experience,* p. 515.

# 24

# Explaining Religious Experience

## *Wayne Proudfoot*

*Reductionism* has become a derogatory epithet in the history and philosophy of religion. Scholars whose work is in other respects quite diverse have concurred in advocating approaches to the study of religion which are oriented around campaigns against reductionism. These campaigns are often linked to a defense of the autonomy of the study of religion. The distinctive subject matter of that study, it is argued, requires a distinctive method. In particular, religious experience cannot properly be studied by a method that reduces it to a cluster of phenomena that can be explained in historical, psychological, or sociological terms. Although it is difficult to establish exactly what is meant by the term, the label "reductionist" is deemed sufficient to warrant dismissal of any account of religious phenomena.

Questions have been raised about this wholesale rejection of reductive accounts and about the theological motivations that sometimes underlie it, but the issues in the discussion have not been sufficiently clarified.[1] Penner and Yonan, for example, take the problem to be crucial for the study of religion, survey the meaning of *reduction* in empiricist philosophy of science, and deplore the negative connotations that have become attached to the term.[2] But they admit that they have found the issue difficult. They show no appreciation of why the attack on reductionism has such an appeal, and thus they are unable to elucidate the discussion. The warnings against reductionism derive from a genuine insight, but that insight is often misconstrued to serve an apologetic purpose. I shall try to clarify the confusion surrounding the term *reduction* as it is applied to accounts of religious experience and to distinguish between the insight and the misapplications that result in protective strategies. A recent essay in the philosophy of religion devoted to the exposure and critique of reductionism will serve to illustrate those misapplications and strategies.

## The Problem

One of the most influential critics of reductionism in the study of religion has been Mircea Eliade. He has argued that the task of the historian of religion is a distinctive one and has contrasted it with what he takes to be the reductionist methods of the social sciences.[3] According to Eliade, a historical or sociological approach fails to grasp the meaning of religious phenomena. Like the literary critic interpreting a text, the historian of religion must attempt to understand religious data on [his or her] own plane of reference. He or she should adopt a hermeneutic method. Just as literary works cannot be reduced to their origins, religious phenomena ought not to be reduced to their social, psychological, or historical origins or functions. Eliade contends that "a religious datum reveals its deeper meaning when it is considered on its plane of reference, and not when it is reduced to one of its secondary aspects or its contexts."[4] He cites Durkheim and Freud as examples of those who have adopted reductionist methods for the study of religion.

Two points are worthy of note: (1) Eliade thinks that what is lost by reductive approaches is the *meaning* of religious phenomena. He praises van der Leeuw for respecting the peculiar intentionality of religious data and thus the irreducibility of religious representations[5]; (2) his examples of reductionist approaches are drawn almost exclusively from history and the social sciences. Theories that purport to account for religious phenomena in terms of their origins or the functions they serve in a particular social context are ipso facto reductionist.

Eliade holds further that religious data represent the expression of religious experiences. Religion is "first of all, an experience sui generis, incited by man's encounter with the sacred."[6] In order to understand religious data on their own plane of reference, the scholar must " 'relive' a multitude of existential situations."[7] Only through such a procedure can the meaning of the data be grasped. To reduce those data to their origins or social functions is to fail to understand them as expressions of religious experience. That understanding can come only from acquaintance. Since Eliade regards religious experience as experience of the sacred, he can summarize his antireductionist position by reference to "the irreducibility of the sacred."[8]

Religious experience is the experience of something. It is intentional in that it cannot be described without reference to a grammatical object. Just as fear is always fear of something, and a perceptual act can only be described by reference to its object, a religious experience must be identified under a certain description, and that description must include a reference to the object of the experience. Eliade employs the term *sacred* to characterize the object of all religious experience. The notorious obscurity of that term need not concern us here, nor need we accept the suggestion that all religious experiences have the same object. The point is that when Eliade refers to the irreducibility of the sacred, he is claiming that it is the intentional object of the religious experience which must not be reduced. To do so is to lose the experience, or to attend to something else altogether.

This point is well taken. If someone is afraid of a bear, his fear cannot be accurately described without mentioning the bear. This remains true regardless of whether or not the bear actually exists outside his mind. He may mistakenly perceive a fallen tree trunk on the trail ahead of him as a bear, but his fear is properly described as fear of a bear. To describe it as fear of a log would be to misidentify his emotion and reduce it to something other than it is. In identifying the experience, emotion, or practice of another, I must restrict myself to concepts and beliefs that have informed his experience. I cannot ascribe to him concepts he would not recognize or beliefs he would not acknowledge.[9] Though historical evidence might turn up to show that Socrates was dying of cancer, no evidence could show that he was afraid of dying of cancer. No such fear could be ascribed to him because he didn't possess the concept of cancer which is presupposed by that emotion.

Consider two examples cited by William James. The first is an experience reported by Stephen Bradley. . . .

> I thought I saw the Saviour, by faith, in human shape, for about one second in the room, with arms extended, appearing to say to me, Come. The next day I rejoiced with trembling; soon after my happiness was so great that I said that I wanted to die; this world had no place in my affections, as I knew of, and every day appeared to me as the Sabbath. I had an ardent desire that all mankind might feel as I did; I wanted to have them all love God supremely.[10]

The second is from Mrs. Jonathan Edwards.

> Part of the night I lay awake, sometimes asleep, and sometimes between sleeping and waking. But all night I continued in a constant, clear, and lively sense of the heavenly sweetness of Christ's excellent love, of his nearness to me, and of my dearness to him. I seemed to myself to perceive a glow of divine love come down from the heart of Christ in heaven into my heart in a constant stream, like a stream or pencil of sweet light. At the same time my heart and soul all flowed out in love to Christ, so that there seemed to be a constant flowing and reflowing of heavenly love, and I appeared to myself to float or swim, in these bright, sweet beams, like the motes swimming in the beams of the sun, or the streams of his light which come in at the window.[11]

Bradley tells of a vision in human shape, and Edwards reports a lively sense of Christ's love, which seemed to glow like a stream or pencil of light. Each of these experiences can only be properly described by reference to Christ and to Christian beliefs. One might try to separate the description of the core experience from its interpretation and to argue that only the interpretation is specifically Christian. But if the references to the Savior, the Sabbath, and God are eliminated from Bradley's report, we are left with something other than his experience. After deleting references to Christian concepts, we have a vision of a human shape with arms extended saying, "Come." Is this any less informed by Christian beliefs and doctrines than was the original experience? Surely the vision of a person with outstretched arms is not some universal archetype onto which Bradley has added an interpretation in Christian terms.[12] Nor can his experience of comfort and salvation be abstracted from his Christian beliefs. Sarah Edwards's experience is not a vision, but it would be inaccurate to describe it exclusively in general terms and to characterize it only as a lively sense of sweetness, accompanied by the sensation of floating in streams of bright light. Her report cannot be purged of references to Christ and Christian beliefs and still remain an accurate description of the experience.

An emotion, practice, or experience must be described in terms that can plausibly be attributed to the subject on the basis of the available evidence. The subject's self-ascription is normative for describing the experience. This is a kind of first-person privilege that has nothing at all to do with immediate intuitive access to mental states versus mediated inferential reasoning. It is strictly a matter of intentionality. It is like the distinction between the words of a speaker and those of one who reports what he says. The speaker's meaning, and his choice of words to express that meaning, are normative for the reporter. The latter may choose to paraphrase or elaborate, but the words uttered by the speaker are authoritative for determining the message. Where it is the subject's experience which is the object of study, that experience must be identified under a description that can plausibly be attributed to him. In the cases cited above, the subject's own words constitute the description. If, however, an observer or analyst describes the experience of another, he must formulate it in terms that would be familiar to, incorporating beliefs that would be acknowledged by, the subject. If challenged, he must offer reasons in support of his ascription of those concepts and beliefs to the subject. He is not responsible for reasons offered in support of those beliefs.

The explanation the analyst offers of that same experience is another matter altogether. It need not be couched in terms familiar or acceptable to the subject. It must be an explanation of the experience as identified under the subject's description, but the subject's approval of the explanation is not required. Bradley's experience might be explained in terms of the conflicts of early adolescence and that of Sarah Edwards as a consequence of her life with Mr. Edwards. No reference need be made to God or Christ in the construction of these explanations. If the explanation is challenged, the one who proposed it is responsible for providing reasons to support it and for showing how it accounts for the evidence better than any of its rivals does. . . .

In the study of religion considerable confusion has resulted from the failure to distinguish the requisite conditions for the identification of an experience under a certain description from those for explaining the experience. The analyst must cite, but need not endorse, the concepts, beliefs, and judgments that enter into the subject's identification of his experience. He must be prepared to give reasons for his ascription of those beliefs and judgments to the subject, but he need not defend the beliefs and judgments themselves. If he proposes an explanatory hypothesis to account for the experience, he need not restrict himself to the subject's concepts and beliefs, but he must be prepared to give reasons in support of his explanation.

## Descriptive and Explanatory Reduction

We are now in a position to distinguish two different kinds of reduction. *Descriptive reduction* is the failure to identify an emotion, practice, or experience under the description by which the subject identifies it. This is indeed unacceptable. To describe an experience in nonreligious terms when the subject himself describes it in religious terms is to misidentify the experience, or to attend to another experience altogether. To describe Bradley's experience as simply a vision of a human shape, and that of Mrs. Edwards as a lively warm sense that seemed to glow like a pencil of light, is to lose the identifying characteristics of those experiences. To describe the experience of a mystic by reference only to alpha waves, altered heart rate, and changes in bodily temperature is to misdescribe it. To characterize the experience of a Hindu mystic in terms drawn from the Christian tradition is to mis-identify it. In each of these instances, the subject's identifying experience has been reduced to something other than that experienced by the subject. This might properly be called reductionism. In any case, it precludes an accurate identification of the subject's experience.

*Explanatory reduction* consists in offering an explanation of an experience in terms that are not those of the subject and that might not meet with his approval. This is perfectly justifiable and is, in fact, normal procedure. The explanandum is set in a new context, whether that be one of covering laws and initial conditions, narrative structure, or some other explanatory model. The terms of the explanation need not be familiar or acceptable to the subject. Historians offer explanations of past events by employing such concepts as socialization, ideology, means of production, and feudal economy. Seldom can these concepts properly be ascribed to the people whose behavior is the object of the historian's study. But that poses no problem. The explanation stands or falls according to how well it can account for all the available evidence.

Failure to distinguish between these two kinds of reduction leads to the claim that any account of religious emotions, practices, or experience must be restricted to the perspective of the subject and must employ only terms, beliefs, and judgments that would meet with his approval. This claim derives its plausibility from examples of descriptive reduction but is then extended to preclude explanatory reduction. When so extended, it becomes a protective strategy. The subject's identifying description becomes normative for purposes of explanation, and inquiry is blocked to insure that the subject's own explanation of his experience is not contested. On this view, to entertain naturalistic explanations of the experiences of Bradley and Edwards is reductionist because these explanations conflict with the convictions of the subjects that their experiences were the result of divine activity in their lives.

Many of the warnings against reductionism in the study of religion conflate descriptive and explanatory reduction. Eliade exhorts the historian of religion to understand religious data on their own plane of reference and contrasts this understanding with the reductive accounts offered by social scientists.[13] Wilfred Cantwell Smith[14] contends that a necessary requirement of the validity of any statement about a religion is that it be acknowledged and accepted by adherents of that religious tradition. This is appropriate if addressed to the problem of providing identifying descriptions of experiences in different traditions, but it is inappropriate if extended to include all statements about religion. . . .

## Protective Strategies

The neglect or refusal to distinguish between descriptive and explanatory reduction constitutes the core of an apologetic strategy. Recognition of the requirement that religious experience and belief must be identified under the description employed by the subject is used to argue that all accounts of religious experience must be acceptable to the subject. This accords with the assumption that in order to understand religious experience one must participate in that experience or reproduce it in oneself.

Smith explicitly formulates the rule that "no statement about a religion is valid unless it can be acknowledged by that religion's believers."[15] He contends that in order to understand the Qur'an as a religious document, one must approach it in the same spirit as a Muslim would.[16] One must read it as if he already believed it to be the word of God. We ought not to study Muslim, Buddhist, or Jewish beliefs and practices but must learn to see the world through Muslim, Buddhist, or Jewish eyes. Understanding requires the scholar to share in the experience or the way of life of a particular tradition and to elicit or reproduce the same in his readers. Eliade describes the task of understanding as a hermeneutic one and exhorts the historian of religion to "relive" the existential situation of those whom he studies.

This requirement gains its appeal from the consideration that a religious experience, belief, or practice must be identified under the description employed by the subject; but it exhibits confusion when it is extended to preclude explanatory hypotheses that differ from those of the subject. In order to understand Astor's experience of a miracle, I must ascribe to him the belief that the event cannot be exhaustively explained in naturalistic terms, but I need not endorse that belief. After accurately citing Astor's description of the event, including his explanation of what he saw, I may go on to propose a competing explanation both of the event and of Astor's perception. To require that any explanation of a religious experience be one that would be endorsed by the subject is to block inquiry into the character of that experience. . . .

Religious beliefs are always to be construed in such a way that they accord with the beliefs we hold to be true. This is clearly a protective strategy. Quine argues for what he calls "the principle of charity."[17] We ought so to assign meanings to the sentences of an alien language that we ascribe to the speakers of that language beliefs that, in the main, accord with our own. At some point it becomes more plausible to assume we have mistranslated than to ascribe to other speakers beliefs that seem widely off the mark. If our translation leads us to ascribe to the speaker such sentences as, "The sunlight is usually brighter at night than in the daytime," or "No one can throw a stone farther than the distance measured by ten paces," then we ought to consider revising the translation to accord with the beliefs that we know to be true and that we ascribe to the speaker. . . .

## Force

In order to elucidate an experience, one must identify it under a description that can be ascribed to the subject of that experience. But when the analyst has given an identifying description of the experience, and has cited the relevant concepts and beliefs while withholding his endorsement of those beliefs, has he really captured the force of the experience? Some would argue that he has not, that to describe the experience of Astor, Bradley, or Edwards in such a way as to understand its force, one must have recourse to the kind of acquaintance or participation called for by Schleiermacher and Otto. A commitment by the analyst to a nonreligious explanation is said to preclude appreciation of the authority of the experience for the subject.

In his remarks on Frazer's *The Golden Bough,* Wittgenstein suggests that the story Frazer tells about the King of the Wood at Nemi is impressive in a way that his proposed explanation of the practice of killing the king is not.[18] Wittgenstein concludes that the satisfaction we seek cannot come from any kind of explanation but only from a description that draws connections between our practices and those of the people whom we are trying to understand. The proper identifying description satisfies where the explanation does not. It is implausible to suggest that such gripping practices rest on mistaken perceptions or theories about the world.

> Even the idea of trying to explain the practice—say the killing of the priest-king—seems to me wrong-headed. All that Frazer does is to make this practice plausible to people who think as he does. It is very queer that all these practices are finally presented, so to speak, as stupid actions.
>
> But it never does become plausible that people do all this out of sheer stupidity. . . .
>
> I think one reason why the attempt to find an explanation is wrong is that we have only to put together in the right way what we *know,* without adding anything, and the satisfaction we are trying to get from the explanation comes of itself. . . .
>
> We can only *describe* and say, human life is like that. . . .
>
> Compared with the impression that what is described here makes on us, the explanation is too uncertain.[19]

The practices themselves are deeper and more gripping than any theories or explanations either we or the practitioners might associate with them.

This is an important point. An explanation must satisfy in that it must account for the force of the experience. It is not necessary for the analyst to share the experience, however, to understand its force. It is the account which must satisfy, and an account can satisfy if it makes clear why the experience has the power it has for the subject. Knowing that my partner takes the log on the trail ahead to be a bear is sufficient for me to understand why it has a dramatic effect on his emotions and behavior. I have elucidated his fear by identifying the object of that fear as he perceives it, and I can see how the fear was occasioned. I can understand his fear without sharing his perception.

The appeal to the force of the experience can be used to serve a protective strategy. D. Z. Phillips argues that religious beliefs are irreducible in the sense that they cannot be explained in nonreligious terms. The impressive character of any religious belief or practice eludes all attempts at explanation.

> One may be interested in investigating the consequences of various religious beliefs for other social movements and institutions, or the historical development of religious beliefs. Yet, such investigations would not be an investigation into the impressiveness of the beliefs. The impressiveness may be elucidated—we have seen how symbol may be placed alongside symbol—but it cannot be explained.[20]

Force or impressiveness is not defined independently but is said to be that which is lost whenever an attempt is made to explain religious phenomena. This remark suggests that what is really distinctive about religious phenomena is their resistance to explanation, or their anomalous status with respect to all natural explanations. No attempt to explain them can be permitted without losing their distinctively religious character. The impressiveness of religious phenomena is identified as that which is lost whenever explanations are proposed for those phenomena.

The rejection of any kind of explanation is presented by Phillips as a plea for neutrality with respect to the truth of religious beliefs and a rejection of reductionism of all kinds. In fact, however, it is not a neutral position at all but conceals a substantial commitment. The function of Phillips's remarks is similar to that of Otto's instructions to his readers. If the experience can be explained, it is not religious. Like *numinous* and *miracle,* the *impressiveness* of religious beliefs, as Phillips uses the term, includes in the rules for its proper application the condition that it will be anomalous with respect to any proposed explanation. . . .

Phillips recognizes that religious experience is constituted by concepts and beliefs, and he urges attention to the grammar of those concepts. He argues that the rules of that grammar must govern any account of the experience. If questions are raised about the validity of beliefs assumed by the subject in his identification of the experience, one has imported issues from outside the religious form of life and ipso facto shown that one does not understand that life. . . .

When the question of how to account for the force of the experience is not employed in a protective strategy, it is a legitimate one. It is likely that no general account can be given which is adequate to capture the force or impressiveness of different kinds of experience. Let us briefly consider two kinds of experience, ordinary perception and the power of a work of art. Both can be gripping and forceful, though in different ways. The authority of perception consists in what we have called, following James, its noetic quality. . . . [T]his quality is best accounted for by the assumption of a causal connection between the perceptual experience and that which is perceived. I will withdraw my claim to have seen a tree if I learn that my visual image of the tree can be traced to some irrelevant cause and that I would have had the same image even if the tree had not been there. The force of my experience of climbing Mount Rainier, as compared with merely imagining the climb, derives from the judgments I make about the connections between myself, the mountain, and the rest of the world. My judgment about how the image in my mind is caused affects the experience, making it more vivid and gripping than if I believe I am just entertaining the possibility of the climb.

Hume thought that belief in a proposition was to be distinguished from merely entertaining that proposition by the greater vivacity of the impression. He illustrates this by comparing the experiences of one who reads a book believing it to be true and another who takes it to be fiction.

> If one person sits down to read a book as a romance, and another as a true history, they plainly receive the same ideas, and in the same order; nor does the incredulity of the one, and the belief of the other hinder them from putting the very same sense upon their author. His words produce the same ideas in both; tho' his testimony has not the same influence on them. The latter has a more lively conception of the incidents. He enters deeper into the concerns of the persons: represents to himself their actions, and characters, and friendships, and enmities: He even goes so far as

to form a notion of their features, and air, and person. While the former, who gives no credit to the testimony of the author, has a more faint and languid conception of all these particulars; and except on account of the style and ingenuity of the composition, can receive little entertainment from it.[21]

Hume is wrong on two counts. It is not a matter of common experience that what is taken to be true is more vivid and lively than what is thought to be fiction. Often novels, plays, and films move us more dramatically than do newspapers or history texts. We do experience something we take to be true in a manner that differs from our experience of something we consider fictional, but that difference is not accurately described by reference to the vivacity of the conception. It is a matter of the connections that we believe hold between what we are reading and the world in which we live. If I read in the paper that a portion of the west-side highway has been closed for repairs, I will alter my route when leaving the city. The murder in a mystery novel may be more vividly portrayed than the murder that took place last night on my block and about which I am now reading in the morning paper, but the latter may have a force and effect upon my emotions and behavior which the novel lacks.

The force of the experience is due to judgments and assumptions about the relation of this experience to the rest of my life and to the world in which I live. Those judgments and assumptions are constitutive of the experience. Wittgenstein and Phillips are correct in calling attention to the fact that the force of the experience is a matter of subtle connections between our concepts and the practices that inform our lives, but they are incorrect in claiming that these connections never involve explanations. The difference between my skiing down a slope and my entertaining the possibility of skiing down the slope is not only a matter of logical or conceptual connection. If I take it to be an accurate perception of what is happening to me now because it stands in a certain causal relation to the slope, the snow, and the terrain I am speeding past, the experience will differ considerably from one in which I am entertaining the possibility of that run, either eagerly or with some trepidation, as I ride up the chair lift. The relevant connections are conceptual, but they include conceptions of causes.

Despite Hume's claim to the contrary, novels, paintings, rites, and other works of art move us deeply even when we are aware that they are fictions. Many different theories have been proposed to account for the force of our experience of art, and it is not possible to examine them here. Wollheim has suggested that the power of a painting, a musical composition, or a ceremony derives from its having been constructed so as to invite the projection and externalization of complex mental states.[22] A work of art succeeds to the extent that it does not foster denial or romanticization but enables a person to experience his or her own inner states with honesty and precision, and so aids in the process of self-discovery. Wolterstorff has proposed that art is best understood as the creation of possible worlds other than the actual one. Fictional characters are denizens of those worlds, and the power of the work derives from the possibilities presented by those alternatives. In either case, a work of art shows something that is true of ourselves and opens up new possibilities, and it can achieve both functions while we recognize it to be a fiction.[23]

Of the two kinds of force we have considered, the noetic quality of religious experience in theistic traditions is closer to the force of ordinary perception than it is to the power of fiction. To experience God or his providential activity is not, from the subject's point of view, to entertain a possible world in which there is a God and he governs events in the world, nor is it to entertain a concept that permits one to externalize certain hopes and fears by projecting them onto another plane. One might suspect that the proper explanation of religious belief and experience would be found along these lines, but it is not the account that would be given by the believer. The experience has a noetic quality for the subject and is taken to reveal something about the world beyond the individual self. In this way, it is similar to the experience of actually skiing down the slope, as contrasted with that of thinking about skiing down the slope. . . .

The force of religious experience is best accounted for by the fact that the criteria for identifying an experience as religious include reference to an explanatory claim. The experience is perceived by the subject as eluding explanation solely in terms of his own mental states but as having been produced in such a way that it supports his beliefs about the world, beliefs that are distinctive of the tradition within which it is being characterized as religious. The experience provides support for and confirmation of those beliefs.

Evidence for the hypothesis that the identification of an experience as religious includes an embedded causal claim is of two kinds. First, the descriptions of religious experience which purport to be neutral with regard to beliefs and explanations include disguised explanatory commitments. Second, critics of reductionist approaches claim that the distinctive character of religious experience and belief is lost when the attempt is made to explain them. This shows that what is distinctive about religious belief and practice for these critics is that they are not amenable to nonreligious explanations. These criticisms provide support for the claim that the distinguishing mark of the religious is, after all, a matter of explanation.

## Explaining Religious Experience

The term *experience* is ambiguous. When I inquire about what a person has experienced at a certain moment, my question is ambiguous between two meanings: (1) how it seemed to that person at that time; and (2) the best explanation that can be given of the experience. This ambiguity is present in our ordinary talk about perception. I may have been frightened by the bear that I saw up ahead on the trail. My friend points out to me that it is not a bear but a log, and my fear subsides. What did I really see up ahead? By one interpretation of the word *see,* I saw a bear. That is the way I apprehended it, and that apprehension accounts for my fear and behavioral response. By another interpretation, what I really saw was a log, and I took it for a bear. I was wrong about what I experienced, and now that I can explain what happened I can correct my mistake.

This distinction is similar to, but differs from, Chisholm's distinction between the comparative and epistemic uses of "appear" words. It differs because Chisholm suggests that the comparative use, the description of how it appears to the subject, is a report of an immediate experience that is independent of interpretation or other beliefs. No such unmediated experience is possible. The distinction drawn here is between one interpretation, which presupposes a particular explanation of the experience, and another interpretation, also assuming an explanation, which is adopted by another person or by the same person at a later time. The perception of the object ahead as a bear was one explanation, and that was replaced by a better explanation when more information became available. That better explanation led to a reinterpretation of the experience.

It is important to note that both senses of *experience* assume explanations. It is not the case that explanation enters only into the second sense. The first, the description of his or her experience as assumed by the subject at the time of the experience, presupposes an explanation. If the distinguishing mark of the religious is that it is assumed to elude natural explanation, then the labeling of the experience as religious by the subject includes the belief that it cannot be exhaustively explained in naturalistic terms. The attempts of scholars as diverse as Eliade and Phillips to preclude issues of explanation from entering into accounts of religious experience and belief are undercut by the recognition that explanatory commitments are assumed in the identification of an experience as religious.

The distinction we have drawn between descriptive and explanatory reduction is tailored to meet this ambiguity. Descriptive reduction is inappropriate because the experience must be identified under a description that can be ascribed to the subject at the time of the experience. The experience must be described with reference to its intentional object. In the example given above, my fright was the result of noticing a bear ahead of me. The fact that the analyst must attempt to formulate a description of the experience which captures the way it was apprehended by the subject does not mean that no explanation is incorporated into the subject's description, nor does it mean that the analyst is not engaged in an inference toward the best explanation in his attempt to arrive at that formulation.

The identification of an experience under a description that can be ascribed to the subject is required before any explanation of the experience can be proposed. Every explanation assumes a description of that which is to be explained. One cannot explain phenomena as such but only phenomena under a description.[24] An event, action, emotion, or experience can be identified only under a certain description, and reference must be made to that description in any explanation that is offered. If the relevant description is not acknowledged, it will be tacitly assumed. The analyst's choice of the appropriate description of an experience or action is not entirely independent of the explanation he goes on to offer. If a practice is completely baffling to me under a certain description, and would be recognizable as a practice common to the culture in which it is ensconced if the description were altered slightly, then I will be tempted to alter it and to ascribe the discrepancy to defects in my observation or in the reports from which I am working. If the evidence for the original description is compelling, I must accept the anomaly and search further for an explanation; if it is weak, I may adjust the description in the interest of overall plausibility. This is the proper point at which to invoke Quine's principle of charity. I want my total account, with its descriptive and explanatory components, to be the most plausible of the available alternatives. I adjust each until I reach a reflective equilibrium.

The recognition that religious experience is constituted by concepts and beliefs permits an optimism with respect to the descriptive task which would not otherwise be possible. There is no reason, in principle, to despair about the possibility of understanding the experience of persons and communities that are historically and culturally remote from the interpreter. The difficulty is not posed by an unbridgeable gap between an experience that can only be known by acquaintance and the concepts in which that experience is expressed. Because the concepts and beliefs are constitutive of the experience, careful study of the concepts available in a particular culture, the rules that govern them, and the practices that are informed by them will provide access to the variety of experiences available to persons in that culture. Though it may be difficult to reconstruct, the evidence required for understanding the experience is public evidence about linguistic forms and practices. We attempt to formulate a description of the experience from the perspective of the subject, but the evidence is, in principle, accessible to us. . . .

If explanation is as central to the study of religious experience as this account suggests, then why has it not been recognized as such? Why is the explanatory component so often disguised or ignored in favor of appeals to a sense or a consciousness that is contrasted with belief? There are two motivations for this procedure: phenomenological accuracy and a protective strategy adopted for apologetic purposes. The first arises from the fact that those who report religious experiences typically take them to be independent of and more fundamental than beliefs or theories. The sense of the infinite or the consciousness of finitude is not apprehended as a theoretical commitment but as an inchoate sense that provides a practical orientation. It seems to the subject to be inaccurate to classify it with inference, inquiry, and hypothesis. Since an understanding of the experience requires that it be identified under a description that accords with that of the subject, it is tempting to assimilate it to the case of sensations, and to assume that sensations are independent of practices and beliefs. For these reasons, phenomenological accuracy appears to some to require that the experience be described so as to make it independent of beliefs.

The appeal to a sense or consciousness that is allegedly innocent of explanatory commitments has an apologetic advantage. If such an appeal could be made, it would be unaffected by any developments in science or other kinds of inquiry. It would, as Schleiermacher said, leave one's physics and psychology unaffected. Religious belief and practice could be seen as derived from this independent experience, and the difficult questions that have been raised for religion by changes in our other beliefs could be circumvented. Rather than seeing the experience as constituted by the beliefs, one could view the beliefs as expressive of the experience. The direction of derivation would be reversed, and that would serve the task of apologetics. If it did not provide a way of justifying religious beliefs and practices, it would at least protect them from the criticism that they conflict with ordinary and scientific beliefs.

As we have seen, the protective strategy used by those who argue that religious experience is independent of concepts and beliefs is parallel to that adopted by those who claim it is permeated by concepts but independent of referential or explanatory commitments. In both cases, accounts of religious experience are restricted to those that would be endorsed by the person having the experience, and consequently the possibility of those accounts conflicting with the claims of the believer is precluded. Whether one describes an allegedly prelinguistic affective experience or confines oneself to elucidating the grammar of a particular religious practice or experience, the result cannot possibly come into conflict with any beliefs or explanations from outside the religious perspective.

A consequence of such strategies is that language that appears to be descriptive may be intended to evoke or reproduce the experience that is purportedly described. Schleiermacher is explicit about his assumption that direct acquaintance is required for understanding the sense of the infinite; thus he sees the need to elicit that sense in his readers. Rhetorical language is carefully constructed, and the speech or essay becomes an edifying discourse, of which Schleiermacher's *On Religion* is a prime example. He regards his evocative language as a catalyst that directs the reader's attention to a sense that is already present but has not been nurtured. In fact, however, the language may be not merely catalytic but constitutive of the experience. If the reader follows Schleiermacher's instruction to attend to the moment before the rise of consciousness and to recognize the unity intuited there, he or she may discover that unity. That discovery ought not, however, to be cited as evidence for the unity of the world or of the infinite. An experience that has been evoked by carefully chosen rhetoric and by assuming a cultural tradition informed by theism cannot be taken as evidence for a unity that is independent of our concepts and beliefs.

Descriptions of doubt, anxiety, or faith in existentialist literature are often employed in a similar way. Kierkegaard displays dazzling literary and analytic skills in the service of edification. His analyses are often designed to elicit experiences and affections in his reader. Just as the spiritual director and the skilled revivalist preacher know how to evoke certain emotions and attitudes, an author can employ rhetorical skills to elicit affections in a reader. That ability presupposes a considerable amount of analysis. Kierkegaard's writings contain very subtle analyses of despair, faith, and doubt. As Aristotle knew, one can often learn more about emotions and attitudes from the orator or poet than from anyone else. Unlike Aristotle's *Rhetoric,* however, Schleiermacher's *On Religion* and most of Kierkegaard's pseudonymous works are written in a rhetorical style intended to elicit that which is being described. Much of the literature in the history and phenomenology of religion can also be viewed in this light. Such terms as *numinous, holy,* and *sacred* are presented as descriptive or analytical tools but in conjunction with warnings against reductionism, they function to preclude explanation and evoke a sense of mystery or awe. They are used to persuade the reader that the distinguishing mark of the religious is some quality that eludes description and analysis in nonreligious terms. Otto's use of *numinous* is an example of how one can employ the term to create a sense of mystery and present it as analysis. Such approaches to the study of religion are offered as neutral descriptions, but they assume not only a theory of religion but also religious theory.

We have distinguished the tasks of description and explanation and have argued that explanation is central both to religious experience and to its study. What kind of explanation, then, might we expect to construct for religious experience? An experience or an event can be explained only when it is identified under a description. And we have concluded that the distinguishing mark of religious experience is the subject's belief that the experience can only be accounted for in religious terms. It is this belief, and the subject's identification of his or her experience under a particular description, which makes it religious. If the concepts and beliefs under which the subject identifies his or her experience determine whether or not it is a religious experience, then we need to explain why the subject employs those particular concepts and beliefs. We must explain why the subject was confronted with this particular set of alternative ways of understanding his experience and why he employed the one he did. In general, what we want is a historical or cultural explanation.

This holds both for discrete, datable religious experiences, of the sort on which James concentrates, and for the identification of an underlying and pervasive religious moment in experience. Why did Stephen Bradley identify his accelerated heart rate as the work of the Holy Spirit? What caused Astor to regard what he saw as a miracle whereas Bingham remained skeptical? Why did Schleiermacher apprehend the moment that precedes thought as a sense of the infinite and discern a feeling of absolute dependence which accompanies all consciousness of the polarity of self and world? For Bradley, we would need to know something about Methodist revivalism in early nineteenth-century New England, about the particular meeting he attended earlier in the evening, and about the events in his life up to that moment. To explain Astor's beliefs about what he saw it would be necessary to acquaint oneself with Roman Catholic teachings on miracles, the significance of the shrine at Lourdes, and the details of Astor's background. To explain Schleiermacher's sense of the infinite, his feeling of absolute dependence, and his apprehension of all events as miracles, one would need to know more about his early years among the Moravians, his study of Spinoza, and the circle of friends in Berlin for whom he wrote *On Religion*. Each of these instances requires acquaintance with the Christian tradition and with the particular forms of that tradition which shaped the person and his experience.

For experiences sought in highly manipulative settings, as in meditative traditions where the training is carefully prescribed and a person is guided by a spiritual director in the interpretation of the states of mind and body achieved by the regimen, explanations of the sort suggested by Schachter's experiment seem clearly relevant. The novice learns to make attributions that accord with the tradition, and he engages self-consciously in manipulations to attain states that confirm those attributions. For seemingly more spontaneous but still relatively discrete and datable experiences in less contrived settings, one would still look to explain the experience by accounting for why the subject makes these particular attributions.... The phenomenologist of religion has often claimed that elaborately contrived ritualistic settings are expressions of the pervasive sense of the sacred or the infinite in human experience, but it seems more likely that the supposedly natural and spontaneous experiences are derived from beliefs and practices in much the same way that an experience is produced in the more disciplined traditions of meditative practice. How did Schleiermacher and others come to think that the sense of the infinite or the sense of finitude was independent of and prior to the beliefs and practices of a culture shaped by theism? His identification of what he takes to be a universal moment in human experience seems clearly to reflect the concept of God as Creator and Governor derived from the Hebrew Bible and the traditions it formed. The consciousness Schleiermacher accurately describes may, upon investigation, turn out to be the product of prior religious beliefs and practices.

Inquiry may demonstrate that some sense or intuition that appears to be independent of beliefs and practices is actually an artifact that developed under particular historical circumstances. Elizabeth Anscombe calls attention to the fact that some of the central concepts of modern moral philosophy, including the distinctively moral uses of *ought* and *right,* have no parallel in Aristotle or in other classical authors. Contemporary moral philosophers debate Hume's claim that one cannot derive ought from is, or Moore's discussion of the naturalistic fallacy, as if they were trying to clarify concepts that are invariant across periods and cultures and that are crucial for moral experience everywhere. Why, then, does that sense of *ought* seem so alien to the moral reasoning we find in Aristotle? Anscombe points out that between Aristotle and Hume our language and practice was shaped by theism, particularly by Christianity. She suggests that the modern concept of moral obligation is not an intuition that is independent of culture and belief, but that it derives from a law conception of ethics, and that that conception assumes belief in a divine lawgiver.

> Naturally it is not possible to have such a conception unless you believe in God as a lawgiver; like Jews, Stoics, and Christians. But if such a conception is dominant for many centuries, and then is given up, it is a natural result that the concepts of "obligation," of being bound or required as by a law, should remain though they had lost their root; and if the word "ought" has become invested in certain contexts with the sense of "obligation," it too will remain to be spoken with special emphasis and a special feeling in these contexts.[25]

The concept of ought, and the related sense of obligation, have survived outside of the conceptual framework that produced them and made them intelligible. The moral sentiments Hume describes and maps so well are artifacts that were formed by earlier beliefs and practices.

It seems quite likely that the feeling of absolute dependence and Otto's sense of the numinous are legacies of belief in the God of the Hebrew Bible and Christian tradition and of the practices informed by that belief. These experiences now appear to be autonomous and independent of that belief and that tradition. At a time in which belief in a transcendent Creator and associated metaphysical doctrines have been rejected by many, the habits of interpretation informed by those beliefs remain firmly entrenched in cultural patterns of thought, action, and feeling. Belief in God as Creator once provided the justifying context for these affections and practices. Now the direction of justification is reversed, and attempts are made to defend the beliefs by appeal to the affective experiences and practices. The sense of finitude, the feeling of absolute dependence, the practice of worship, and the grammar that governs the use of the word *God* are appealed to in order to justify the traditional religious statements without which this sense, feeling, practice, and grammar would not be intelligible.

These are only some suggestions of the kind of explanation that might be offered of religious experience. While one might venture a hypothesis to account for Bradley's accelerated heart rate or the recovery that Astor witnessed, that approach will not yield an explanation of their experiences. What must be explained is why they understood what happened to them or what they witnessed in religious terms. This requires a mapping of the concepts and beliefs that were available to them, the commitments they brought to the experience, and the contextual conditions that might have supported their identification of their experiences in religious terms. Interest in explanations is not an alien element that is illegitimately introduced into the study of religious experience. Those who identify their experiences in religious terms are seeking the best explanations for what is happening to them. The analyst should work to understand those explanations and discover why they are adopted.

# Notes

1. See John Y. Fenton, "Reduction in the Study of Religion," *Soundings* 53 (1970): 61–76; and Hans H. Penner and Edward Yonan, "Is a Science of Religion Possible?" *Journal of Religion* 52 (1972): 107–33.

2. Penner and Yonan, "Is a Science of Religion Possible?"

3. See Mircea Eliade, *The Quest* (Chicago: University of Chicago Press, 1969), pp. 1–53.

4. Eliade, *Quest,* p. 6.

5. See Eliade, *Quest,* p. 35.

6. Eliade, *Quest,* p. 25.

7. Eliade, *Quest,* p. 10.

8. See Mircea Eliade, *Patterns in Comparative Religion,* trans. R. Sheed (New York: Meridian, 1966), p. xiii, "To try to grasp the essence of such a phenomenon by means of physiology, sociology, economics, linguistics, art, or any other study is false; it misses the unique and irreducible element in it—the element of the sacred."

9. The ascription of unconscious beliefs or desires presents special problems. For a good discussion, see Arthur W. Collins, "Unconscious Belief," *Journal of Philosophy* 66 (1969): 667–80. Even in these cases, the beliefs and desires must be described in terms that the subject would understand and that could plausibly be attributed to him or her.

10. William James, *The Varieties of Religious Experience* (New York: Longmans, Green, 1902), pp. 189–90.

11. James, *The Varieties of Religious Experience,* p. 276.

12. Eliade assumes the existence of archetypal patterns that are given different interpretations in different cultures. See Eliade, *Patterns in Comparative Religion.* The identification of such patterns is highly arbitrary, however, and encourages the scholar to ignore the contextual details of religious experience.

13. Explanatory reduction is permissible, but descriptive reduction is not. Eliade, however, decries explanatory reduction, while his practice of treating symbols and rites as universal archetypes, abstracted from their social and cultural contexts, amounts to descriptive reduction. This is precisely the wrong combination.

14. See Wilfred Cantwell Smith, *Religious Diversity,* ed. W. G. Oxtoby (New York: Harper and Row, 1976), p. 152, and *Faith and Belief* (Princeton, NJ: Princeton University Press, 1987), p. 97.

15. Smith, *Religious Diversity,* p. 146.

16. See Smith, *Religious Diversity,* p. 31.

17.  Willard van Orman Quine, *Word and Object* (Cambridge, MA: MIT Press, 1960), p. 59.

18.  See Ludwig Wittgenstein, *Remarks on Frazer's* The Golden Bough, ed. R. Rhees, trans. A. C. Miles and R. Rhees (Retford, Engl.: Brynmill, 1979), pp. 1–9.

19.  Wittgenstein, *Remarks on Frazer's* The Golden Bough, pp. 1–3.

20.  D. Z. Phillips, *Religion Without Explanation* (Oxford, Engl.: Basil Blackwell, 1976), p. 151. (Eds.: see the article by Phillips in Part II of this volume.)

21.  David Hume, *A Treatise of Human Nature,* ed. L. A. Selby-Bigge, rev. ed. P. H. Nidditch (Oxford, Engl.: Oxford University Press, 1965), pp. 97–98.

22.  See Richard Wollheim, *On Art and the Mind* (Cambridge, MA: Harvard University Press, 1974), pp. 84–100; and *The Sheep and the Ceremony* (Cambridge, Engl.: Cambridge University Press, 1979).

23.  See Nicholas Wolterstorff, *Works and Worlds of Art* (Oxford, Engl.: Clarendon Press, 1980).

24.  See Arthur Danto, *Analytical Philosophy of History* (Cambridge, Engl.: Cambridge University Press, 1965), pp. 218–32.

25.  G. E. M. Anscombe, "Modern Moral Philosophy," *Philosophy* 33 (1958): 6.

# Bibliography

Abraham, William J. "Religious Experience," in his *An Introduction to the Philosophy of Religion*. Englewood Cliffs, NJ: Prentice-Hall, 1985.

Allen, Diogenes. *Christian Belief in a Postmodern World: The Full Wealth of Conviction*. Louiseville, KY. Westminster/John Knox Press, 1989.

Alston, William P. "Christian Experience and Christian Belief," in *Faith and Rationality: Reason and Belief in God*, ed. Alvin Plantinga and Nicholas Wolterstorff. Notre Dame, IN: University of Notre Dame Press, 1983.

———. "The Fulfillment of Promises as Evidence for Religious Belief," *Logos* 12 (1991): 1–26.

———. "Perceiving God." *The Journal of Philosophy* 83 (1986): 655–65.

———. *Perceiving God: The Epistemology of Religious Experience*. Ithaca, NY: Cornell University Press, 1991.

———. "Psychoanalytic Theory and Theistic Belief," in *Faith and the Philosophers*, ed. John Hick. London: Macmillan, 1966.

———. "Religious Diversity and Perceptual Knowledge of God." *Faith and Philosophy* 5 (1988): 433–48.

———. "The Role of Reason in the Regulation of Belief," in *Rationality in the Calvinian Tradition*, ed. Hendrik Hart, Johan Van der Hoeven, and Nicholas Wolterstorff. Lanham, MD: University Press of America, 1983.

———. "What's Wrong with Immediate Knowledge?" *Synthese* 55 (1983): 73–95.

Audi, Robert. "Direct Justification, Evidential Dependence, and Theistic Belief," in *Rationality, Religious Belief, and Moral Commitment: New Essays in the Philosophy of Religion*, ed. Robert Audi and William J. Wainwright. Ithaca, NY: Cornell University Press, 1986.

Barbour, Ian. *Myths, Models and Paradigms*. New York: Harper & Row, 1974.

Beardsworth, Timothy. *A Sense of Presence*. Oxford, Engl.: The Religious Experience Unit, 1977.

Bowker, John. *The Sense of God: Sociological, Anthropological, and Psychological Approaches to the Origin of the Sense of God*. Oxford, Engl.: Clarendon Press, 1973.

Brakenhielm, Carl-Reinhold. *Problems of Religious Experience*. Stockholm: Almqvist & Wiksell, 1985.

Broad, C. D. *Religion, Philosophy and Psychical Research*. New York: Harcourt, Brace, 1953.

Clark, R. W. "The Evidential Value of Religious Experience." *International Journal for Philosophy of Religion* 16 (1984): 189–202.

Clark, Stephen R. L. *The Mysteries of Religion: An Introduction to Philosophy Through Religion*. Oxford, Engl.: Basil Blackwell, 1986.

Conway, David Alton. "Mavrodes, Martin, and the Verification of Religious Experience." *International Journal for Philosophy of Religion* 2 (1971): 156–71.

Davies, Brian. "Experience and God," in his *An Introduction to the Philosophy of Religion.* Oxford, Engl.: Oxford University Press, 1982.

Davis, Caroline Franks. "The Devotional Experiment." *Religious Studies* 22 (1986): 15–28.

———. *The Evidential Force of Religious Experience.* New York: Oxford University Press, 1989.

Donovan, Peter. *Interpreting Religious Experience.* New York: Seabury Press, 1979.

Evans, C. Stephen. *Subjectivity and Religious Belief.* Grand Rapids, MI: Eerdmans, 1978.

Evans, Donald. "Can We Know Spiritual Reality?" *Commonweal* 13 (July 13, 1984): 392–96.

———. *The Logic of Self-Involvement.* London: SCM Press, 1963.

Ewing, Alfred C. "Awareness of God." *Philosophy* 40 (1965): 1–17.

———. *Value and Reality: The Philosophical Case for Theism.* London: Allen & Unwin, 1973.

Flew, Antony. *God and Philosophy.* London: Hutchinson, 1966.

Frankenberry, Nancy. *Religion and Radical Empiricism.* Albany, NY: State University of New York Press, 1987.

Freeman, Eugene, ed. "The Philosophy of Mysticism." *The Monist* 59, No. 4 (October 1976), entire issue.

Geisler, Norman, and Winfried Corduan. "God and Experience," in their *Philosophy of Religion.* 2d ed. Grand Rapids, MI: Baker, 1988.

Gill, Jerry H. "Mysticism and Mediation." *Faith and Philosophy* 1 (1984): 111–21.

———. *On Knowing God: New Directions for the Future of Theology.* Philadelphia: Westminster, 1981.

———. *The Possibility of Religious Knowledge.* Grand Rapids, MI: Eerdmans, 1971.

———. "Reasons of the Heart: A Polanyian Reflection." *Religious Studies* 14 (1978): 143–57.

———. "Religious Experience as Mediated." *Christian Scholar's Review* 13 (1984): 349–59.

———. "Response to Perovich." *Faith and Philosophy* 2 (1985): 189–90.

———. "Tacit Knowing and Religious Belief." *International Journal for Philosophy of Religion* 6 (1975): 73–88.

Goulder, Michael, and John Hick. *Why Believe in God?* London: SCM Press, 1983.

Gutting, Gary. "The Presence of God and the Justification of Religious Belief," in his *Religious Belief and Religious Skepticism.* Notre Dame, IN: University of Notre Dame Press, 1982.

Hardy, Alister. *The Spiritual Nature of Man.* Oxford, Engl.: Clarendon Press, 1979.

Hasker, William. "On Justifying the Christian Practice." *New Scholasticism* 60 (1986): 129–44.

Hay, David. *Exploring Inner Space.* Harmondsworth, Middlesex (Engl.): Penguin, 1982.

———. "Religious Experience Amongst a Group of Post-Graduate Students: A Qualitative Study." *Journal for the Scientific Study of Religion* 18 (1979): 164–82.

Heaney, James. "Faith and the Logic of Seeing-As." *International Journal for Philosophy of Religion* 10 (1979): 189–98; also published in *Sophia* 18 (1980): 33–41.

Helm, Paul. "Religious Experience." *Sophia* 16 (1977): 1–6.

Henle, Paul. "Mysticism and Semantics." *Philosophy and Phenomenological Research* 9 (1948–49): 416–22.

Hepburn, Ronald. *Christianity and Paradox.* London: Watts, 1958.

———. "Religious Experience," in *Encyclopedia of Philosophy,* ed. Paul Edwards. New York: Macmillan, 1967.

Hester, Marcus, ed. *Faith, Reason, and Skepticism*. Philadelphia: Temple University Press, 1991.

Hick, John. *Faith and Knowledge*, 2nd ed. Ithaca, NY: Cornell University Press, 1966; reissued 1987.

————. *An Interpretation of Religion: Human Responses to the Transcendent*. London: Macmillan; New Haven, CT: Yale University Press, 1989.

————. "Rational Theistic Belief Without Proofs," in his *Arguments for the Existence of God*. New York: Herder & Herder, 1971.

————. "Religious Faith As Experiencing-As," in *Talk of God*, Vol. 2, 1967–68 (Royal Institute of Philosophy Lectures), ed. G.N.A. Vesey. London: Macmillan, 1969; reprinted in John Hick, *God and the Universe of Faiths: Essays in the Philosophy of Religion*. New York: St. Martin's Press, 1973.

Hoffman, Robert. "Logic, Meaning and Mystical Intuition." *Philosophical Studies* 5 (1960): 65–70.

Hook, Sidney, ed. *Religious Experience and Truth: A Symposium*. New York: New York University Press, 1961.

Horsburgh, H.J.N. "The Claims of Religious Experience." *Australasian Journal of Philosophy* 35 (1957): 186–200. (Reprinted in *A Modern Introduction to Philosophy*, 3rd ed., eds. Paul Edwards and Arthur Pap. New York: Free Press, 1973.)

James, William. *The Varieties of Religious Experience*. New York: Longmans, Green, 1902.

Jones, C.P.M. "Mysticism, Human and Divine," in *The Study of Spirituality*, eds. Cheslyn Jones, Geoffrey Wainwright, and Edward Yarnold. Oxford, Engl.: Oxford University Press, 1986.

Katz, Steven T., ed. *Mysticism and Philosophical Analysis*. New York: Oxford University Press, 1978.

————, ed. *Mysticism and Religious Traditions*. New York: Oxford University Press, 1983.

Keeling, L. Bryant, and Mario F. Morelli. "Beyond Wittgensteinian Fideism: An Examination of John Hick's Analysis of Religious Faith." *International Journal for Philosophy of Religion* 8 (1977): 250–62.

Kellenberger, James. *The Cognitivity of Religion: Three Perspectives*. Berkeley, CA: University of California Press, 1985.

————. "The Ineffabilities of Mysticism." *American Philosophical Quarterly* 16 (1979): 307–15.

————. "Problems of Faith." *Canadian Journal of Philosophy* 6 (1976): 417–42.

————. *Religious Discovery, Faith, and Knowledge*. Englewood Cliffs, NJ: Prentice-Hall, 1972.

Kessler, Gary E., and Norman Prigge. "Is Mysticism Everywhere the Same?" *Sophia* 21 (1982): 39–55.

Kristo, Jure. "The Interpretation of Religious Experience: What Do Mystics Intend When They Talk about Their Experiences?" *Journal of Religion* 62 (1982): 21–38.

Kvanvig, Jonathan L. "Credulism." *International Journal for Philosophy of Religion* 16 (1984): 101–10.

Kvastad, Nils Bjorn. "Philosophical Problems of Mysticism." *International Philosophical Quarterly* 13 (1973): 191–207.

Lane, Dermot. *The Experience of God: An Invitation to Do Theology*. New York: Paulist Press, 1981.

Levine, Michael. "Can There Be Self-Authenticating Experiences of God?" *Religious Studies* 19 (1983): 229–34.

Lewis, H. D. *Our Experience of God*. London: Allen & Unwin, 1959.

Lewis, H. D., and C. H. Whitely, "The Cognitive Factor in Religious Experience." *Proceedings of the Aristotelian Society* (Suppl.) 29 (1955): 59–84.

Long, Eugene T., ed. *Experience, Reason and God.* Washington, DC: Catholic University Press, 1980.

Losin, Peter. "Experience of God and the Principle of Credulity: A Reply to Rowe." *Faith and Philosophy* 4 (1987): 59–70.

Mackie, J. L. "Religious Experience and Natural Histories of Religion," in *The Miracle of Theism: Arguments for and against the Existence of God.* Oxford, Engl.: Clarendon Press, 1982.

Martin, Charles B. *Religious Belief.* Ithaca, NY: Cornell University Press, 1959.

Martin, Michael. "The Principle of Credulity and Religious Experience." *Religious Studies* 22 (1986): 79–94.

Matson, Wallace. "Authority and Experience," in his *The Existence of God.* Ithaca, NY: Cornell University Press, 1965.

Mavrodes, George. *Belief in God: A Study in the Epistemology of Religion.* New York: Random House: 1970.

Melchert, Norman. "Mystical Experience and Ontological Claims." *Philosophy and Phenomenological Research* 37 (1977): 445–63.

Miles, T. R. *Religious Experience.* New York: Macmillan, 1972.

Miller, Richard B. "The Reference of 'God'." *Faith and Philosophy* 3 (1986): 3–15.

Moore, Peter. "Mystical Experience, Mystical Doctrine, and Mystical Technique," in *Mysticism and Philosophical Analysis,* ed. Steven T. Katz. New York: Oxford University Press, 1978.

Oakes, Robert A. "Mediation, Encounters, and God." *International Journal for Philosophy of Religion* 2 (1971): 148–55.

———. "Mystical Experience and Rational Certainty." *Religious Studies* 12 (1976): 311–18.

———. "Mysticism, Veridicality, and Modality." *Faith and Philosophy* 2 (1985): 217–35.

———. "Religious Experience and Epistemological Miracles: A Moderate Defense of Theistic Mysticism." *International Journal for Philosophy of Religion* 12 (1981): 97–110.

———. "Religious Experience and Rational Certainty." *Religious Studies* 12 (1976): 311–18.

———. "Religious Experience, Self-Authentication, and Modality *De Re:* A Prolegomenon." *American Philosophical Quarterly* 16 (1979): 217–24.

———. "Religious Experience, Sense-Perception, and God's Essential Unobservability." *Religious Studies* 17 (1981): 357–67.

O'Hear, Anthony. *Experience, Explanation and Faith.* London: Routledge & Kegan Paul, 1984.

Otto, Rudolf. *The Idea of the Holy,* trans. J. W. Harvey. New York: Oxford University Press, 1958.

Owen, H. P. *The Christian Knowledge of God.* London: Athlone Press, 1969.

Penelhum, Terence. *Religion and Rationality.* New York: Random House, 1971.

Perovich, Anthony N., Jr. "Mysticism or Mediation: A Response to Gill." *Faith and Philosophy* 2 (1985): 179–88.

Peterson, Michael, William Hasker, Bruce Reichenbach, and David Basinger. "Religious Experience: What Does It Mean to Encounter the Divine?" in *Reason and Religious Belief: An Introduction to the Philosophy of Religion.* New York: Oxford University Press, 1991.

Pike, Nelson. *Mystic Union: An Essay in the Phenomenology of Mysticism.* Ithaca, NY: Cornell University Press, 1992.

————. Review of *Mysticism and Religious Traditions,* edited by Steven T. Katz. *Faith and Philosophy* 2 (1985): 317–20.

Pojman, Louis P. "A Critique of Gutting's Argument from Religious Experience," in *Philosophy of Religion: An Anthology,* ed. Louis P. Pojman. Belmont, CA: Wadsworth, 1987.

Proudfoot, Wayne. *Religious Experience.* Berkeley: University of California Press, 1985.

————. "From Theology to a Science of Religions: Jonathan Edwards and William James on Religious Affections." *Harvard Theological Review* 82 (1989): 149–68.

Robbins, J. Wesley. "Does the Existence of God Need Proof?" *Faith and Philosophy* 2 (1985): 272–86.

————. "John Hick on Religious Experience and Perception." *International Journal for Philosophy of Religion* 5 (1974): 108–18.

Rowe, William. "Religious Experience and the Principle of Credulity." *International Journal for Philosophy of Religion* 13 (1982): 85–92.

Runzo, Joseph. "World-Views and the Epistemic Foundations of Theism." *Religious Studies* 25 (1989): 31–51.

Runzo, Joseph, and Craig K. Ihara, eds. *Religious Experience and Religious Belief: Essays in the Epistemology of Religion.* Lanham, MD: University Press of America, 1986.

Smart, Ninian. *The Religious Experience of Mankind.* New York: Charles Scribner, 1979.

Smith, John E. *Experience and God.* New York: Oxford University Press, 1968.

————. *Reason and Empiricism* (The Aquinas Lecture). Milwaukee, WI: Marquette University Press, 1967.

————. *Reason and God: Encounters of Philosophy with Religion.* New Haven, CT: Yale University Press, 1961.

Staal, Frits. *Exploring Mysticism.* Harmondsworth, Middlesex (Engl.): Penguin, 1975.

Stace, Walter T. *Mysticism and Philosophy.* London: Macmillan, 1961.

Swinburne, Richard. "The Argument from Religious Experience," in his *The Existence of God.* Oxford, Engl.: Clarendon Press, 1979.

Taber, John A. "The Philosophical Evaluation of Religious Experience." *International Journal for Philosophy of Religion* 19 (1986): 43–59.

Taliaferro, Charles. "Kenny and Sensing God." *Sophia* 25 (1986): 11–16.

Taylor, A. E. "The Argument from Religious Experience," in *Arguments for the Existence of God,* ed. John Hick. New York: Herder & Herder, 1971.

Trethowan, Dom Illtyd. *Mysticism and Theology.* London: G. Chapman, 1975.

Trueblood, D. Elton. *The Logic of Belief: An Introduction to the Philosophy of Religion.* New York: Harper & Row, 1942. (See Chapter 12, which is reprinted as "The Evidential Value of Religious Experience" in *A Modern Introduction to Philosophy,* 3rd ed., ed. Paul Edwards and Arthur Pap. New York: Free Press, 1973.)

Tugwell, Simon. "Faith and Experience I–XII." *New Blackfriars* (Aug. 1978–Feb. 1980).

Underhill, Evelyn. *Mysticism.* New York: New American Library, 1955.

Wainwright, William J. *Mysticism: A Study of Its Nature, Cognitive Value and Moral Implications.* Madison, WI: University of Wisconsin Press, 1981.

————. "Mysticism and Sense Perception," in *Contemporary Philosophy of Religion,* ed. Stephen M. Cahn and David Shatz. New York: Oxford University Press, 1982.

————. *Philosophy of Religion.* Belmont, CA: Wadsworth, 1988.

————. "Stace and Mysticism." *Journal of Religion* 50 (1970): 139–54.

Webb, Mark O. "Religious Experience as Doubt Resolution." *International Journal for Philosophy of Religion* 18 (1985): 81–86.

Wiebe, D. "The Religious Experience Argument." *Sophia* 14 (1975): 19–28.

Wilson, Kirk Dallas. "John Hick on 'Total Interpretation'." *New Scholasticism* 52 (1978): 280–84.

Woods, Richard, ed. *Understanding Mysticism*. Garden City, NY: Doubleday, 1980.

Yandell, Keith. "Experience and Truth in Religion," in his *Basic Issues in the Philosophy of Religion*. Boston: Allyn & Bacon, 1971.

———. "Religious Experience and Rational Appraisal." *Religious Studies* 10 (1974): 173–87.

———. "Some Varieties of Ineffability." *International Journal for Philosophy of Religion* 6 (1975): 167–79.